The *Uninformed*
VOTER

ROBERT LEVINE

outskirts
press

Previous books by Robert A. Levine

Aging Wisely

Shock Therapy for the American Health Care System

Resurrecting Democracy

Defying Dementia

Aging with Attitude

The Uninformed Voter is dedicated to my wife Anne-
My always muse, friend, lover, companion and inspiration.

Table of Contents

Preface

THE UNINFORMED VOTER demonstrates how voter apathy, unwillingness to spend time learning about candidates and issues, and general lack of knowledge of how government works has led to the decline of democracy. Citizens take universal suffrage for granted and have neglected their responsibility to acquire necessary information prior to voting. Too often, voting is an exercise in tribalism with partisanship directing citizens' votes. When surveys are taken of the information Americans have regarding government structure and important historical events, the positions candidates and their parties have on critical issues, it is amazing how uninformed citizens are. Immigrants applying for citizenship are much more knowledgeable about these vital matters.

Democracy is being challenged now by populism and nationalism internally and autocratic systems of government externally. If it is to survive and thrive as envisioned by the Founding Fathers and the philosophers of the Enlightenment, citizens of democratic states must become more involved in politics and more knowledgeable about the pertinent issues of the day. Some suggestions are made in The Uninformed Voter to entice citizens to learn and vote, perhaps changing some of democracy's structure to make it more competitive in an evolving, complex world.

The recent onset of the deadly Corona virus pandemic has put even more stress on democratic norms and procedures. With vacillating leadership in Washington, Americans are often uncertain about the roles demanded of them in this devastating situation. Small groups of citizens are disregarding medical advice about mitigation of the contagion, ignoring state government requirements for social distancing, facemasks and sheltering indoors unless one is an essential worker. To push for opening the economy and to proclaim their independence, these citizens are thumbing their noses at the majority who are following government directions, putting themselves and their fellow citizens at greater risk of being infected by the virus.

Robert A. Levine

Democracy- A System in Peril

"there is no government so subject to civil wars or intestine agitation as democratic or popular government, ...or demands more vigilance and courage for maintenance as it is." Rousseau[1]

Introduction

Democracy comes from the Greek word demokratia meaning a government where the people hold power.[2] In its present form, however, it has not produced effective governance in the states that have adopted its principles and structure, its vulnerabilities exposed and exploited by those seeking power. Currently, after a century of wars and economic upheavals, nationalism and populism are flourishing in countless democratic nations. And given Brexit, both Britain and the European Union face trying times. In addition, the dysfunction in Washington in recent years may merely be a preamble of what is in store for America. But after decades of apparent stability, why does liberal democracy appear to be faltering? (The term liberal democracy does not indicate left wing governments, but its classical meaning: nations with capitalist economies that value human rights, innate dignity of the individual, justice, freedom, rule of law, and universal suffrage.[3])

Ultimate control of liberal democracies is supposedly in the hands of the electorate. However, numerous voters have little knowledge of government and politics, and do not gather data regarding the issues and candidates before going to the polls. These individuals can be termed politically uninformed, democracy's Achilles' heel. Seduced by sound bites, overt lies, conspiratorial advertising, and emotional appeals, many citizens have difficulty separating fact from fiction, often voting against their own interests and those of the nation. In addition, they are often drawn to and believe fake news, nearly half of Americans getting non-vetted information from Facebook.[4] Tribalism has also infected much of the electorate, directing the way people vote.

Furthermore, extremely affluent political activists and corporations use their funds to dominate political advertising, pressuring the electorate to support particular candidates and ideas. Once elected, lawmakers are in thrall to lobbyists and special interests, doing their bidding instead of that of their constituents. Given voters' ignorance of political matters and their power to choose officials and policies in democratic states, changes to the present system should be considered in order to make the act of voting more rational and effective, with citizens who are more aware of the consequences of their votes. Because of chaotic governing, failed promises and intrusive inequality, only 19 percent of Americans in 2018 said they could trust the government.[5] The nominees for president offered to the voters by the political parties in the United States in 2016 were symptomatic of the bankruptcy of the democratic process.

Since the American Constitution was written and ratified over two centuries ago, the world has changed dramatically. Yet in spite of the establishment of universal suffrage and amendments to the original document, the Constitution still does not sufficiently reflect the technological advances of the last two centuries. No adjustments have been made in how citizens' votes are employed to elect government officials, though new options are available. The Constitution itself remains a hand-written product of an age of horse-drawn carriages and wind-driven ships. This would not matter except that the government instituted by the Founding Fathers has not been able to deal satisfactorily with the challenges arising in this new age. Democracies globally face similar situations.

Aside from democracy's inadequacies exemplified by the conflicts and gridlock in Washington, there are also the disappointing attempts to implant this Western enlightenment concept in the infertile soil of the Middle East, Africa, and Asia. In addition, autocracies have emerged out of democratic states in Russia, Turkey, Hungary, the Philippines, Venezuela and other nations. Over the last half century, a number of other democracies have languished economically or politically, being unable to provide their citizens with needed improvements in the quality of their lives despite free elections. And economic inequality has mounted in virtually every democratic state, along with corruption, inefficiency, and partisanship, the consequence of uninformed voters.

Francis Fukuyama's conviction expounded in his 1989 essay about 'the end of history,' touting the inevitable success and triumph of liberal capitalist democracy, appears to have been a mirage.[6],[7] Interestingly, after its ascendency over fascism and communism, democracy's problems and decline have come about not from external forces, but from its own faulty underpinnings. A survey of 3000 scholars and political scientists asked to evaluate the democratic system in 178 nations in 2018 found that democracy's decline was gaining momentum in one third of these countries.[8] 2.5 billion of the world's people were living through a process of 'autocratization,' where the attributes of democracy were being curtailed and liberal democracy was being supplanted by unilateral rule.

In the United States, the checks and balances built into the system by the authors of the Constitution have not been sufficient to generate the necessary compromise between political parties and to defend equity, justice, and the rule of law. Rankings of liberal democracy had the United States falling from 7th in 2015 to 31st in 2017, a precipitous drop.[9] There was concern by experts that Congress would be unable to control executive overreach, with the executive branch showing less respect for the Constitution and compliance with the judiciary. The 2016 election was assessed as being only 'somewhat' free and fair. A bipartisan poll commissioned by Bush and Biden in June 2018 revealed that half of Americans believed the United States was in danger of being transformed into a nondemocratic, authoritarian nation.[10] 55 percent perceived democracy as being weak, with 68 percent thinking that it was getting weaker. Big money's malign influence on politics and racial discrimination were noted as the major factors subverting democracy.

The Founding Fathers did not envision democracy or universal suffrage for the nation they were shaping. In fact, the idea of everyone voting and participating in politics was anathema to the prominent figures of that era. The privilege of voting was initially granted only to white adult male property holders, or white male taxpayers.[11] Thus, many men, all women, and all blacks were not given the franchise in this new nation deemed a republic rather than a democracy. Economic qualifications were included as a prerequisite for voting because the Founders believed that owning property freed individuals to execute independent decisions.[12] They also thought propertied citizens were more likely to cast their ballots in the public interest. (Similar systems restricting the franchise were employed in Great Britain and later in France.)

Did the Framers not consider that property-holders might vote in ways to help them preserve or increase their wealth, rather than in the best interests of the nation? Actually, it was probably a matter of social class that determined who would have the franchise. Those writing the laws perceived members of their own stratum as most suitable to assess candidates for office. They were afraid demagogues might convince the mass of people to vote for them by stoking their fears and making outlandish promises. There was also concern that votes of poor people might be bought by politicians or that those less affluent might vote in ways injurious to property-holders. James Madison noted in *Federalist Number 10*- "The most common and durable source of factions has been the various and unequal distribution of property."[13] In favoring a republic over a democracy for the United States, Madison further said that "It may well happen that the public voice, pronounced by the representatives of the people, will be more consonant to the public good than if pronounced by the people themselves."[14] His words reflect the distaste Madison and the other Founders had for mass democracy.

Despite safeguards instituted to block transition to a democratic state, those defenses were breached over time and the Republic evolved into a democracy. Suffrage was extended, first to all white men, then to black men with the XV Amendment in 1870, and finally to women with the XIX Amendment in 1920. America had been transformed on paper to a nation with near universal suffrage (the ability of blacks in the South to freely vote required the Voting Rights Act of 1965). The question now is how or if the political process can be revised to improve governance. As politicians pander to the masses in democracies, long-term needs may be disregarded. For example, taxes may not be raised, or may even be cut, though money is essential for vital programs and the national debt is ballooning. Globally, people are nearsighted in what they view as paramount, unable to accept delayed gratification and a better world for their children and grand-children through current sacrifices. Of course, politicians may promise their constituents that by electing them, their wishes can be attained and that no sacrifices will be necessary. To get elected and re-elected, the can of financial pain may be kicked down the road by these politicians, with the burdens falling on later generations.

Indeed, the fears of America's Founding Fathers regarding democracy have been realized repeatedly in different settings. Universal suffrage and the democratic process have not provided fair and equitable modern states that meet the needs of their citizens. The possibility of developing successful polities has been subverted by voters' lack of knowledge when they go to the polls, the primary reason democracy does not work adequately. The system cannot operate efficiently and productively when numerous citizens are unaware of critical issues and the qualities of the candidates whom they must judge. Too many voters are unwilling to educate themselves about the characters and stances of those vying for office before casting their ballots. As the political philosopher Jason Brennan notes, "Universal suffrage incentivizes most voters to make political decisions in an ignorant and irrational way, and then imposes these ignorant and irrational decisions on innocent people."[15] (The rest of the citizenry.)

Donald Trump, a celebrity television personality, populist and nationalist, raging against Wall Street and Big Business ultimately obtained the Republican presidential nomination in 2016, without a majority of GOP primary voters.[16] A sexual predator, he denigrated immigrants and minorities, praised various dictators and was supported by white supremacist groups.[17] Hillary Clinton became the Democratic candidate, bringing a history of ethical problems to the table, her ties to Wall Street reinforced by enormous speaking fees from financial firms. [18] One wonders how the political system of the United States had corroded to the point that these candidates were the choices of the major political parties to lead the nation. Neither one demonstrated that democratic mechanisms had produced able, competent and ethically esteemed nominees.

Additional evidence of democracy's failings is Americans' disgust with politicians and the institutions of government over which they supposedly have control, along with the low regard in which citizens hold federally elected officials and legislative bodies. A Gallup Poll in November 2013 reported that public approval of Congressional performance had reached a new low of 9 percent.[19] A NORC Poll from the University of Chicago in 2014 found that only 23 percent of Americans had a great deal of confidence in the Supreme Court, 11 percent in the executive branch and 5 percent in Congress.[20] Public perception of the Senate was in a similar range.[21] In May of 2017, a Pew Poll showed trust in government remaining near historic lows.[22]

Yet even though surveys have repeatedly revealed Americans' extreme dissatisfaction with both branches of Congress, incumbents are regularly returned to office. In elections for the House in 2014, 96.6 percent of incumbents won their races.[23] In the Senate, 23 of 26 incumbents were re-elected. And 98 percent of House incumbents won in 2016.[24] This disconnect is another indication of democracy's insolvency, with few accomplished candidates offered to voters.

Certainly, democratic institutions in the U.S. are badly in need of repair. The design of the government, with all its checks and balances, has led to polarization and partisan gridlock, making effective governing difficult and frustrating. The Electoral College mechanism, that awarded the election to a president who had lost the popular vote by a considerable margin, also needs to be overhauled. In addition, money's overarching influence in politics has to be neutralized before the system is completely rigged in favor of the affluent. And the probity of voting procedures has been compromised with voter identification laws and gerrymandering that skew elections and disenfranchise many voters. Another problem is that each state has its own regulations regarding voting and its own technology, run by political workers. The Electoral Integrity Project based on the contests of 2012 and 2014 ranked the U.S. 52nd of 153 nations in terms of fairness of its balloting.[25] There is also the issue of Russia and possibly other nations meddling in our elections to aid their favored candidates.

One hundred and fifty years ago, most American men participated in the democratic process with social equality prevalent.[26] Current surveys reflect the change, with America 28th of 35 developed nations in the percentage of its population voting in national contests. (In income equality it is 32nd.) Young Americans are cynical about the political system and indifferent to its status.[27] In the U.S., politics for many citizens has become a spectator sport, though the election of Trump as president in 2016 appears to have mobilized people of all political stripes. However, less than a third of Americans born after 1980 believe it is important to live in a democracy and choose leaders in free elections, with Western Europeans evincing similar feelings.[28] And worldwide, American concepts of democracy have been losing support.

Truly effective governing in democratic countries is difficult be-cause of the inefficiency, corruption, and partisanship that invariably develop. These features, however, are merely symptoms of the disease responsible for much of democracy's problems. After all, corruption and inefficiency are not only characteristic of democratic governments, and ideologues are ubiquitous in every type of polity. The critical illness that plagues democracies is disengagement of numerous voters from the electoral process. Citizens in democratic states are often apathetic, po-litically oblivious, or misinformed when they go to the polls (if they go to the polls), lacking knowledge of the issues and the candidates for whom they are casting their ballots. In fact, they are usually ignorant of politics in general and the workings of their governments. These uninformed voters do not act as a check on corruption, do not demand efficiency in government performance, and are easily misled by politicians to em-brace partisanship. In fact, the majority of voters in democratic nations can be considered politically incompetent.[29]

Interestingly, many of those who lack political insight are often unaware of their ignorance and may even think they are informed regarding matters about which they have no knowledge. The false in-formation they profess to have may reinforce the choices they make at the polls and the way they live their lives. Scientific studies have verified this conduct which is called the Dunning-Kruger effect after the men who initially described it.[30]

One example of voters' non-comprehension are in those areas of the country where large segments of the population are dependent on federal government largesse for their survival but vote for politicians who want smaller government and to cut programs the people need.[31] That is, if they vote at all. In general, people who most require gov-ernment transfers are least likely to vote. In Harlan County, Kentucky, 54 percent of resident's income came from government programs in 2016 such as Social Security, Medicaid, food stamps (SNAP), and earned income tax credits. Yet the voters in 2016 cast their ballots overwhelmingly for Trump and the Republicans who wanted to curb these programs.

The voters seem unaware how they got the food stamps and other federal benefits that help them live day to day, backing the GOP because of cultural issues and gun rights. In other words, they are motivated by right-wing tribalism which works to their economic detriment. And this is true year after year in many rural counties throughout the nation where the people do not understand the ways in which government helps them. They listen to conservative radio and television stations that rail against big government and wasteful spending and believe whatever they hear. Though they are receiving government welfare, they associate that with blacks and minorities in urban areas, not with what they are getting. And they resent the fact that the government has been unable to stem the decline in their communities.

The phenomenon of an uninformed electorate explains why the present democratic model is incompatible with capable governing, despite its freedom and the system's attraction for many of the world's peoples living under oppressive regimes. Citizens in the dark regarding the issues when voting, frequently elect officials who are unprepared, inept, partisan, and sometimes venal to run their nations' governments. Not surprisingly, these officials often do not perform competently in the positions for which they have been chosen.

Currently, democracy universally may be at a tipping point, with autocratic states arising from democratic nations by the will of the people--those who are not aware or do not care about the freedom they are surrendering. And remaining democracies must deal with nationalism and populism, along with citizens' fear of globalism.[32] A degree of nationalism is not necessarily negative among citizens of a country connected by a national identity. But nationalism becomes a problem when extreme and minorities are deprecated, harassed or persecuted because they are different and their heritage and culture may vary from the majority.

The recession of 2007-2008 heightened the anxiety of blue collar workers worldwide, producing a profound loss of faith in democracy.

Working people lost jobs, their homes, savings, and saw little hope for the future. Populism and nationalism became more attractive to these people, searching for leaders who might help them. Indeed, twelve years after the recession, individuals in a number of countries remain without work or trapped in dead end jobs, providing them with no optimism about what lies ahead. Surveys have shown support for democracy in Eastern Europe is tepid at best, with 'illiberal' politicians' ascendant.[33] And some democracies, like Brazil, are being destroyed by extensive corruption of the political classes, doing the bidding of dishonest businessmen.[34] Where the population is disillusioned by the failures of democracy, autocracy finds fertile ground.

There are some analysts who question whether the system in place in America can truly be designated democracy. Is it democracy when elected officials do whatever is possible to keep people from the polls who might vote for the other party? Is it democracy when gerrymandering is permitted by the courts to guarantee victory for one party in an engineered district? Is it democracy when affluent citizens are allowed to use their money to control the political dialogue under the supposed banner of free speech? Is it democracy when a president can get elected when losing the popular vote by nearly three million ballots because of an arcane law devised over two and a quarter centuries ago? Is it democracy when senators from the 26 least populous states, representing 18 percent of the nation's citizens can determine the laws of the land? Is it democracy when the vast majority of citizens want sensible gun laws and the NRA lobby dictates what is acceptable? Is it democracy when economic inequality is so great that that the top 10 percent of the population owns 70 percent of the nation's wealth?[35]

What changes are necessary in America and globally to establish democratic political systems that work? Two objectives are paramount- politically knowledgeable voters and candidates for office who are ethical, efficient, and effective. However, if the first goal can be achieved, the second will follow.

Uninformed Voters- Political Ignorance

(Information utilized in this and succeeding chapters is mainly from American sources.) In a policy analysis from the Cato Institute in 2004 entitled *When Ignorance Isn't Bliss- How Political Ignorance Threatens Democracy*, Ilya Somin noted that "Inadequate voter knowledge prevents government from reflecting the will of the people in any meaningful way."[36] With exceedingly short memories as well, voters at times appear not to recall, or ignore previous ethical lapses, moral misjudgments, and frank criminal activity by officials and politicians, as some are returned to office by their constituents after this conduct. Not surprisingly, there is a correlation between political knowledge, acceptance of democratic principles, participation in one's community, and voting.[37]

Uninformed voters have doomed democracies to missteps and malfunctions that make it challenging for them to compete in a complex world, where men and women of the highest caliber are needed to run governments. Instead, democracies wind up with candidates and officeholders who are adept fund-raisers, masters of rhetoric, manipulative and partisan in their views, but who are not innovative, bold, and progressive in the way they govern. As examples of ineptitude, a survey of leading economists from the Initiative on Global Markets in 2014 agreed thirty-six to one that the Obama stimulus had been successful in reducing unemployment.[38] Yet when Obama asked for further infrastructure spending to stimulate the economy during the recession, it could not be passed over GOP opposition in Congress.[39] And policy makers in the European Union continued to follow a path of austerity the majority of economists had rejected.[40]

There are a number of reasons voters are devoid of information about the government, candidates and issues in the United States. A critical factor is the absence of national standards in the schools seeking proficiency in history and civics.[41] And lack of civic knowledge due to deficient education is connected to a decrease in voting, volunteering, and more distrust of government among younger citizens.[42] A decline in the quality of journalism in America also contributes, where there are attempts at false equivalency regarding the ideas of the two parties: ie: the reality of global warming and its effects on the planet vs denial and support for fossil fuels. The proliferation of online news sites spewing fake news also advances political ignorance. And political advertising may confuse Americans. It is estimated the Koch brothers spent from $300 to $400 million dollars promoting their political ideas in the 2018 election cycle, up from about $250 million in 2016.[43] A Bloomberg Poll in 2015 revealed that 78 percent of respondents wanted the Supreme Court to turn off the spigot of political spending.[44]

In addition, since many voters believe their votes are inconsequential, it may be considered rational for them not to spend their time learning about government and politics. However, it is likely that most of these voters do not analyze the reasons why they are uninformed to try and excuse their conduct. As Jason Brennan notes in his book *Against Democracy*- "In a democracy, individual citizens are nearly powerless."[45] Therefore it makes sense for voters not to acquire knowledge about government or politics.

Though America is seen by much of the world as the prototype of advanced democracy, many of its citizens are disinterested or lazy when it comes to vetting the candidates they support and understanding important issues. The ignorance of the electorate is actually breathtaking when Americans are asked questions about politics, history, geography, and current events though it is likely citizens in other democratic states would fare comparably if questioned.

(Polls tracking citizens' political knowledge may show statistical differences depending on how questions were asked and the period when the poll was taken.)

As evidence of political ignorance, a Pew Research Poll in 2012 found that only 53% of Americans knew Republicans wanted smaller and less intrusive government and 43% knew the GOP had a majority in the House at that time but not in the Senate.[46] In a 2011 Citizenship Test from Newsweek, nearly one third of respondents could not name the vice-president, just 12% could name one of the writers of the Federalist papers, only 20% knew Woodrow Wilson was president during World War I, and 27% understood the reasons for the Cold War.[47] 39% realized a Senate term lasted six years, 14% knew the size of the House of Representatives, only 19% could define one power of the federal government, 37% were aware there were nine justices on the Supreme Court, 30% identified the Constitution as the supreme law of the land, 6% knew how many amendments the Constitution had, 41% could name the Speaker of the House, and just 33% realized America's economic system was capitalism.

A poll by the National Constitution Center in 2007 reported that two thirds of Americans could not identify the three branches of the federal government nor a single justice of the Supreme Court, and 91% could not name the Chief Justice.[48] More than a third of respondents could not describe any First Amendment rights, 42% believed the Constitution designated English as America's official language, 25% thought Christianity was the official government religion established by the Constitution, and only 40% knew there were one hundred senators.[49] In a Pew Poll also in 2007, 36% were aware Vladimir Putin was president of Russia and just 21% could identify Robert Gates as Secretary of Defense.[50] Two years after the Cuban Missile Crisis, only 38% of Americans realized the Soviet Union was not a member of NATO and in 2003, about 70% of Americans were not cognizant of the passage of the prescription drug law.[51]

Continuing on, a CNN poll in 2011 found Americans believing foreign aid on average accounted for 10% of government spending and one in five thought it was 30 percent when actually it was less than 1%.[52] And a month before the 2014 election, with the economy a major issue, 27% of Americans thought the unemployment rate was 9% and nearly 20% said it was 12%, when the correct rate was 5.9%.[53] (Nearly half of citizens had it dramatically wrong.) Furthermore, a Rasmussen poll less than two months prior to the 2014 election revealed that only 63 percent of Americans knew which parties controlled the Senate and House.[54]

Though the U.S. economy had rebounded from recession under Obama, with its strongest six months of growth since 2003, and unemployment had dropped considerably, most American voters blamed the president for stagnant middle-class earnings in October 2014.[55] The fact that a gridlocked Congress with the House controlled by Republicans would not support Obama's proposals to boost the minimum wage, extend unemployment insurance, and fund a stimulus program to address the crumbling infrastructure, was lost on the citizens who faulted Obama. And Democrats paid dearly in the 2014 election for the electorate's lack of knowledge.

Perhaps even more disheartening as a sign of voter obliviousness (if that is possible), a Public Policy Poll in 2013 revealed that nearly a third of Republicans in Louisiana blamed Obama for the federal government's inept handling of Hurricane Katrina.[56] Of course, he was not president until three years after Katrina's devastation, with Bush occupying the White House when the hurricane struck. The poll had 29% blaming Obama, 28% blaming Bush, and 44% uncertain who to blame. But how could Louisianans have forgotten government actions that had affected them in such a major way just a short while earlier?

In November 2015, a Public Religion Research Institute Poll revealed that 72 percent of Americans thought the economy was still in recession, though it had ended six years earlier.[57] A Bloomberg News poll had 34 percent of Americans wrongly believing unemployment was higher than when Obama became president, with 53 percent of Republicans agreeing. Actually, when Obama took office in January 2009, the unemployment rate was 7.9 percent, rising to 10 percent later in the year.[58] When the Bloomberg Poll was taken, unemployment was 5 percent. Could it be that a large percentage of Americans were getting their information from the wrong sources, or getting none at all?

It is not just the general population that is ignorant about politics and government, but highly educated people as well. A study in the 1990s of over 3000 Ivy League students in face-to-face interviews on the eight campuses found half of them unable to name their home state senators, and a third not knowing John Major was Prime Minister of Britain.[59] Forty-four percent could not name the Speaker of the House and 35 percent did not know the Chairman of the Federal Reserve. Twenty-three percent were unaware the Supreme Court had nine justices and 18 percent could not name a single justice. A similar survey of University of Florida and Florida State graduates conducted by phone had even more disappointing results.[60] Just 20 percent could name both of Florida's senators and 10 percent knew Lincoln had written the phrase- "a government of the people, by the people and for the people." Only 10 percent were aware Lyndon Johnson initiated the 'Great Society.' Two thirds did not know there were nine justices on the Supreme Court and could not name even one justice. Eighty percent of Florida graduates were also unable to name Alan Greenspan as Chairman of the Federal Reserve.

There are a number of other misconceptions that influence how people vote. A survey of Fox News viewers in 2013 had 49 percent believing that cutting waste and fraud in the federal government could eliminate most of the national debt.[61] The general population thought that more than 25 percent of the federal budget went for foreign aid, when it was less than 1 percent; 5 percent funded PBS and NPR, when it was 0.01 percent; pensions and benefits were thought to cost 10 percent when it was actually 3.2 percent. Many uninformed Americans believed that 40 percent of American workers were employed by the federal government, when it was really about 2 percent. These ideas had been instilled by Republicans and right-wing media.

Another sobering concept comes from a Pew Poll published in October of 2016.[62] The survey found only 36 percent of Americans cared a great deal about climate change in spite of thirty years of publicity by scientists and activists, with 97 percent of scientists believing man-made global warming is a threat to the planet. Political ignorance and scientific ignorance appear to go hand in hand. A Gallup Poll in 2014 found that 42 percent of Americans believed God created human beings in their current form 10,000 years ago, rejecting the Theory of Evolution.[63] Interestingly, in 2008, three quarters of the Republican candidates for president declared a belief in evolution.[64] In 2012, it had dropped to a third, and in 2016 it was just one- Jeb Bush. These are America's leaders rejecting scientific data.

Trump supporters see him as a deficit hawk when he talks about cutting funds for Public Broadcasting, the N.E.A. and legal aid, though they would not significantly affect the deficit. And in December 2016, 52 percent of all GOP voters believed Trump had won the popular vote, which Clinton won by nearly 3 million.[65] 37 percent of college educated Republicans thought Trump had won the popular vote and 60 percent of those with a high school education. The Public Policy Polling organization in a post-election survey found 60 percent of Trump voters did not know or did not believe the stock market had soared to record heights under Obama.[66] And 34 percent of Republicans according to Public Policy Polling believed that "a secretive power elite with a globalist agenda is conspiring to rule the world through an authoritarian world government."[67, 68] In a poll by Monmouth University in March 2018, 74 percent of respondents across the political spectrum admitted to believing that a 'Deep State' of unelected officials existed within the Federal Government, secretly controlling and regulating policy.[69] This is a disturbing finding suggesting a lack of faith in the government and a willingness to accept conspiracy theories. Surveys have also shown that Americans are clueless about the degree of inequality in the country.[70] The Walton family is more affluent than 42 percent of American families combined.

Another Pew Poll in June 2017 revealed no major improvement in citizen's political knowledge during this period of apparent intense interest in politics.[71] Only 62 percent knew Paul Ryan was Speaker of the House, 45 percent that Neil Gorsuch was a Supreme Court Justice, and 44 percent that Tillerson was Secretary of State. 47 percent knew of Mueller's role, 37 percent that Macron was French president, 45 percent what the Freedom Caucus was, and 37 percent knew the unemployment rate. (The questions were framed as multiple choice with four possibilities, which means that actual knowledge was undoubtedly lower.)

Aside from the fact that many Americans pay little attention to the news, others tend to have a 'confirmation bias' or 'desirability bias' that leads them to listen to news sources that reinforce the views they already had or credit information they want to believe--a selective exposure to the media (likely the result of tribal culture).[72] With the ubiquity of Internet, cable television, and talk radio, they can easily find sources that confirm the 'facts' they believe, which are sometimes an alternative reality. They are only willing to trust ideology-based news with a perspective similar to their own. Views of experts or academics may be dismissed if they conflict with deeply-held ideas. People have difficulty dealing with cognitive dissonance, where new concepts may make sense but clash with ingrained beliefs, upsetting an individual's value system.

Many Americans do not esteem intelligence or expertise, believing that common sense can provide solutions to most problems. And Americans frequently are suspicious and untrusting of the educated and wealthy elites, of scientists and experts in various fields. Some of this may be due to the average citizen feeling left behind (and possibly disrespected) by those educated or affluent. They believe, not unreasonably, that many of the nation's laws and regulations have been established in a way to help already wealthy individuals accumulate more wealth.

Additional studies and polls exploring citizens' information about politics, foreign affairs, and government functions merely reinforce evidence that major deficiencies exist. Though the data above may appear somewhat repetitive and redundant, voters devoid of basic knowledge about the workings of government and inattentive to critical issues, elect America's legislators and executives to craft its laws, conduct policy, and govern its citizens. A significant proportion of the shortcomings noted were because citizens did not pay enough attention to relevant world and national news, or political programming, or were not discerning about 'fake news.' A Pew Research Center survey in 2018 of over 5000 American adults revealed that recognizing whether news is factual or an opinion is challenging for a majority of Americans.[73] Five factual news statements were recognized as such by only 26 percent of respondents, 35 percent aware five statements were opinion. Those most knowledgeable about politics were most likely to be right about which statements were factual and which were opinion. Those who trusted national news organizations did generally better in choosing facts and opinions.

The ignorance of Americans regarding political issues makes them particularly vulnerable to attack ads targeting candidates during election season. Many citizens accept the lies and half-truths put forth by the Super PACs and anonymous 501(c)(4) organizations and cast their votes for candidates on that basis. As the 2014 midterm elections were in their closing days, according to the Center for Public Integrity more than seven of ten television advertisements in battleground states with Senate contests attacked candidates for these offices, with both parties vilifying their opponents.[74] Unfortunately, the strategy was mostly successful because voters did not realize which messages were accurate and which were lies.

Certain elections affirm citizens' lack of knowledge about politicians' ethical and criminal disputes as well as their stances on critical issues. If they do know about character flaws in these candidates, they disregard the breaches of conduct that have occurred, indicative of the cynicism or apathy infecting many voters. A few examples follow. (The chapter on corruption will examine this in more detail.)

In the 2018 Congressional elections, two Republican Congressmen under indictment for campaign finance fraud and insider trading, Duncan Hunter of California and Chris Collins of New York were re-elected by their districts.[75]

Republican Rick Scott was elected governor of Florida in 2010 and again in 2014 by a 1.3 percent margin despite his tenure as CEO of Columbia/Health Corporation of America when it was hit with $1.7 billion in fines for Medicare fraud, the "largest health care fraud case in U.S. history."[76] Scott was forced to resign, walking away with a large severance package and denying responsibility for the company's actions.

He never served prison time for the fraudulent conduct though he was in charge of the company. Scott spent $13 million of his own money in the 2014 governor's race, a media blitz that likely won the election for him.[77] After being ousted at HCA, he set up 32 urgent care clinics and backed legislation as governor that would refer Medicaid patients to these clinics, a blatant conflict of interest.[78] He also claimed to have placed his investments in a blind trust which was shown to be false. In 2018, he ran for the Senate against Democrat Bill Nelson and won by a tiny margin necessitating a manual recount, again using much of his own money.[79]

Democratic Congressman Charlie Rangel of New York was re-elected in 2010, 2012, and 2014 in spite of being named one of the most corrupt members of Congress by Citizens for Responsibility and Ethics in Washington (CREW) a number of times.[80] The Congressional Ethics Committee in November 2010 found him guilty of eleven ethics violations.[81]

Republican Spencer Bacchus, Congressman from Alabama, was re-elected in 2012 and 2014 though he had profited financially from insider trading with information obtained in Congressional hearings.[82]

Democrat James Trafficant, an Ohio Congressman, from 1985 to 2002, was indicted for taking bribes from the mob while working as a sheriff before running for Congress.[83] He was caught on tape talking about taking money and signed a confession, but was found innocent by a jury. While in Congress, "he was convicted of bribery, racketeering, and tax evasion." Even so, he continued to be reelected by large margins by his constituents. Though a criminal, he was able to connect with politically oblivious voters.

One of the most recent egregious illustrations of political 'chutzpah' was the campaign in 2015 by Democrat Joe Ganim for Mayor of Bridgeport, the largest city in Connecticut. Having been convicted of extortion, racketeering, and bribery during a previous twelve years as mayor, and after spending seven years in prison, Ganim ran for his old position, beating his nearest rival by more than a two to one margin.[84]

The House Banking Overdraft Scandal that broke in 1992 involved many House members overdrawing their bank accounts and basically taking interest-free uncollateralized loans which were not paid back for months.[85] The vast majority of these compromised House members were re-elected when they next ran for office.

These are a few instances, merely the tip of the iceberg, where uninformed voters did not know or ignored politicians' corrupt activities, returning them to office in spite of their crimes. One of the questions raised by these elections besides the role of political ignorance is whether character in politics counts any more. If someone running for office has the same tribal affiliations and beliefs as a voter, will that person support the candidate even if he or she is corrupt or lacking a moral or ethical compass?

The citizens of European democracies are also deficient regarding political information, as surveys about participation in the European Union have shown. In a poll in the spring of 2013, only 46% knew their rights as citizens of the E.U. and just 52% were aware that citizens of member states elected the European Parliament.[86] Another study reported that only 52% of Europeans realized the president of the Council of the European Union changed every six months and 62% knew the number of member states.[87]

The vote on Brexit by British citizens in 2016 also highlighted the degree that voters can be uninformed or irrational. Many of them were remorseful after the referendum to leave the E.U. and wanted it repealed.[88] They had not understood the economic ramifications of their votes. Then after years of wrangling among Conservatives in Parliament, the Party could not reach a decision on how to separate Great Britain from the E.U.[89] This was an example of democracy at its worst, with an ignorant and unreasonable electorate having decided on Brexit against their own interests and incompetent politicians unable to come to an understanding to bring Brexit to fruition. Questions of sovereignty and national pride seemed to have won out over future economic growth and participation in a large market. The election of Boris Johnson and the Conservative Party in 2019 appears to have finally settled the Brexit question.

Amazingly, in 2008 a survey found that 20 percent of British teenagers thought Winston Churchill was a fictional character and 58 percent believed that Sherlock Holmes was real.[90]

France provides an example of politically illiterate citizens revolting against the democratic process in 2018 and 2019.[91] When Emmanuel Macron's government decided to impose a tax on gasoline to fight global warming, 'yellow vest' demonstrators peacefully protested in the streets of the cities. But this deteriorated into rioting and fighting the police by some groups, destroying property, burning cars, and looting. Many of the participants were from rural areas and could not afford the increased costs of the new tax. They were also unhappy with a number of Macron's reforms which were market-based to try and open up France's constrained economy. Macron backed off on the gasoline tax to assuage the protesters, but democracy is yet to provide answers to the numerous complaints of the working and middle classes in France.

Few Latin American nations have lengthy histories of democracy, with intermittent military coups interrupting the process of representative government. And corruption in Latin American democracies is endemic, reaching its pinnacle in Brazil. After former President Luiz da Silva was convicted of corruption and sentenced to nine and a half years in prison, 30 percent of Brazilians said they would still vote for him for president the following year.[92],[93] In the 2018 election, Jair Bolsonaro won, an incipient fascist willing to trample freedom and human rights.

In the newer democracies in Asia, Africa, and the Middle East, citizens' knowledge of politics and government is meager, with segments of the population illiterate. Additionally, television, the Internet, and newspapers, as sources of news and information, are not available for many citizens, or skewed in their depiction of events. Leading parties in India nominate candidates who have been indicted for major crimes such as murder or assault.[94]

Interestingly, it appears that the twenty-four-hour news cycle and the information revolution via cable television and the Internet has had little effect on Americans' grasp of political issues.[95] According to the Pew Research Center in 2011, the low level of Americans' political awareness has remained virtually unchanged over more than fifty years.[96] Most of the electorate does not delve into the background of candidates, nor learn about the issues. They do not properly value the franchise inherited from their forebears, taking the ability to vote for granted. Citizens are generally unwilling to analyze why candidates may deserve, or not deserve, their support. Though data about candidates and their positions may be available in newspapers, on public television and radio programs, online, and in books, prospective voters are usually averse to doing the required fact-finding.

As it would require time taken from active and passive entertainment, Americans are lax about educating themselves regarding forthcoming elections. Sports, games, and television shows appear to be more important than news and politics. (In 2014, American adults watched an average of 4 hours and 36 minutes of television daily, Europeans slightly less.[97] The numbers have probably changed with the ubiquity of cellphones. In fact, a study in 2019 of over 2400 Americans revealed the vast majority spending over 4 hours a day on cell phone apps.[98]) Even voters with advanced degrees, scientists, academics, professionals, and corporate executives, often do not explore the issues and candidates before voting.

Voting

Many Americans, whether educated or not, do not vote on a regular basis. Less than 60% of the population casts ballots in presidential elections, falling to below 40% in off year contests.[99] The midterm election of 2018 was unusual, with 47 percent of those eligible voting, the highest total in over fifty years.[100] The U.S. ranked 120th of 169 countries for which data was available on the percentage of voter participation in recent balloting.[101] (In the presidential election of 2016 only 55 percent of those eligible voted.[102]) The diminished number of voters might be partially due to the two-step process to register and vote in some states.

In addition, thirty-four states, mostly controlled by Republicans, have placed restrictions on voters, making them prove their identities before allowing them to register and vote.[103] And only certain documents are accepted as proof. Reduced hours for registration and voting and fewer polling places have also made it more difficult for minorities, students, and those with disabilities to vote, all of whom generally support Democrats. And those fewer venues for voting are usually located in areas convenient for white voters and less so for minorities. With complete control of many state governments, gerrymandering of Congressional and legislative districts is standard practice for Republicans, making their votes count more. In the election of 2018, Democratic candidates obtained 54 percent of the votes in State Assembly Districts, but wound up with only 37 percent of the seats.[104] Voter suppression has been a powerful tool for the GOP, helping them maintain continuing control of many states and punching above their weight in most elections. However, simple apathy and lack of initiative is the reason many Americans neglect to vote.

The percentage voting in party primaries is even lower than in general elections. Because the numbers are so small, citizens with specific agendas willing to cast ballots may be able to hijack the primaries, choosing candidates with extreme views to represent their parties. With radical activists playing an important role in the primaries, mainstream officeholders have shifted their views to the right or left, fearful of being overthrown by insurgents. These small aggregates of party activists present a danger to democracy, as they are firmly fixed in their views and refuse to compromise. Increased partisanship in Congress and state legislatures in recent years can be traced in large degree to the primary system and activists willing to vote. Their control of state legislatures has also allowed them to draw the boundaries of state and Congressional districts (gerrymandering) making many elections almost moot. Gerrymandering and restrictive voter laws make a mockery of the democratic process, but help the GOP win elections. (In North Carolina, Republicans and Democrats have had roughly equal vote totals in Congressional elections prior to 2018. Yet partisan gerrymandering gave the GOP ten House seats and the Democrats only three.[105]) Strengthening representative democracy with one person, one vote is no longer the mantra being followed in supposedly democratic America. It has been superseded by 'do anything to win' even if it subverts democracy. And partisan gerrymandering has significant policy ramifications on both federal and state levels.[106]

Numerous Americans who do not bother to vote, or who vote with minimal information, believe their votes are meaningless and will not change the outcome of elections. They see the large sums of money Super PACs and other groups spend backing candidates, funded by wealthy individuals or corporate interests, and are convinced their own votes do not count for much. Citizens accept that politicians of both parties kowtow to those who provide them with financing, fueling feelings of indifference and alienation among countless voters. Why waste time voting or learning about the candidates when they are in the pockets of the lobbyists and special interests who are sources of funding. Some potential voters also cannot find candidates who represent their views. And anyway, their one vote among millions will not accomplish anything.

Because of uninformed voters, democratic governments perform poorly, with the quality of officeholders declining. Important legislation cannot get enacted and the government shuts down periodically. According to Gallup polls in 2015, just 8 percent of Americans rated the honesty and ethics of members of Congress as high or very high, and only 32 percent were satisfied with the direction the United States was going.[107] The chaos caused by Trump has made Washington even more dysfunctional.

Another study by Professor Martin Gilens of Princeton and Professor Benjamin Page of Northwestern shows that the wealthy elite and business interests have substantial independent impacts on government policy, while the general electorate has limited power to bring about change, even when desired by a majority.[108] Thus, America has evolved in some ways into an oligarchic system rather than a democracy. And the Supreme Court's Citizens United and McCutcheon decisions has permitted affluent Americans and corporate entities to pour unlimited funds into political campaigns either openly or anonymously, enhancing the power of the top 0.01 percent.

The 2018 midterm elections reinforced the notion that the United States was strongly divided between liberals and conservatives, urban and rural citizens, reflected in the politicians who were elected.[109] The Democrats won the House overwhelmingly while the Republicans increased their seats in the Senate. This is a recipe for more gridlock. Though the majority of the population supports the Democrats, Republicans control the rural vote and dominate geographically as shown by the results in the House and the Senate. Tribal allegiance and unwillingness to compromise can be expected. With this divide, governance is likely to be even more difficult, citizens becoming more dissatisfied with the political system labeled democracy.

2

Brief Philosophic Perspectives and the Evolution of Democracy

"The vigor of government is essential to the security of liberty."
Hamilton[110]

THROUGH THE YEARS, philosophers and political analysts have had various assessments regarding the functionality of democracy and whether its precepts could provide the basis for practical and stable systems of government. Plato was not an admirer of democracy as he revealed in *The Republic* over two thousand years ago. "Tyranny arises naturally out of democracy."[111]

Aristotle also argued against democratic states with the majority ruling. In *The Politics* he showed concern about democracies where the law might not be followed and demagogues arose.[112] The people can become as a monarch not controlled by law, and master over more ethical, honest citizens. Then "the decrees of democracy are the directives of tyranny....The law ought to rule over all."[113] "The democratic idea of justice is in fact numerical equality, not equality based on merit...whatever the majority decides is final and constitutes justice."[114]

Machiavelli's *The Prince* from the 16th century notes that "whoever organizes a state…must assume that all men are wicked and will act wickedly whenever they have the chance to do so."[115] This does not sound as if he were trumpeting a call for democracy.

Thomas Hobbes in *Leviathan* in the 17th century described the need for men to have a stronger power to control them, as their natural condition is "Warre…of every man against every man."[116] They have to submit to a single man or single assembly for protection from their fellow men.

Spinoza, in the 17th century favored democratic forms of government because they preserved men's natural equality and freedom.[117] He did not believe some men inherently more able to govern than others. In addition, he thought popular assemblies could enact legislation more wisely than other bodies. Democracy was "of all forms of government the most natural and the most consonant with individual liberty."[118]

John Locke in *Two Treatises of Government* also in the 17th century was a strong proponent of democracy, influencing America's Founders. He noted- "Every man, by consenting with others to make one body politic under one government, puts himself under an obligation to everyone of that society, to submit to the determination of the majority."[119] "No government can have a right to obedience from a people who have not freely consented to it."[120]

John Adams, the second president of the United States, helped found the republic. He worried about the possibility of transition to democracy. He wrote in a letter in 1814- "Remember, democracy never lasts long. It soon wastes, exhausts, and murders itself. There never was a democracy yet that did not commit suicide. It is in vain to say the democracy is less vain, less proud, less selfish, less ambitious, or less avaricious than aristocracy or monarchy… Those passions are the same in all men, under all forms of simple government, and when unchecked, produce the same effects of fraud, violence, and cruelty. When clear prospects are opened before vanity, pride, avarice, or ambition, for their easy gratification, it is hard for the most considerate philosophers and the most conscientious moralists to resist the temptation."[121] It is worse, of course, when the leaders are immoral and their actions promote their own interests instead of what is beneficial for the nation's citizens.

John Stuart Mill in the 19th century thought happiness for the maximum number of people should be the aim of government.[122] "Happiness is the sole end of human action....and the test by which to judge all of human conduct."[123] States should allow freedom of speech, freedom of character, freedom of thought and discussion, and freedom of action. He saw the dangers of democracy and mass society as being a tyranny of the majority, self-repression and conformity. In society, threats came not only from legislative or state coercion, but from social coercion as well. Though Mill believed in universal suffrage and democracy, he thought people with more education and greater knowledge should be given greater voting power. "No government by a democracy ....ever did or could rise above mediocrity except insofar as the sovereign Many have let themselves be guided....by the counsels and influence of a more highly gifted and instructed One or few."[124]

Mill affirmed that expansion of the franchise was inevitable and should be applauded. "But though every one ought to have a voice- that every one should have an equal voice is a totally different proposition."[125] He thought the level of education should ascertain the number of votes a person should be accorded. "It is not useful, but hurtful, that the constitution of the country should declare ignorance to be entitled to as much political power as knowledge.... everyone is entitled to some influence, but the better and wiser to more than others."[126] Though Mill was committed to liberal democracy as the optimum political system, he recognized the danger of populism and hoped that extra votes for the educated elite would be protective.

A current political philosopher at Brown University, David Estlund, has suggested in an essay, *Why Not Epistocracy?* that while democracies are generally fair and usually make good decisions, it might be sensible to transition to a system slightly less fair that made even better decisions more frequently.[127] He labeled this system epistocracy, meaning government by the knowledgeable, believing a polity controlled by 'educated' voters would likely function more effectively than democracy. This concept seems faulty by conflating education with knowledge about politics, as did J.S. Mill. People educated in specialized fields, ie: nuclear physics, art history, and the like, may know less about politics than a high school dropout who pays more attention to the world around him or her. Estlund was reluctant to abandon democracy, even if epistocracy seemed to be a more rational form of governing.

Jason Brennan, a political philosopher at Georgetown, in his book *Against Democracy*, argues unreservedly for epistocracy.[128] He believes it is reasonable to restrict political power of the irrational, the ignorant, and the incompetent to improve government and policies. Universal suffrage is not necessarily the best way to choose a government. Public welfare is more critical than fairness and people's feelings. Those who are politically uninformed should not have the ability to make choices that affect the lives of others, deciding who should govern and policies that should be followed.

Bryan Caplan, an economist at George Mason University, believes most voters are irrational rather than ignorant when they make choices in the voting booth, examining this concept in his book, *The Myth of the Rational Voter*.[129] Voters have systemic biases that move policies in certain directions.[130] They may be more impressionable than expected, accepting false or skewed information as valid because they are pleased by the way a candidate sounds, looks, or dresses. Indeed, voters' beliefs may not emerge coherently from the facts. This may be due to irrationality, but can also be from ignorance, a lack of interest or dismissing evidence.

The idea that humans are irrational in their decisions has come from many sources, reinforced by the behavioral psychologists Daniel Kahneman and Amos Twersky.[131],[132] Though their work was applied particularly to economics, it is true in the way people make all their choices, including political ones. Everyone has biases that influence decisions, emotions and past experiences playing a role. In picking candidates to support, the wording of slogans may strike emotional chords, eliciting positive or negative reactions. A study at University College London suggests that rational behavior may depend on the ability to override automatic emotional reactions to stimuli.[133] Can citizens with more knowledge about politics and government act more rationally than others when voting?

That our decisions are rational has also been challenged by Steven Sloman and Philip Fernback in their book *The Knowledge Illusion*.[134] They believe human beings seldom think for themselves, instead tending to think in groups. Because existence is becoming more complex, with knowledge in many areas expanding geometrically, men and women are unable to master the flood of information and thus depend on experts to explain the universe and how things work. In addition to scientific data, facts regarding politics, economics, technology, and what is happening in the world come from sources other than our own experiences. And many of our beliefs are molded by groups of which we are a part instead of our own thought processes. Even scientific facts may not change people's ideas of reality, as we have seen with global warming.

Illustrating this mind set, avid partisans are bound to political tribal cultures that have specific world-views and provide information for their adherents, making it unnecessary for individuals to gather their own data on different issues and candidates. These cultures stamp their supporters with defined identities, making it difficult for tribal members to adopt contrasting ideas or switch political parties.[135] And each tribe gets its news from designated sources, with major differences in how matters are interpreted. Many people vote for a particular party's candidates because their family, friends and neighbors also back that party. In certain regions of the country, voting for a party's candidates verge on automatic.

Large proportions of GOP and Democratic tribal cultures adhere to rigid opposing social beliefs, such as on abortion, same sex marriage, and gun control. Because of these differences, they demonize each other and have trouble communicating and compromising on other issues. Tribal members' economic interests may not motivate them to vote for candidates as much as stances on social issues. There are some who see the nation's elections as a cultural civil war, with white rural Christian America fighting against urban diversity and demographic changes.[136] Tribal cultures may have different viewpoints on morality and virtuous conduct, believing themselves morally superior to opposing tribes.[137] In fact, differing convictions may be seen as sinful, leading to disdain and even hatred for other tribes, prompting social separation, in-group loyalty and an unwillingness to work with opponents. This problem escalates when morality is perceived in absolute terms. Political tribal adherence has grown over the years, substituting for other groups that have faded but once provided a sense of community and belonging.[138] These included unions, churches, clubs, lodges, VFWs, and so forth.

The survival of democracy globally requires citizens to be knowledgeable about politics and history and realize past sacrifices made to preserve liberty. American leadership of the free world and its participation in multinational organizations to guarantee freedom of other democracies is now being questioned.[139] Trump is not a fan of history and has publically excoriated NATO allies because of deficient military spending.[140] With the Cold War having ended twenty-five years ago, many Americans believe geopolitical competition is no longer important. In 2016, 57 percent of Americans wanted to avoid international entanglements and let other nations get along the best they could. Angela Merkel of Germany in 2017 said that Europeans must stand alone and take their fate into their own hands.[141]

Americans also seem to have forgotten the balanced system existing between government and the markets that brought prosperity in the 20th century.[142] Jacob Hacker and Paul Pierson in their book, *American Amnesia*, detail how repeated attacks on Washington by Republicans and conservatives have made people angry at government, blaming it for the nation's problems and wanting it reduced in size. Government rules and regulations are disparaged, and responsibilities of the government and its agencies to build infrastructure, collect taxes, provide funds for research and development, assure the safety of cars, planes, food, water, drugs and workplaces are not considered. Insuring the banks, consumer protection, making certain the markets are working smoothly are denounced by those who want the markets to be completely free and open, and the government to play no role. But even the guru of capitalism, Adam Smith, believed government regulation of markets was needed, as long as the laws were "just and equitable," and "in favor of the workman."[143] Smith also saw the need for government revenue through taxation, the sources being 'rent,' profits and wages.[144]

Another market icon, F.A. Hayak, fervently opposed central planning, but saw no reason affluent societies could not guarantee a minimum income for all citizens. [145] "Outside and supplementary to the market system," this would not endanger freedom. Hayak perceived similarities and threats to liberal democracy from fascism, communism, and socialism and the need for market-based economies. However, he believed there was a role for government in ensuring the welfare of citizens. He wrote- "the case for the state's helping to organize a comprehensive system of social insurance is very strong.... There is no incompatibility in principle between the state's providing greater security in this way and the preservation of individual freedom."[146] Though the GOP wants government downsized with a free market unconstrained by regulations, this would allow the extremely affluent greater control of the economy and political system.

Ilya Somin in *Democracy and Political Ignorance* notes- "Effective democratic accountability requires voters to have at least some political knowledge."[147] Somin's solution to the problem of political ignorance is to shrink the size and scope of the federal government and decentralize its functions, devolving them to the states and municipalities. A Gallup Poll in 2009 had 57 percent of Americans believing government was attempting to do too many things that could be handled by individuals and businesses.[148] Somin insists that- "Democratic control of government works better when there is less government to control."[149]

However, Somin's solution does not address uninformed voters, nor provide a method of neutralizing their perverse effects on democracy. Conservative voters at political rallies have been heard to shout "keep government hands off my Medicare," showing a total lack of understanding about government and Medicare. Politically illiterate voters (among others) are also drawn to politicians who promise to reduce taxes, increase Medicare spending and cut the national debt, though the objectives are contradictory.

Democracy to Autocracy

In previously democratic nations now governed by autocrats elected by the citizenry, political ignorance always plays a role. This may be the result of apathy, with an unwillingness to take the time to study the candidates and issues before voting. Or there may be a presumption that people's votes are meaningless and elections are managed by those in power. Because the media in some states are under the thumb of the autocrats they may not always deliver accurate information. Whatever the cause of voter ignorance, it has been responsible for the demise of democracy and rise of autocracy in a number of nations.

Russia

Since Putin attained power, a shackled media has made it difficult to be politically educated. And nationalism induces many citizens to forgo information and follow the 'party' line at the ballot box. Indeed, nationalistic beliefs are reinforced by the controlled media.[150] For example, reporting on Russia's roles in the Ukrainian separatist conflict and the war in Syria. Though Putin's grab of the Crimea and his machinations involving neighboring states met with approval by his countrymen who saw Russia projecting strength, they did not know the entire story. [151],[152] People were fed lies and false information, voting for particular candidates because they wanted strong leadership, disregarding restrictions on freedom. (Putin's previous position as a KGB operative never seemed to give Russians pause about supporting him.) The Russian Orthodox Church has also backed Putin, and vice versa. Putin's policies mirror Russian ambitions over centuries of expansionism and national greatness constrained by economic weakness under the Czars, the Communists, and the current system.[153]

Sanctions by the West in reaction to Putin's belligerent moves and the drop in the price of oil have greatly damaged the Russian economy.[154] There has been little middle class growth since Putin's ascension to power. Though the nation's wealth has increased, most of the gains have gone to those already affluent and allied with Putin. In 2016, Russia was in the midst of its longest recession in twenty years.[155] Material goods taken for granted in people's lives were not accessible or affordable. And with its citizenry growing older, one third of Russians were surviving on disproportionately low pensions. The working age population, shrinking by one million citizens annually, is anticipated to equal pensioners by 2030, not a good long-term prognosis for the economy. However, the recession and Russia's economic problems have not significantly dented Putin's popularity, his approval ratings at 83 percent in March 2016.[156]

Despite the nation's financial situation, Putin committed Russian soldiers and armaments to wars in the Ukraine and Syria, and there has been a military build-up and modernization.[157] With Putin in command of all the levers of power, there have been relatively few protests. Opposition political figures have been murdered or jailed along with journalists who crossed Putin. As further evidence of the acceptance of autocracy, Stalin is being rehabilitated, the perception of his rule evolving.[158] He is being lauded because Russia was a super-power during his reign. The repression and fifteen million citizens killed in his prisons and gulags are felt to be gross exaggerations by a majority of current Russians (52 percent) who are fed a steady diet of his achievements. Whether democracy's flame will burn again in Russia remains to be seen.

Turkey

Turkey is a prime example of democracy morphing into autocracy with power placed in one man's hands. Many Turks support President Erdogan and others from his AKP Party because they believe Islam will benefit.[159] Even news of corrupt behavior can be dismissed or over-looked (though these reports are often suppressed) by Turkish voters if the candidates are perceived as devout Muslims.[160]

Erdogan ended a cease-fire against the Kurdish PKK group in August 2015 to stir up nationalist sentiment and perhaps more votes for his AKP Party in November elections.[161] The AKP soared to 49.4 percent in the election after Erdogan's actions and calls for stability.[162] Numerous Turks believe the voting was tainted, but the majority he received in parliament helped him attain more direct power for the presidency. In a January 2016 speech, Erdogan used Hitler's Germany as an example of what a strong president can accomplish, raising fears about his objectives.[163]

Taking over independent newspapers and TV stations that opposed him, in March 2016 the government seized control of Zaman, the newspaper with the largest circulation.[164,165] Within two days, Zaman began publishing propaganda-like articles favorable to Erdogan.[166] Dozens of journalists are now in prison because their reports questioned Erdogan's policies. Unfortunately, in making arrangements with Turkey to control immigration, E.U. negotiators downplayed his power grab, suppression of human rights and freedom of expression.[167]

In the summer of 2016, an attempted coup by elements of the military was quickly suppressed.[168] Erdogan used the coup as an ex-cuse to purge tens of thousands of men and women from the military, the police, prosecutors and the judiciary, teachers and other govern-ment employees, claiming they had supported the action against him. In April 2017, Erdogan narrowly won a referendum for constitutional amendments transforming the country's parliamentary system into a presidential one, granting Erdogan even more extensive power.[169]

(Keep in mind that Putin and Erdogan originally gained their positions through free elections and the democratic process. Once they held the reins of power, they took control of the intelligence agencies, police, courts, legislatures, and media.)

Poland and Hungary

Some Eastern European nations previously under Communist rule are brushing aside democratic norms and moving in authoritarian directions. Poland is one of these states.[170] The right-wing Law and Justice Party has ignored decisions of its Constitutional Tribunal (which can evaluate the nation's laws) and has manipulated its membership and the appointment of judges, disregarding admonitions of the E.U. Parliament. An attempt to purge Supreme Court judges was foiled in July 2017 when President Andzej Duda vetoed two bills passed by parliament.[171] This is likely to come up again.

Hungary is another Eastern European nation that has turned to autocracy after a short democratic interval. Viktor Orban's Fidesz Party attained power through elections in 2010 and since then the government has abandoned democratic practices, enacting new laws and constitutional changes.[172] All control and executive functions are now in the hands of Fidesz. In July 2013, the European Parliament passed a resolution reprimanding Hungary for flouting European values, Hungary essentially ignoring the assertion. Though Fidesz appears to have the backing of most Hungarian citizens, it is hard to know how much of this is due to its control of the media. In the elections of 2014, Fidesz and Orban won 133 of 199 parliamentary seats.[173] The Jobbik Party, even further to the right, won an additional 24 seats. Orban calls his government an 'illiberal democracy,' which is strongly nationalistic and populist. He has taken to demonizing George Soros, a Hungarian Jew who has supported a number of NGOs and Central European University in Budapest. Soros would like Europe to be composed of transparent democratic states which Orban opposes.

Venezuela

Venezuela's leaders also gained power through democratic means, then continued to rule as autocrats, jailing opponents on spurious charges and regulating the media.[174] This began with Hugo Chavez who maintained control of the state for fourteen years, until he died of cancer in 2013.[175] His acolyte, Nicholas Maduro succeeded him in a contested election, using managed media to burnish his image.[176] As new legislative elections approached in December 2015, Maduro barred leading opposition candidates from running for office on various trumped-up charges. [177] The head of the opposition, Leopold Lopez was given a fourteen year prison sentence with other opposition figures jailed as well.[178]

Venezuela is currently a failed state, with conflict between the opposition legislature and Maduro's executive branch and judiciary. The economy worsens daily and there is persistent civil unrest.[179] Frequent demonstrations against Maduro have been occurring in major cities, with the military intervening and fatalities occurring.[180] Inflation is exploding and many foods and medications are unavailable to the general population. A new body was elected in July 2017 to revise the constitution and keep Maduro in power.[181] Numerous Venezuelans have left the country for more stable nations. As of August 2019, total chaos was approaching.

Philippines

Rodrigo Dutarte was elected president in May 2016, transforming the Philippines into a dictatorship, with violence supposedly aimed at drug users and dealers.[182] He had been mayor of Davao City for twenty-two years, ruling in a similar fashion, claiming he had personally killed drug dealers. Though Dutarte won the presidency with 39 percent of votes cast, he was far ahead of other candidates. He has vowed to kill all drug users, dealers, and criminals, and has given orders to the police to follow through on his promise. However, many innocent people are being murdered, simply settling personal scores. Dutarte does not appear to have any cohesive domestic or foreign policy, seems unstable emotionally, and often determines plans on the spur of the moment. As another illustration of political ignorance, polls in May 2017 revealed that 80 percent of the Philippine public supported and trusted Dutarte in spite of his encouraging vigilante slayings, misogynistic comments, and erratic behavior.[183]

The examples above are merely a few instances where democracy evolved into autocracy with the assent and complicity of the populace. Similar to autocracies are 'pseudo-democracies' where people vote for officials but there is no transfer of power. Iran is a model of this, where a religious cleric, Supreme Leader Ayatollah Khomeini is responsible for major decisions.

Past Autocracies

Past transitions of democracy to autocracy also demonstrate the failings of the democratic process, as despots were able to subjugate their nations in spite of supposed constitutional safeguards. In Germany in the 1930s, lack of knowledge by the citizenry, politicians who may have been fooled as well, and an ancient chief of state, all played roles in the Nazi rise to power.[184] Aside from a rabid faction of supporters, many Germans refused to believe Hitler's ranting actually represented Nazi policy until it was too late. Though Hitler and the Nazi Party did not initially have a majority of Germans behind them, they were able to manipulate the democratic system of the Weimar Republic in 1933 and take over the government. Once they were in power, democracy was dead, with all vestiges of freedom eliminated. From that point on, nationalism and ideology enmeshed most Germans in the Nazi web.

A decade earlier, Mussolini had come to lead Italy through democratic means.[185] He was asked by King Victor Emmanuel III to form a right-wing coalition government, even though Mussolini's Fascist

Party was in the minority. Prime Minister Mussolini was given dictatorial powers from the democratically elected legislature for a year. Subsequently, he gradually abolished the trappings of democracy and made himself the autocratic head of state, using the secret police and even the Mafia to eliminate opposition.

Democracy in Asia and the Third World

Generally, democracy in much of Asia, Africa, and the Middle East is a travesty, with fraudulent elections endemic. Autocrats have gained control 'democratically' in many of these states, remaining as leaders for years afterward. In most Moslem nations, women do not have full rights despite laws that have been enacted. The democratic process is obviously flawed on that basis alone. There is also continued strife between different religious and ethnic groups, with killings of members of minority sects and assassinations of their leaders. This is true in Iraq, Afghanistan, Pakistan, Bangladesh, Lebanon, Yemen, and Tunisia, all supposed democracies. Advocates for secular reform, or Western ideas have also been killed by religious zealots in these 'democratic' nations.[186] There is unwillingness by radical Islamists to trust the ballot box in a contest of ideas, as they consider the Koran the source of all law. In Pakistan, the law prescribes the death penalty for blasphemy, though vigilante action will often mete out justice before the courts.[187]

In a number of these countries, the concept of nationhood is weak compared to tribal, religious, and sectarian ties, which makes democracy problematic. Freedom of religion, the press, and free speech, are not countenanced. Religious leaders in these states can also order their followers to vote for particular politicians or parties, limiting free thinking and choice. In addition, judicial systems are heavily politicized, favoring well connected or wealthy citizens. The rule of law is not standard.

India

India can be employed as a brief snapshot of how democracy functions in the Third World. As the most populous nominal democracy, India's inefficiency and corruption are notorious--an immense government bureaucracy demanding bribes to get anything done. Though India has been a democratic state for well over half a century, much of its population remains impoverished and illiterate, with survival a daily struggle aside from a growing middle class.[188] Infrastructure is shockingly poor, a major deterrent to economic growth.[189] In fact, sanitation, sewage systems and basic services are lacking in much of the country.[190] Talmudic government regulations have also had negative effects on businesses. As further economic obstacles, many foreign companies have been excluded from competing against inefficient Indian counterparts that would lower prices for consumers.

Elected in May of 2014, a right-wing Hindu nationalist party (BJP) controls the central government. Its leader and Prime Minister, Narendra Modi, was Chief of Gujarat State when a massacre of Moslems occurred, possibly encouraged by Modi, who did little to stop it.[191] There are also currently state laws prohibiting the killing of cows, animals sacred to Hindus, where Hindu extremist governments are dominant.[192] Rumors about cow killings have led to attacks and murders of Muslims. Hindu radicals have also killed writers and intellectuals who favored a secular state, instead of one based on right-wing Hindu ideas.[193],[194] Despite India's laws, those born into the lower castes are still treated poorly, as are members of minority groups and women.[195] Modi has become increasingly authoritarian and appears to be aiming for a right-wing nationalist Hindu nation with himself in the seat of power. In August 2019, Indian troops took over the Muslim state of Kashmir, previously administered by India but disputed by Pakistan. Both nations are nuclear-armed.

Japan

Japan has been a democracy since World War Two. For virtually this entire period, one party, the conservative Liberal Democrats, has controlled the government.[196] Though its economy was once booming, structural problems make future prosperity questionable and necessary adaptations have not been forthcoming.[197] In spite of an aging population and low fertility rate, young immigrants have not been welcomed in sufficient numbers to pay for the safety net of the elderly. Japan's debt is enormous and ultimately unsustainable without more young people to generate taxes and invigorate the economy. Women have been encouraged to enter the work force in greater numbers to partially compensate for the labor shortages.[198] By April of 2016, it was evident Prime Minister Abe's program 'Abenomics' was not working, as the value of the yen soared and central bank efforts to stave off deflation were unsuccessful.[199] The way the government handled the nuclear disaster at Fukashima was a fiasco as well whose effects will reverberate for years.[200] Currently, under nationalist pressure, Japan is whitewashing atrocities in its history textbooks that occurred during World War II.[201]

Singapore

Singapore is another democracy that has essentially been a one party state since achieving independence from British rule a half century ago.[202] The People's Action Party led initially by Lee Kuan Yew and then his son, Lee Hsien Loong, has been in power for five decades. Though dissatisfaction was evident because of unemployment, lack of affordable housing and the increased cost of living prior to the 2015 election, the People's Action Party again coasted to victory.[203] Singapore's economic transformation during the Lee's fifty year rule has been notable, but there has been lack of transparency and there have been restrictions on freedom of expression. The majority of Singapore's citizenry seems willing to accept the trade-off of a strong economy, minimal crime, and decent health care for the limitations of a near autocratic state.

The above examples provide a brief overview of autocracies and some troubled democracies, including Japan and India which are considered triumphs by some political analysts. Autocratic states in Africa which often followed democratic elections were not discussed. However, democracy's defects are universal and underlying its difficulties everywhere is a lack of knowledge by citizens about vital issues and the frequent election of incompetent or corrupt officeholders.

Though democracy has been shown to be flawed, the question should be asked whether liberal democracy is gaining adherents or is presently in worldwide retreat (notwithstanding Fukuyama's hypothesis of the end of history). Certainly, if it is losing believers and its strength is dissipating, those would be reasons for trying to breathe new life into democratic practices, propelling democracy to compete more effectively with autocratic systems. On the other hand, if democracy is doing reasonably well in its current form in confronting other political models, there would be less of a rationale to bring about significant change, even if its mechanisms were imperfect. However, democracy indeed appears to be in decline and needs to be revitalized.

In January 2018, as in the twelve previous years, Freedom House's annual report, *Freedom in the World,* showed shrinkage of global political rights and civil liberties.[204] The report noted that 71 countries had net declines in civil liberties and political rights, with only 35 showing gains. Worldwide, a number of large, economically powerful, or regionally influential nations regressed, a pattern noted since 2006. Affected were freedom of expression, the rule of law, civil society, and limits on personal autonomy. Open disdain for democratic standards also occurred more frequently. Even major democratic states curbed some freedoms to fight the threat of terrorism. Authoritarian leaders promoted nationalism to bolster their positions and media freedom was severely constrained in many nations. Eighty-eight of

195 countries evaluated were designated free by Freedom House, representing 45 percent of the world's population, 58 nations or 30 percent were partly free, and 49 or 25 percent were not free.

During the past century, particularly after World War II, America had been the champion of democracy, the leader in spreading its principles and practices. At this time, however, the United States must be considered at least partially responsible for democracy's retrenchment. This is in spite of evidence that a number of factors contributed to the waning of democracy, many of them beyond America's reach and power to influence. Nevertheless, the United States is no longer perceived as the font of freedom it once was by friendly nations and oppressed peoples. The democratic shining star has lost its luster, its ideals and values appearing to have been trampled by the nation's obsession with immigration and the war on terrorism. And Donald Trump as America's leader has not burnished the nation's reputation.[205]

Certainly, some of America's fabled allure had already faded prior to its focus on terrorism and immigration. There was Vietnam in the sixties and seventies that made people wary of America's values and power. Many citizens in other countries also regarded the U.S. as a hotbed of Philistinism, its residents driven by the desire to acquire money and material goods. And the nation's belief in individualism and self-reliance had caused it to neglect assistance for the poor and downtrodden. American capitalism seemed to emphasize every person for him or herself, rather than a sense of community and cooperation. And there was the gun culture that refused to be constrained by common sense laws. But people globally still generally admired Americans because they were successful, and the United States remained a relative bastion of freedom and the land of (slightly diminished) opportunity.

However, freedom was further tainted by policies of the federal government. First on the list was the use of torture in interrogating suspected terrorists.[206],[207] Some of these men had been kidnapped from the streets of friendly nations, without permission of their authorities. There was rendition as well, with the transport of suspects to different countries, some that employed torture and others that turned a blind eye toward its use.[208] In addition, stood Guantanamo, where American adversaries were imprisoned for indefinite terms without a trial.[209]

And of course there was the invasion of Iraq, destabilizing that country and resulting in countless deaths and injuries.[210] The rationale had been the belief that Saddam Hussein had weapons of mass destruction, which, however, were never found, and that he supported Al Qaeda, a contention never shown to be valid. True, Saddam had been a loathsome dictator, killing and torturing his own citizens and invading neighboring countries. But what gave America the right to attack this nation halfway around the world, bringing chaos and death to its citizens and leaving behind a pseudo-democratic state where sectarian violence and bombings seem unending. In fact, the birth of ISIS was likely a reaction to the American adventure in Iraq.

There were also the drone strikes on foreign soil, killing citizens of sovereign nations along with terrorists, with or without approval from the leaders of these states.[211] Labeled collateral damage, non-combatants, women, and children were injured or killed by U.S. missiles targeting enemies. Certainly, terrorists were 'taken out' by these operations, some of whom may have been plotting against the U.S. But these methods of warfare did not endear America to the populace of other nations. Spying on friend and foe as well as U.S. residents was another action that earned America approbation from its own citizens and those around the world.[212] And being the supposed avatar of democracy and freedom, the very concept of democracy suffered when America ignored its values and ideals in its conduct.

Adding to the negative perception of democracy has been the dysfunction in Washington and inability of American government to get things done. Naked partisanship pervades both Houses of Congress and has filtered down to state levels, making it difficult to pass necessary legislation. The extreme right-wing of the GOP seems to hold the party hostage to its desires and whims. The world also sees the proliferation of Super PACs and 501(c)(4) organizations with unlimited spending by affluent individuals and corporations to influence the outcomes of elections.[213] And the election of Trump as president with his America First mantra disillusioned people worldwide. In addition, there is financial inequality in America greater than in any other democracy, with laws favoring the rich. Sadly, many Americans see the 'American dream' as out of reach given the way the nation has evolved.[214] And citizens of other countries ask, is this the way democracy should be practiced? Is this the political system we want to embrace?

Efforts by the Trump administration to cut down on immigration by separating families at the border, taking toddlers and children from their parents, further blackened foreigner's views of America.[215] This cruel behavior was meant to dissuade families from illegally entering the United States, but it evoked a negative reaction worldwide. As of July 2019, many children had still not been united with their parents and it was uncertain when this would take place.

China's power and stature has grown as well during this period. The system of state capitalism with its thriving middle class has appeared eminently successful to citizens of third world nations. This is in spite of widespread corruption, spiraling debt, lack of freedom, the absence of equality, and pollution of China's soil, air, and water.[216] All that foreign nationals seem to notice are economic growth and undreamed of wealth. To many poor people, the Chinese political and economic models appear more attractive for their nations than the Western concept of democracy.

In Europe, dissatisfaction with democracy has led to a surge in voting for nationalist and populist parties.[217] Antipathy toward immigrants, government corruption, and the inability of politicians to produce a better life for their constituents were the starting points, leading citizens to look for avenues other than the mainstream political parties to vent their frustrations.[218] The flow of immigrants, many of whom live insular lives and have not integrated into the culture of the nations where they were allowed to settle, has heightened support for nativist parties.[219] These parties look for their inspiration to Russia, rather than to America and democracy.[220]

And nationalism and right-wing autocratic parties have not been limited to Europe. In India, Narendra Modi's BJP Party won the national election on a platform of Hindu power, along with economic reform. Though the Liberal Democratic Party has ruled Japan almost continuously since World War II, it has become increasingly nationalistic under Prime Minister Abe since 2012. Israel has also evolved into a more right-wing nationalistic state. Of course, religious intolerance in many Muslim 'democracies' in Asia and Africa makes the required freedoms and practices impossible to implement. In South America, the retreat from democracy of leftist origin brought Chavez and then Maduro to Venezuela, Morales to Bolivia, and Ortega to Nicaragua.[221] On the right is Bolsonaro in Brazil.

Thus, it is evident that democracy is in decline, with nationalism, populism, fascism, and state capitalism growing in appeal, and a number of autocratic regimes suppressing freedom. The leaders of these states promise their citizens jobs along with pride, stability, and heightened economic development, though it is questionable whether they will be able to deliver on their pledges. However, democracy, with America as an example and leading proponent, does not seem to be a desirable alternative for many citizens of these nations. Of course with Trump as president, having issued many pernicious executive orders, alienated allies, and spoken badly of many other nations, the democratic system appears much less attractive.

On the other hand, though liberal capitalist democracy contains significant flaws, when working properly, no other political system offers its freedoms, the rule of law, and the opportunities for individual advancement based on merit. As leader of the 'free world' for decades, the ball has always been in America's court to advocate for democratic change and it seems that the United States has dropped the ball. Whether there will be other chances in the future is uncertain. However, given the fall-off in democracy's appeal to people around the world, major structural changes in its format will be necessary to restore its allure and make it the method of choice for fair and just governance.

3

The Strange Presidential Election of 2016

"Democracy is beautiful in theory, in practice it is a fallacy....
The truth is that men are tired of liberty." Benito Mussolini[222]

THE UNITED STATES presidential election of 2016 was unlike any previous contest, reinforcing democracy's failings and affirming why uninformed voting must be addressed if democracy is to survive as a viable political system. Recognizing the defects in character, faults and missteps of both candidates of the major parties, many voters selected whom they believed the lesser of two evils. Others eligible simply did not vote, the turnout rate of 55 percent the lowest in twenty years.[223] And still others accepted at face value Trump's promises of change and his depictions of Hillary Clinton. These fueled Trump's upset despite his lies and exaggerations, lack of experience, apparent instability, and misogyny. There has never been a presidential contest where the two candidates of the principal parties were as damaged or unappealing.

As illustrations of the strangeness of this election, Donald Trump, a serial philanderer with a foul mouth, who had bragged about groping women, was avidly supported by the religious right and Evangelicals as he pledged to place conservatives on the Supreme Court. His character seemed inconsequential to these 'pious' individuals. And this celebrity billionaire braggart from New York, who had employed undocumented workers on his projects and had not paid some of his contractors, was backed by white working men in the industrial heartland. With Trump playing to white identity politics, they believed his vow to restore jobs that had been transferred abroad and to deport undocumented immigrants. Populism, nationalism and patriotism generated enthusiasm and connected Trump to the white masses. Many of these people lacking higher education, the left-behinds, were angry, depressed and anxious about their lives. They were middle and working class, both men and women with financial pressures who were unsuccessful, either unemployed or in low-paying jobs. Politics as usual had not worked for them. But many of them did not comprehend what Trump stood for, his persona, his temperament, his lies, and his lack of knowledge about government.

Though officials of organized labor backed Clinton, much of the rank and file voted for Trump. And James Comey's comments about FBI investigations of Clinton and Russian hacking with the release of disparaging information, appeared to heighten her loss of credibility. Fake news from the Russians and right-wing sites that tarred Clinton with ethical offenses also hurt her, as well as the lies and fake news from the Trump team. In other nations she would have been victorious anyway, accumulating nearly three million more popular votes than Trump.

Interestingly, voters who disapproved of both presidential candidates voted solidly for Trump.[224] In a survey prior to the election, 51 percent of white working class citizens did not think Trump had a 'sense of decency,' yet he won three quarters of this group. And though they also disapproved of his treatment of women, they still voted for him. Many considered him a 'jerk' but felt he would do more for them than Clinton. Voting for Trump was felt to be a vote against the status quo and a desire for change. Racism was probably not the primary reason most of his supporters backed him, though it did influence some.

During the campaign, the transition and as president, Trump also waged a war against the media, declaring they were spreading fake news and were the 'enemy of the American people.'[225] Unlike any other president, his hammering of the media was constant, with tweets, at press conferences, and with offhand remarks. He wanted to destroy the influence of the media, so that his take on the news would be authoritative. Tribalism also played an important role in defining political reality, as sources of news for opposing tribes were different. And sorting through the tsunami of false news was not easy. Truth was less of an absolute than usual in politics and depended on one's viewpoint.

Though a divergence in perception regarding the seriousness of problems facing the nation would be expected for Trump and Clinton supporters, the gulf between the two groups was enormous on major issues according to a Pew Poll after the election.[226] For instance on climate change, 14 percent of Trump adherents viewed it as significant, vs 66 percent of Clinton's. Terrorism was 74 percent for Trump backers vs 42 percent for Clinton's, racism 21 percent vs 53 percent, gun violence 31 vs 73 percent, inequality 33 percent versus 72 percent. It was as if many of the Trump and Clinton advocates were living in alternative universes.

The Primaries

The battle for nominations of the two parties started in early 2015, though actually they had been conducted covertly since the election of 2012. Candidates were aiming to gain early momentum by doing well in the Iowa caucuses at the end of January, and the February 2016 primary in New Hampshire, the first in the nation. Both entailed 're-tail campaigning: meeting with residents of these small states, shaking hands and holding rallies. When the game began in 2015, there were seventeen candidates vying for the top Republican spot, the largest presidential field ever for any political party--Jeb Bush and Ted Cruz the frontrunners with Donald Trump possibly the best known because of his television series.

Though Trump stood out from other GOP aspirants with his rhetoric, given his lack of experience, his chances of winning were dismissed by most pundits. In addition, populism was not part of the usual Republican playbook and it was believed party zealots and officeholders would not support him. However, he had a loyal and vocal following among voters that grew as his campaign continued. He also had a mantra, 'Make America Great Again' that appealed to citizens discouraged with the direction of the nation. In January 2016 he said "I could stand in the middle of Fifth Avenue and shoot somebody, okay, and I wouldn't lose any voters, okay,"[227] an indication of the extent of his ego and the loyalty of his base. He was a great candidate for uninformed voters, appealing to their emotions, denigrating knowledge and skewing the truth.

Hillary Clinton was considered the overwhelming choice for Democrats, believed to have both the experience and gravitas necessary for the position. There was also some feeling among Democrats and women that she deserved the nomination, after having lost to Obama in 2008. Much of the Democratic establishment backed her, including the Democratic National Committee. Though Bernie Sanders presented himself as a populist of the left, major party figures thought his rhetoric and policies were too extreme for him to be a viable nominee.

With the large number of Republican candidates, victory in any primary did not require a majority. However, because of the size of the field, it was difficult getting name recognition and publicity regarding policy statements. Five candidates dropped out in January with poor polling numbers. Then, despite leading in the polls, Donald Trump lost to Ted Cruz in the Iowa caucuses, 27.8 percent to 24.7, with Marco Rubio in third place with 22.8 percent.[228] Three more GOP aspirants left the race afterwards, failing to gain any traction. Among Democrats, Hillary Clinton beat Sanders 54 percent to 45 percent in Iowa.

In New Hampshire on February 9 Trump won by a huge margin, though he obtained only 35 percent of primary ballots cast.[229] However, his nearest opponent was John Kasich with 16 percent. On the Democratic side, Bernie Sanders won a crushing victory, beating Clinton 60 to 38 percent.[230] Sanders' accomplishment was asserted by many to result from his residence in neighboring Vermont, rather than any inherent appeal to voters.

Another three GOP candidates withdrew after New Hampshire. Then, after coming in fourth in South Carolina, Jeb Bush left the race. When Rubio lost Florida, his native state, on Super-Tuesday, he also dropped out, leaving only Trump, Cruz, and Kasich in contention. Between March and the end of May, Trump continued to rack up victories and gain delegates to the point where his steam-roller seemed unstoppable. When he won the Washington primary on May 26, he had more than 1,237 delegates in his pocket, guaranteeing the nomination though he had only garnered 41 percent of primary votes cast.[231] A celebrity with no political chops but a powerful theme of 'Make America Great Again' was now the GOP candidate for president.

By June 6, Hillary Clinton had clinched the Democratic nomination. Having 2,383 delegates, she had amassed the necessary total with 1,812 won in primaries and caucuses and 571 super-delegates who had pledged support.[232] Many of Sanders' adherents were reluctant to champion Clinton in the general election, believing she was not progressive enough and had obtained victory in a questionable fashion.

Analysts who had previously dismissed Trump's candidacy now presented various rationales about why he had emerged victorious. One reason was that with so many contestants vying for the nomination, Trump was conspicuous because he was not a politician but a well-known celebrity. And, unlike his opponents, he was comfortable using television to his benefit. As a celebrity, the TV networks focused on his rallies and what he had to say, cutting into other programming when he was giving a speech. The networks realized his appearance brought millions of eyeballs to their stations. This meant more free media exposure for Trump.

Another reason Trump did well was his populist approach to America's problems. He made it seem as if his main interest was helping the 'little guy,' the working men and women (particularly the men) who had been abused and damaged by large corporations that had seen them as disposable. He railed against companies who had moved their factories abroad to lower costs, throwing American workers by the wayside, some of whom had been loyal employees for decades. His wrath was also turned against trade agreements transacted by both Democratic and Republican administrations.

He declared he was opposed to the Trans Pacific Partnership Free Trade Agreement and asserted he would abandon it.[233] (He did not appreciate that TPP was an attempt to contain Chinese expansion and that opting out would hand China a victory.) His jeremiads against free trade and globalization were completely antithetical to long-standing GOP convictions and policies. Trump also accused China of unfair trade practices and currency manipulation, the latter actually a problem of the past. He threatened to impose heavy tariffs on Chinese goods to equalize subsidies China's government provided to companies and their stealing of intellectual property. Though many Republicans were aghast at his proposals, his base loved them and cheered wildly at his rallies. Trump's attacks on Wall Street and the big banks also revved up his populist supporters.

In addition to bringing manufacturing jobs back, Trump stated he expected coal mining to flourish again, even though the price of natural gas was undercutting coal as a fuel and it had become less economically viable. The price of renewable energy had also plummeted and was approaching the cost of fossil fuels, many utilities in the process of switching. Renewables actually created more jobs than did coal mining, but Trump was more interested in harvesting votes than absorbing data regarding energy. Trump claimed as well that global warming was a hoax perpetrated by China to damage America's economy and when he was elected he would scrap the Paris Accord on climate. Trump also declared the nuclear agreement with Iran and lifting of sanctions had been a disaster.

Another comment generating exuberant responses from Trump's audiences was his pledge to eliminate ISIS, saying he would carpet bomb them (even though that was not feasible since ISIS was embedded in many towns and cities in Syria and Iraq). Trump declared he had a secret plan for destroying ISIS, but would not give any details. He insisted he knew better than America's generals how to fight ISIS.

A major part of Trump's routine was to denigrate Obama and his policies along with Hillary. These remarks always energized spectators who had come to see him. He stated that Obamacare was failing and he would overturn and replace it with something better. However, no specifics were given. Trump asserted Obama's environmental regulations had cost millions of American jobs and that Hillary and the Democrats would increase rules and regulations in every sphere. Trump also loved conspiracy theories and was one of the 'birthers' who contested Obama's origins, years before Trump himself ran for the presidency. He adhered to the paranoid style in American politics noted decades earlier by Richard Hofstadter and used regularly by the 'radical right.'[234]

The primary debates produced opportunities for Trump to stand out against the field of GOP opponents. Showing disdain for political correctness, he belittled the other candidates, calling them names and making fun of their anatomic characteristics and looks. Though such comments might have sounded a death knell for a candidate in the past, the media paid attention to him because of his remarks and his supporters loved it. He said Jeb Bush was low on energy and called Marco Rubio little Marco, making it sound as if he were talking about his sexual apparatus. He insinuated Carly Fiorina's face was ugly and repeatedly referred to Ted Cruz as 'Lying Ted.' Trump labeled Clinton 'Crooked Hillary' and attacked her work as Secretary of State.

Trump also declared he would ban Muslims from entering the country to protect America and spoke about greater scrutiny of Muslims already in the U.S., perhaps having a watch list to keep them under surveillance. He proclaimed as well he was not averse to torturing suspected terrorists to get them to reveal information. Trump made it seem as if America were in danger of constant Islamic attacks, though less than one hundred Americans had been killed in terrorist incidents by Muslims since 9/11.[235] In fact, attacks by white supremacists were more of a threat, but disregarded by Trump.

Even more energizing to supporters were pledges to deport all undocumented immigrants he claimed were taking jobs from Americans, labeling them rapists, criminals, and drug dealers. Another aspect of his plan was to build a wall along America's southern border to keep out new immigrants. (This was at a time when more Mexicans were returning to Mexico than coming into the United States, with a net loss of 140,000 from 2009 to 2014.[236]) And ignoring government statistics, Trump said America was in the midst of a terrible crime wave and only he would be able to make citizens safe. Actually, violent crime was at an all-time low according to data from the FBI.[237]

Though promising to Make America Great Again and bring jobs back, Trump did not define how he was going to fulfill his pledges. The media did not interrogate him or his surrogates on how his objectives were going to be accomplished, allowing him to get away with talking in generalities. And his Republican opponents seemed incapable of deflecting his barbs or denting the armor Trump wore at every debate. Trump also received verbal support from alt-right groups and white supremacists, and refused to disassociate himself from them.

As Trump made progress in his campaign and attained the nomination, he interacted less with the press, reluctant to answer their questions. Aside from the debates where he received a disproportionate amount of interest, Trump's main way of communicating with his supporters and the press was through Twitter. This social media staple permitted him to reach millions of followers with short messages (tweets) of 140 characters or less, blasting people and media entities he felt were disrespectful to him.

During the 'invisible primary' season in 2015, news outlets had given Trump unusually high exposure since his polling numbers were low during this period.[238] Getting far more good press than faultfinding and critical analysis, exhaustive coverage by the media pushed Trump to lead the pack of GOP candidates in the polls by the time the real primaries began. There was little fact checking of his comments and when he made outrageous statements that were false. (Political scientists believe media exposure the year prior to the primaries is an important predictor of success, especially if it focuses on a candidate's favorable attributes, as it bestows credibility and helps fund raising. Before the primaries, it was estimated that eight of the mainstream media, five of the top newspapers and three TV networks, provided $55 million to Trump in free publicity.[239] This does not include hundreds of other papers and cable TV.)

On the other hand, Democrats during the invisible primary period received less than half the attention from the media as given to Republicans and Trump.[240] Even though Trump's outlandish outbursts for the most part were repetitive and broke no new ground, he was a celebrity different than the other candidates. There was one important negative element, however, not highlighted. He refused to release his tax information. The Shorenstein Center on Media, Politics, and Public Policy noted- "Trump is arguably the first bona fide media-created presidential nominee. Although he subsequently tapped a political nerve, journalists fueled his launch."[241] Nonetheless, as Trump ascended in the polls and became more politically powerful, he criticized the media over his coverage.

At its onset, Bernie Sanders' campaign was generally disregarded by newspapers and television. It was thought Hillary had the Democratic nomination locked up and that he would only be an annoyance: an inconvenient candidate. Then, as his campaign gathered steam, he gained more coverage which overall was generous and positive.[242] In contrast, commentary on Hillary's activities and statements were the most detrimental of anyone running. Her negatives from the media outpaced positives in eleven of the twelve months of 2015, undoubtedly why many voters viewed her unfavorably. For journalists, she was old news, a figure that had been part of the political establishment forever.

Many Democrats were angered by the process for the presidential race.[243] The rules gave convention votes to super-delegates who were party officials, officeholders, past officeholders, and important donors.

And many delegates elected in state primaries or caucuses were not bound to specific candidates, or could change their support after the second or third round of voting at the convention. These rules made the selection process less democratic with outsider candidates, like Bernie Sanders, at a distinct disadvantage.

The Election Campaign

The campaign for president between Clinton and Trump was one of the ugliest in history. Some of the language used and comments made were beyond what was previously considered acceptable. In addition, unpredictable factors influenced the voting. Actors outside the country (Russian intelligence and Wikileaks) who detested Clinton and supported Trump, aided his campaign. There was also the earthquake of populism rocking the world which added to Trump's momentum. And his mantra, 'Make America Great Again' seemed to catch fire. In retrospect, Clinton's campaign was deficient in numerous ways with her arrogant belief she could not lose against this celebrity with no political experience, with little knowledge of how government worked, and even less of foreign affairs and the military.

However, Clinton could not duplicate the emotional bond this billionaire formed with many working class Americans. Her support came from the political class, youth, minorities, and informed voters, the latter group choosing her because they were afraid of Trump. Though she emphasized 'identity politics' in her campaign, she did not focus on the white working class and their resentment of the elites and globalization. She also did not address the issue of perceived racial preferences angering white workers.

The calendar of circumstances and events involving both campaigns prior to the election reads like fiction, unanticipated occurrences requiring evasive and complicated explanations. On July 6, Director James Comey declared the FBI was ending its examination of Clinton's emails.[244] This was related to her use of a private server while Secretary of State against department regulations. Comey said the FBI

would recommend to the DOJ that Clinton not be prosecu
actions did not rise to a criminal level. This would have
news for her except that Comey added that she had been careless
in using her private server. The Trump campaign railed that Clinton
should have been indicted and that her political connections had kept
charges from being filed. The chants at Trump rallies of 'Lock Her Up'
started soon afterwards. On July 12, Sanders endorsed Clinton, agreed
to work for her and asked his supporters to back her. Subsequently,
Obama, Michelle, and Biden in addition to Sanders campaigned for
Clinton, but could not generate the enthusiasm seen at Trump rallies.
Nonetheless, poll numbers pointed to a Hillary victory.

During the Republican convention on July 21, Trump accepted the
nomination with blistering attacks against 'Crooked' Hillary and the
Obama administration, promising to reverse much of what Obama had
put in place. Just before the Democratic convention July 24, Debbie
Wasserman-Schultz, Chair of the Democratic National Committee, resigned because of pressure from progressives regarding her support
for Clinton, rather than neutrality in the race.[245] Wikileaks release of
20,000 DNC emails a few days earlier revealed Schultz and the party
establishment had been in Clinton's corner, helping her beat Sanders.

Within two weeks, Clinton was forced to deal with another issue
that tarnished her image. Additional released emails questioned her
ties to the Clinton Foundation while Secretary of State.[246] There were
intimations she had encouraged 'pay to play' arrangements, where
people who contributed to the Foundation were given access to
Clinton or high officials at the State Department. These emails were
made public by Judicial Watch, a conservative legal group. Clinton denied any 'pay to play' agreements and emphasized the charitable work
the Foundation had been doing. However, even prior to Clinton's run
for office, there had been misgivings about her role at the Foundation,
its funding, and the way it had been spending its money.[247]

Notwithstanding Clinton's troubles, on August 17, concerned with
poll numbers showing him behind, Trump decided on a major restructuring of his advisors.[248] Cory Lewandowski had been fired in June and

replaced by Paul Manafort. But in August, Trump hired Steve Bannon, Breitbart News CEO and Kelly Anne Conway as campaign managers. Bannon was known to be aggressive politically and Conway was a public relations veteran who would help with women. Breitbart and Bannon were considered voices of the alt-right. From that point on, Trump seemed more disciplined, staying on message with scripted speeches and fewer spontaneous outbursts.

Clinton ran into a firestorm after remarks at a New York campaign event which were publicized on September 10.[249] She had characterized half of Trump's supporters as a 'basket of deplorables,' stating they were racist, homophobic, sexist, xenophobic, Islamophobic- you name it. She declared Trump had given a public platform to these people, tweeting and retweeting their "offensive, hateful, mean-spirited rhetoric." Clinton soon moderated these comments, realizing she had offended millions of people. She admitted that many of Trump's backers were normal Americans who believed the political system was ignoring their needs. This was yet another indication of her inability to run a smart campaign.

The first debate between Clinton and Trump took place September 26. Though a majority of pundits thought Clinton won, it was not an overwhelming victory.[250] Focus groups, however, labeled Clinton the clear winner.[251] On October 2, the New York Times printed an analysis of Trump's 1995 tax returns, claiming he had paid no federal taxes for years.[252] He had taken a $915 million loss on these returns that could have helped him avoid taxes up to 18 years. Trump's team asserted the Times had obtained the records illegally and were acting as agents for Clinton's campaign. But making these public did not appear to influence voters.

Several days later, on October 7, Wikileaks provided emails to the news media of private speeches Clinton had given to Wall Street banks for lucrative fees.[253] Some of her public positions conflicted with what she had told the bankers. She was not as tough on Wall Street as she would have liked voters to believe. The information came from hacked emails of John Podesta, Clinton's campaign chair.[254] Transcripts were also made available of talks she had given to Goldman Sachs and Deutsche Bank. A spokesman for Clinton claimed Wikileaks was acting in concert with Russia and Trump to try and derail her candidacy. Subsequently it was shown Russia was interfering in elections in Europe as well as the U.S.[255] Putin wanted to discredit the democratic process and break up the E.U. and NATO.

Also on October 7, Trump's conversation about women during an interview for Access Hollywood became public, having been caught on tape in 2005.[256] Trump claimed that as a star, he was a magnet for beautiful women. He just started kissing them and could do anything he wanted, including grabbing them by the 'pussy.' Trump also described how he went after a married woman to try and f--- her. Though his lewd comments engendered negative press and anger from feminists, they did not influence his supporters.

Trump dismissed his remarks as 'locker room talk' between guys that meant nothing. But some Republicans withdrew support, suggesting Trump drop out of the race, which he rejected. Most amazing was the way evangelicals continued to see Trump as the preferred candidate, with Clinton considered almost demonic. There was a strong element of hypocrisy in the willingness of religious believers to back Trump, a serial adulterer and sexual predator who had been married three times. Was it because of the seat on the Supreme Court at stake?

The second debate on October 9 had greater hostility evident.[257] In a Town Hall format, Clinton and Trump bandied about insults, repelled attacks, and provided several policy positions. Prior to the start of the debate, Trump held a press conference with several women who had accused Bill Clinton of sexual crimes. When Trump was asked about the tape of his sexual comments by moderators, he said he had never acted that way and it was just talk he claimed was embarrassing. Trump noted he was being accused of using sexually inappropriate words, while Bill Clinton had been guilty of sexual transgressions and Hillary had viciously attacked Bill's accusers.

Clinton went on to mention Trump's mocking of a disabled reporter, his demeaning attacks on a Muslim Gold Star family who had lost a son in Iraq, his fat shaming of women, and his character assassination of a Mexican-American judge handling a suit against him. Clinton reinforced the idea Trump would be divisive for the nation while she would bring people together. Trump replied that Clinton was all talk and no action. Going further, he said he would appoint a special prosecutor to investigate her if he won the presidency, claiming deletion of emails on her private server while Secretary of State was criminal. Clinton admitted she had made a mistake with her actions, offering further excuses which made it seem as if she might have been lying.

No presidential debate in the past had ever reached this level of venomous personal attacks. Another issue that confounded Clinton was the disparity in what she had told Wall Street bankers in private speeches and her public declarations. Trump interrupted her justifications by saying she had been lying and had been caught, an effective riposte. Subsequently, however, Trump was forced to admit he had used a federal loophole to avoid paying income taxes, employing depreciation as a write-off. He believed this made him a smart businessman. A major disagreement flared over Russia and the conflict in Syria. Clinton wanted an inquiry of Russia for possible war crimes, while Trump defended Russia's actions. In a survey following, Clinton appeared to have won the second debate, 42 percent to 28 percent.[258] Politico had Hillary leading Trump by five percentage points.

Afterwards, a number of women charged that Trump had touched them in a sexual manner over the years, or had treated them as sexual objects.[259] Contestants from the Miss Teen USA Pageant said on several occasions Trump had walked into their dressing room while they were naked. Trump denied the accusations, saying the New York Times published fiction and engaged in character assassination to aid Hillary. He threatened to sue the women who had made these claims to prove they were false. Trump's support remained steady, as many Trump enthusiasts believed Clinton was even worse.

The third presidential debate occurred on October 19. A CNN/ORC poll had Clinton winning, 52 percent to 39 percent,[260] most other polls in agreement. There was discussion of the Supreme Court appointee, gun rights, and the interpretation of the Second Amendment. But the major bombshell was Trump's refusal to say he would accept the outcome of the voting.[261] He declared the election was rigged and he would decide afterwards whether to accept the results. These comments repudiated a basic principle of American democracy: the peaceful transfer of power after an election. Clinton labeled Trump's remarks typical of past behavior when he had not gotten his way.

She also attacked Trump as a puppet of Putin and asked him to denounce Russia's attempts to influence the election. Trump responded by labeling Clinton a puppet and said it would be good for America if he and Putin could work together. Trump was found by fact checkers to have exaggerated or lied on many comments during the debate, such as health care premiums increasing 60 to 100 percent over the next year, and having tens of thousands of ISIS aligned Syrian refugees in the country.[262] He claimed as well that his economic proposals would not raise the national debt because he was going to create so many jobs. Speaking of Clinton's private email server, he stated she was guilty of a very serious crime and in addition, $6 billion had vanished from the State Department while she had been in charge.

Clinton was also shown to have been mistaken or exaggerating with some of her remarks, asserting when her husband had been president, the country had been on the road to eradicating the national debt. Without proof, she said that Trump had used illegal workers to construct the Trump tower. Declaring her fiscal plan would not add to the national debt, she stated Trump's plans would increase the debt by $20 trillion. There were numerous other comments on both sides either wrong or misleading. Whatever was said though, Clinton was believed to have been victorious, with more knowledge of policy and government. Still, she was seen as an establishment figure who did not connect with working people.

Though the debates stood out in people's minds because both candidates were facing off, they were only a small part of the campaigns. The candidates and surrogates held rallies around the country, Trump concentrating more on the swing states. His rallies were massive affairs, with wildly enthusiastic turnouts. Sometimes, the rallies turned violent if opponents of Trump were seen, and it appeared he encouraged some of this behavior. He still claimed the election process was rigged and was unsure whether he would concede to Hillary if he didn't win.

When he excoriated Clinton at his gatherings, her name continued to be greeted with chants of 'Lock her up.' Though questions had been raised of Russian involvement in the hacking and release of DNC material, Trump asked the Russians to hack Hillary's emails to get back information she had deleted. Never before had a presidential candidate asked a foreign power to become involved in an American election, his supporters ignoring his comment. When he said the election was rigged, Trump was right, though he didn't mean it was rigged to help him. In addition to data captured by Russian hackers and released through Wikileaks that embarrassed Clinton, the election was rigged by Comey's divulgences and by other FBI employees who favored Trump and provided information to right-wing media.[263]

Trump kept emphasizing he would bring manufacturing jobs back to America and would expel illegal immigrants, two important issues for his base. The idea of building a wall along the border Mexico would pay for always evoked wild cheers. He also pledged to abrogate NAFTA and other trade pacts and negotiate better deals. China would no longer be able to eat America's economic lunch by currency manipulation, subsidizing Chinese products for export, and stealing intellectual property. Any nation conducting trade unfairly would have to pay the price with tariffs on their products and a ban on some goods. Trump also declared the Second Amendment was sacred for him, but guns would be banned if Hillary were in charge. And the mantra of making America great again was repeated over and over.

His type of campaigning could be called 'revival tent' politics, where he was like an evangelist preaching to crowds who were already converted. The crowds participated in the show yelling out responses to Trump's questions and repeating his lines. He was a master manipulator of people with whom he had personal contact. His supporters saw him as witty and charming, his charisma giving them hope he could bring about change that would help them and 'clean up the swamp' in Washington. But many outside his base viewed him as petty and vindictive, vengeful towards those who had crossed him, and willing to mock and shame opponents.[264] They were worried that his use of power might restrict individual liberties and freedoms.

In spite of Trump's large, enthusiastic crowds, Hillary continued to run ahead in the polls by two to eight points. Her campaign organization believed getting her adherents to vote would be the key to victory, the 'ground game' that would be decisive. She continued to focus on 'identity politics,' addressing minorities, young people, gays, and the educated populace in her speeches. States like Michigan, Wisconsin, Ohio and industrial areas that had previously voted Democratic, received minor attention, as her organization thought she had these locked up. Her failure to effectively compete in 'rust belt' states that had lost jobs would later come back to haunt her.[265] Many working class men and women viewed her as deceptive and evil, and voted for Trump even if they considered him a deeply flawed figure.

However, the working classes were not the only Trump supporters.[266] Just 35 percent of his voters had household incomes at or under $50,000 annually, the median for the nation. About two thirds came from the more affluent segment of the electorate, many of them making over six figures. Though 69 percent of his voters lacked college degrees, this was the same as the overall Republican pool. So it was not just blue collar whites and working class voters responsible for Trump's victory, though they did play a significant role.

Though Clinton had adequate funds for advertising and get out the vote efforts, she did not spend her money wisely, convinced that states and counties with large populations of white workers Obama had won would remain in her column. But instead they moved to Trump en masse, who had reached out to them. Clinton's plans to grow jobs were more detailed and made more sense than Trump's, but she never could get voters to listen to her message in critical states. More than anything was a lack of trust between Clinton and white working class voters. They believed she favored minorities over whites and would provide more help to blacks and Hispanics than whites if she were president. Cultural issues were another selling point for Trump. White working class voters were mostly against abortion and same sex marriage, did not care about feminism or gay rights, and harbored a streak of racism, openly or covertly. And there was alarm that Hillary would restrict gun rights, reinforced by Trump's advertising and fake news sites. There was also fear of a female president among uneducated white men.[267]

In a surprising turn of events that may have determined the election, James Comey on October 28 sent a message to Congress that the FBI was analyzing a batch of Clinton's emails.[268] He noted these might have been relevant to her use of a private server, but did not say whether the emails contained any classified material, or anything new or of interest. They had been found on the computer of Anthony Weiner, husband of Clinton's aide, Huma Abedin. Coming just eleven days prior to Election Day, the statements re-raised the question of Clinton's trustworthiness for many voters. At his rallies, Trump focused on this, intimating Clinton had jeopardized national security and criminal charges might result. On October 28, Real Clear Politics average of national and state polls had Clinton leading Trump by 5.2 percent.[269]

Following the release of Comey's message, the race tightened further and on October 30, Clinton led the Real Clear Politics average polls by just 4.3 percent.[270] Then Fox News falsely reported on November 2 that an FBI probe of the Clinton Foundation was occurring that might lead to an indictment.[271] Subsequently, the news anchor, Bret Baier, offered an apology on November 4, saying there was no FBI probe of the Clinton Foundation. But damage had already been done, with social media and other sites having spread the fake news. Average poll numbers had Clinton leading Trump by only 1.8 percentage points on November 5.[272] On November 6, three days prior to the election, Comey released another statement that the FBI investigation had not uncovered new information regarding Clinton.[273] The question was whether Comey's exoneration had come too late to help her. Indeed, on Election Day, November 9, Trump was elected president.[274]

The campaign for president was fought for the most part in fourteen states both parties viewed as winnable.[275] Barely a third of the electorate resided in these states, and just four, Florida, Ohio, Pennsylvania, and North Carolina, consumed 71 percent of spending on campaign ads, and 57 percent of visits from candidates. All of these states went to Trump. The other thirty-six states were believed too solidly Republican or Democratic to be worth contesting. When Trump needed money at the start of his campaign, or for blanketing the air waves in the swing states just before the election, it came in unlimited amounts from a hedge-fund manager, Robert Mercer, an ardent Trump supporter.[276] Some analysts believe Trump would not have won without Mercer's help. And with the turnout diminished, attracting a small number of those who stayed home could have shifted the election the other way.[277,278]

The factors responsible for Trump's victory will be examined by political scientists in the years ahead, a large degree of uncertainty likely to remain. Were Clinton's email scandals decisive? Did Comey's actions destroy Hillary's chances? Did the Clinton Foundation problems play a role? How could she have made those speeches to Wall Street? Benghazi? How much did Russian hacking help Trump? Did the wave of populism sweeping the world elevate him? Did Hillary and her team run a pitiful campaign neglecting to highlight her strengths? Voter approval numbers for both candidates were dreadful, with Trump's worse. A CBS/NY Times Poll in March of 2016 showed Trump with a favorable rating of 24 percent vs unfavorable of 57 percent, Clinton's numbers being 31 percent vs 52 percent.[279] She was not seen as ethically upright by many voters, some considering her arrogant. Her campaign did not find ways to reverse those perceptions.

Clinton's campaign mistakes as much as Trump's appeal to his supporters probably underlay Trump's victory. Though he connected with his base, he was vulnerable on a number of counts not exploited effectively by Clinton's team. First of all, he was not the successful businessman he claimed to be. And, unlike any other presidential candidate, why had he refused to show his taxes? An article in February

2017 reported- "There is little mystery as to why Trump has broken with custom and refuses to release his tax returns. A record of his colossal tax breaks, associations, deals, and net worth reside in these forms. It may turn out that deals.... will haunt his presidency no less than his grotesque conflicts of interest or any of the possible connections to Russia."[280] Trump declared his triumphs as a businessman would help him run the nation, bring back jobs, and change trade pacts to favor America. But if he had failed as a business tycoon, his claims would have been invalid. Hammering away at this issue was an important missed opportunity for the Clinton campaign.

Secondly, Clinton didn't focus on how Trump's promises did not make financial sense.[281] There was no way he could produce a multi-trillion dollar tax cut as he described, reduce the national debt, spend a trillion dollars on building infrastructure, grow the military, protect Social Security and Medicare, and end Obamacare. Where was the money going to come from without a huge ballooning of the national debt? Trump was recycling supply-side, trickle-down voodoo economics, which had not worked in the past.[282] Yet Clinton did not repeatedly assail this line of reasoning.

Clinton also did not emphasize the scope of Trump's lies and exaggerations revealed by independent fact-checkers. Organizations measuring the truthfulness of important statements by each candidate noted that Trump lied three quarters of the time and Clinton about one quarter. Trump's lies, however, were more substantial, greatly exceeding the normal hyperbole of politicians. Trump also made racist comments, encouraged violence by his backers, and was thought by many in his party not to have the temperament or judgment to be president. But in spite of Trump's remarks and behavior, many Americans believed his promises to bring back jobs and make America great again, identifying with him emotionally. Though he stated that his successful business career qualified him to be president, his casino businesses went bankrupt a number of times with losses of investors' money. Trump Airlines also failed as did Trump Institute and 'Trump University,' scamming students who paid with federal loans.

And Trump's real estate business was known to have stiffed contractors and small businessmen.

On the other hand, Clinton also had a number of concerns regarding her ethics and judgment. The most damning was her employing a personal server and unprotected emails while Secretary of State, the head of the FBI labeling her careless. There was also a question of a tie-in between the State Department and the Clinton Global Initiative when she was Secretary, with donors to the latter having access to department officials. As another issue, Clinton had excoriated women her husband had slept with, rather than blaming him for the missteps. And there were her ties to Wall Street banks.

In addition, she did not attack Trump vigorously enough for his comments that the election process was rigged and he might not accept the results. This was an extraordinary repudiation of American democracy and did not fit with the idea of fair play. And why did Trump go out of his way to praise Putin and deny that Russian hacking had influenced the election? Another element Clinton should have addressed was Trump's dependence on Twitter for communicating, bypassing the press corps, unhappy to have to respond to probing questions. It was much easier to describe one's thoughts in 140 characters than to have to explain policy in detail.

The media, which had made Trump in the first place, were also not combative enough in pointing out his lies, exaggerations, and contradictions, in many ways normalizing him as a candidate. They did not take him to task when he spoke of illegal or unconstitutional actions, such as surveillance of Muslims, torture of terrorist suspects, and jail terms or removal of citizenship for flag burning. Once Trump had grown in stature and power, he no longer needed the press, and intimidated them into disregarding many of his impractical, unreasonable, or uninformed remarks and actions. His labeling of the media as "the enemy of the people" also encouraged his base to attack journalists verbally or physically.

The media also spent an inordinate amount of time focusing on Clinton's problems, reinforcing negative views voters might have had.

Comparable attention was not paid to Trump's business failures, his refusal to release his taxes, possible non-payment of taxes, his charitable foundation's lack of donations and its self-serving uses by Trump, his admiration for Putin and cozying up to this dictator, the hacking of the DNC by the Russians and the release of material that damaged Clinton, the fact that many of Trump's products had been made abroad while he had been promising to bring jobs back to America, and so forth. Attempting to equate the two candidates and treat them fairly, the media gave credibility to some of Trump's outrageous statements and blatant lies, making uninformed voters believe that what he said was valid. The media saw Trump more as a celebrity than politician and cut him slack because of that.

With Trump's campaign hitting the right notes with voters and with all the mistakes Clinton made, another factor was that Obama did almost nothing to build up and energize the Democratic Party during his years in the White House. Though he had brought the nation back from the brink of Depression and the economy was improving, he did not mobilize the grass roots and did not work with senators, members of Congress, governors, mayors, and legislators to develop a strong and lasting political organization that could compete effectively with the GOP. State legislatures and governorships were overwhelmingly in Republican hands, gerrymandering districts after the 2010 census and controlling local politics. Not only did Hillary Clinton lose the presidency, but the Democrats lost the House and the Senate as Obama was ushered out of the White House.

This political tsunami occurred with unemployment at its lowest level in years, median wages increasing, Wall Street reformed, and the stock market booming. Yet millions of citizens felt left behind, disaffected, discouraged and demoralized. Many of them had voted for Obama, believing his policies would benefit them. For a man who had been a community organizer and whose campaigns had featured strong grassroots support, Obama's failure to develop the Democratic Party can be seen as a major deficiency that aided Trump and the GOP and led to the repeal of many of Obama's progressive accomplishments. Did

Democrats misread the working and middle classes? Bernie Sanders was able to capture them, which means a populist message (similar to Trump's) might have brought many of them into the Democratic fold. Obama's bailout of the auto industry saved millions of jobs for workers in the rust belt. Why then did these states vital to winning the Electoral College and presidency go to Trump?

When all the votes had been counted, it turned out Clinton won the popular vote by a huge margin of nearly 3 million votes.[283] Trump received 45.94 percent of the vote, with Hillary ahead of him by 2.1 percent, the highest percentage for a losing candidate in modern history. However, with Trump doing well in the swing states, he won the Electoral College 304 to 227. Despite the confirmed results, Trump claimed he won the popular vote in a 'massive landslide victory.'[284] He declared Clinton's lead was due to illegal voting, with no proof offered. It appeared to be all about Trump's ego and refusal to accept the loss of the election count in terms of the popular vote.

The Trump victory was a resounding defeat for the nation's labor unions, which had spent over $100 million to try and beat him.[285] Yet voters from union households supported Clinton over Trump by a margin of only 51 percent to 43 percent. This disconnect between union leaders and membership, may be part of the reason for the slide in union power, notwithstanding Republican antagonism, right-to-work laws, and the rise in populism. If the Democrats are going to overturn the GOP majority in the Senate and defeat Trump in 2020, they are going to need avid backing from labor. If union leadership cannot do a better job communicating with members about their needs and solidifying the politics of the union movement, both the Democrats and unions will be in even more trouble. One group that came through for Trump were the evangelical Christians, who voted for him at an 81 percent rate, despite his admitted sexual predation, adultery, divorces, and lack of religiosity.[286]

There is also no question that Russian hacking and use of social media interfered in the electoral process, though their impact is uncertain. Together with Wikileaks and Julian Assange, the Russians did whatever they could to damage Clinton and the Democrats.[287] Trump downplayed Russian involvement, not wanting it to seem as if he had needed outside help or that he would be ingratiated to them. In fact, he refused to accept information from the U.S. intelligence agencies, declaring they had been wrong on Iraq and were wrong on the source of the hacking and whether it was designed to help him.[288] His refusal to believe the CIA and FBI, and his admiration for Putin put him at odds with members of both political parties, his positions perplexing. There was some thought the Russians might have some compromising photos or information about him, or that he might have financial ties to Russian oligarchs.

Prior to leaving office, Obama finally placed sanctions on a number of Russians and the FSB and GRU agencies believed responsible for hacking American computers to influence the election.[289] Thirty-five Russian intelligence agents were also expelled. Whether his retaliatory actions were proportional to Russian attempts to undermine the election is questionable. Trump, who refused regular intelligence briefings, said he would meet with some leaders of the intelligence communities to learn more about the hacking. It is unclear why Comey and the FBI had made statements regarding Clinton's emails and avoided any focus on the Trump team's contact with Russian officials prior to the election.[290] The information was not made public until after Trump was installed in office.

That much of the Republican establishment and traditionalists voted for Trump given his stances contrary to GOP principles was somewhat surprising. Free market dogma, a cornerstone of Republican doctrine, was abandoned by Trump and replaced by nationalist and populist concepts that appealed to the white working and middle classes.[291] As The Economist noted, Trump had been opposed to trade deals for decades, a protectionist who favored tariffs to help domestic industries. [292] He viewed globalization and trade pacts as a boon for multi-national corporations, raising their profits but hurting their workers, while benefiting underdeveloped nations like Mexico and China. Trump saw the nation's trade deficits as evidence America had been duped by other countries, because of poor negotiating tactics or unfair conduct.

In mid-January, as Obama was preparing to leave office, his approval rating was among the highest in years, 62 percent.[293] On the other hand, Donald Trump's approval rating three days prior to inauguration was the lowest of any recent president at 40 percent according to a CNN/ORC poll.[294] A Washington Post/ABC News poll also had Trump's handling of his transition at 40 percent, indicating that he was the least popular president-elect of the last seven occupants of the White House.[295] Other polls were in a similar range.[296] Trump tweeted in response that the polls were rigged, unwilling to accept results of multiple surveys.[297]

Obama's rating prior to his inauguration in 2009 was 84 percent, Bill Clinton's 67 percent, and George W. Bush's 61 percent.[298] Most Americans (53 percent) felt Trump's shaky management of the transition, along with his comments and actions after the election, made them less confident he would be able to function well as president. His constant fighting with the media and apparently thoughtless and confrontational remarks via Twitter were believed to have damaged his image with the public. In addition, his love fest with Putin and his battles with America's intelligence agencies took some luster off the Trump façade.

In an NBC/Wall Street Journal poll two days prior to Trump's inauguration, almost 70 percent of Americans disapproved of his use of Twitter,[299] often unclear whether his messages represented official policy. And he employed Twitter to attack people with whom he disagreed. In the same poll, only 30 percent were confident Trump had the right policies and goals for his upcoming job and 32 percent believed he had the right personal characteristics to lead the nation.[300] A Pew Poll after the election had just 30 percent satisfied with the way Trump conducted himself during the campaign, compared to 43 percent for Clinton.[301] Never before in Pew post-election polls did the loser have a higher grade than the winner. Unlike other presidents-elect,

Trump's frequent attacks on critics, journalists, and political opponents revealed his disdain for democratic norms.[302] In the same realm was his acceptance of torture of suspected terrorists and refusal to accept refugees into the country. Trump also suggested that flag-burners be jailed or lose their citizenship, both unconstitutional infringements on freedom of speech as previously ruled by the Supreme Court.[303] And his declared admiration for a number of the world's dictators indicated a major shift away from support for democratic principles.

4

American Political Corruption

"A Crime is a sinne, consisting in the Committing (by Deed or Word) of that which the Law forbiddeth, or the Omission of what it hath commanded....Ignorance of the Law of Nature Excuseth no man; because everyman that hath attained to the use of Reason, is supposed to know, he ought not do to another, what he would not have done to himself."
Leviathan, Thomas Hobbes[304]

CORRUPTION IS A universal problem, possible in every financial transaction and the political processes of every nation. Whether legal or illegal, some individuals are always looking for an edge whenever money exchanges hands or there is an opportunity for gain. Government officials are no different than the population at large in terms of ethics and morality (though many citizens may disagree with that assessment). If there is a chance to obtain extra income by some action or scheme, many will proceed, particularly if there is a low probability of exposure. In countries where the rule of law is generally observed, the amount of fraud and corruption is less than in states where the law is easily subverted. In most democracies, including America, the number of uninformed or uninterested voters enhances political corruption as politicians assume their actions will not affect their standing with their constituents. Fraud and corruption poison democracies because perpetrators believe they can escape detection and not be penalized. Deceit and illegal conduct also occur because some individuals are convinced the risk-reward ratio makes it worthwhile to take chances. Corruption is more common in autocratic states where criminals may elude punishment through connections, bribery of officials or witnesses, or by intimidation of witnesses or law enforcement officers.

Surprisingly, it is easy to hide money in the U.S. obtained through illegal activities, though offshore accounts are often utilized.[305] Certain states, particularly Delaware, Nevada, and Wyoming, try to attract corporations and wealthy Americans to use their financial institutions to shield assets. Anonymous shell corporations can be established inexpensively. Estimates are that about 8 percent of the world's wealth, more than $7.6 trillion, is stashed in offshore accounts. Though the United States pressures other countries to share information, the U.S. has not signed on to new standards for exchanging financial information, thus allowing money laundering and corruption to go undetected.

Various types of political corruption take place in democracies. Elections may be stolen, with rightful winners deprived of victory. With computerized voting machines, hacking is now an issue. A second type of fraud is the selling of votes or influence by elected or appointed officials in return for money, gifts, or promises of future well-paying jobs. Politicians who have been enticed may support particular projects, laws, and funding of programs. Special interests or lobbyists are often the seducers. In a third type of corrupt activity, politicians take bribes from people doing business with the government. Officials may also avoid prosecuting citizens who have committed financial crimes if they receive campaign contributions or payoffs.

Sexual harassment or sexual demands may also be made by politicians on female or male staff members, leading to unwanted relationships, or workers quitting. Lobbyists and government contractors may provide sexual favors to officials or aides in exchange for desired actions. Undoubtedly, other types of corruption target lawmakers or appointed officials, as political power is always corrupting and the lure of money, sex, or additional power may be hard to resist.

Using the United States again as an example, stealing votes and fixing contests occurred in presidential elections in the past, as well as Congressional, state, and municipal balloting. When big city machines were more powerful, local, municipal, and state elections were often preordained, with the bosses choosing winners. Most powerful were Boss Tweed and Tammany Hall in New York, Tom Pendergast in Kansas City, James Michael Curley in Boston, Huey Long in Louisiana, and Richard Daley in Chicago.[306] Following the Civil War, corruption permeated American politics at every level.[307] Political machines ran the big cities, collecting graft and bribes while dispensing patronage jobs. Irish Catholics, nearly 25 percent of New York's population, were corralled by Tweed's men as soon as they stepped off the boat. Given money, liquor, and help finding work, they had a strong allegiance to Tammany Hall and voted as directed. Many public works projects were controlled by Tweed, who held a number of positions in the city and placed his own men in others. In his heyday, he was more powerful than the mayor.

At one time, patronage helped the bosses guarantee votes for a particular candidate. The bosses simply told their followers whom to vote for, with balloting that was not actually 'secret.' Some bosses or politicians would buy votes with small sums of money, food, or other gifts. (This strategy is still used in third world 'democracies.') Or legal ballots could be removed after voting was complete and ballot boxes stuffed with votes for candidates backed by the bosses. In addition, extra ballots could be placed for non-existent citizens or residents of the district who had died. Votes could also be miscounted by monitors employed by the bosses.

A 'lawful' form of corruption is gerrymandering (discussed elsewhere), utilized by both parties when they control a state's legislature and governorship. The boundaries of House and legislative districts are redrawn every ten years after a census. Placing most of a racial or ethnic group strategically can almost guarantee a party's candidates will win certain districts. Gerrymandering has been particularly effective in states controlled by conservative Republicans.

Because voters are generally uninformed about candidates' positions or contested issues, politicians seek to use inaccuracies or falsehoods to gain supporters. Many voters are willing to overlook lies and exaggerations, believing these are universal characteristics of politicians. Polifact, started by the Tampa Bay Times in 2007, checks comments made by presidential candidates and other major nominees and rates them in terms of what is false and what is true.[308] During the 2016 election campaign, 70 percent of Trump's statements were found to be false, with only 4 percent completely true. 26 percent of Clinton's statements were deemed false.[309]

1876 Presidential Election

The 1876 victory of Republican Rutherford B. Hayes over Democrat Samuel Tilden in their presidential contest was blatantly fraudulent.[310] Tilden attained nearly 300,000 more popular votes than his opponent and would have won the presidency with one additional electoral vote. However, under Reconstruction, Republicans controlled three Southern states, Florida, Louisiana and South Carolina, and the boards responsible for certifying votes. The election and presidency went to Hayes because Republican electoral boards threw out enough Democratic votes to hand Hayes the victory. The deadlock ended when Hayes agreed to terminate Reconstruction, allowing white Democrats to again control the governments of the Southern states.[311]

Nixon-Kennedy

The Richard Nixon-John Kennedy presidential contest in 1960 also generated suspicion of fraud, some analysts believing Nixon may have actually won. The two candidates were separated by only 113,000 votes out of 68 million cast. Skeptics postulate that Mayor Daley's machine in Chicago piled up votes for Kennedy along with Lyndon Johnson's followers in central Texas. In Cook County, Illinois (Chicago), Kennedy won by a suspicious landslide of 450,000 votes.[312] Republicans refused to accept the voting, but could find no proof of significant fraud. This does not mean the election was untainted, as local election boards could have altered the vote count without being detected.[313]

Bush-Gore

The presidential election of 2000 between Al Gore and George Bush was another dirty affair, a triumph of the 'do whatever's necessary' approach by Bush and his guru, Karl Rove. The first victim of this strategy was John McCain, the only other credible GOP candidate. After McCain won the New Hampshire primary, in South Carolina there were whispered stories of marital infidelity by McCain, assertions he was anti-religious and had fathered an inter-racial child. Not unexpectedly, Bush took South Carolina.[314] During the general election campaign, Bush attacked the Clinton Administration over the American undertaking in Somalia, declaring in the second debate- "I don't think our troops ought to be used for what's called nation-building."[315] (An interesting comment from a man who involved America in a much more extensive venture in Iraq.) Bush pledged to bring moral integrity back to Washington and promised to stand against abortion, against activist judges, and for faith based initiatives.

On election night, the outcome was unclear. Bush had 246 Electoral College votes and Gore 255, with 270 needed for victory. Florida, with 25 Electoral votes was the key to election, but the result was too close to call.[316] Though Bush led in Florida in the initial count by about 1000 votes, a month of court challenges and recounts were necessary before he was declared victorious. When recounts were halted, Bush was ahead by 537 votes, 0.009% of the state's ballots.[317] With a strongly partisan Republican, Katherine Harris, supervising the recounts and Bush's brother, Jeb, as governor, questions were raised about the fairness of the process. The Florida House of Representatives also voted on a party line basis to certify the state's electors for Bush. Though the Florida Supreme Court ordered a statewide manual recount on December 8, the next day the U.S. Supreme Court ruled 5 to 4 to stay the recount, the conservative majority choosing Bush.[318] By preventing a hand recount, the Supreme Court determined the outcome of the election--the counties whose votes were in question, strongly Democratic. Gore lost though he polled over 500,000 more votes nationally than Bush.[319]

Justice Stevens wrote in dissent- "Although we may never know with complete certainty the identity of the winner of this year's presidential election, the identity of the loser is perfectly clear. It is the Nation's confidence in the judge as an impartial guardian of the rule of law."[320] The consensus of analysts is that, if Nader had not been running, Gore would have won the states lost by narrow margins, including Florida, Tennessee and New Hampshire.[321] Hoping Nader would siphon off votes from Gore, GOP groups paid for advertising extolling Nader in several states. In Florida, Nader had 97,488 votes, far exceeding the 537 votes giving Bush victory.[322]

Executive Branch Transgressions

A report in Political Science Quarterly in 2012 examined the frequency of modern day presidential scandals, noting that between 1972 and 2008, eighty-seven had occurred, the president involved in sixteen. [323] Clinton was entangled in seven (three sexual, three political, one financial), while Nixon, Reagan, Ford, George H.W. Bush were all caught up in single incidents, Jimmy Carter and George W. Bush in two each. Cabinet members and cabinet rank officials were often implicated in disreputable actions, the White House Chief of Staff a recurrent actor.

Nixon, Watergate, and Agnew

The infamous Watergate Scandal, a major blow to American democracy, showcased depravity and corruption on the presidential level by Richard Nixon.[324] In June of 1972, burglars were caught in the offices of the Democratic National Committee in the Watergate building in Washington trying to bug the phones and steal documents to aid Nixon's re-election.[325] While it is unclear whether Nixon knew about this 'espionage' beforehand, afterwards he worked to cover it up. This included trying to keep the F.B.I. from probing the episode with the help of the CIA, destruction of evidence, and discharging staff members unhelpful to his efforts at concealment. Though early disclosures suggested presidential crimes, the electorate voted for Nixon, since his opponent, George McGovern, was a weak candidate. And Nixon swore that he and the White House staff had known nothing of the break-in. Nixon won the 1972 election by a wide margin, the illegal activity ludicrous because it had been unnecessary and amateurish. After their failed attempt, Nixon's Committee to Re-elect the President, was mockingly called CREEP.[326]

The cover-up by Nixon was an abuse of presidential power and obstruction of justice, Nixon lying about his involvement. Subsequently, seven Watergate conspirators were indicted, with five pleading guilty and avoiding trial, having been coerced by Nixon's aides to do so. In January of 1973, the other two were convicted. However, investigative reporters Bob Woodward and Carl Bernstein of the Washington Post began digging further, along with Judge John J. Sirica and members of a Senate committee.[327] Under intense stress, some conspirators began to cave. A few of Nixon's aides testified before a grand jury, including White House Counsel, John Dean.[328] They revealed Nixon had known about the operation, had tried to hide it, but had taped all the discussions in the Oval Office.

At this point, prosecutors wanted those tapes. Through the summer and fall of 1973, Nixon claimed executive privilege gave him control of the tapes. However, pressure mounted from the Senate investigating committee, Sirica, and independent special prosecutor, Archibald Cox. When Nixon fired Cox, a number of other DOJ officials resigned in protest in what became known as the Saturday night massacre.[329] Nixon finally capitulated and yielded some tapes to investigators. By early 1974, Nixon's cover-up was in disarray. On March 1, a new special prosecutor convinced a grand jury to indict seven former members of Nixon's staff. Nixon was labeled an unindicted co-conspirator, the grand jury unsure a sitting president could be indicted.

In July, though the Supreme Court ordered Nixon to release all the tapes, he refused. Given his recalcitrance, the House voted to impeach him, charges including "obstruction of justice, abuse of power, criminal cover-up, and several violations of the Constitution."[330] With his own party, Republicans in Congress, pressuring him, Nixon finally surrendered the tapes on August 5, showing definitive proof of his complicity. Expecting conviction by the Senate, Republicans persuaded Nixon to resign.[331] Six weeks after having been sworn in as new president, Gerald Ford pardoned Nixon for any illegal acts committed while in office.

The reason Gerald Ford became president was because Nixon's running mate, Spiro Agnew, had been forced to resign as vice president in October of 1973 due to charges of bribery and corruption while Baltimore county executive, governor of Maryland and vice president.[332] Soliciting kickbacks from contractors given county work, he had received payoffs from engineers with state business and bribes even while vice president. Agnew resigned on October 10, pleading nolo contendere to the charges against him, the legal equivalent of guilty. Attorney General Richardson read a catalogue of evidence then asked the judge for leniency, part of the agreement structured the day before. Agnew escaped prison, his only punishment a $10,000 fine for tax evasion and the blot on his name. House minority leader, Gerald Ford, succeeded Agnew as vice president, and president after Nixon's resignation.

The amount of dirt and illegal activities by the nation's highest officials, seen constantly on television news, disgusted citizens and made many wary of the democratic process. Some in the young 'Woodstock generation' dropped out, communal living, drugs and sex the answer for them. Even today, cynicism and suspicion of government remains ingrained in many citizens.

Iran-Contra

Though Watergate is considered the pre-eminent American political scandal of the 20th century, violations of the law did not end there. The next major illegal presidential action was the Iran-Contra affair during the Reagan administration.[333] Reagan, a staunch anti-communist, was incensed by the Cuban-backed Sandinistas of Nicaragua and determined to defeat them.[334] However, twice after 1982, Democratic Congresses passed the Boland Amendment, limiting activities by the CIA and Defense Department in Nicaragua. Directly contravening the law, Reagan instructed National Security Advisor, Robert McFarlane, to take measures to bolster the Contras in their fight against the Sandinistas.

At war with Iraq, Iran had secretly asked to buy weapons from the U.S, despite an arms embargo and history of enmity since the Iranian revolution in November 1979.[335] And at the time of the request, Iranian-backed terrorists held seven Americans prisoner in Lebanon. Though his cabinet was split over the idea, Reagan supported shipping arms to Iran in return for release of the hostages. This was in spite of a vow never to deal with terrorists, knowing that sending arms to Iran violated the embargo. Over 1500 missiles had gone to Iran by the time the scheme was exposed, with three hostages being released.

In November 1986, a Lebanese newspaper published an article about covert activities involving Iran, Lebanon and the U.S, Reagan angrily denying the story. However, he retracted his denial a week later, declaring the exchange had not been an arrangement of arms for hostages. By his reversal, Reagan's veracity and straightforwardness was no longer accepted by many Americans. During this time, Attorney General Edwin Meese found that only $12 million of the $30 million paid by Iran had gone to the U.S. Oliver North, a lieutenant colonel on the National Security Council, had been redirecting Iranian funds from the arms sales to the Contras. This had been done with the okay of National Security Advisor John Poindexter, believing Reagan would have agreed.

Though Poindexter resigned and North was dismissed, the media and Congress would not stop probing, wondering how Reagan could not have known of these activities. The Tower Commission, appointed by Reagan and headed by former Texas GOP Senator John Tower, investigated the affair. They concluded that Reagan's detachment from management of operations by his staff had allowed diversion of funds to have occurred without his knowledge. But this was not the end. For the next eight years, Independent Counsel Lawrence Walsh studied Iran-Contra, charging fourteen people close to Reagan with various crimes. However, North was freed on a technicality and six pardons were issued by President Bush, including McFarlane and former Defense Secretary Weinberger. In spite of engaging in federal crimes, Reagan's approval rating leaving office was the highest of any president since Franklin Roosevelt.[336]

Bill Clinton Scandals

Bill Clinton's presidency was notable for its scandals, many related to sexual predation.[337] However, Whitewater was an investment scheme of buying land for future development in Arkansas while Clinton was governor. The Clintons had been partners with James McDougal and his wife in this real estate deal since 1978.[338] In time, McDougal became a client of Hillary Clinton at the Rose Law Firm in Little Rock where she handled his failing savings and loan company, Madison Guaranty. In 1994, a special counsel was appointed to investigate Whitewater.

McDougal claimed that while governor, Clinton had asked him to bring Hillary more business. Testimony from McDougal, Hillary, lawyers from the Rose Law Firm, and officers of Madison Guaranty were conflicted regarding how Hillary had obtained the Madison account. (Madison eventually went bankrupt, with taxpayers on the hook for more than $60 million.) Because of the partnership between McDougal and the Clintons in the land deal, questions of conflict of interest arose regarding Hillary representing McDougal and the bank. Questions also were generated about why the Clintons had been involved with McDougal, since he had been indicted a number of times in real estate scams and eventually convicted. Hillary was also attorney for McDougal and Madison in cases that came before the Arkansas Securities Commission, an agency under Governor Bill Clinton's aegis.[339]

During Clinton's presidency, Hillary and others involved in Madison and Whitewater testified a number of times before the Resolution Trust Corporation, the Federal Deposit Insurance's inspector general, and Senate Whitewater committee. Clinton himself also testified, different versions given by various parties. Conflicting stories also emerged over Hillary's handling of another convoluted McDougal land deal called Castle Grande. Sham transactions had falsely raised profits at McDougal's troubled bank leading to multiple convictions for fraud in 1996, including McDougal and his wife. Though there were several changes in Hillary's version of what she had done related to the McDougals, Madison and Whitewater, as well as her billing and work at the Rose Law Firm, no charges were filed against Bill and Hillary after years of probing, costing the government $70 million. Multiple investigators and special counsels concluded that though Whitewater had benefited from criminal transactions, evidence was insufficient to implicate President Clinton or Hillary.[340]

Bill Clinton's sexual escapades before and during his presidency and lying about them, almost brought his administration to an early end. Prior to the 1992 presidential election, Gennifer Flowers publically asserted she had been Clinton's mistress for years.[341] He strongly denied this and Hillary stood by his side supporting him during a television interview, enhancing his credibility. (Six years after this denial, during a deposition with lawyers for Paula Jones, Clinton admitted having once had sex with Flowers in the 1970s.)

In May of 1994, Paula Corbin Jones brought a lawsuit against Clinton, claiming sexual harassment while he was governor of Arkansas and she was a clerical worker.[342] Other women who accused Clinton of sexual offenses were Kathleen Willey, a White House volunteer, who claimed Clinton had groped her in a hallway in 1997, Arkansas attorney, Dolly Kyle Browning, who reported a long affair with Clinton prior to his marriage but only ending in 1992, and Juanita Broaddrick, who alleged Clinton had raped her in 1978, though she had brought no charges. Though Clinton dismissed all these allegations, in January 1999 Paula Corbin Jones agreed to an $850,000 settlement from Clinton to end her suit. Attention then focused on Clinton's affair with Monica Lewinsky.

The saga began when Lewinsky, a twenty-one-year-old, became an unpaid intern at the White House in June 1995.[343] By November, Clinton and Lewinsky had started a sexual relationship lasting into 1996. Both were deposed by Jones' lawyers in 1998 and denied sexual contact.[344] Clinton publically declared he had never had sex with Lewinsky and had not tried to cover anything up. However, Lewinsky had been friendly with a woman co-worker at the Pentagon, Linda Tripp, who recorded their telephone conversations where Lewinsky had unburdened herself about the affair. Tripp betrayed Lewinsky by delivering the tapes of their confidential exchanges to the special prosecutor, Ken Starr. With these in hand, Starr questioned Lewinsky again, offering her immunity from perjury charges related to her previous testimony.

Given his possession of the tapes, Lewinsky had no choice but to cooperate and reveal the details of her affair with Clinton.[345] Her description of where they had sex, people they had passed, and phone calls Clinton had taken, reinforced her credibility and truthfulness. In his report, Starr alleged Clinton had perjured himself at least five times relating to the affair in his Paula Jones deposition in January of 1998, and another three times during his grand jury appearance in August of that year, and had lied in a television statement to the American people.

Starr's report went to Congress, suggesting there were grounds for impeachment, including perjury, obstruction of justice, witness tampering, and abuse of authority. In October and November of 1998, the

House Judiciary Committee reviewed the report and sent a written inquiry to Clinton about a number of points. His answers were legalistic and contentious, and on December 12, the committee recommended impeachment on a party-line vote. Polls had shown the public to be against impeachment, but the House voted in favor on December 19. Clinton became the second president to be impeached, the other being Andrew Johnson (Lincoln's successor).

Clinton's Senate trial began in January 1999. Testimony was limited and on February 12, the Senate rejected impeachment in a close vote. However, Judge Wright, who had dismissed the Paula Jones case, found Clinton in contempt for denying the Lewinsky affair when testifying in January 1998, and ordered him to pay Jones' lawyers $90,000.[346] The day before Clinton left office in January 2001, he acknowledged false statements in the Jones case and agreed to have his law license suspended for five years along with a $25,000 fine. Clinton's presidency will forever be tarnished by his lack of sexual restraint, numerous lies and attempts at cover-up.

John Edwards

John Edwards, previously a personal injury lawyer, in 1998 was elected Senator from North Carolina, labeled 'Sexiest Politician Alive' by People Magazine in 2003. In 2004, he was picked by John Kerry to be his running mate as vice president, losing to Bush and Cheney. [347] Soon afterwards, his wife, Elizabeth, was diagnosed with breast cancer. However, by 2006, Edwards was running for the Democratic presidential nomination. In March of 2007, Elizabeth announced that her cancer had recurred, but she and her husband wanted the campaign to continue. Meanwhile, Edwards was having an affair with Rielle Hunter, a videographer covering his campaign.

Hunter gave birth to a child in 2008, claiming Edwards as the father which he denied. Subsequently, he dropped his presidential bid and disclosed he was indeed the father of Hunter's child. At the same time, he separated from his wife who died shortly afterwards. In June

2011, Edwards was indicted on six charges of utilizing almost a million dollars in campaign funds to conceal his affair, pleading not guilty. The case went to trial in 2013, describing the sordid details of his affair and attempted cover-up while his wife was dying. He was acquitted on one count of fraud, with a mistrial on the others, but was required to reimburse the Treasury for his campaign funds.[348] At that point, he announced a return to the practice of law.

Donald Trump is currently president (2020) and his criminal activities including obstruction of justice, campaign spending violations, and impeachment will not be discussed.

Arrogance of Power

Watergate, Iran-Contra, Clinton and Edwards' sexual escapades were all examples of arrogance of power, where people holding high offices believe themselves above the law and able to flout rules and societal mores. Abuse of office and arrogance of power are common attributes of politicians, corporate executives, and financial gurus (probably universal human characteristics- 'power corrupts' and so forth).

Senator Ted Kennedy's 'accident' at Chappaquidick, where he was driving after drinking at a party and his passenger Mary Jo Kopechne drowned, is another example of arrogance by a politician who never paid a price for his conduct. He did not report the incident to authorities until the next morning, never had a test of his alcohol level, and denied culpability for the death. In spite of this, citizens of Massachusetts returned Kennedy to office afterwards, disregarding his actions and seemingly not caring that he had evaded the law and caused someone's death.

Vice-President Cheney shot a man in February 2006 in an apparent hunting accident, yet did not notify the police for hours. The episode was not investigated until the following day. Though Cheney admitted imbibing alcohol while handling his weapon, he made no statement to law enforcement agents after the shooting and an alcohol level was not drawn. It was another case of a powerful man perceiving himself as above the law and getting away with misconduct.

When forming his cabinet in 2009, Obama found ethical and possible criminal actions involving some of his choices, forcing him to drop these men from consideration. Because they previously held government posts, they may have felt themselves immune to scrutiny. Arrogance of power may also explain the willingness of most politicians to disregard ethical considerations in dealing with lobbyists and special interests, believing their actions will not become general knowledge, or will not incite their constituents. The same conviction may also explain sexual indiscretions by many politicians. Indeed, the majority of criminal or ethical mistakes, sexual harassment or affairs by politicians likely have never come to light.

President George W. Bush demonstrated disregard for tradition and the law, trying to increase powers of the presidency with what some described as 'creeping autocracy.'[349] Using the threat of terrorism as rationale, Bush claimed surveillance and investigative powers requiring no oversight, no consultation with Congress and no judicial review. Though some officials at the Justice Department objected on Constitutional grounds, they were overruled by Attorney General John Ashcroft.[350] Using Article 2 of the Constitution, which delineates powers of the president, Bush asserted his expanded authority was inherent in his role as Commander in Chief.[351]

The administration also declared other controversial actions within the purview of the president, including imprisonment of enemy combatants at Guantanamo, rendition of suspected terrorists, military trials of belligerents, and use of coercive interrogation techniques on possible terrorists.[352] The Supreme Court, however, in July of 2006, established its control in these matters.[353] The Court said military tribunals for terror suspects contravened the law and Geneva Conventions.[354] But in new legislation the president proposed after the Court decision, he asked for the same authority the Court had struck down.[355],[356] These were opposed by prominent members of his own party. In response, the president asserted that Republicans rejecting his legislation were putting America at risk and "hindering the fight on terrorism."[357]

A conservative legal scholar, Jack Goldsmith, who headed the DOJ's Office of Legal Counsel from October 2003 until resigning in June 2004, wrote a scathing indictment of the Bush administration's efforts to expand powers of the presidency. (The OLC provides opinions on the legality of government strategies and conduct.) In his book, *The Terror Presidency*, Goldsmith asserts Bush, Cheney, Gonzales and their aides ignored international agreements (the Geneva Conventions), the Constitution, and Congressional mandates in such matters as torture of prisoners, detention of enemy combatants and domestic surveillance.[358]

Bush also claimed nearly unlimited power to manage the war in Iraq, requesting that Congress fund everything he asked for in that regard. He ignored the fact that the Constitution grants Congress the power of the purse specifically to check the president's authority to conduct war. Other questionable maneuvers were Bush's statements when he signed legislation, presenting his concept of the laws and how he intended to execute them. If accepted by other branches of government, these 'signing statements' would increase presidential power and could subvert Congress's intentions in passing legislation. A bipartisan panel of the American Bar Association stated "President Bush was flouting the Constitution and undermining the rule of law by claiming the power to disregard selected provisions of bills he signed."[359]

Before invading Iraq, President Bush was reluctant to ask for Congress's approval to go to war, believing he had authority to act on his own. Only after outcries from senators of both parties did he agree to get consent.[360] However, the resolution submitted to Congress, though asking for prior authorization, claimed inherent presidential power "under the Constitution to defend the national security interests of the country,"[361] making it appear that approval from Congress was unnecessary. In every area possible, Bush tried to augment the power of the president, with or without Congressional and judicial assent. Were these not a form of corruption?

Though President Obama decried Bush's use of executive power and signing statements on the campaign trail in 2007 and 2008, he acted in the same manner as president.[362] He used signing statements to protect what he saw as the executive domain against intrusion from Congress, particularly in foreign affairs.

Overt Corruption in the Executive Branch

During the 19th century, winning candidates could distribute patronage jobs to their supporters. With the Pendleton Civil Service Reform Act in 1883, most sub-cabinet positions were awarded after merit testing. A Civil Service Commission from both parties vetted the exams and chose people for non-policy making jobs.[363] The Reform Act also prohibited government employees from contributing to political parties or participating in political activities. However, officials in the executive branch were in charge of contracts for government services, as well as awarding rights for oil and gas drilling on public land or in continental waters, and mineral rights. These functions provided opportunities for bribery and corruption.

The Teapot Dome Scandal during the Harding administration in the 1920s, involved the Secretary of the Interior, Albert Fall, leasing land and drilling rights to oilman Harry Sinclair in Wyoming, and Edward Doheny in California, without open bidding.[364] A Senate investigation found that Fall received $400,000 in 'loans' for assisting these men with their leases. Throughout the last century, scandals involving cabinet or sub-cabinet personnel occurred periodically, usually regarding government contracts given without competitive bidding. But other corrupt activities also occurred.

Michael Deaver, President Reagan's former deputy chief of staff, was found guilty of perjury in September 1988 after lying to Congress and a Federal grand jury regarding lobbying work after leaving the White House. The judge, a Reagan appointee, gave Deaver a suspended prison sentence, a $100,000 fine and 1,500 hours of community service.[365]

Over the years, a number of scandals occurred in the Department of Housing and Urban Development, poorly managed since its inception. Samuel Pierce, HUD secretary during the Reagan administration, allowed political appointees to utilize their positions for personal gain and was guilty of similar actions himself.[366] Abuses occurred in subsidy and co-insurance programs, mortgage lending, and construction. Losses from corruption and fraud under Pierce's 'supervision' were estimated between $2 and $6 billion.

Other government officials on the take included James Watt, Secretary of the Interior, who made nearly a half million dollars assisting clients in obtaining subsidies for three HUD-related projects, and Edward Brooke, a former Republican Senator from Massachusetts who made $183,000 for 'consulting' work on two HUD projects. An independent counsel's probe into corruption at HUD produced seventeen convictions, three of them HUD under-secretaries.[367]

Henry Cisneros was HUD secretary under President Bill Clinton from 1993-1997.[368] He resigned to handle allegations he had lied to the FBI about money to a former mistress. Pleading guilty in 1999, he was fined $10,000 and escaped prison.

Lewis "Scooter" Libby, assistant to President George W. Bush and chief of staff to Vice President Dick Cheney, resigned in October of 2005 after indictment on five counts, including perjury and obstruction of justice.[369] He was sentenced to thirty months imprisonment in June 2007, convicted on four of the five counts. The case was related to the outing of Valerie Plame, a covert CIA agent, to allegedly punish her husband, Joseph Wilson, a diplomat who opposed the Iraq War and discredited Bush's assertion that Saddam Hussein had nuclear weapons.

In 1978, after Watergate, Congress passed the Inspector General Act, having independent observers in federal departments and agencies to expose corruption, fraud, waste, and abuse.[370] These individuals were supposed to have unlimited access to all necessary records. However, during the eight years of the Obama administration, many departments and agencies blocked access to facts and reports, including personal credit data, grand jury testimony, and wiretap information. This impaired some investigations, with IGs fighting for the data they needed. The OLC defended this conduct on the grounds that protected knowledge might become public. But government officials need to be held accountable, with exposure of corruption or ineptness the province of the IGs.

Congressional Corruption- Congress, Lobbyists, Special Interests

The Congressional Ethics Committee, an oversight body charged with reducing ethical lapses and corruption in Congress, has been woefully ineffective, with three members from each party and lacking support from GOP and Democratic leaders. In February 2010, the Ethics Committee cleared five Democratic and two Republican members of Congress of violations after they had taken campaign contributions from companies to which they had earmarked hundreds of millions of dollars, much of it in no-bid contracts.[371]

Charles Rangel, a Democrat from New York, involved in multiple ethical lapses and tax violations, was allowed to retain chairmanship of the House Ways and Means Committee until he stepped down under pressure from other Democrats in March 2010.[372] After re-election, he was censured by Congress but not expelled, finally retiring in 2016.

In another deadlock, the House Ethics Committee refused to appoint a special panel to investigate charges that Congresswoman Cathy McMorris Rodgers, the House's fourth ranking Republican, had improperly combined campaign and official funds in her re-election campaign and GOP leadership race.[373]

The Chair of the Federal Election Commission (F.E.C.), Ann Ravel, declared in May 2015 that a paralyzed commission was unable to perform its job.[374] Though this agency regulates how political money is raised and spent, she said it was impossible for the F.E.C. to rein in abuses as equal representation from the two parties meant partisan gridlock. The three GOP members repeatedly voted against pursuing important fundraising and spending violations.[375]

Even casual observers recognize corruption is endemic in Washington, as well as in the statehouses and city halls. Contaminating both Republicans and Democrats, the degree of involvement is perhaps determined more by who holds power at the moment than by some inherent moral difference between parties. The last few decades, however, saw more GOP members implicated, with the K Street Project, the Abramoff scandals, the defense contractors' scandals, the PMA lobbying group scandal, as well as ethical and illegal activities by many individual members of Congress.

While politicians should be like Caesar's wife, above suspicion, many of them are no better than streetwalkers, willing to take payment from any john that comes along, bestowing whatever favors are desired. Lobbyists and special interests have joined with these acquiescent politicians to subvert the premises of democracy- that each person's vote has equal weight with every other and that elected representatives will serve the interests of their constituents and the nation instead of enhancing their own personal power and wealth.

Corrupt behavior on the GOP side of the ledger has included that of Jack Abramoff, Congressmen Randy Cunningham, Bob Ney, Tom DeLay, and a number of Congressional staffers, while the Democrats have weighed in with Representatives Maxine Waters, Rangel, and William Jefferson, who stashed some of his bribery loot in his freezer.[376] Congressmen Dan Rostenkowski, James Traficant, Jim Wright, and other Democrats also enjoyed extra paydays in the recent past when they were ascendant in Washington. In June 2010, twenty members of the Congressional Black Caucus, all Democrats, introduced a resolution to limit powers of the Office of Congressional Ethics and prevent release of most of their investigative reports.[377] Thus party or race is no guide to integrity. Even religion, worn proudly on their sleeves by some politicians, is no predictor of ethical behavior. And if we accept the 'cockroach theory,' we can assume scores of other miscreants of both parties continue to exist hidden in the crevices of the

House while their less fortunate corrupt brethren have been exposed to the light of day.

In fact, there are few 'clean' politicians in Washington who refuse to break bread with lobbyists, or who decline contributions from special interest groups. And earmarks, those peculiar devices of Washington officeholders that benefit special interests, once metastasized at an alarming rate into Federal legislation, perhaps less blatantly recently because of legislative changes. Pork and earmarks are prerogatives of elected officials that seem corrupt, but are staunchly defended by many legislators. Pork is money appropriated specifically for pet projects of senators or members of Congress benefiting their home districts or special interests. When inserted secretly or at the last moment into the plethora of paragraphs constituting a Congressional bill, these appropriations become earmarks, though the 2007 ethics law decreed transparency. Usually of little value to the nation, these measures waste tens of billions of dollars of taxpayers' money. In 2010, the GOP congressional leadership banned the practice because of negative publicity they created.[378]

Even with the scope of political scandals, far-reaching reform to make legislators and their staffs more responsive to the electorate and less beholden to lobbyists and special interests does not appear to be on the horizon. Though promised by both Democratic leadership and the GOP over the years, restrictions on lobbying by former government officials and limiting bundling of campaign contributions are still only promises.[379] In 2016, Trump also pledged to drain the Washington swamp, but seems more inclined to populate the city with billionaires.

Who are these lobbyists and special interests that undermine the democratic process and whose voices are heard above those of the electorate? Lobbyists are intermediaries for special interests or advocacy groups who attempt to influence legislation and executive actions or win government contracts. They are often former members of Congress, senators, or staff members, high-level employees of government agencies or departments, or retired military personnel. Because of their previous positions, they have access to legislators and members of the executive branch or top military officers.

Special interests include a multitude of corporations seeking government contracts for products or services, government subsidies or tax breaks, protection from foreign competitors through tariffs or import restrictions, or the waiving of environmental regulations. Business associations may have similar objectives. Unions and labor groups are special interests that want to maintain or raise wages or want protection from low-wage workers abroad. Farmers may want subsidies for their crops or protection from imports. Cities, states and counties, foreign governments, social and religious groups, health organizations, environmental groups, the National Rifle Association and gun control groups, and countless others also act as special interests. To promote their own concerns and values, they provide campaign funds to officials friendly to their views and may be willing to mobilize voters to support them.

The drive for re-election requires huge sums of money, and members of Congress and senators feel indebted to those who contribute. Anyone or any group providing significant aid gets access to the official, perhaps a willingness to craft legislation benefitting that person or group, and maybe a willingness to block other legislation perceived as harmful. This *quid pro quo* makes legislators resistant to campaign finance reform, which along with lobbying reform, could change the political structure now in place and significantly reduce corruption. Along with campaign help, many politicians and staffers also accept personal blandishments from lobbyists, such as trips, dinners, and direct financial rewards (now supposedly prohibited), or the promise of plush lobbying jobs in the future. And the nation's real problems are unaddressed. According to the Federal Election Committee, $7 billion in total was spent on the 2012 election by candidates, parties and outside groups.[380]

President George W. Bush had fundraisers designated as Pioneers, who supplied $200,000, or Rangers, who contributed $100,000 for his campaigns.[381] They delivered these amounts by bundling funds from friends and associates to circumvent campaign financing laws. Ken Lay, of Enron, was a major contributor to Bush and many indicted or convicted white-collar criminals give regularly to one or both parties. Total spending on the 2010 midterm elections reached $4 billion, according to the Center for Responsive Politics.[382] The 2014 midterm election only cost $3.7 billion.[383] Since the Citizens United and McCutcheon decisions, it has become easier for individuals or corporations to contribute to candidates in unlimited amounts through Super PACs or 501(c)(4) organizations, with the ability to remain anonymous. [384],[385]

The list of federal officials who graduate to become lobbyists is extensive. Many are rewarded for work that benefited special interests, while others are hired for potential clout in dealings with government agencies. An example of the first scenario was GOP Representative Billy Tauzin of Louisiana, who helped shepherd the Medicare prescription drug bill through Congress in 2003. He retired afterward to become president of PhRMA, the drug industry lobby, where he commanded millions in salary and benefits.[386] An example of the second was conservative Republican John Ashcroft, who had been a senator from Missouri and attorney general for President Bush. Upon leaving government, he started a lobbying firm in the fall of 2005.[387] Though Ashcroft had been head of DOJ a short time earlier, his firm represented Oracle in attempts to persuade the Justice Department there were no antitrust implications in a billion-dollar acquisition it wanted. Needless to say, Oracle's quest was successful.

The Center for Public Integrity reported in January 2006 that "more than 22,000 companies and organizations had utilized 3,500 lobbying firms and more than 27,000 lobbyists since 1998."[388] Over 2200 former federal employees registered as lobbyists from 1998 to 2004, including 273 previous members of the White House staff and almost 250 members of Congress and heads of federal agencies. During this period, 50 percent of senators and 42 percent of congressmen who left office became lobbyists, 52 percent of Republicans and 33 percent of Democrats:[389] a revolving door between government and lobbying firms. Total spending by lobbyists reached $2.38 billion in 2005, the yeoman's share going to Republicans.[390]

For the 2008 election campaign, Democratic candidates received more money from lobbyists than Republicans, as contributors who wanted access believed Democrats were more likely to win.[391] In 2009, according to the Senate Office of Public Records, the top twenty industries alone spent $2.22 billion on lobbying to convince public officials to acquiesce to the needs of special interests.[392] The 2010 midterm election saw the lion's share of funding by special interests and lobbyists go to the GOP. In 2014, data from the Center for Responsive Politics revealed there were 11,800 lobbyists, and $3.24 billion had been spent on lobbying by special interests.[393]

While not all politicians are tied to lobbyists and special interests, the vast majority are, and even the most righteous have to cooperate to some degree if they want to get re-elected. Money is the mother's milk of politics, necessary to finance campaigns unless the person running is inordinately wealthy and willing to fund it him or herself. National parties solicit funds to distribute to their committees as well as to individual candidates. In addition to the GOP and Democratic National Committees, there are Republican and Democratic congressional campaign committees and senatorial campaign committees, raising and disbursing funds for candidates. Members of the House and Senate also raise money for struggling colleagues through so-called leadership PACs.[394]

In addition to huge sums the two parties spent on recent campaigns, special interests and affluent individuals with particular objectives provided advertising in support of candidates for various offices through Super PACs and 501(c)(4) groups. The identities of most of these donors remain secret. This so-called 'dark money' was of critical importance in competitive races for the Senate in 2014 as noted by the Brennan Center for Justice.[395] In ten of the hardest fought contests, dark money supplied up to 89 percent of outside funds: over $127 million. Advertising was provided by donations to organizations operating as nonprofits, not required to disclose their sources of funding and whose primary purpose is not supposed to be political.[396] These organizations, primarily Republican in orientation, often try to appear of grassroots origin, although they had been created by political operatives and financed by special interests working in the shadows.

With enormous amounts spent on targeted congressional and senatorial races, these 501(c) groups may at times decide the composition of Congress while keeping donors hidden. They also helped engineer GOP takeover of many state legislatures and governorships. Though the electorate wants limits on campaign spending, the very affluent corporations, and other special interests will continue to pour money into the political process, believing their investments are worthwhile. According to a Gallup Poll in 2014, 79 percent of Americans, from the right, left, and middle, want campaign finance reform.[397]

When the virus of corruption infects some members of a group, it encourages corrupt behavior in others, with the idea that they too can evade censure or penalties for their actions. Those involved in proscribed activities turn a blind eye to what colleagues are doing, unwilling to investigate or punish possible unethical or illegal conduct. They are afraid that exposing a peer's disreputable deeds will cause the spotlight to be turned on their own corrupt endeavors. There is also a veneer of acceptability covering the stain of unethical activities when there is a belief that others in a peer group are similarly engaged.

Three scandals in particular show how extensive venal behavior is among officeholders with accountability lacking. One was the House bank overdraft scandal in the late '80s and early '90s, in which hundreds of members of Congress issued 20,000 bad checks without penalties or fees.[398] Among those with overdrafts was Dick Cheney, who became vice president under George Bush, Newt Gingrich, and Tom Foley, the Democratic House speaker at that time. Another scandal was the savings and loan debacle in the late '80s. Five senators, dubbed the Keating Five, defended in a federal regulatory investigation a corrupt bank owner and real estate mogul, Charles Keating, who had made large contributions to fundraising groups for them.[399] The senators, including John McCain, were later rebuked by the Senate

Ethics Committee for bad judgment, and Senator Alan Cranston of California was rebuked for breach of ethics, but they were never significantly disciplined.

There was also the quaint Abscam scandal in 1978-1980, the result of a sting operation by the FBI caught on tape that sent six members of Congress and a senator to prison for conspiracy and taking bribes.[400] The sting involved bogus Arab sheiks, mobsters, dishonest elected officials and politicians, all too willing to accept piles of hundred dollar bills for legislative favors. One of the corrupt Congressmen, a Philadelphia Democrat 'Ozzie' Meyers, was caught on tape uttering an unforgettable line- "Money talks in this business and bullshit walks." Currently, similar actions are performed by lobbyists for special interests who are a bit more sophisticated in their approach to corrupt politicians.

Another kind of corruption that is a mix of political and corporate transgressions are citizens' loss of privacy through social media companies and the use of private data for political purposes by these companies. Though Facebook under Mark Zuckerberg and Sheryl Sandberg is the leader in selling private information of users to advertising firms, other software companies, and even foreign governments, it appears that all social media entities engage in similar conduct. If a person utilizes social media, he or she can expect that a loss of privacy occurred. It is bad enough when peoples' information is used by advertising companies to target them to buy something, but political advertising and covert suggestions, falsehoods and fake news are also employed by domestic political enterprises and foreign governments to influence the way people vote. Russia was the main culprit in the 2016 presidential election, aiding Trump in his presidential bid and it is likely their activities have continued. But China and Iran may also use Americans personal and corporate data in nefarious ways, stealing intellectual property and people's financial information as well as attempting political manipulation. High-tech companies should be held responsible for the misuse of private data and must find ways to protect users of social media.

5

Additional Rot

"If there be no penalty annexed to disobedience, the resolutions or commands which pretend to be laws will, in fact, amount to nothing more than advice or recommendation." Federalist Papers, Number 15, Hamilton[401]

CORRUPTION DESCRIBED IN the executive and legislative branches of the federal government is merely a small fraction of politically illicit behavior that occurs. The question remains how some corrupt politicians can be re-elected after their tainted and fraudulent conduct is exposed. Uninformed voters either do not know about these actions, or do not care. A few recent scandals will be mentioned.

Michael Grimm, an incumbent Republican Congressman from Staten Island in New York City, won his race for re-election in 2014, 55 to 42 percent in spite of having a twenty count indictment pending against him for tax fraud.[402] After pleading guilty to felony tax evasion, he resigned from Congress at the end of 2014.[403] In 2017, the next election, he decided to run again for Congress in the same district but lost.

In September 2013, Trey Radel, a Florida Republican was found to possess cocaine and resigned from Congress. Previously, he had voted in favor of GOP legislation that would make food stamp recipients urinate in a cup to prove they were not taking drugs.[404]

Senator Robert Menendez, Democrat of New Jersey, was indicted on multiple charges of bribery and corruption in April of 2015, pleading not guilty. There had been prior allegations he had paid for prostitutes and engaged in sex parties in the Dominican Republic.[405] In the new case, a donor, Salomon Melgen, provided over $750,000 in campaign contributions to Menendez and the Democrats.[406] This was in return for Menendez trying to influence Medicare regarding a billing dispute of $9 million involving Dr. Melgen. There was a hung jury at his trial and Menendez won his Senate seat again in 2018.

Rick Renzi, an ex-Republican Congressman from Arizona, was convicted in June 2013 on seventeen counts of extortion, racketeering, money laundering, and embezzlement, and sentenced to three years in prison.[407] Reinforcing the disconnect between religion and corruption, Renzi was a strict Roman Catholic, with twelve children, and was staunchly against abortion.

Democratic Representative Frank Balance of North Carolina was given a three year prison sentence after pleading guilty to conspiracy, mail fraud, and money laundering in 2005.[408]

Jesse Jackson Jr, a Democratic Illinois Congressman, received thirty months in prison in 2013, pleading guilty to wire and mail fraud, tax cheating, and making false statements. Jackson misused three quarters of a million dollars of campaign funds for personal expenses.[409]

Pennsylvania Democratic Congressman Chaka Fattah was found guilty in June 2016 of money laundering, fraud, and racketeering.[410] He had used federal grant money and non-profit funds to reimburse an illegal $1 million loan, and to benefit family and friends.

Congressman Frank Guinta, a New Hampshire Republican, in May 2015 was asked by his party to resign because of an illegal contribution of $355, 000 from his parents in the 2010 election.[411] The F.E.C. fined him $15,000.

The Chairman of the House Transportation Committee, GOP Congressman Bill Shuster of Pennsylvania, dated a top lobbyist for the airline trade association in 2015.[412] While this in itself was not corrupt, he was involved in negotiations for a major restructuring of the Federal Aviation Administration at the same time. Though Shuster said the woman did not lobby him about airline matters, the statement lacked credibility. Shuster was divorced in 2014 after twenty years of marriage, having been chastised by House Speaker John Boehner in 2010 about his partying with female lobbyists. Shuster's father, Bud Shuster, who represented the Pennsylvania district before his son, resigned from the House in 2001 after accepting gifts and allowing preferential access to a former aide who had become a lobbyist.

Aaron Schock, an ex-Republican Representative from Illinois, in November 2016 was indicted on twenty-four counts by a federal grand jury, including wire fraud and theft of funds.[413] Schock had resigned from Congress the previous March when the information became public.

Corrine Brown, a Democratic Congresswoman from Florida, was sentenced to five years in prison in December 2017 for stealing money from a sham charity she operated for personal expenses.[414] She had been convicted on eighteen criminal counts, including filing false tax returns, mail and wire fraud. She represented her district in Congress for nearly a quarter century.

Sexual harassment and sex crimes by government officials occur fairly frequently. As mentioned earlier, arrogance of power allows politicians to believe they are untouchable. Many feel their power and position make them attractive to others and those they pursue for sexual relationships should be honored by the attention they are receiving.

GOP Speaker of the House from 1999 to 2007, Dennis Hastert, was involved in sexual crimes before election to Congress, committing financial crimes during and after service in the House.[415] Once second in line for the presidency, his office was a fountain of corruption while he was in Congress. Personally involved in real estate deals with partners in Illinois, he used an earmark to fund a highway interchange a mile from land he had purchased, realizing a huge profit from his transaction.[416] He also protected Tom DeLay and other disreputable Republican Congressmen, firing members of the Ethics Committee when they reprimanded DeLay in 2004. As the author of the 'Hastert rule,' he would not allow bills to be voted on by the House unless they were passed first by a majority of Republicans, not permitting Democratic input.[417] After leaving Congress, he became a lobbyist.

His indictment resulted from lying to the FBI and illegal bank transfers. This was to conceal sexual crimes while a high school wrestling coach in Illinois. He abused at least four male students and was using the money withdrawn to pay for silence of one of his victims. Hastert was a family values, born-again Christian conservative, so hypocrisy can be placed on top of his criminal acts. In October of 2015, he pleaded guilty to violating federal banking laws[418] and was sentenced to fifteen months in prison.[419] Sexual misconduct was not pursued because the statute of limitations had run out. A number of his Republican colleagues wrote testimonials to the sentencing judge, praising Hastert's character and public service, hoping the judge would show him mercy.[420]

Senator John Ensign, Republican of Nevada, resigned his Senate seat in 2011 while being investigated for ethics violations.[421] He was a member of the Senate GOP leadership and had previously demanded President Clinton resign after his trysts were exposed. Ensign had had an affair with his best friend's wife while both were working for him. Subsequently, Ensign and his family tried to cover up matters by giving money to the staffer, Doug Hampton, and getting him a lobbying job. In that position, Hampton lobbied Ensign, a violation of federal law. In 2011, Hampton was indicted and reached a plea deal the following year. He and his wife eventually divorced, Ensign escaping punishment.

Senator David Vitter, Republican of Louisiana, a family values conservative, confessed to using an escort service to procure prostitutes in Washington.[422] Admitting his actions, he said he asked and had received forgiveness from God and his wife. He was re-elected to the Senate three years later and ran for governor in 2015, losing to a Democrat in a runoff.

Senator Larry Craig, another conservative, family values Republican from Idaho, pleaded guilty to 'disorderly conduct' in August 2007. He had been arrested in June in an airport bathroom, having made sexual advances to a plainclothes officer in an adjoining stall.[423] Fined $500 by the court, he was given a year's probation and resigned from the Senate in September. Subsequently, he had to repay almost $200,000 in campaign funds and was penalized $45,000.[424]

Representative Mark Foley, a Republican from Florida, resigned in 2006 when it was revealed he had been sending lurid, sexually inappropriate email messages to under-age Capitol Hill pages.[425] Foley was known for pushing tougher penalties for sexual predators of children and helped design legislation protective of children on the Internet.

In 2017, there were a flood of sexual harassment allegations in all walks of life. President Trump, Democratic Senator Franken, Democratic Representative John Conyers, and Senate candidate Alabama Republican Roy Moore were all accused, with more politicians undoubtedly involved. Moore had been implicated in pedophilia by nine women.

Another opportunity for corruption is the ability of corporate and wealthy donors to fund national conventions of the two political parties.[426] Besides the public aspects of the convention, there are many venues where businesspeople can meet and greet politicians at parties, dinners, and other sheltered gatherings. Approximately $150 million was spent on each convention in 2016, bankrolled by private entities. The Inauguration is another event where financial contributions lead to mixing of corporate and political bigwigs to the benefit of both.

To chronicle all the crimes committed by officials in state and local governments would entail a manuscript of thousands of pages.

A report in May 2006 noted that more than 2000 investigations into public graft were active by the FBI.[427] Over 1060 government officials were convicted of criminal acts in 2004 and 2005. The ubiquity of corruption in municipal, county and local governments is mind-boggling, with reports in the news on a daily basis. Between 1998 and 2007, a public group called Integrity Florida found that 1762 Florida officials had been convicted of public corruption.[428] In the same time frame, New York had 2522 officials convicted, California 2300, Illinois 1828, and Pennsylvania 1563.[429]

Four of the last seven governors in Illinois have gone to prison because of corrupt acts. Included were Democrat Rod Blagojevich, impeached in 2009 and convicted in 2011 on a number of charges, among which were trying to sell Obama's Senate seat. (Blagojevich was pardoned by Trump in 2020.) Also in the group were Republican George Ryan, governor from 1999-2003 and convicted afterwards of racketeering while in office. Democrat Dan Walker, governor from 1973-1977, pleaded guilty to bank fraud after leaving office, and Democrat Otto Koerner, governor from 1961-1968, became a judge afterwards until he was convicted of bribery during his tenure as governor.[430]

In January of 2015, Republican Governor Bob McDonnell of Virginia was sentenced to two years in prison for public corruption.[431] McDonnell and his wife had accepted expensive gifts and $175,000 in loans from a constituent in exchange for promoting a nutritional supplement. Though it would seem that individuals or corporations giving officeholders money or expensive gifts in exchange for special treatment of some kind would be considered illegal, as of April 2016 this was not a settled issue.[432] The Supreme Court took up McDonnell's case on appeal, with the governor claiming a First Amendment right to accept the gifts, and that his efforts to promote the product had been official acts, not quid pro quo.[433] Based on the questioning of the justices, they seemed to believe McDonnell's conduct fell into the realm of normal behavior by politicians and that he was not guilty of a crime. However, this same Court produced the Citizens United and

McCutcheon decisions permitting unlimited political contributions by wealthy donors on the grounds that this was free speech. In June, the Court overturned McDonnell's conviction, allowing him to be retried, finding the government's interpretation of the bribery statute 'boundless,' saying it could interfere with normal political activity.[434]

After the McDonnell reversal, the lobbyist Jack Abramoff who was convicted of fraud and conspiracy in 2006 and went to prison, declared the Court didn't get it when it came to influence peddling and buying of politicians.[435] The Court's willingness to excuse McDonnell's conduct as usual for politicians showed a naivete about how things worked in the real world and how money and gifts resulted in recipients doing favors for the donors. The ruling will make it difficult to convict those who bribe politicians, making corrupt activity more likely.

Edwin DiPrete, Republican governor of Rhode Island from 1985-1991, went to prison after pleading guilty to eighteen felony counts of bribery, extortion, and racketeering.[436] Speaker of the Rhode Island House, Democrat Gordon D. Fox, pleaded guilty in March of 2015 to receiving bribes, wire fraud, and filing a false tax return.[437] He faced a three year prison sentence.

Democratic governor Edwin Edwards of Louisiana, released from prison in 2011 after serving eight years for bribery and extortion, subsequently lost a run for Congress.[438]

Arch Moore, Jr, GOP governor of West Virginia, served three years in prison, pleading guilty to five felony charges relating to acceptance of illegal payments during his campaign.[439]

Republican John Rowland, governor of Connecticut from 1995 to 2004, served ten months in prison after pleading guilty to corruption charges. In 2014, he was convicted of a role in an election fraud case and was subsequently sentenced to thirty more months.[440]

Texas Attorney General Ken Paxton, a conservative Republican, was indicted for felony securities fraud by a grand jury in August 2015.[441] He was also charged with acting as an investment advisor without registering with the state securities board. Prior to becoming attorney general, he had apparently misled clients regarding investments.

Federal regulators filed civil charges against Paxton in April 2016 for securities fraud.[442]

Also in August of 2015, the Democratic Attorney General of Pennsylvania, Kathleen Kane, was arraigned on charges of perjury and leaking secret grand jury information.[443] This was to retaliate against a previous Republican prosecutor she believed had disrespected her. Facing criminal charges, she threatened an investigation into embarrassing emails from elected state politicians, including judges and prosecutors that contained racist and homophobic jokes and photos of nude women.[444] In August 2016, she was found guilty of nine criminal charges.[445] However, due to her nascent investigation into the inappropriate emails, two state Supreme Court justices and a host of other officials resigned from their positions, afraid of information that was going to be released.

New Mexico Republican Secretary of State Dianna Duran, was charged in August 2015, with embezzlement, fraud, money laundering, and campaign finance violations.[446] Money raised for her campaigns wound up in personal accounts, much of it lost at casinos, including nearly $300,000 in 2014 and about half that amount the year before. Previously, a number of high state officials, all Democrats, went to prison for kickbacks, money laundering, and fraud.[447]

The New York State government in Albany has been a hotbed of corruption for years, with little prosecutorial drive to indict the top perpetrators. Occasionally, a senator or assemblyman has been penalized for misdeeds, but the culture has remained unchanged. Democrat Eliot Spitzer vowed to clean up Albany but resigned as governor in 2008 after it became known he had patronized prostitutes.[448] Democrat Alan Hevasi, State Comptroller from 2003-2006, went to prison for twenty months in 2010, guilty of taking a $1 million payoff from a pension fund investor in return for business in the state pension fund.[449]

Democrat Sheldon Silver, Speaker of the State Assembly for two decades and one of the most powerful politicians in New York State, was indicted in February 2015 by a grand jury on charges of fraud, extortion and kickback schemes.[450] At trial, he was found guilty on all counts[451] and sentenced to twelve years in federal prison.[452] Three months after Silver's indictment, the GOP leader of the State Senate, Dean Skelos, left office after arrest on federal corruption charges.[453] He was convicted of bribery, extortion, and conspiracy.[454] The new Speaker, Carl Heastie, was subsequently accused of benefitting from his mother's crime of embezzling $90,000 from a non-profit agency to buy an apartment.[455] When his mother died, Heastie sold the apartment at a profit of nearly $200,000, neglecting to pay back the agency. He also spent campaign funds inappropriately: a tab at a Manhattan go-go club, servicing his BMW ($30,000 over nine years), $51,000 for mileage reimbursement, and $150,000 with no details given.[456]

Then U.S. attorney, Preet Bharra, whose office obtained the convictions of Silver and Skelos, stated that corruption in Albany was "deep and systemic."[457] He noted that fraud and payoffs were the result of the ability of legislators to earn outside income, a lack of transparency with weak disclosure requirements, and concentrated power. Governor Andrew Cuomo, had promised to attack corruption in New York politics when he was elected. However in 2014, he abruptly disbanded the anti-corruption Moreland Commission he had established when it went after people close to him.[458],[459] The panel had found sham corporations set up by legislators with government money, businesses buying legislation through targeted campaign contributions, and legislators billing the state for travel expenses already paid by their campaigns.[460] Subsequently, one of Cuomo's top aides, Joseph Percoco, and eight others were indicted for bribery, fraud, and lying to federal agents.[461] Interestingly, after the convictions of Silver and Skelos, the ethics panels of the State Assembly and Senate took no action to address future corruption.[462] In fact, the Senate's panel had not held a meeting since 2009.

Thus, corruption continues to run rampant in New York with supposed reformers neglecting to aggressively pursue miscreants. Officials who have been found guilty of crimes and gone to prison, continue to collect state pensions, with the Assembly unwilling to change the law for employees in the pension system.[463] Yet New York citizens keep electing the same corrupt politicians to office over and over, unaware of their misdeeds or ignoring them.

Governor Scott Walker of Wisconsin signed a bill in 2015 that protected politicians from secret investigations to uncover corruption.[464] Similar to grand jury proceedings, this had worked successfully in the past. While he had been executive of Milwaukee County, six of his associates had been convicted of criminal activities through this pathway. The bill ending these probes was enacted by Republicans in the state legislature on a party-line vote, though it had been in place since the mid-19th century. Official misconduct, bribery, campaign finance offenses and so forth, will no longer be subject to the same scrutiny the old law provided.

As of May 2016 in Alabama, Governor Robert Bentley and House Speaker Michael Hubbard were under investigation for criminal charges and ethical misconduct.[465],[466] Bentley was involved in sexual misbehavior as well and resigned in April 2017.[467] Hubbard was convicted on twelve felony charges, using his office for soliciting work and investments, and pushing bills that would aid clients of his consulting firm.[468] He received a four year prison sentence and $200,000 in fines. Previous Democratic Governor Don Siegelman had been convicted of bribery and went to prison after a trial in 2006 based on questionable evidence.[469] Fifty-two former state attorneys-general from both parties asked Congress to examine whether Siegelman was targeted for political reasons, as they found the evidence ludicrous. Karl Rove had pushed the indictment and GOP prosecutors and judges were happy to go after a Democrat who had won in Alabama.

In New Jersey, top aides to Governor Christie were indicted by federal prosecutors for arranging to have the George Washington Bridge partially closed for several days in 2013, causing massive traffic tie-ups. This was to punish the mayor of Fort Lee for not supporting Christie's bid for re-election.[470] At the trial in September 2016, lawyers for prosecution and defense claimed that Christie, a former prosecutor, knew about the incident and may have been involved in planning it. Christie denied knowledge of the scheme until months afterwards. A Christie appointee who was executive director of the Port Authority, David Wildstein, pleaded guilty and two of Christie's top aides were found guilty at trial in November 2016.[471]

Though apparently not illegal, Republican Secretary of State Brian Kemp's conduct while running for governor of Georgia against Democrat Stacey Abrams was highly unethical.[472] The Secretary of State supervises elections in Georgia and Kemp refused to step down from his position while being a candidate, a major conflict of interest. In the run-up to the election, Kemp purged hundreds of thousands of voters from the rolls for various reasons, done covertly, with those purged not notified. The majority of these were minority voters who likely would have supported Abrams. In some minority voting stations, provisional ballots were gone early, with long lines waiting to vote. Kemp's victory in the race was by less than 2 percent, which certainly was affected by those voters purged. Suppression of minority voting was not just an issue in Georgia but was instituted in twenty-four states by Republicans since 2010.[473] These included Florida, North Dakota, Wisconsin, Kansas and Texas. Republicans benefitted from these measures in federal, state, and municipal elections.

Another illustration of corrupt or at least unethical behavior was the attempt by the Republican Governor of Missouri, Mike Parsons, to overturn State Constitutional amendments that were passed by Missouri's citizens by referenda in 2018.[474] One amendment restricted the amount in gifts that lobbyists could give to lawmakers who had to abide by the state's open records law. The second was the creation of the position of nonpartisan state demographer who would be responsible for redrawing the state's legislative districts in a fair way instead of the gerrymandering that provided Republicans with supermajorities in both Houses of the State Legislature. Governor Parson was so upset with these amendments that he declared he was thinking of making it more difficult for citizens' referenda to be on the ballot.

Though as noted, municipal corruption is too widespread to tackle in these pages, three examples previously discussed should be reemphasized because they were so outrageous. Revealing voter ignorance or disregard of facts, three mayors of major cities who were convicted felons, guilty of crimes like extortion, bribery, money-laundering, and tax evasion, were returned to office after serving prison sentences: Joe Ganim of Bridgeport, Connecticut, Buddy Cianci of Providence, Rhode Island, and Marian Barry of Washington, D.C. The crimes had occurred during previous periods in office, yet their constituents had few qualms about voting for them.

Unfortunately, judges in the American court system also engage in criminal behavior. They show favoritism, are involved in ethical missteps, and accept sub-rosa bribes, particularly when they are elected officials and need campaign funds. A quid pro quo often develops between those who have contributed money and sitting justices. A prime illustration was the buying of a West Virginia Supreme Court Justice by Don Blankenship, the CEO of Massey Coal Company with a $50 million judgment pending against it.[475] Blankenship funded the campaign of Brent Benjamin, a virtual unknown, with $3 million. Thus in a race against an incumbent justice, Warren McGraw, Blankenship got Benjamin elected to the state Supreme Court. Benjamin subsequently did not recuse himself from the Massey case and cast the deciding vote overturning the verdict. (In 2015, Blankenship was tried in federal court and convicted of criminal conspiracy.[476])

Judges all over the country on different level courts have also been bought by corporate interests or wealthy ideologues, skewing the law to favor corporations. And special interest money sponsors advertising even in non-partisan judicial elections, blanketing the airwaves with ads supporting conservative candidates who perceive justice through a rightward-looking lens.[477] In addition, President George W. Bush loaded the federal courts with conservative justices who tend to rule for business against consumers and workers. A Harvard Law Review study showed that federal appeals courts after Bush were five times as likely to back employers in discrimination cases by employees.[478] The justices in these cases had not been bought; their rulings resulting from their ideological leanings. On the other hand, many liberal or centrist Obama nominees for the courts were not confirmed by a highly partisan GOP Senate. Trump and a Republican Senate have also packed the courts with additional conservative judges.

Sham Corporations, Tax Havens, and Government Involvement

In April 2016, an enormous leak of documents from the Mossack Fonseca law firm in Panama showed how money from affluent individuals, criminals and politicians was being laundered and hidden in offshore accounts (the Panama Papers).[479] A number of leaders of democratic and autocratic nations were discovered to be utilizing these accounts to avoid taxes, to shield their assets from the public eye, and to hide ill-gotten gains. The law firm used Panama and Caribbean islands for offshore accounts, as their legal systems did not allow disclosure of money to investigators from foreign governments. Some American states are being used as tax havens as well. Thus, in order to curb corruption and tax avoidance, the U.S. has to pass laws ensuring transparency in all bank holdings reciprocally with foreign governments and the O.E.C.D. This will not end corruption, but will make it slightly harder to hide illegally obtained wealth and evade taxes.

Financial Corruption

Another manifestation of corruption in America has been the failure of appropriate federal and state agencies to pursue individuals guilty of financial crimes.[480] While the banks, hedge funds, and other institutions for whom these people worked have been penalized with large fines, those responsible for the corrupt actions have not been indicted. This is particularly troubling regarding those at the top who had to have known about the criminal activity. With all the fraudulent loans approved prior to the 2007 recession and the bundling of low grade mortgages falsely into highly rated financial instruments that deceived investors, not a single perpetrator has gone to jail. And lies to investors by executives at failing financial firms did not result in criminal charges. Similarly, currency manipulation by the banks resulted in fines, but no prison terms. Wall Street and the banks were bailed out by the government while the little guys who could not keep up with their mortgages had their homes foreclosed. Though the Department of Justice may have been fearful of destroying major financial institutions that might affect the economy adversely, merely fining them does not deter fraud and predatory practices.[481] How can citizens have faith in government when they see corrupt businessmen and financial executives going unpunished?

Illicit activity is seen as well in manufacturing firms, automobile companies, and pharmaceutical corporations. Because of safety problems not revealed by executives or engineers, some who used these products were injured or killed. Fines have been imposed on these companies at times, but those responsible have avoided prison. To ensure that laws and regulations are followed and safety and the environment is a priority, government has to prosecute businessmen and women, and demand harsh terms if they are found guilty. Too often, firms disregard safety issues, believing suits by injured persons or fines by government are merely the cost of doing business.[482]

There have also been instances where companies paid fines for defrauding individuals and/or the federal government, but have continued to receive government funds. This happened in private educational institutions that lied to students about opportunities they would provide while saddling them with backbreaking debts from government loans. And drug companies have been penalized for promoting ineffective or dangerous drugs, costing the government hundreds of millions of dollars as well as impairing patient health. Federal agencies must go after those who have broken the law along with the chain of command above them: to put them in prison so others will know that more than money is at risk with corporate crimes.

While corruption enmeshes government at all strata in the United States, there is a symbiotic relationship between executives of financial institutions and politicians that fosters illegal conduct in both realms. One hand washes the other but cannot clean away the stain of dishonest behavior that allows cash to flow. Money is given to legislators who craft the laws that allow financial institutions and their top personnel to make money in various ways,[483] lobbyists often acting as the conduits. In addition, figures in the executive and legislative branches direct contracts to companies that donate money to their campaigns, or provide jobs to people in their districts. Promises of jobs to lawmakers also help companies obtain contracts, or have legislation enacted favorable to them.[484],[485],[486]

Nobel Prize winner and Columbia Professor Joseph Stiglitz in March 2016 suggested six ways to reform America's corrupt financial system excerpted from his book *Rewriting the Rules of the American Economy*.[487] First was the importance of curtailing 'Too Big to Fail' by breaking up large financial institutions whose risks are underwritten by the federal government. Second was Regulating the Shadow Banking Sector and Ending Offshore Banking. Third was Bringing Transparency to All Financial Markets. Fourth was Reducing Credit and Debit Card Fees. Fifth was Enforcing Rules with Stricter Penalties. Sixth was Reforming Federal Reserve Governance. With the financial industry and politicians still intertwined, these are not likely changes.

Americans like to think of their country as an exemplar of clean government, notwithstanding the evidence given. However, in an independent rating by the Corruption Perception Index of Transparency International in 2014, the United States came in as the seventeenth least corrupt state.[488] Most European nations, the Scandinavian countries, Canada, Australia, and New Zealand all ranked lower than the U. S. in the degree of political graft and bribery. In America, corruption infests all three branches of government, executive, judicial, and legislative, at all levels, federal, state, and municipal, with the money of special interests often determining the outcome of elections. The chances are clearly remote that lobbyists and special interests and their money will be eliminated from the political dialogue in the near future.

The examples given of corruption in American politics is not all-encompassing though it continues to occur regularly. It may seem surprising to many citizens that corruption is so ubiquitous in America. But those surprised have not been paying attention. In politics, money is the root (and route) of corruption. Permissive laws that allow the affluent to bend politicians to their will, as in Citizens United and the McCutcheon rulings must be overturned. The McDonnell decision by the Supreme Court that declared expensive gifts and large sums of money given to elected officials as normal politics must be reversed. Stringent restrictions should be placed on lobbyists and special interests in terms of how they interact with officeholders and their staffers at all layers of government. For these actions to take place, voters are needed who are politically informed, who understand the workings of politics and government. These citizens are more likely to elect honest officials willing to fight for the necessary laws and penalties to reduce corruption. It will not be easy.

6

Corruption in Other Democracies

"It is a common failing of men not to take account of tempests during fair weather."
Niccolo Machiavelli[489]

A BRIEF SURVEY of political corruption in democratic nations other than America will reinforce the fact it is universal in nature and even more pervasive in many other states. Some of the highest officers of other democracies, including presidents, prime ministers and cabinet ministers, have been and are involved in criminal conduct. In fact, elected officials at every level are willing to cheat in various ways to gain or enhance their wealth. To some extent, the degree to which corruption flourishes depends on the longevity of the democracy, the strength of its legal system, its political culture, and its laws against corrupt practices. In many democracies venality is driven partially by the need for politicians to obtain campaign funds, though personal gain is usually the main factor. If there are opportunities for politicians to enrich themselves because of their positions, these will often be seized, ignoring chances of discovery or possible penalties. The political traditions of the nation are also considerations, and if others are known to be taking advantage of their offices, colleagues are more likely to follow this path.

Examples of corruption given below merely skim the surface of malfeasance in a number of democracies. While campaigning, officials may promise to reduce corruption, then find it harder to attack than previously imagined. In addition, many if not most are seduced by the power and perks of their new status, and re-election, or aspiring to higher offices becomes paramount. Promises made may be abandoned and ethics compromised in the pursuit of campaign funds and greater affluence. And stopping abuse may become less important to those interested in climbing the political ladder. One does not want to antagonize tainted colleagues who might be useful in the future.

Theft and fraud by politicians in democratic nations should shock no one and will occur until politically informed voters arrest it. The leaked 'Panama Papers' in 2016 revealed the ubiquity of corrupt politicians looking for ways to hide their wealth, along with other criminals, oligarchs and autocrats.[490] Democracies do not provide enough safeguards and penalties to prevent illegal behavior by politicians, whose self-interest overrides responsibilities to their constituents as they lie, deceive, and steal.

A report in *Foreign Policy* in December 2016 noted that corruption, bribery and graft were growing worldwide, a major impediment to the global economy.[491] According to the IMF, bribes of about $1.5 trillion changed hands every year, equivalent to about five percent of global GDP. This facilitated other evils such as drug smuggling, human trafficking, and terrorism. Civil societies had difficulty enforcing anti-bribery laws and government transparency was often deficient. The pattern of illegal practices in many countries was often remarkably similar, particularly in adjacent geographical regions with comparable cultural attributes.

This chapter will summarize some instances of corrupt actions by democratically elected high officials in different nations, focusing on the central governments.

Canada

Though Canada has a reputation for enjoying a clean political system, it has had its share of scandals. Nigel Wright, Prime Minister Stephen Harper's chief of staff resigned in 2013 after having given a senator nearly $90,000 to repay false expense claims and avoid censure.[492] In June of 2015, after reviewing expense accounts of 116 sitting and recently retired senators, Canada's auditor general found over a quarter had major 'irregularities.'[493] Nine were so serious auditors suggested they be referred to the police for possible criminal charges. In the 1990s, Conservative Progressive Prime Minister Brian Mulroney accepted bags of cash from an aircraft lobbyist. Proclaiming his regrets later over "a serious error in judgement" Mulroney was not prosecuted.[494]

Europe

Though many Europeans are stupefied by the sums of money spent on American political campaigns and the abuse it breeds, a similar pattern occurs in European nations, perhaps to a lesser degree. A European Union report in 2014 declared that corruption on the continent was 'breathtaking,' costing the European economy about $162 billion yearly.[495] According to EU analysts, 76 percent of Europeans believed corruption was ubiquitous. During two years prior to the report, hundreds of thousands of Europeans demonstrated against corruption in the streets of the Czech Republic, Bulgaria, and Romania. And they brought down the government of Slovenia.

France

Political corruption in France is widespread. Ex-conservative President Nicholas Sarkozy, head of state from 2007 to 2102, was involved in illegal campaign financing and several other scandals.[496] Sarkozy was charged with accepting $67 million in funds from Libyan dictator Quaddafi, questions also raised regarding illegal funding of

Sarkozy's 2007 campaign by Lilanne Bettencourt who at age 91 was France's richest woman.[497] Other potential charges include influence peddling and corrupting officials.[498] Jacques Chirac, like Sarkozy a former right-wing president, and one of his prime ministers, Alain Juppe, were both convicted of illegal political financing after having left office.[499] Another of Chirac's Prime Ministers, Edouard Balladur was investigated for an alleged role in a kickback conspiracy involving the sale of French warships to Pakistan. On the left, Socialist Minister of the Budget Jerome Cahuzac, responsible for uncovering tax evaders, resigned in 2013 when found to have more than $1 million in offshore accounts.[500]

Valery Giscard d'Estaing, finance minister and then president of France from 1974-81, was accused of accepting diamonds from Central African Republic dictator, Jean Bokassa, and then granting him asylum in France.[501] He was never charged with a crime. Francois Fillion, a candidate of the right in the 2017 presidential race, was caught in a financial scandal involving many politicians.[502] Fillon paid his wife and children nearly $1 million from the public payroll over several years for no-show jobs. The scandal was named Penelopegate after Fillon's spouse. Nepotism has been a tradition for French politicians, with at least 20 percent of members of parliament, and probably more, hiring family members or those of colleagues who do the same.

Germany

Helmut Kohl, Christian Democratic Chancellor from 1982-1998, who negotiated unification of Germany, admitted in 1999 he had received millions in illegal contributions, but refused to divulge donors.[503] Kohl controlled a number of secret accounts and doled out money to individuals and party organizations in disregard of the law.[504] Though paying a fine, he never went to prison.[505] In the EU's first anti-corruption report in 2014, Germany was highlighted because of its revolving door activity from government to corporate positions.[506] The report noted "the political commitment to really root out corruption seems to be missing."[507] German law not only permitted bribery outside the country until 1999, but also made it tax deductible.[508] As of 2011, Germany was one of three G20 countries not to have ratified the UN Convention Against Corruption.[509]

Gerhard Schroeder, Social Democratic Chancellor from 1998 to 2005 joined the board of the Russian company, Gazprom, after being defeated for re-election.[510] Two weeks post-defeat, he also became board chairman of a conglomerate created to construct a pipeline in the Baltic Sea to transport Russian natural gas to Germany.[511] It was clearly unethical for a former German head of state to participate in leadership roles of Russian companies that had dealings with Germany. Schroeder has professed admiration for Vladimir Putin whom he described as a "flawless democrat." In fact, Schroeder sided with the Russians on their annexation of Crimea and military actions in eastern Ukraine, criticizing German policies.

The ties between German government and top automobile companies became more evident in 2015 when Volkswagon was found to be cheating on mileage and emissions claims.[512] All other German car makers were also discovered to be cheating. Government and auto firms engage in free flow of personnel back and forth, allowing special consideration for these companies responsible for one in seven German jobs. False data provided by the company was detected in road testing by American analysts.

Pressured by its car companies, Angela Merkel's government strong-armed the E.U. to overturn an agreement on curbing carbon emissions, postponing inception of some rules for six years and delaying development of less polluting cars.[513]

Great Britain

British political corruption in the last several decades has included a phone hacking scheme involving government ministers, deceptive political party funding, and members of parliament taking bribes.[514] And still endemic is governmental acquiescence to overseas bribery for UK businesses to win contracts.[515] The phone hacking scandals resulted from media companies trying to obtain gossip about celebrities and breaking news stories before their rivals. A survey in 2013 found 65 percent of citizens believing corruption in the UK was increasing, with one in twenty Britons admitting bribing officials.[516] Both Conservative and Labor Parties have apparently offered access to government ministers to major donors and opportunities to influence legislation, as well as chances at peerage (becoming a Lord).[517] Two former Foreign Secretaries, the Conservative Party's Sir Malcolm Rifkind and Labor Party's Jack Straw, were caught on film in 2015 by a reporter in a sting operation, revealing willingness to provide services to a non-existent Chinese company in exchange for cash.[518]

Probably the most jaw-dropping news of corruption in the UK surfaced in 2009, showing that many members of Parliament and government ministers padded their expense accounts.[519] Fraud included fake receipts, mortgage costs on second homes, double-dipping, construction bills, travel and entertainment spending, and so forth. Five Labor MPs and two Conservative Peers went to prison for claiming fraudulent expenses.

Italy

Italy has a history of corruption at all layers of government. Relationships exist between elected officials, the judiciary, and Mafia, with bribes and payoffs passing in both directions. Public works projects often go to corrupt firms, with cost overruns and poor quality resulting. Frequently, workers on these projects also have to kick back to their employers to get their jobs. Affluent citizens have been able to avoid punishment for white collar and other crimes because of their connections, the incompetence of the judiciary, and venality of some judges.

Silvio Berlusconi, a media magnate and one of Italy's wealthiest men, was Italy's right-wing prime minister three times intermittently for a total of nine years from 1994 to 2011. His first conviction for lying about membership in a subversive lodge came in 1990, extinguished by amnesty.[520] In 1998, he received a two year nine month sentence for bribing tax inspectors. Overturned on appeal, he could not be retried because the statute of limitations had expired. In 2002 and 2005, he was acquitted of false accounting when his own government changed the law under which he was being tried. Berlusconi was sentenced to four years in prison for tax fraud in 2012, and in 2013 was sentenced to seven years for paying an underage prostitute for sex, but has not served any prison time with appeals likely to take years.[521]

Giulio Andreotti, a Christian Democrat was prime minister seven times.[522] In 2004, after a gripping trial and two appeals, Andreotti was acquitted of being a member of the Mafia, protecting the mob, and having ordered the murder of a journalist who had delved into his criminal activities.[523] Italy's highest court declared that the statute of limitations protected him from prosecution.

Bettino Craxi, Italy's Socialist prime minister from 1983-1987, fled to Tunisia after being accused of taking over $100 million in bribes. Convicted in absentia, he received a twenty-seven-year prison sentence.[524] His Socialist Party and its government ministers took kickbacks for public contracts, with the Christian Democrats and Communists also involved in a system known as 'Bribesville.'[525] This scandal in the early 1990s, resulted in disintegration of the previously dominant Socialist and Christian Democratic Parties.[526]

Spain

A democratic state since Franco died in 1975, Spain has endured more than its share of political corruption. Prime Minister Mariano Rajoy's right-wing Partido Popular government in 2013 was accused of kickbacks and money laundering, with incriminating documents by the former party treasurer, Luis Barcenas, published in El Pais, Spain's leading newspaper.[527] There was a huge slush fund through which construction companies gave politicians illegal payments. Millions of Euros went to Partido Popular officials, members of Parliament, ministers, former Prime Minister Jose Maria Aznar as well as Rajoy. Barcenas was also found to have transferred a portion of 22 million Euros obtained illegally and stashed in a Swiss bank back to Spain during a tax amnesty. [528] A 2014 EU survey revealed that 95 percent of Spaniards were convinced corruption was extensive.[529] Because white collar crimes may take years to come to court, Spaniards believe perpetrators get away with criminal activity. The ex-head of the Catalan Parliament, Jordi Pujol, allegedly siphoned money from government contracts into secret accounts. One of his sons carried bags with 32 million euros across the border into Andorra, where the accounts were located.

Greece

Greece is a nation where corruption is a way of life, with tax evasion and cheating the government by citizens and businesses commonplace and acceptable. The patronage system has also bloated the public sector with numerous unnecessary employees, and along with excessive government spending and pension benefits, have driven Greece to the brink of bankruptcy. The E.U.'s Central Bank and the IMF have repeatedly come to the government's rescue. A report in 2013 documented resale of contraband oil by Greek oligarchs, to whom the state gave special tax breaks to support the shipping industry.[530] For years, the state lost billions in taxes when the oil was sold at the going price and the sellers made huge profits. Analysts estimated that tax evasion by the elite was equivalent to about a third of the public debt. The media in Greece are also controlled by oligarchs who keep tax evasion cases covered up.

In 2013, Greek prosecutors began pursuing corruption more avidly, ignoring resistance from government officials.[531] Senior members of the Greek military have been investigated regarding kickbacks for defense contracts. Akis Tsochatzopoulos, a previous defense minister, was convicted of money-laundering in October of 2013, an unlikely verdict in a nation where top government politicians are rarely prosecuted. Prosecutors have been trying to recover some of the bribe money from politicians, businessmen and military officers implicated. Of particular interest were deals for tanks and submarines valued at $6.8 billion, but believed bought at inflated prices in return for kickbacks. A former defense ministry official told a magistrate "I took so many bribes that I've lost count." Another lower-ranking defense ministry official was discovered to have bought a private jet with kickback money.

Eastern Europe

A number of nations in Eastern Europe, formerly behind the Iron Curtain, have had difficulty changing their culture and adapting to democratic systems, as corruption had been normalized under Communism. When the Soviet Union collapsed and state enterprises were privatized, cunning men who understood the workings of capitalism pounced and bought these companies inexpensively, becoming newly constituted oligarchs. From positions of economic strength, their money bought cooperation from pliant government officials, helping growth of their businesses and increasing their wealth. In some of these nations, politicians demanded pieces of the pie, achieved through bribes, kickbacks, and other corrupt dealings. However, sometimes they bought or were given portions of the privatized businesses and became oligarchs themselves. Corruption and criminal activity was and is everywhere, with politicians and businessmen willing to do almost anything to make money. Romania, Bulgaria, Poland, Hungary, Ukraine, the Czech Republic, and Slovakia, in addition to the Balkan nations were all involved, with high government officials participating in this orgy of self-enrichment.

Africa

Corruption is prevalent in all African democracies. Financial rewards are required by those in power in return for access and favors. Even petty bureaucrats expect their due for merely performing the functions of their offices. There are also stolen elections in many of these so-called democracies, where the tradition of voting politicians and parties into and out of office is a concept of relatively recent vintage. Those holding office are able to appoint the judges and the people who set the rules, count and tabulate votes, and determine the winners of elections.

South Africa

According to an alliance of eight labor unions and twenty-nine NGOs in June 2015, South Africa was having an epidemic of corruption.[532] The office of the president and cabinet officials were infected, the germ spreading throughout the government, businesses, and trade unions. The leadership of the ANC was in denial, allowing billions of dollars to be diverted from services for the poor into the hands of the already affluent. In March 2016, South Africa's highest court declared that President Zuma had violated the Constitution by failing to repay millions the government had spent for renovations to his home.[533] Reports have also circulated about friends of Zuma offering to provide cabinet positions for politicians in return for payoffs.

Under severe pressure, Zuma resigned in February 2018 with Cyril Ramaphosa assuming the presidency. Whether he is capable of reversing the tide of corruption remains to be seen.

Nigeria

Nigeria, the most populous state in Africa, is exceedingly corrupt and graft-ridden, ranked 136 of 175 nations by Transparency International.[534] The nation's economy is dependent on oil exports, but when oil prices soared, much of the profits were siphoned off by government officials. Education and health care, both severely underfinanced, were not improved. The military has failed to adequately combat an insurrection in the north by Boko Haram, partially because of poor leadership, but also because the army lacks enough modern weapons. Funds were diverted by government leaders and military personnel. A new president, Mohammadu Buhari, was elected in March of 2015, but given the ubiquity of corruption along with the drop in oil prices, ameliorating the lot of Nigerian citizens will be difficult.

The Business Anti-Corruption Portal has shown that corruption in Nigeria infests all of society, with oversight and prosecution unable to curb fraud, graft, and bribery.[535] 'Facilitation' payments to officials are expected for any government services. Contracts and commercial suits are also hard to enforce in Nigerian courts, because of inefficiency, dearth of personnel, and corruption. Not surprisingly, there is no transparency in tax administration, with rampant evasion and bribing of officials. And the police head the list of venal institutions.

Kenya

Kenya is another African country gripped by corruption. In a survey released in April 2015, 75 percent of Kenyans declared most or all of the police were dishonest, along with 46 percent of government officials and members of Parliament.[536] A Kenya Travel Guide in 2014 noted the average urban citizen had to pay sixteen bribes a month to handle everyday affairs.[537] All of Kenya's first three presidents were considered corrupt.[538] Jomo Kenyatta was the first president after independence in 1963. When fertile lands stolen by British colonists from the Kalenjin tribe were returned, Kenyatta gave them to his own clan and tribe (the Kikuyu) instead of the original owners. Appropriating a portion for himself, he became one of the largest landowners in the country. Corruption was also extensive during the administration of Daniel arap Moi, Kenya's second president. Mwai Kibaki was voted into office as third president in 2002, pledging to end corruption. In the three years after his first election, Kibaki's cabinet members spent $14 million buying new Mercedes for themselves. Results of the 2007 balloting, when Kibaki was re-elected, were believed to have been falsified.

The fourth president, Uhuru Kenyatta, Kenya's richest man and Jomo's son, was elected in 2013.[539] He won with 50.07 percent of the vote, questions again raised about fraud. Kenyatta was wanted by the International Court at the time of his election for crimes against humanity, having instigated tribal violence after the previous election, resulting in 1200 deaths. However, Kenyatta has never faced justice.

The continuing rape of the country by elected officials was noted in a parliamentary report in November, 2015 showing graft and fraud growing.[540] Millions of dollars in government funds had disappeared in excessive overcharges for everyday items. This was besides ministers skimming additional millions from various contracts. The money from a $2 billion Eurobond which was supposed to be utilized for infrastructure improvements also vanished.

Congo

Joseph Kabila, president of the Congo for two terms, was not allowed by the Constitution to run for a third term and was due to leave office in December 2016.[541] However, after he and his family had looted millions of dollars, he was afraid to step down, concerned he could be tried for corruption, go to prison, and much of his wealth could be clawed back. Perhaps he also imagined going back to driving a taxicab, which he did before ascending to the presidency.

Other African democracies, such as Liberia, Ghana, Senegal, Namibia, and Tunisia face enormous corruption problems. With a long history of colonial exploitation of every nation on the continent, it is not surprising that democracy, a Western concept, has had difficulty taking hold and that corruption remains endemic, along with poverty and illiteracy.

Middle East

Turkey

A non-military strongman, President Recep Tayyip Edogan, currently has Turkey in his grip, a corrupt autocrat who uses Islam to hide abuses.[542] His party, the AKP with Islamist roots, now dominates

Turkey's political system. Crony capitalism is rampant, with government contracts going to Erdogan's friends, supporters, and family. Journalists critical of Erdogan have been jailed, the military purged of opponents by using false documents.[543]

Non-compliant members of the judiciary and prosecutors investigating members of his cabinet, Erdogan and his son on corruption charges have been removed.[544].[545] After an Erdogan electoral victory in 2015, more authoritarian measures and control of opposing media properties occurred.[546] Dozens of Turkish journalists were imprisoned for crimes such as insulting the president or criticizing his policies. The Prime Minister, Ahmet Davutoglu, resigned in early May 2016,[547] opposed to the imprisonment of dissidents, academics and journalists who disagreed with Erdogan, or had insulted his honor. Later in the month, Parliament voted to strip immunity from lawmakers, allowing them to be prosecuted.[548]

In July 2016, an attempted coup by the military was thwarted by units loyal to Erdogan and the Islamists.[549] Erdogan used the coup attempt to fire hundreds of thousands of officers and enlisted men from the military, along with additional prosecutors, judges, policemen, school teachers, and others he believed hostile to his rule. Turkey has morphed from a democratic state to a dictatorship, with voters having handed power to an autocrat who has robbed them of their freedom.

Iran

Iran is a pseudo-democracy, unelected religious leaders determining who is eligible to run for elected offices, severely limiting choices. Control of many businesses has been placed in the hands of the Republican Guard, giving it the ability to run strategic industries, commercial services, and black market transactions.[550] Thus, what is supposed to be a free enterprise system is not really free. The Supreme Leader Khamenei has appointed many Guard members to sensitive political posts, depending on it to suppress internal dissent and civil unrest. In all likelihood, it was instrumental in fixing the 2009 presidential election in favor of Ahmadinejad. According to a prominent Iranian economist, Saeed Leylaz, Ahmadinejad's administration was one of the most graft-ridden in the history of the Middle East.[551]

Israel

In December 2015, the Jerusalem Post reported Israel as among the most corrupt OECD nations.[552] Abuse was believed worsening by most Israelis, 73 percent saying government had been captured by special interests. Twelve percent noted they had paid bribes the past year and declared political parties the most dishonest institutions in society. Religious bodies were also perceived as highly corrupt. Previous Prime Minister Olmert, who left office after allegations of graft, was sentenced to eight months in prison in May 2015 for fraud and breach of office.[553] In a separate case, he received a six year sentence for bribery while mayor of Jerusalem.[554]

In 1997, Israel was ranked 10th in honesty by Transparency International.[555] By 2007, it had fallen to 34th. In June 2016, a French businessman on trial for fraud, Arnaud Mimran, claimed he gave Netanyahu 170,000 Euros while the latter was serving as Israeli Finance Minister.[556] Numerous other elected officials have been indicted in the past for corruption or sexual misconduct, with some found guilty and imprisoned and others absolved. Prime Minister Netanyahu is again (2019-20) under three separate investigations for corruption and running for re-election.[557,558]

Asia

Pakistan

Corruption at all government levels and businesses is overwhelming in Pakistan. The National Accountability Bureau (NAB) Chief in 2012 declared 8-11 percent of the nation's GDP was lost to corruption.[559] This did not encompass indirect losses from agriculture, the revenue department, land grabbing and encroachments, loan defaults, overstaffing, ghost schools, ghost employment, wealth tax losses, and customs duties, which would raise the tally considerably. Politicians and government bureaucrats participated avidly in fraudulent activities, as did individuals in the private sector. Transparency International noted in 2014 that South Asia, which included Pakistan, was the worst region of the world when it came to corruption.[560] To conduct any business, bribery of officials was required.

Though there are agencies fighting corruption, there is a lack of political will by the government, and staffing and budget are inadequate for the job. In addition, political interference makes the battle generally ineffective. The judiciary is also not perceived as being independent and is thought to shield politicians and wealthy business figures from prosecution.[561],[562]

The Pakistan Institute of Legislative Development and Transparency (PILDAT), a group that promotes good government, has claimed every national election from 1970 to 2008 was rigged or flawed.[563] (Subsequent contests had not been evaluated.) They noted stability would not come for the country until balloting was perceived by the public as fair and credible. In a number of elections, the resources of the state, the military and intelligence agencies were utilized to shape results and place candidates they favored in office.

When the Panama Papers were leaked in April 2016, it was revealed that three of Prime Minister Nawaz Sharif's children had offshore shell companies concealing wealth and escaping taxes.[564] In July 2017, Sharif relinquished his office after the Supreme Court declared him disqualified by corruption allegations.[565] However, his brother was first in line to take over party leadership.

India

India is another democracy in South Asia where corruption has long been a way of life.[566] Every interaction with civil 'servants' include bribe money as part of the encounter. A series of scandals under Prime Minister Singh from 2009 to 2014 weakened the governing Congress

Party, undermining government institutions.[567] Though a right-wing Hindu party, the BJP, with Narendra Modi as head, gained national power in 2014 the population continues to be dissatisfied with overt corruption. [568]

During riots in Gujarat State in 2002, over 1000 Indian Muslims were killed; and Modi pushed Indian Criminal Justice agencies to harass his critics. This has continued unabated since he came to national power and points to an abuse of power unsurpassed in Indian history.[569] After the nation became independent in 1947, in an attempt to develop domestic industries, new companies had to obtain licenses.[570] This stifled competition and foreign investment, and bribery became an integral part of doing business. The Congress Party, which dominated Indian politics for decades, did little to suppress venality and bribery. The BJP Party with its history of corruption does not seem to be the entity to change things, with Modi becoming increasingly autocratic.

South Korea

South Korea's problems with corruption involve both government and large family-dominated business conglomerates known as chaebols that control much of manufacturing and services.[571] Their illicit behavior includes tax evasion, bribery, and price fixing. Chaebols such as Samsung, LG, and Hyundai, are thought to be so powerful that Korea's anti-corruption agency has no jurisdiction over them. However, businessmen and high-ranking government officials have been convicted of corruption in recent years, including former Prime Minister Han Myeong-sook and Economy Minister Park Young-joon.

According to Transparency International, the political environment in Korea is laden with corruption, 70 percent of South Korean households agreeing.[572] In May of 2015, South Korea's Prime Minister Lee Wan-koo resigned and was indicted after allegedly receiving a bribe from a businessman.[573] The number two official in the government, Lee was the second prime minister in President Park's administration forced to resign. In November 2016, a secret advisor to President Park, Choi Soon-sil was arrested on charges of extorting bribes from Korean companies.[574] Choi was considered a religious charlatan who exerted control over Park, embarrassing Korean citizens. After huge demonstrations, Park was impeached by Parliament in December 2016 for having played a role in the scandal.[575],[576] Subsequently in 2018, a court sentenced her to a prison term of twenty-four years for corruption.[577] Two former Korean presidents in the 1990s also wound up in prison for corrupt actions.

Japan

Japan has been controlled by a single party, the Liberal Democrats (LDP) since the institution of democracy in 1955, aside from a hiatus of eleven months from 1993-1994 and 2009-2012.[578] This dominance has led to arrogance by the leadership and 'arrangements' between government officials and business executives. Even so, Japan was rated as the 18th least corrupt nation by Transparency International in 2008.[579] But dirty politics is ingrained, causing little outrage in the populace and allowing corrupt politicians to remain popular and be re-elected. Bid-rigging and kickbacks between politicians, bureaucrats and construction companies on public works contracts is routine.

One of the biggest Japanese corruption scandals embarrassed the Recruit Company and LDP in 1988-1989, forcing Prime Minister Takeshita to resign.[580] In the Recruit affair, 70 politicians and insiders received stock before the company was listed, greatly profiting after it went public. Takeshita's closest aide was prosecuted for tax evasion when millions of dollars of gold bullion and bearer bonds were discovered in his house. A top LDP official, Kiochi Kato, retired after allegations he had laundered money and his major advisor pressured a construction company to build him a new home in exchange for a construction deal. However, in 2003, Kato was voted back into office.

Ministry of Finance officials in the 1990s were arrested after demanding that bankers take them to call girl restaurants.[581] The bankers also gave $100,000 to administrators for warnings about investigations into bad loans. But construction transactions remain the main source of corruption. In 2006, 90 percent of road contracts were awarded without bidding. And nearly 60 percent of over 1200 bureaucrats involved were given jobs by construction firms after leaving government.[582] Many public work projects were subsequently deemed unnecessary, with excessive costs building them.

Under Prime Minster Shinzo Abe, corruption has continued. In 2007, the Minister of Agriculture, Forestry and Fisheries committed suicide rather than submit to questioning over dubious spending.[583] Two ministers who followed him resigned because of unexplained expenses. In January 2016, Akira Amari, the minister for economic revitalization and one of Abe's closest aides resigned over charges of corruption and misconduct.[584] Accused of taking hundreds of thousands of dollars to help a construction company resolve a dispute with a public agency, he was the fourth minister in Abe's cabinet to step down. Though Japan may be considered cleaner than many other states, corruption is a river that runs through the government and society that needs to be dammed.

Indonesia

Indonesia transitioned to democracy in 1998 after Suharto's autocratic rule ended, corruption and graft remaining endemic.[585] Transparency International's Corruption Perception Index in 2014 had Indonesia ranking 107 of 175 nations. A favorite refrain of anti-government protesters when they demonstrate is KKN, an abbreviation standing for corruption, collusion, and nepotism, which entangle the country's politicians, officials, and judiciary.

In 2003, a government agency, the Corruption Eradication Commission (KPK) was established by the national government to investigate corruption. When it extended its reach to high-level police executives and politicians, claims were made that the KPK itself was corrupt, attempting to discredit it. The former chief justice of the

Constitutional Court, Akil Mochtar, was sentenced to life imprison-ment for criminal activity and money laundering by the Corruption Court in July 2014, the first time a sentence of this harshness was im-posed upon a major official.[586] It was hoped this would deter fraud, kickbacks, and bribery prevalent in the police, judiciary and parlia-ment. Indonesia's current president, Joko Widodo, called Jokowi and elected in 2014, was previously a mayor and governor of middle-class background. Though expected to continue the push against corrup-tion, Indonesia has a long road to travel.

Philippines

The Philippines are close geographically to Indonesia and also with a long history of corruption.[587] In 2013, the nation ranked 94 on Transparency International's Corruption Perception Index. However, the World Economic Forum's 2013-2014 Global Competitiveness Report had bribery and fraud as the second most serious obstacle to doing business, lack of infra-structure the first. The dictator, Fernando Marcos and his wife Imelda, made the Philippines their own private fiefdom during his rule from 1972-1986, with raging corruption led by Marcos himself.

Winning the presidency in 2010 by promising honest governance, Benigno Aquino was dogged by high-level scandals,[588] every govern-ment department succumbing to bribes, payoffs, and kickbacks. Military procurement provided opportunities for dishonest officers to acquire wealth by colluding with suppliers, a common scenario. Though the government has a number of anti-corruption agencies and anti-graft laws, these laws have not been effectively enforced.[589] Corruption is widespread among the national police force, with solici-tation of bribes and other illegal acts. Also lawmakers are tagged for misappropriating funds.[590] A businesswoman, Janet Lim-Napoles, was arrested in August of 2013 on assertions she redirected $140 million away from poverty reduction programs to politicians.[591] The Philippine Center for Investigative Journalism reported that 504 candidates in the May 2013 election had at some point been charged with corruption or other crimes. More than half were elected to office, among them seventeen already convicted.

Rodrigo Duterte became president of the Philippines in June 2016, promising to clean up crime and drug use.[592] However, he has been encouraging vigilante action, urging citizens to kill criminals, drug pushers, and drug users. Policemen have been supported in executing suspects rather than bringing them to trial. Duterte claimed that he personally killed citizens suspected of being drug dealers or criminals when he was mayor of Davao.[593] As of December 2016, it was estimated over 5,000 people had been murdered by police and vigilantes, some of them innocent victims of personal vendettas. The extra-judicial murders have continued through 2020 with Duterte's approval.

Malaysia

Malaysia has a history of corruption dating back to independence from the British, with one party rule, Muslim domination, and suppression of civil liberties. The nation became even more authoritarian under the rule of Mohamad Mahathir, elected Prime Minister five times, and in office twenty-two years starting in the early 1980s.[594] Recent Prime Minister Najib Razak is being investigated at home and abroad for massive corruption, graft, and money laundering.[595] A full $681 million was found diverted from a government fund into Razak's personal bank account. In addition, more than $150 million in luxury real estate was purchased through shell companies by Razak's stepson and a family friend.[596] Swiss investigators have discovered about $4 billion misappropriated by Razak and Malaysian public officials and transferred into Swiss bank accounts. A parliamentary investigating committee in April 2016 reported billions of dollars in the sovereign wealth fund unaccounted for, with Razak heading the fund's advisory board.[597] The Malaysian Attorney General, appointed by Razak, absolved him of any criminal activities, but investigations continue in other countries.[598]

In a 2018 election, Razak was defeated and Mahathir Mohamad returned to office as prime minister though he was in his nineties. A thorough investigation of Razak and the missing funds can be expected.

Corruption in other Asian democracies, including Taiwan, Bangladesh, Myanmar, Sri Lanka, and Singapore, will not be addressed. Aside from Singapore, heavily regulated and managed by the government, it can be assumed the level of corruption is similar in the countries mentioned to those in geographic proximity. Myanmar is an evolving democracy with the military still controlling the levers of power. The National League for Democracy, won the general election in 2015 led by Aung San Suu Kyi, but this should not affect corruption.[599] And there is evidence of genocide against the Muslim Rohingya minority by the Buddhist military.[600]

Latin America

Corruption in a few democratic states will be briefly examined. As in other regions, the incidence is too extensive to be fully considered.

Brazil

Brazil is a young democracy, emerging from a military dictatorship in 1985, the world's fifth largest nation in population and land mass. Corruption has infiltrated every level and agency of government, an article in Forbes noting that graft in Brazil was estimated to cost the nation $53 billion in 2013.[601] The report described diversion of public funds to buy political support for the regime of President Luiz da Silva (Lula) and pay off election debts. The investigation, started in 2005 by the Public Ministry, the Federal Police, and the Brazilian Court of Audit, revealed that $43 billion of public money was believed siphoned off in a cash-for-votes scandal.[602]

Under President Dilma Rousseff in 2015, probe of a kickback scheme was found to involve dozens of politicians and Petrobas, the state-run oil company.[603] At least $800 million in bribes were paid to lawmakers. The leaders of Brazil's lower House and Senate were targets of the inquiry along with Senator Fernando Collar who was forced to resign as president in 1992 because of a different corruption scandal.[604] Also under investigation were 21 federal deputies and twelve senators as of March 2015.[605] Politicians who reached plea bargains described how funds were disbursed to top officials, the Workers' Party and other parties.[606] In August 2015, prosecutors revealed that Eduardo Cunha, Speaker of the lower House of Congress, had pocketed at least $40 million for himself and associates in bribes and kickbacks from Petrobas.[607] Cunha laundered the money through an evangelical megachurch he controlled.

Though President Rousseff did not gain personally from the Petrobas scheme, her popularity plummeted and demonstrations calling for her resignation attracted hundreds of thousands.[608] Calls for impeachment grew when she appointed former President Luiz da Silva as her chief of staff [609] to provide him with immunity from criminal charges. However, a federal judge blocked da Silva from taking the position. In December 2015, Cunha, the Speaker of the lower House, (though accused of kickbacks and bribes), initiated impeachment proceedings against Rouseff.[610] She was charged with using funds from state bank accounts to manage budget shortfalls but not in any self-enrichment plans like her accuser. Subsequently, the lower House of Congress voted to impeach Rouseff.[611] Her vice-president, Michel Temer, from the PMDB Party who assumed the presidency, also appeared to be involved in graft, as did the leading members of his party, cabinet officers, and Congressional officials.

In May 2016, Cunha was ordered by the Supreme Court to step down as Speaker of the lower House of Congress because of the corruption charges.[612] Ten months later, he was sentenced to fifteen years in prison.[613] The PMDB Party which was set to rule, appeared to be equally or more corrupt than Rosseff's Worker's Party, which they were replacing.[614] Temer's anti-corruption minister, Fabiano Silveira, was forced to resign at the end of May 2016 when a covert recording showed he had tried to obstruct the Petrobas investigation.[615]

A number of other senior political figures, including former President Jose Sarney, appear to have participated in the Petrobas bribery scheme. Temer had also been embroiled in a different corruption case with calls for him to leave office or face impeachment like Rouseff.[616] However, Temer was given protection from prosecution by a vote of lawmakers in August 2017 to prevent more turmoil in the country.[617] But perhaps the most striking of all the legal proceedings occurred in July 2017 when former president, Luiz da Silva, one of Brazil's iconic figures, was sentenced to nine and a half years in prison for corruption.[618] In spite of his conviction, as of January 2018, he was in first place in the upcoming presidential race with 36 percent of voters supporting him.[619] In March of 2019, former president Michel Temer was arrested for participation in the political corruption scandal known as Carwash that had brought down so many high government figures. Companies looking for business with Petrobas were paying three percent of the value of their contracts as bribes, hundreds of millions of dollars changing hands.[620]

As of April 2016, 60 percent of the 594 federal legislators elected in 2014 were under investigation for an array of crimes.[621] Besides bribery, these included illegal deforestation, electoral fraud, kidnapping, homicide, embezzlement, and torture.[622] However, in spite of the indictments, it is unusual for federal legislators to wind up in prison, given the special standing members of Congress enjoy. And in Brazil, as in other nations, politicians involved in corruption scandals are often re-elected, their constituents ignorant of their actions or not caring.

Not only were politicians and businessmen on the take, but judges, prosecutors, policemen, and other public employees. Electrobras, the nation's biggest power utility, also seems to have had a system of bribes and kickbacks in place similar to Petrobas. Four journalists who probed corruption were murdered in 2015, with none of the assailants caught.[623] Stamping out graft and bribery in Brazil will be an enormously difficult task, given the number of participants and apparent public indifference.

In October 2018, a former military officer and right-wing populist Congressman, Jair Bolsonaro, was elected president of Brazil.[624] A strong law and order candidate, he has shown contempt for human rights, the nation's indigenous population, the environment, and is racist, misogynistic and homophobic. With many stances similar to Donald Trump, he admires military dictators, backs gun rights, is anti-abortion, and has garnered support from the country's evangelicals. Some analysts see him as a budding fascist and he intends to use military officers to staff important positions.[625] Democracy has not seemed to work in Brazil, with tribalism and political illiteracy allowing corruption to fester at every level of government. Whether democracy will survive Bolsonaro's regime is an open question.

Mexico

Mexico is a narco-state with vast economic potential, a nation held back because it is drowning in crime. Drug cartels and criminals are running wild, with most government agencies infiltrated by gang members, officials paid to provide information, or intimidated to do so. A number of cities and states are controlled by the gangs, with politicians as figureheads. Murders and rapes are common and more than 20,000 people are known to have disappeared over the last twenty years, the number undoubtedly much higher.[626] Kidnappings for ransom occur frequently, as does extortion of businessmen. A PBS documentary in 2015 reported 164,000 homicides between 2007 and 2014, the vast majority related to the drug trade.[627]

While many murders result from turf wars and grudges between rival gangs, thousands of innocent civilians have been killed by accident or mistaken identities. And little is done about the killings or disappearances, as incestuous connections between the police and gangs are the norm.

More than forty students vanished in Iguala, a Southern Mexican city in September 2014 trying to get buses to take them to a political rally.[628] A brief investigation determined the city's mayor had ordered the police to kidnap the students and deliver them to a local gang because they had criticized his wife. Though the mayor, his wife, and a number of police officers have been arrested in the case, no traces of the students have been found. The case was reviewed by an international committee of law enforcement experts who rejected the official conclusion, noting physical evidence contradicted the government's version of events. [629] A member of the committee declared the episode revealed the degree of impunity in state security forces when they acted in league with organized crime.

A more sophisticated panel of international experts established by the Inter-American Commission on Human Rights was invited by President Nieto after the first failed inquiry to examine the evidence and help Mexican authorities resolve the question of the students' disappearance.[630] However, the government did not cooperate and it seems that high-level officials did not want the truth about these mass murders to come out.

The PRI Party, considered extremely corrupt, dominated Mexico for decades aside from a hiatus of a few years, and in 2018 controlled eighteen of Mexico's thirty-two states, as well as the national government.[631] Vigilantes have organized in many states and armed themselves to fight the gangs, the population welcoming them since the police have been ineffective.[632] Besides killings by vigilantes, the army has executed without trials thousands of civilians believed to be drug dealers, a number of innocents adding to the totals.[633] It appears the central and state governments control the media and can have them minimize stories of political corruption and drug related crime, making citizens feel safer.[634] Investigative articles are often suppressed and criticism of the government limited. According to an independent good government group, Fundar, Nieto spent nearly two billion dollars on media advertising over his five year term.

Corruption has also appeared on the doorstep of Nieto, mansions having been built for his wife and finance minister in an exclusive Mexico City neighborhood by a company that had obtained hundreds of millions of dollars in government business.[635],[636] A former Mexican governor, Humberto Moreira, was arrested in Spain in January 2016, on charges of money laundering and misuse of public funds.[637] As governor of Coahuila state, Moreira had borrowed billions of dollars, much of it unaccounted for. Two of his finance secretaries had been arrested in Texas for money laundering, one of whom pleaded guilty. Given his political connections, the government in Mexico was unable to go after Moreira for his corrupt actions. Thus, Spain imprisoned him and denied bail. The Spanish police built a strong case against him after the Mexican attorney general stated there was no evidence with which to charge him. In October 2016, the governor of the State of Veracruz, Javier Duarte, believed to have stolen tens of millions of dollars of state funds, resigned and vanished as a warrant was issued for his arrest.[638] Veracruz had been a hotbed of violence under Duarte with at least seventeen journalists having been murdered.

Testimony at the trial of the drug king, El Chapo, in New York in 2018 reinforced the degree of corruption in the government, the military and law enforcement agencies. Those on the take included prison guards, airport officials, police officers, prosecutors, tax assessors and military personnel.[639] Bribes from hundreds of thousands to millions of dollars were disbursed to high officials, including generals, the public security director in charge of the war on drugs, the chief of Mexico City's federal police, and so forth. President Nieto was also said to be involved.

Only twelve percent of crimes in Mexico are even reported, the police considered impotent or corrupt. Approximately 98 percent of homicides go unsolved. With law enforcement and other governmental agencies involved in illegal activities and providing immunity or even aiding the criminals, Mexico's fight against corruption and violence seems to be a losing battle. However, a new president took office in December 2018, Andres Manuel Lopez Obrador, known as AMLO.[640] A populist and a man of the left, he is likely to take a different approach to the drug scourge and its accompanying violence. Whether he will be successful against a plague that has infiltrated all of Mexican society is an open question. Drugs, corruption and uninformed voters have so far kept Mexico from becoming a viable democracy.

Argentina

Argentina is yet another democracy where corruption has made deep inroads. It was ranked 105th by Transparency International on its Corruption Index in 2012.[641] In 2011, a Supreme Court Justice was discovered owning six apartments utilized as brothels. Also in 2011, the Securities and Exchange Commission charged Siemens Corporation with bribing two Argentine presidents, Carlos Menem and Fernando de la Rua, with $100 million to secure contracts for a $1 billion national identity card. Eighty-one percent of Argentines consider law enforcement deficient. 60 percent believe they can pay off police officials to avoid infractions and 13,000 police officers have been arrested for various crimes.

In June 2014, Vice President Amado Boudou was charged with abuse of power in obtaining control of a firm printing the nation's currency.[642] An economy minister under President Christina Kirchner was sentenced to four years in prison when large sums of currency were found in her bathroom. It was reported in 2013 that the personal wealth of Presidents Nestor Kirchner (now deceased) and his wife President Christina Fernandez de Kirchner had multiplied more than ten times since they took office.[643] Apparently, a friend had been handed construction projects by the presidents and they were given kickbacks. Christina Kirchner attributed the gains to lucky moves in real estate and profits from hotels they owned. In April 2016, an Argentinian prosecutor sought to investigate former President Kirchner for money-laundering, implicated by a wealthy construction magnate.[644] In May, she and other officials were indicted on charges of manipulating the Central Bank to strengthen the Argentinean peso to help her political party.[645] Further indictments were handed down by a judge in December 2016.[646]

Argentina was in deep financial trouble under the Kirchners' regime and had been censured by the IMF for falsifying its economic data. In an October 2015 presidential election, conservative Mauricio Macri beat Kirchner's candidate. [647] But with such deep-seated corruption at the highest levels of the government even before the Kirchners, the question is whether democratic processes can possibly bring about the reform needed to clean up the country? In fact, Macri has been implicated in the Panama Papers scandal, having hidden money in off-shore accounts.[648] Where will the impetus come for change?

Venezuela

Venezuela is an autocracy that evolved from a democratic state. All the centers of power, the media and military are under the control of Nicholas Maduro, the leader elected to succeed Hugo Chavez in what was believed to have been a fraudulent contest.[649] With the price of oil having plummeted in 2014-2015, the economy is a disaster. Inflation is rampant, food and popular goods in short supply. A former bus driver, Maduro has blamed Venezuela's economic problems on a conspiracy by the United States and has arrested scores of opposition leaders, including a number of elected officials, without any evidence of crimes.[650] Street crime and corruption are rife, the population suffering greatly. Millions of Venezuelans have emigrated from the country, seeking security and a place to make a living.

The opposition presented two million signatures to the National Election Board for a recall referendum on Maduro which he initially ignored.[651] The Electoral Panel (which Maduro appointed) ended the drive for a referendum in October 2016 and the Supreme Court declared it could bypass the nation's Congress in approving the national budget.[652] Maduro's intransigence will make it much more difficult to turn around the moribund economy and restore democracy.

Chile

Since Augusto Pinochet's ouster, Chile has been considered one of the least corrupt Latin American nations.[653] However, that reputation was badly tarnished in 2015. Michelle Bachelet, the leftist president elected on a platform of reducing inequality, saw her son accused of utilizing his influence to obtain a $10 million loan for a land deal that generated profits of millions of dollars over a few weeks. And the right-wing opposition party, the Independent Union, had one of its supporters, a large financial firm, charged with money laundering, tax fraud, and bribery, resulting from a scheme to fund the party. In addition, a major mining company headed by Pinochet's son-in-law, Julio Ponce Lerou, allegedly made illegal payments to a number of politicians on the right, as well as to members of Bachelet's coalition.

The revelations shocked the populace, unaccustomed to seeing top political figures mired in the quicksand of corruption. In January 2016, Bachelet's daughter-in-law Natalia Compagnon was charged with fraud for issuing false invoices for her business to evade $170 million in taxes.[654] A Latin American business magazine noted, "Whether they're from the left, center or right, the members of a small elite have the money and power in their hands."[655] Reporters have been highlighting illegal activities of prominent politicians, affluent individuals, and major companies for over a year, embarrassing those in power. Meanwhile, the Chilean Senate passed a 'gag law' in April 2016, prohibiting revelation of information about judicial investigations.[656] Violators face long prison sentences, while many corrupt politicians and business executives remain free.

Peru

Peru is among the most corrupt Latin American nations, with a number of presidents and high government officials involved in kickback schemes, particularly involving construction projects. Odebrecht, the Brazilian construction conglomerate, has built much of Peru's infrastructure after bribing the country's presidents and other officials to obtain the jobs.[657] In April 2019, ex-President Alan Garcia who served two terms as president, committed suicide by shooting himself in the head when the police came to arrest him. At least three other Peruvian ex-presidents have also participated in construction kickback scandals with Odebrecht. The company was also implicated in bribery of high officials to obtain construction contracts in Ecuador and Colombia as well as Brazil.

Every nation in the developed and undeveloped world whether democratic or autocratic must deal with corruption. It is a particular problem for democracies, whose goals are supposed to be more concerned with fulfilling lives and material benefits for their citizens. Corruption makes the objectives of democracy difficult to achieve, giving those with wealth, status, or political connections an advantage over the rest of the population. And with corruption ingrained in every democracy, significantly reducing or eliminating it will require a change in the structure and practices of the system. Otherwise, politicians will continue to be seduced by bribes and graft, getting re-elected with tainted money and accumulating wealth while the needs of their constituents are not addressed. The populace must take an interest in politics and become knowledgeable about the corruption in their nations, using their power at the ballot box, assuming the elections are legitimate.

7

Partisanship and Polarization

"The best argument against democracy is a five-minute conversation with the average voter." Winston Churchill[658]

ACCORDING TO VARIOUS polls during the last decade, pluralities to small majorities of Americans identify themselves as centrists, moderates, or independents. The variability in statistics are probably related to how the surveys were conducted and questions asked, what year data was collected, and whether bias was present in the polling organizations. Notwithstanding, moderates and centrists were usually the largest bloc. This means extremists in both political parties, generally the most vocal, do not represent most of the citizenry, though avid partisanship among politicians makes government dysfunctional.

In October 2013, an NBC News/Esquire poll had 51 percent of Americans labeling themselves as centrists, 44 percent of whom did not believe their views were represented by either party. A poll by The Third Way published in May 2014, had 37 percent moderate, 42 percent conservative and 21 percent liberal.[659] Forty-two percent of millennials identified as moderates in this survey. These were the youngest group, seeming to indicate America will be growing more moderate in the future. Similarly, non-white and Hispanic participants described themselves as moderate by a plurality of 44 percent.

A poll by the Pew Center in April 2015 revealed 39 percent of Americans considered themselves independents, 32 percent Democrats, and 23 percent Republicans.[660] The data came from interviews with more than 25,000 citizens. The percentage of independents, which had surpassed Democrats and Republicans some time ago, continued to increase. In more than seventy-five years of Pew polling, this was the highest percentage of independents ever reported. White men preferred the GOP, white women the Democrats. Those with post-graduate or college degrees leaned Democratic as did racial minorities and those religiously unaffiliated. Millennials also favored Democrats 51 to 35 percent. Mormons and white evangelical Protestants were overwhelmingly Republican. White Southerners and white men without college degrees tended to be Republican, and there was a GOP bias of four percentage points among citizens over sixty.

Though centrists may represent the largest political group in America, animosity and partisanship between parties is the strongest it has been in decades according to a Pew Study in 2016 and a Washington Post poll in 2017.[661],[662] Party members associate negative qualities with members of the opposing party, a rising tide of mutual antipathy making it challenging for the two parties to govern together.[663] Survey data in 1970 showed that though Republicans and Democrats were hostile to each other, their mutual dislike was mild.[664] However, negative feelings between party members have increased over the years, more so since 2000--the process labeled 'affective partisan polarization' or negative polarization by political scientists. Antipathy toward the opposition party is a major motivating factor for partisans, and it is difficult for democracy to function as each side demonizes the other and compromise is a struggle.[665]

Various surveys show a plurality or majority of Americans are not extremists or partisans, but the partisans are more politically active than their moderate brethren. Their agendas are the ones debated in the halls of government, determining the laws that are or are not enacted. A CBS poll in 2011 had 85 percent of Americans favoring compromise by politicians to get things done, including 75 percent of Republicans.[666] However, their message was apparently not transmitted to politicians in Washington and state capitals. Another factor driving partisanship is that the wealthy top one percent is politically zealous and contributes large sums to officeholders and candidates with views similar to theirs.[667]

Partisanship is also more evident now because the percentage of Americans labeling themselves 'consistently conservative' or 'consistently liberal' has doubled in the last twenty years from 10 to 21 percent. [668] In addition, Democrats and Republicans are more likely to socialize with people having similar political positions. There are also media voices that amplify differences between the parties and benefit from the 'climate of bitterness.' Polarization in both Houses of Congress is at its highest level in nearly a hundred and fifty years.

In many democracies, 'identity' is the critical determinant of how individuals cast their ballots.[669] People vote for politicians because they share the same religion, race, or ethnicity. These factors may be more important than whether candidates are honest or competent or have the same positions on issues, though often voters are in the dark about these aspects because they have not investigated them. Identity politics reinforces partisanship, particularly in nations riven by tribal, religious, or ethnic hatreds and fears.

American politics has become more tribal in the last quarter century, dominated by partisans in both parties. Touting their own values, each tribe has its own facts regarding history, economics, and science. Beliefs about climate change and global warming is an example. Members of each tribe tend to think similarly and have similar interpretations of events and views about political figures, as well as comparable personality traits. Interestingly, CT scans of brains in each group show similar structural changes.[670] Conservatives tend to have larger amygdalas, part of the limbic system involved in processing emotions, such as fear, anger, disgust and pleasure. Liberals tend to have a larger anterior cingulate cortex, an area of the brain that deals with uncertainty, handling conflicting information, impulse control, morality and ethics. In both tribes beliefs can be changed, but it is difficult when brains may process information differently.

'Tribalism' has been critical in the growth of partisanship. In the past, citizens' identities evolved through families, communities, churches, employment, unions, clubs, lodges, and so forth. People were part of something greater than themselves. But these bonds have been sundered by modern society. Divorce and single parent families are common. Small towns and rural communities are in decline, with young people moving away. Church participation is lessening and jobs no longer secure. This lack of connection and of belonging to something has impacted Americans negatively. Alcohol and drugs have been an escape for some and others have chosen to be active members of political parties, adopting the characteristics of their 'tribes.' Social media may also augment the stances partisans take. This makes it harder to compromise or see the humanity and understand the positions of opponents. Many members of political tribes have joined not because of policy, but because the party consisted of people who were similar to them in terms of class, religion, race, or region.[671]

Webster's New Twentieth Century Dictionary describes a partisan as "1) one who takes the side of, or strongly supports a side, a party, or another person: often said of an unreasoning, emotional adherent. 2) blindly or unreasonably devoted. Partisanship is 1) the strong supporting or endorsement of a side, party, etc. 2) a strong, often unreasoning, attachment. 3) blind loyalty."[672] My personal definition is slightly different: Partisanship is an unbending or absolute belief regarding the correctness of a principle or principles by an individual or group that does not sanction compromise with opposing views. This can encompass political stances, social tenets, religious convictions, nationalism, and so forth.

In all likelihood, partisanship is in the eye of the beholder, with some partisans unaware they are so-characterized by others. To moderates, the description partisan is an ugly connotation, while ideologues or partisans may see it as a badge of honor. Barry Goldwater in his acceptance speech to the GOP convention in 1964 defended extremism and partisanship. "I would remind you that extremism in the defense of liberty is no vice. And let me remind you also that moderation in the pursuit of justice is no virtue!"[673] His words set the tone for future conservative partisans. But who are these partisans of the right and left? What attributes separate them from each other and make them opponents?

Republicans-Right Wing

In the United States and most democracies, conservative partisans stand for smaller government, reduced government spending, and lower taxes. Unfettered capitalism with fewer regulations by government to control business activity is also desired. There is a belief as well that people should be responsible for their own needs, rather than depending on government. In addition, individual rights trump those of the community when there is a conflict. Consumer protection laws are thought to be superfluous, as those buying merchandise should be capable of making their own decisions. The market will select out companies whose products are inferior or dangerous. Free trade between nations is also important.

Power and authority should be devolved more to the states, except for defense and foreign affairs. And states should permit local and municipal governments to assume as much responsibility as possible in spheres such as education, zoning, building codes, and whatever else they can handle. Special programs in early education and K-12 to work with disadvantaged children are not a priority for rightists, who place the onus on families for children's inability to learn. The right to own and bear arms is another central tenet of conservative partisans.

A strong currency, balanced budgets, and limitations on government debt are major precepts (though obviously not always observed). There is considerable antagonism toward unions and laws appearing to favor them. In fact, a number of American states have passed 'right to work' laws that make it difficult for unions to organize. Workman's compensation benefits should also be curtailed as these payouts reduce incentives for laid-off workers to find jobs during the period they receive support. In addition, right-wingers are generally hostile to regulations forcing businesses to operate in environmentally friendly ways, most conservatives refusing to accept global warming as a fact. They do not want to restrict carbon-producing fuels through regulations or taxes, believing that will have negative economic repercussions.

Law and order has always been a crucial issue for the right and growth of the prison population was testimony to the way they sold Americans on their solution for crime. Drug treatment, education, and employment for young offenders were bypassed in favor of imprisonment, particularly for men of color. The U.S. has the highest rate of incarceration of any developed country and a generation of young black men lost opportunities to build successful lives.[674] (However, many conservatives and liberals now agree the pendulum has swung too far and are pushing reform for non-violent offenders.[675])

The Tea Party movement during the first two decades of the 21st century consisted of far-right partisans who refused to compromise with the left. Stronger in the House than Senate, they forced a sixteen day government shutdown in October 2013 when they could not agree on a spending bill with Democrats.[676] (The Budget Office estimated the shutdown cost taxpayers $2 billion.) Because of gerrymandering by state governments controlled by the GOP, a number of Congressional districts in the South and West are fiercely conservative. This explains the preponderance of conservative partisans in the House and proportionately fewer in the Senate as senators are elected by entire states. Congressional districts will change after the census in 2020. If the majority of state governments remain in GOP hands, gerrymandering will make Republican command of the House more likely. Maximizing a party's power by the way legislative maps are drawn can have major policy ramifications.[677]

Socially conservative partisans are frequently lumped together with economic conservatives, as their voting patterns are often similar. However, this combination should not be automatically con-flated, as their beliefs are not always congruent. Indeed, individuals and groups may have opposing views in the social and economic spheres- ie: fiscally conservative but socially liberal, or vice versa. The tenets of social conservatives are generally religiously based. They tend to be members of religions which are conservative in their world views- Evangelical Protestants, Roman Catholics, Mormons, Orthodox Catholics, Orthodox Jews and devout Muslims.

Social conservatives are vehemently (and sometimes violently) anti-abortion, believe homosexuality is a sin and are against same-sex marriage. They are often opposed to teaching evolution, preferring 'creationism,' intelligent design, or similar doctrines, and object to the 'big bang' theory. The GOP supports these positions, since much of their base are social conservatives. (Only 43 percent of Republicans think the theory of evolution is valid.[678]) The Bible is often accepted literally and many social conservatives believe the world is less than ten thousand years old, with humans and dinosaurs co-existing in the past.

Evangelical Protestants, virtually all socially conservative, vote overwhelmingly for the GOP.[679] Two thirds of evangelicals identify as Republicans. However, the number of evangelicals appears to be shrinking, as more Americans label themselves religiously unaffiliat-ed.[680] Even so, 46 percent of Republicans currently are evangelicals.[681] Seventy percent of Mormons consider themselves Republicans or lean Republican along with 69 percent of white voters who attend religious services at least once per week, with only 41 percent of white voters who rarely or never visit a house of worship.[682] Exit polls showed 80 percent of evangelicals[683] and religious voters backed Trump, not-withstanding his adultery, divorces and three wives, use of obscene language, lack of church attendance, and ignorance of the Bible.[684]

Democrats- Left-Wing

As expected, partisans on the left take numerous opposing positions to those on the right. Government spending on social programs and taxes to sustain these expenditures are considered essential. The size of the government is not an issue as long as it functions well and provides needed benefits for citizens. Protection of entitlement programs like Medicare, Medicaid, and Social Security are critical to liberals and partisans on the left, though many centrists are similarly inclined. In fact, expansion of these programs would be considered desirable. Universal health insurance such as Medicare for all is an important tenet for many leftists.

Alignment with labor is automatic for left-wing adherents, who see workers at the mercy of big business. Though the union movement in America has been in decline for some time, politicians on the left would like a revival of organized labor. To accomplish this, elimination of right to work laws would be needed, along with strengthening of existing unions, and legislation making it easier for unions to organize. In the past, the relationship between unions and the left was symbiotic, with leftist officeholders helping to enact laws favoring unions, and unions supporting left-wing politicians with campaign contributions, canvassing, and get-out-the-vote efforts. Generous unemployment compensation benefits were another way the left helped workers and justified union backing. Though labor leaders for the most part supported Clinton and the Democrats in the 2016 election, many white working men went for Trump.

Regulation of banks and big business, along with enhanced consumer protection laws are also consequential for leftists. They perceive the recession of 2007-2008 as mainly the fault of the banking industry and inability of the regulatory agencies to monitor them. The left wants to prevent large financial institutions from investing in speculative securities for their own accounts (as mandated in Dodd-Frank). This way, there would be less risk of banks failing and needing government assistance. According to the left, consumer protection laws should encompass a number of different areas in financial agreements. Simplification should be provided when fine print in contracts is not lucid, or where the public does not fully grasp the arrangements. These would include mortgages, insurance policies, annuities, consumer loans, borrowing from credit cards, and payday loans. The language in these contracts and loans should be clear and concise, so people are aware of their obligations.

Environmental protection is a serious concern for left-wing partisans. Included are immediate issues like controlling pollution and toxic byproducts of industrial production, along with long-term climate change. The latter's danger to the earth and scientific basis is accepted as fact. People should not continue to use fossil fuels for power and transportation without considering its effects on the planet. Alternative energy sources are growing cheaper every year and should be employed to replace fuels producing carbon dioxide and methane.

Reducing financial inequality is another quandary for the left, as there does not seem to be a simple way to bridge the vast gulf between the top 0.1 percent and the bottom 50 percent. However, before social explosions occur, just solutions must be found. No one should have to go without life's necessities, nor be unable to pursue higher education. And the political process should not be controlled by the very wealthy, willing to spend unlimited funds to sell their views. Many Democrats favor significantly higher taxes on those who are extremely wealthy.

Co-existing with inequality is the specter of racism in America that never seems to go away in spite of a black man having been elected president. Poverty, drug use, and violence among black and Latino populations seem omnipresent, with high unemployment rates and poor educational attainment. This is also true for rural white citizens, particularly men. Without education to compete in today's technologically propelled world, blacks, Latinos and poor whites will remain on the bottom rungs of the economic ladder indefinitely. Society must improve the K-12 educational system to capture those youths always behind the curve. Some of this results from parental neglect, particularly in single parent families where the mother or father is working two or three jobs. Head Start and other preschool programs are critical.

Policing must also become color-blind and not target black and Latino youths without reasonable suspicion. The 'black lives matter' movement was born in 2015 after a number of police shootings of unarmed black men.[685] The justice system must change as well, with less imprisonment of young black men for non-violent crimes, greater balance in sentences for blacks and whites and more attempts at rehabilitation.[686]

In general, left-wing partisans are secular in their approach to social problems. They believe in strict separation of church and state, and do not want religion to dictate how social issues are addressed. Fervently pro-choice, they affirm that women should have control over their bodies and pregnancies, with contraception universally offered as part of health care. Homosexuality is accepted as within the spectrum of normal behavior and same-sex marriage is supported. Leftists want scientific subjects backed by evidence taught in the public schools.

Most leftists in their hearts would like a gun-free society in America, but realizing that is impossible, accept possession of guns by civilians with certain limitations. Licensed guns should be used for protection in the home or externally if one has a dangerous job. Rifles and pistols can also be employed for hunting or sport shooting. Assault rifles and large capacity ammunition clips should be banned. Before a weapon is purchased, there should be thorough background checks and a waiting period. No one with a history of a felony, domestic abuse, or mental illness, should be allowed any type of gun.

As evidenced by the 2016 election, leftists must pay more attention to problems of the white working class, and cultural and religious issues important to them. Though the stances that define liberals and conservatives are long-standing and straightforward, Trump and the current Republican Party have discarded many of the hallmarks of conservatism such as free trade and lowering of budget deficits and the national debt. Instead, Trump's emotions seem to drive government policy.

Causes of Polarization

Alan Abramowitz, a professor of Political Science at Emory University, believes the polarization dominating American politics reflects the changes that have occurred in the nation's culture and society over the last several decades.[687] He points to the growth of racial and ethnic diversity, and the increasing divide in religious and moral values. Through immigration and the higher fertility rate of non-white citizens, the demographic make-up of the nation has been transformed, America close to no longer having a Caucasian majority. With these changes, the two political parties appear to have different constituencies holding differing world views. The partisans in each party are more aligned and homogeneous in their positions on major issues, and further apart from the opposing party. Republicans can be characterized as the party of white men, with Democrats the party of women and citizens of different ethnic and racial backgrounds. At times, it seems as if the politicians in each party are speaking separate languages when they talk about the needs of the nation and solutions they believe necessary.

Given the life experiences of non-whites, with higher rates of unemployment and poverty, less access to health care, reduced educational achievement and inferior housing, it is not surprising the Democratic Party wants to reverse the conditions responsible. To improve matters, more government spending is necessary, with higher taxes to generate revenue. Republicans, on the other hand, are the party of the status quo. By fighting immigration, they hope to keep America white for as long as possible. And by GOP opposition to tax increases, people of color may have greater struggles to reach the middle class or even affluence through improved education, better health care and housing. (A more educated population would also enhance the economy, with higher incomes augmenting consumer spending.)

Two other political science professors, Morris Fiorina and Samuel Abrams are convinced the electorate in America has not grown more polarized since the 1970s, though the political class is more partisan.[688] According to them, the aggregate of voters currently appears similar to that of forty years ago, partisanship fluctuating within a narrow band. Where tracking of individual issues in surveys has been possible over time, centrist opinions appear to be favored in both parties. However, there has been sorting of partisans within the parties, with self-labeled Republicans more conservative and self-labeled Democrats more liberal. Though overlap of opinions is now less common among ordinary members, the divide between the two parties' politicians has become even greater. As recently as 2012, survey data indicated a quarter of Democrats could be considered 'pro-life' and a third of Republicans as 'pro-choice.' However, Democrats running for office now are generally more liberal and GOP candidates more conservative, moderate middle politicians having melted away.

Though partisanship has always existed in politics, it was not too long ago that members of the GOP and Democratic Parties socialized, with comity between them instead of animus. Politicians attempted to understand the positions of their opponents instead of demonizing them. Of course, that was when the face of the Republican Party was formed by New England moderates rather than extreme conservatives from Texas and the South. Is polarization of the political class permanent or will there be movement back toward the center over time?

The Need for Political Parties

In every modern democracy, political parties are a fact of life. It would be impossible for governments to operate without them. But parties do not have to devolve into organizations controlled by ideologues. Parties serve an administrative purpose, grouping together individuals with similar beliefs to elect candidates for local, regional and national offices who will promote common ideas. They provide members opportunities to run for office themselves with backing from an organization, or to nominate others whom they would support. The larger a nation, the more important parties are, since sheer numbers make it extremely difficult for solitary voices to be heard. In a party, people can propound their views at a local level, and if there are enough adherents, the message filters through to a regional and perhaps national level. If the party achieves power, these beliefs can be turned into law. Primaries run by the parties also allow sorting of candidates with comparable ideas so one person will be chosen to carry the party's banner in the general election and the vote for that position will not be divided. Parties should be agents of stability in society, allowing people to 'work within the system' to bring about change.

Some political scientists describe parties as having three parts: the party-in-the-electorate where affiliated voters and low level activists reside, the party-in-government consisting of the party's elected officials, and the party-as-organization where workers and volunteers raise money, educate and propagandize voters, develop policy proposals and map strategy.[689] Through their educational and propaganda roles, parties try to convince the general public about the validity of their viewpoints so they will vote for party candidates. Party organizations also mobilize voters and get them to the polls.

All legislative bodies are structured along party lines. Legislators of each party try to choose leaders who concur with their views and in turn receive appointments to committees that increase their power. If an elected official is defeated for office or decides not to run, he or she may be given a job in the executive branch by other party officeholders. Party members may also be appointed to the judiciary or obtain positions outside of government (lobbyists).

Notwithstanding the necessity of parties and their positive roles, there are unwelcome aspects. Parties can institutionalize divisiveness already existing and enhance discord within government, legislative bodies, and throughout entire nations. Their promotion of ideology also binds members in philosophical strait jackets, compelling them to adopt narrower world views and be less open to competing ideas.

Parties are almost secular religions, with codes of beliefs and rationales for action. Parties become destructive of democratic principles when ideologues control the direction and objectives of the organizations. Unfortunately, American political parties, particularly Republicans, have become more extreme over the last several decades, with unwillingness to compromise on most issues.

'Politics stops at the water's edge' used to be a precept of American politics.[690] It meant foreign policy would be bipartisan, and both parties would be united in the way the country dealt with the world. Daniel Webster may have first said something similar in attempting to get citizens to enlist in the military during the War of 1812. "Even our party divisions, acrimonious as they are, cease at the water's edge." For most of American history, the president and secretary of state have set foreign policy and expected support from both political parties.

However, the degree of extremism in the current GOP and their refusal to back Obama on foreign policy, led to a strict party line vote on the Iran Nuclear Treaty in 2015. It began when Republican Speaker John Boehner invited Prime Minister Netanyahu of Israel to address a joint session of Congress with a speech against the treaty, going behind the back of the president.[691] This invitation to a foreign leader was unprecedented.[692] Netanyahu advocated stricter sanctions instead of a deal with Iran. However, the treaty was subsequently negotiated with five other world powers. But when a vote came up in Congress to ratify the treaty, the vote was almost completely on a party line basis.[693] Democrats had enough votes in the Senate to filibuster a rejection so the president did not have to veto the measure, but partisanship had intruded into foreign affairs. Trump said the treaty did not protect American interests and failed to certify Iran's compliance in October 2017, throwing the treaty into a divided Congress to decide what to do.[694] As of August 2018, of all the signatories to the Iran nuclear agreement, the United States was the only nation refusing to abide by the treaty and considering new sanctions on Iran.

Another example of extreme partisanship was the Terry Schiavo incident.[695] Though it was and is difficult to pass legislation in Washington, a special law to protect a single brain-damaged patient in a vegetative state was debated and enacted over two days by both Houses of Congress in March 2005. Congress was called back to Washington by GOP leaders for an emergency session and President Bush flew back from vacation in Texas to sign the bill. This legislation, important to social conservatives, forbid the removal of this poor woman's feeding tube, ignoring wishes of her husband and her own apparent desire, siding with Schiavo's parents. The bill was meaningless from a legal standpoint, but was hailed by Christian conservatives and scored significant political points. Subsequently, the request to continue the feeding tube was denied by the court system, Schiavo dying shortly afterward.

GOP Senator Ted Cruz of Texas, who ran for president in 2016, is among the most partisan of any recently elected Senators. He has used his power to throw monkey wrenches into government functions like a spoiled child unable to have his way. These actions were fueled by overt hostility to President Obama and Cruz's willingness to halt government services to prevent any Obama victory.[696] In addition to leading a government shutdown in 2013 by refusing to fund operations unless money was stripped from Obamacare, he blocked nominees for cabinet posts and ambassadorships, as well as funding for the State Department.[697] In September 2015, he threatened another shutdown unless federal money was eliminated from Planned Parenthood.

Partisanship exists in every type of polity, though it may be suppressed in autocratic states where dissent from official policy is not tolerated. In democracies with freedom of speech and expression, there may be more opportunity for conflict between ideologies. Unfortunately, in some nations considered democratic, there may be restrictions on freedom of expression. Certain subjects may be considered taboo, and challenging special texts or satirizing religious or historical figures forbidden by law or custom. These limitations often exist in Muslim states. They may also be seen related to royalty or figures of high status in constitutional monarchies. In Western democracies, partisanship is between the left and right, liberals and conservatives. In Muslim 'democracies' partisan battles may be between secularists and Islamists, between different sects of Islam, or those who espouse different interpretations of Islam. And the battles may be marked by violence.

The stirrings of partisanship probably originated when men clustered in organized societies and disputes arose between groups with diverse views, who followed different leaders, or worshipped different gods. Depending on the strength of their beliefs, compromise might or might not have been possible, and fights might have erupted to settle disagreements. Blood feuds between people also existed pre-history, when proper respect was not shown to a leader, or when some personage felt insulted or dishonored, or when women were violated. As social groups increased in size, ideological contrasts morphed into political parties and partisanship, with sides arguing for their ideas instead of physical fights for dominance. However, even today partisan positions can result in violence in 'civilized' societies when people cannot legally get their way (murdering of abortion providers, beatings of homosexuals, bombing of government buildings).

The Development of Parties and Partisanship in America

In the colonies in the 1770s, partisanship was rampant, the division between colonists who favored independence and Tories who desired continued rule by England. This led to verbal, written, and physical conflicts between adherents of opposing views. After the Revolutionary War and failure of the Articles of Confederation, the formation of a new order was tasked to political leaders of the thirteen states. America's Founders were men of the enlightenment willing to compromise to midwife the birth of a new nation. In writing the Constitution, the document that gave coherence to that nation, they were able to bridge great differences—between North and South, urban and rural, and varying visions of what America would become.

There is no mention of political parties in the Constitution. As

Jethro Lieberman notes in his book *The Evolving Constitution*; the "two party system... came about largely independent of the law."[698] The historian John D. Hicks declared in 1933 that "the two party system was not ordained by the Constitution, (nor was a division into political parties)...desired by some of those who first guided the nation's destinies."[699] America's early leaders did not view political parties positively and were not sure of the role they should play. Some were quite hostile to the concept which they saw in a naive way as causing conflict and dissension among men, rather than merely reflecting differences already present. [700] Yet the organization of people coalescing around particular ideas and supporting like-minded candidates suggested the necessity of political parties if chaos was to be avoided. Indeed, soon after the first government was elected with Washington as president and Congress in place, nascent parties could be discerned.

By the presidential election of 1796, there were two dominant parties locked in combat, and individuals who had cautioned against them were influential in their formation. George Washington warned against them in his farewell address from the presidency. "I have already intimated to you the danger of Parties in the State, with particular reference to the founding of them on Geographical discriminations. Let me now take a more comprehensive view and warn you in the most solemn manner against the baneful effects of the Spirit of Party, generally.

"The Spirit, unfortunately, is inseparable from our nature, having its root in the strongest passions of the human Mind."[701]

Washington's words fell on deaf ears as political pragmatists understood parties were needed in order to govern. Besides, danger developed not from the parties themselves but when ideologues in the parties refused to compromise on important issues, making it more difficult for government to operate. The first two parties were the Federalists, led by Treasury Secretary Alexander Hamilton, and the Republicans headed by Secretary of State Thomas Jefferson.[702]

The Early Years of the Republic

In the initial sessions of Congress during Washington's first term, there were shifting alliances of senators and representatives on various proposals that made it challenging to pass legislation. This necessitated constant negotiations and horse trading over each bill. A formal grouping of like-minded persons was the obvious answer to simplify the process. The power of the central government was the major issue, opposing views like magnetic poles attracting those with similar beliefs. Hamilton, who favored federal primacy, believed it was important for the federal government to assume the states' debts, find a way to retire them, and to form a national bank to bolster America's commerce. John Adams, a Federalist, was the first 'party man' elected President in 1796, though the party was more of a loose affiliation.

Agrarian interests, led by Jefferson and Madison, were wary of this bloc that wanted to centralize power and began recruiting adherents at a state and local level, as well as Congress, to build a national party. In response, Federalists organized belatedly, which probably caused Adams to lose the Presidential election of 1800 to Jefferson and his Republicans. The campaign was one of the most vicious in American history, the first time power passed from one party to another.[703] Ethical considerations and propriety were disregarded in charges and countercharges before Jefferson won in the House of Representatives. The political scientist John Aldrich noted- "by 1800 elections were publicly and undeniably partisan, ….impelled by the attempts of Hamiltonians and Jeffersonians to win a consistent pattern of victories on policy."[704]

After Jefferson's presidency, the Republican (Democratic) Party remained dominant on a national level, with Madison and then James Monroe elected president, each for two terms, with control of both Houses of Congress. The Federalists won few seats in the House and Senate. Though there was essentially one national party in 1824, multiple candidates were put forward for president by state legislatures. John Quincy Adams' victory came despite Andrew Jackson winning a plurality of the popular vote. Henry Clay's support for Adams in the

House of Representatives gave him the presidency, Clay subsequently being appointed Secretary of State.[705]

Mid 19th Century

With Martin Van Buren helping Jackson reorganize the Republicans, (now called the Democratic Party), Jackson was elected president in 1828. This was the first mass political party, a highly structured organization whose strength lay in the emerging middle class, instead of elite gentleman farmers of the Jefferson and Madison eras. Rather than fixed guiding principles, its objective was to appeal to a majority of voters to win elections. Victory meant power, patronage, and direction of policy. The election of Jackson effected a major innovation in American politics: development of the 'spoils system.'[706] The Whigs, composed of remnants of the Federalists, organized in a similar fashion and when the new Republican Party was created a few years later, it followed the same model. Many politicians in this period saw "government service as a rich opportunity to line their own pockets at the public expense."[707]

The Whig Party, shepherded by Daniel Webster and Henry Clay, and similar to the Federalists, were locked in combat with the Democrats through the 1830s and 1840s. Each tried to gain an advantage among a greatly enlarged electorate resulting from elimination of property holding as a qualification for voting. The Whigs labeled Democrats as too elitist and asserted that common citizens should control the government. As described by political scientists John F. Bibby and L. Sandy Maisel in their book *Two Parties-or More*: "The parties engaged in popularized campaigning—torchlight parades, rallies, picnics, campaign songs, and slogans like 'Tippecanoe and Tyler too.' In this atmosphere of partisan mobilization, voters began to see themselves as either Whigs or Democrats."[708] "Political campaigns became a form of entertainment, generating interest and enthusiasm that spilled over into participation."[709]

Slavery became the dominant partisan issue during the 1850s.

The Republican Party, opposed to slavery, was born in the Midwest, composed mostly of former Whigs with some northern Democrats and members of splinter groups. Officially, the party was initiated at a meeting in Ripon, Wisconsin, in March of 1854 and quickly gained adherents throughout the north.[710] Republicans and Democrats battled for the presidency in 1856, with John C. Freemont, the first Republican candidate, losing to James Buchanan, who was corrupt and partisan.[711]

In the presidential contest of 1860, Republicans highlighted corruption under Buchanan and emphasized the integrity of their candidate, 'Honest Abe,' elected sixteenth president, beating northern Democrat Stephen Douglas. The southern Democratic Party split with its northern faction, running John C. Breckinridge as its candidate, with another offshoot, the Constitutional Union Party, nominating John Bell.[712] With four candidates running, Lincoln won with a plurality of 39.8%, which translated to 59.4% of the Electoral College vote.

Once the Civil War was over, the structure and ideas of the two national parties were fixed in place. From that point on, because of its stand against slavery, and its role in the Civil War and Reconstruction, Republicans remained essentially a party of the north and west until well into the 20th century, while the Democrats maintained a strong base of support in the south.

Post Civil War Era- The Gilded Age

After the Civil War, Republicans controlled the presidency until Democrat Grover Cleveland's election in 1884. Its popularity rested on its 'reputation as the party that had freed the slaves and saved the union.'[713] But there were divisions among Republicans about how to deal with the Confederate states and their leaders. When President Andrew Johnson's plans allowed the Confederate elite to gain ascendancy in the South, radical Republicans in Congress passed the Reconstruction Acts dictating how governments in Confederate states were to be administered. Granting suffrage to black men and with migration of northern white 'carpetbaggers' to the south, Republicans maintained power in most of the Confederacy.

By 1872, the push to continue Reconstruction began to lose momentum, economic issues paramount reinforced by the Depression of 1873. The following year, Democrats won a majority of seats in the House, Democratic control also reasserted in a succession of Southern states. In addition to the 'solid south,' Democratic supporters included Catholics, urban workers, and immigrants. Republican strength came from commercial interests- both big and small businessmen, northern Protestants, western farmers and those hostile to immigration.

Late 19th and Early 20th Centuries

From 1880 to 1900, Republicans and Democrats alternated as president every four years, but from 1896 through 1912, the GOP occupied the White House. When Democrats put forth the candidacy of William Jennings Bryan in 1896, they had returned to their rural, populist roots. However, Democrats showed little affection for the cities and their problems, alienating the other half of their core constituency: urban labor and Catholics. Given their rhetoric and policies, the Democrats were left in the wilderness until Woodrow Wilson rescued them in 1912, assisted by a split in the GOP. Republican support of high tariffs had brought them the votes of the working classes (who believed tariffs would save jobs), and backing of business.

Though Republicans were in control of the legislative and executive branches of government early in the 20th century, there was conflict between the progressive wing and traditional conservatives. The most prominent progressive was Senator Robert La Follette of Wisconsin. In 1912, when Theodore Roosevelt was unable to unseat his successor, William Howard Taft, as GOP candidate for president, Roosevelt ran as the nominee of the Progressive Party, labeled the Bull Moose Party. The main impetus of the party was political reform: to end collusion between establishment politicians and big business. Roosevelt drew more votes than Taft, but this division allowed the Democrat Wilson to win with a plurality of 41.8%.[714]

Early to Mid 20th Century

After eight years of Democratic ascendancy under Wilson, the GOP regained power with Warren Harding as president in 1920, followed by Calvin Coolidge then Herbert Hoover. Withdrawing America from the world stage, Republicans were seen as the party of prosperity and stability. However, the Great Depression, which began with the stock market crash in 1929, changed the political dynamic, Republicans blamed for this financial and human disaster. And Hoover seemed impotent in attempts to correct the economic downturn, joblessness and despair blanketing the country.

Democrat Franklin Roosevelt was elected president by a solid margin in 1932. For the next two decades, Democrats remained on top with Roosevelt and then Harry Truman. Under the mantle of the New Deal, with the country reeling and social unrest a concern, Roosevelt used his mandate and majorities in both Houses of Congress to raise spending on programs to provide jobs and reduce unemployment. Other legislation included the FDIC to re-establish confidence in the banking system, the SEC, the Tennessee Valley Authority, and measures to improve collective bargaining. Possibly the crowning achievement of the New Deal was passage of the Social Security Act to provide income for retired workers, the disabled and dependent children.

In the '30s, the two national parties acquired the positions they would assume on domestic issues for the next century. The metamorphosis occurred gradually, but the final changes and ultimate shape were forged in the cauldron of the Depression. The partisan stances they would subsequently take could be foreseen in actions during this most stressful time for the nation. The Democrats of Jefferson and Jackson, who had argued for limited central government and restricted spending, had been transformed into a party that saw expansive government and increased social spending as the way to bring Americans better and more secure lives. The Republicans, heir to the legacy of the Federalists and Whigs, who under Hamilton and Adams had encouraged a powerful federal government, had morphed into the party of small government and reduced spending. The Democrats, rural and agrarian in the 19th century, and backing slavery and secession, had become the party of the urban poor, unions and minorities, though the Southern wing retained its old beliefs. The GOP, whose base had once been in Northern cities, who under Lincoln had fought the Civil War to free the slaves and had been the party of social action, now battled against Social Security and other programs that would assist the least able, finding its greatest support in small towns and rural America.

Roosevelt was re-elected in 1936, 1940 and 1944, Democrats maintaining control of Congress until 1946. The start of World War II in 1941 ended the Depression, America achieving victory in Europe and the Pacific in less than four years. After the Depression and anguish of war, the country was ready for a period of peace and prosperity, but the advent of the Cold War, Berlin airlift and then Korean War in 1950, meant tranquility was unattainable. The United States had gone from being an isolated giant, separated from the world by two wide oceans, to an international power with interests and security concerns everywhere.

In 1948, the Democratic Party splintered over civil rights, the southern segregationist wing fighting northern liberals. Truman tried for compromise at the convention, but when a strong plank for civil rights was adopted, thirty-five southern Democrats bolted and established the States' Rights Party- the Dixiecrats.[715] Governor Strom Thurmond of South Carolina was chosen as their presidential nominee. In the November election, Thurmond was victorious in four Southern states, Alabama, Louisiana, Mississippi and South Carolina. The defection of the Dixiecrats presaged a later shift in political alignment, where the once solid Democratic South was to become an equally solid GOP South.

With a burst in the homestretch, Truman defeated Republican Thomas Dewey and splinter opponents in 1948, retaining the presidency for the Democrats. Truman brought a touch of the common man to the country's highest office, making decisions on the basis of pragmatism and common sense. One of his most quotable statements is "the buck stops here." Many elements of his agenda, called the Fair Deal, were thwarted by a conservative Congress uninterested in social progress or expanded government power.

The '50s and '60s

General Dwight D. Eisenhower returned the GOP to power in 1952, defeating Democrat Adlai Stevenson for the presidency and winning a second term in 1956. A moderate Republican who was a pragmatist like Truman, Eisenhower was able to keep the right wing of his party in check during his eight years in office. He brought an end to the Korean War in July of 1953 and accomplished integration of Little Rock High School in 1957. He also appointed Earl Warren as Chief Justice of the Supreme Court in 1953, whose decisions advanced civil rights and voting rights, changing the character of America.

In 1960, the pendulum swung back to the Democrats, with John Kennedy defeating Richard Nixon for president. The first Roman Catholic and youngest candidate to reach that office, Kennedy brought glamour and vitality to the White House. His missteps over the Bay of Pigs invasion of Cuba and early commitment of American forces to South Viet Nam were overshadowed by his careful and successful maneuvering with Khrushchev during the Cuban missile crisis in 1962, averting a disastrous outcome. He also initiated the Peace Corps and tentative steps to further civil rights. His assassination in November of 1963 shocked America and thrust Vice-President Lyndon Johnson into the Oval Office.

Johnson defeated Republican Barry Goldwater in the 1964 presidential election by portraying him as too far right to be trusted with nuclear weapons. (Goldwater, while losing the campaign invigorated the conservative movement with his feisty rhetoric and principled behavior.[716]) Enamored of Roosevelt's New Deal, Johnson's victory allowed him to pass legislation encompassing the Great Society and War on Poverty. This included Medicare and Medicaid, major civil rights and voting rights legislation, liberalization of immigration laws, creation of the National Endowments for the Arts and Humanities, and federal aid to education.[717]

The 60s and 70s

Tension simmering within the Democratic Party over civil rights boiled over again in 1968, when George Wallace, segregationist governor of Alabama, mounted a bid for president under the banner of the American Independent Party. Wallace hoped to appeal not only to racist Southerners, but to blue collar workers and those fed up with 'hippie' protests against the Vietnam War, crime, riots in the cities, civil rights demonstrations, and government spending.[718] He had exceeded expectations in 1964 in a number of Democratic primaries in the North, riding the white backlash to civil rights activism.[719] In the 1968 election, his American Independent Party won ten million votes, half of them from Northern states, with 13.5% of the overall vote and carrying five states in the Deep South.[720] Rejoining the Democratic Party, in 1972 Wallace pursued its presidential nomination. He did quite well in primaries in the South and Midwest, but an assassination attempt left him paralyzed and in a wheelchair.

However, the GOP realized the magnetism of the earlier George Wallace to white voters of the South and adopted what might be called its 'southern strategy' which has continued to the present. This emphasized state's rights, limits on federal government, an acknowledgment of the role of religion, and no further expansion of civil rights. Western and Midwestern states have also been drawn to these concepts. Republican Richard Nixon attained the presidency in 1968 at the height of the Vietnam War and social unrest at home, re-elected in 1972 as Republicans used their Southern strategy with code words to get their message across. Though Nixon became pre-occupied with exiting the Vietnam morass in a face-saving way, he managed to pass some important domestic legislation, including the EPA (Environmental Protection Agency) and expansion of Social Security.[721] His foreign policy was marked by the opening to Communist China and agreement with the Soviets on nuclear weapons restrictions. However, he also backed the military overthrow of the democratic government of Chile because of its socialist leanings. And the agreement with North Vietnam in 1973 was also on the table for Nixon in 1969 and was rejected, leading to unnecessary casualties on both sides.

Nixon never captured the affections of Americans, depicted in political cartoons with a swarthy face, and unable to escape the nickname 'Tricky Dick.' Enmeshed in what was termed the Watergate scandal, in August of 1974 he resigned, facing the prospect of impeachment. Gerald Ford assumed the presidency and pardoned Nixon soon afterwards. Jimmy Carter, who defeated Ford in 1976, was a southern farmer who had been governor of Georgia. Though honest and honorable, he was not a great administrator and indecisive at times. A Washington outsider, he lacked a power base in the Democratic Party and had difficulty with the wheeling and dealing of the political process. Fate was also unkind to him, throwing the energy crisis and Iran-hostage crisis into his lap.

Party reforms after 1968 eliminated the secretive coalition building that determined the parties' presidential candidate.[722] The majority of delegates to the conventions were now chosen in primary elections. Candidates had to campaign throughout the country, exposing themselves and their views to gain delegates to support them. This process appeared to increase democracy, but actually restricted choices in the general elections. With ideologically charged partisans voting in greater proportions in the primaries, the candidates chosen were not always electable.

8

Recent Partisanship

"Man is capable of changing the world for the better if possible, and of changing himself for the better if necessary," Viktor Frankl[723]

The Reagan-Bush Years- The 80s and Early 90s

Once a liberal Democrat, Reagan converted to conservative Republicanism and was elected California governor in 1966 after a lifetime in the entertainment industry. Capturing the GOP nomination for president in 1980, he fashioned a resounding victory over Carter and John Anderson, a third party candidate. With a grand vision of smaller federal government, lower spending and lower taxes, he never-the-less presided over a major expansion in government size, with the largest increase in national debt since World War II. During his term in office, Reagan oversaw a build-up of American weaponry and military might, and many of the Great Society's anti-poverty programs were slashed, while income taxes were cut for the most affluent Americans.[724]

Reagan's popularity leaving office was partially transferred to Vice President George Bush, elected president in 1988, defeating

Michael Dukakis in a landslide victory. Bush highlighted Dukakis's stance against the death penalty. In the nefarious Willie Horton ads, he blamed Dukakis for a rape and armed robbery committed by a convicted African-American murderer, Willie Horton, during a weekend 'furlough' from prison. The Prison Furlough program had actually been started by another Massachusetts governor in 1972 and Dukakis ended it. But the Horton ads were effective in turning public opinion against Dukakis as most Americans were uninformed about the actual sequence of events that had occurred.

During Bush's administration, the first Iraq War was launched with an overwhelming military force to liberate Kuwait from Saddam Hussein. With Communism vanquished and the venture in Iraq easily successful, America's stature and power was at its height. However, domestically, the economy retreated into recession in 1991 and 1992. Bush also alienated his conservative base by allowing tax increases to pass after his "read my lips" pledge in the 1988 election.

Political Parties in the '90s

One of the most impressive third-party forays in American history occurred in 1992 when Ross Perot, a Texas billionaire, challenged George Bush and Bill Clinton for the presidency. With a folksy, down-to-earth style, he used infomercials with charts and graphs as well as regular advertising and television interviews to make points about the sorry state of the country, telling the electorate America was in "deep voodoo."[725] Ahead of Bush and Clinton in the polls in June, questions about his personality made voters wonder if he had the temperament to be president and his percentages in the polls began to drop. Perot struck a populist chord against the loss of jobs, telling voters to listen for the "giant sucking sound" of American jobs heading south to Mexico should NAFTA be ratified. Perot was the choice on 18.9 percent of ballots, garnering nearly 20 million votes on Election Day.

Using the mantra "It's the economy, stupid," Bill Clinton burst onto the scene in 1992, defeating Bush and Perot. With little national exposure as governor of Arkansas, Clinton established himself as a centrist Democrat with an appeal to independents. Emphasizing problems of the economy, along with the importance of increasing productivity and investing in education and infrastructure, he was able to unite Democrats behind him while the GOP was fractured and unenthusiastic about Bush. On Election Day, Clinton won 42.9 percent of the popular vote versus 37.4 percent for Bush. In addition, Clinton coattails brought control of both houses of Congress to the Democrats. He presided over a major expansion of the economy, with a booming stock market and tax revenues producing large budget surpluses.

The midterm election of 1994 brought Republicans back into control of Congress, riding in on Newt Gingrich's Contract with America.[726] Gingrich colored all issues in partisan ink, trying to block Clinton's initiatives. In fact, growth of conservative ideologues started with Gingrich's shutdown of government in 1995 due to an impasse over the budget, but partially related to Clinton's snub of Gingrich on an Air Force One trip to Israel.[727] After Clinton was reelected in 1996, conservatives milked the Whitewater investigation and then his dalliance with Monica Lewinsky, the latter resulting in impeachment proceedings that heightened polarization.

The New Millennium

The 2000 election was a triumph of the 'sleazy' approach to campaigning by Republicans George W. Bush and his guru Karl Rove.[728] Gore lost the presidency though he had polled over 500,000 more votes nationally than Bush. The GOP maintained control of both houses of Congress throughout Bush's first term, allowing a number of his initiatives to be enacted. One was passage of Medicare Part D, the Medicare Modernization Act, which provided Medicare drug coverage.[729] Though contrary to conservative convictions, politicians thought it would be helpful in gaining support from seniors. However, it produced a large increase in government expenditures and blocked Medicare from negotiating prices with pharmaceutical companies. It seemed when voters were worried about the economy, they favored the Democrats, but when social issues drove people to the polls, the GOP had an advantage.

President Bush ran for reelection in 2004 against John Kerry, helped by a tailwind from the 9/11 disaster and the fight against terrorism. What the public did not understand because of Republican spin and misrepresentations was that Saddam Hussein did not have weapons of mass destruction or a connection to Al Qaeda. In addition, they did not realize the invasion and occupation of Iraq may have reduced American security rather than enhancing it, encouraging growth of radical Islam and recruitment of new jihadists. (This was shown in a National Intelligence Estimate in September of 2006.) Kerry did not use the issues of Iraq and terrorism to his advantage and there was a public perception of him as vacillating and indecisive.

During the campaign, Bush emphasized his role as a wartime president, willing to make hard decisions to protect the country. The 'victory' in Afghanistan removing the Taliban from power, had been accomplished with a minimum of troops and few casualties, but Iraq was a different story. On May 1, 2003, less than two months after the invasion of Iraq, Bush landed a jet on an aircraft carrier in a photo op, making his 'Mission Accomplished' speech.[730] But war in Iraq persisted with deadly consequences. After Bush's performance and Rumsfeld and Cheney's optimistic slants on the war, Kerry could have gone after Bush like a bulldog. But his comments were never hard-hitting enough. And Kerry's failure to respond immediately to the lies and innuendos about his service record cost him dearly in votes and credibility. Bush's victory in the 2004 election helped the GOP add to their majorities in the Senate and House.

The Midterm Election of 2006

There were significant issues separating the two parties in the 2006 midterm election, but aside from Iraq, substance was generally lacking in campaign advertising. The focus was on slogans and sound bites repeated endlessly. Continuing a trend begun in the 1980s, the election was marked by negative characterizations, attack ads and dirty tricks.[731] The ads online, on radio, TV, and through mailers, were filled with deliberate distortions, inaccuracies, and outright lies by the campaign committees of the two parties and independent groups.[732]

Though middle-class feelings of economic insecurity and the specter of Congressional corruption helped propel the Democrats to victory, there was little question the war in Iraq and Bush's poor standing with the electorate were determining factors in many congressional and senate races. The Democratic victory was not because most citizens had confidence in them. Instead it was because of the negative perception many Americans had of the Republicans, stemming from the poor job they had done running the country.

In January 2007, Bush announced the deployment of additional military personnel to Iraq to try and control the insurgency. It was hoped that 30,000 more combat troops known as the 'surge' would help the Iraqi Army tamp down sectarian violence and increase security.[733] Despite Congressional opposition and polls showing public resistance, the new plan under the leadership of General David Petraeus was generally successful. Many Sunni fighters joined the so-called Awakening Councils and fought on the side of the Americans. After his election in 2008, Obama persevered with this strategy, though he had initially been against the troop buildup. With violence decreasing, he started withdrawing combat units in 2010.

The Election of 2008 and the Obama Years

Though Hillary Clinton was the initial favorite among Democrats, Obama's ability to mobilize young people and minorities, his prodigious Internet fundraising ability, and the power of his oratory made a fight for the nomination a near certainty. When Obama won the Iowa caucuses in January 2008, it became evident his appeal extended to predominantly white rural Midwestern states. By June, with multiple super delegates choosing to endorse him, Obama had nailed down the nomination. John McCain, the big winner on GOP Super Tuesday primaries in February of 2008, soon had amassed enough delegates to secure the Republican nomination. In a major surprise he selected Sarah Palin, governor of Alaska, as his vice-presidential partner. Though this energized his conservative Republican base, it left much of the country wondering about her qualifications to be president should the need arise.

The battle between Obama and McCain was dirty and expensive, with attack ads from both sides, Obama's citizenship and religion challenged by Republicans. Though the wars in Iraq and Afghanistan were significant issues, the overriding concern of the electorate was the economy. Both candidates highlighted the need for transforming the culture in Washington, each claiming to be a stronger agent of change. In addition to Obama raising $778 million for his 2008 presidential campaign (McCain over $380 million),[734] he used the Internet and social networks to obtain support of young voters. On Election Day, Obama easily beat McCain.

Obama was inaugurated in January 2009 with Democratic majorities in both Houses of Congress. Republicans, however, were in lockstep against any measure he favored. And Democrats did not have sixty votes needed in the Senate to overcome possible filibusters. With the recession and unemployment top concerns of the electorate, Congress passed a federal stimulus package of over $700 billion, a compromise by Obama to garner support. A number of analysts thought the amount was inadequate to lift the economy, but conservatives in Congress refused to increase the stimulus further. Most economists believe the stimulus along with the bank bailout under Bush and actions of the Federal Reserve prevented an economic collapse that might have mirrored the Depression.

The soaring cost of health care and uninsured Americans made health care reform a priority for Democratic partisans. But the way legislation was developed in Congress and the bill's final structure became a public relations disaster for Obama and bonanza for the GOP. Though the CBO asserted the measure would save money over the years and reduce the budget deficit, a majority of citizens believed it would raise costs and lower quality of care, and so were opposed to what its detractors labeled 'Obamacare.' The fact the bill also made health insurance mandatory enraged libertarians and citizens hostile to expansion of federal government power. In reality, the law was complex, difficult to understand, and without upfront savings.

The attempt to address global warming and formulate an energy policy also ran into strong resistance from the GOP. While the House passed a cap-and-trade bill to try and deal with carbon emissions, the Senate never considered similar legislation. Many Republicans were not convinced of the reality of global warming (and still remain doubtful). In fact, the GOP opposed every major piece of Democratic legislation, never offering their own programs and sticking to their mantra of no new taxes and cutting government spending. The two parties could not even agree on extending Bush's tax cuts for the middle class, the GOP insisting wealthiest Americans be included, even though this would increase the budget deficits and national debt.

Republican strategy paid off on Election Day 2010 when they achieved a majority in the House and took back five Senate seats, making it even more difficult for Democrats to pass legislation. Of course, it was just as difficult for the GOP to enact laws, making governmental gridlock possible. The Republicans had won the election because they had remained on message, emphasizing their desire to lower taxes, cut spending, and reduce the deficit, but giving no specifics. Repealing the ACA was also high on their agenda.

The Tea Party, the amorphous conservative partisan group, supported many Republicans and elected some of their own members who had triumphed in state primaries against candidates deemed not conservative enough. Senator Bob Bennett of Utah was eliminated in an April convention, with Mike Lee winning the primary and general election. Marco Rubio, with Tea Party backing, forced Governor Charlie Crist to run as an independent, losing to Rubio in the general election. Rand Paul in Kentucky defeated the organization candidate supported by Mitch McConnell in the primary and beat his Democratic opponent on Election Day. Though the Tea Party generated enthusiasm among GOP partisans, there were negative aspects to its ideas and image, causing problems for some of the primary winners it had backed.

In the Senate GOP primary in Delaware, Tea Party adherent, Christine O'Donnell, eliminated Representative Mike Castle, a moderate expected to easily win the Senate seat against Democrat Chris Coons. Instead, Coons handily beat O'Donnell because of her apparent dabbling in witchcraft, financial problems, and misreading of the Constitution. In Nevada, virtually any Republican could have beaten Democratic Senate Majority Leader Harry Reid, who was quite unpopular. But Tea Partier Sharon Angle was so strange and unpredictable, Reid was reelected. Angle made misstatements, avoided questions from the press, and spoke of 'Second Amendment remedies' if Congress didn't change. Similarly in Colorado, Democratic incumbent Michael Bennet retained his Senate seat against Tea Party favorite Ken Buck, whose statements disturbed many voters. And the same pattern held in a number of races for the House.

After the new Congress was seated in January 2011 with a strong Republican majority in the House and Democrats with a narrow majority in the Senate, ideologic constraints made it difficult to get bills passed. The GOP was adamant about cutting $60 billion in discretionary spending, while Democrats were reluctant to approve that magnitude of reduction, believing it would stunt the economic recovery.[735] There seemed to be no understanding by budget cutters of the need to fund education, infrastructure, and basic research, all necessary for future prosperity. And neither party was willing to attack the unfunded liabilities of Medicare and Social Security.

Simultaneously, the states were also pursuing reductions in spending in partisan fashion to balance their own budgets. Some of this came at the expense of public service workers, many of whom had enjoyed benefits disproportionate to those in the private sector. Most public service unions agreed to givebacks to help cut the deficits, but GOP leaders were not always satisfied. In Wisconsin and a number of other states, they passed right to work laws and tried to end rights to collective bargaining to weaken the unions.[736] To underscore the political motivation behind these moves, Republican Governor Scott Walker did not include police and firemen's unions in his bill to end collective bargaining, two groups that had backed his election bid.[737],[738]

In Kansas in 2012, conservative Sam Brownback and the GOP legislature passed large unfunded income tax cuts as did several other states, with advantages for small businesses and bonanzas for the wealthy. Conservative ideologues expected these cuts to enhance economic activity, create tens of thousands of new jobs, and lead to more revenue (trickle-down).[739] Unfortunately, this pie in the sky did not materialize and Kansas was left with huge budgetary deficits. In addition, Kansas' job growth lagged behind the rest of the nation,[740] with state services suffering and education taking a major hit. The whole concept of trickle-down economics was a mirage foisted on the public by conservative partisans. Many voters bought this idea and supported Republicans who advocated this approach. However, this led to badly needed tax increases in 2017 to fund Kansas schools, the legislature overriding Brownback's veto.[741]

More Obama

When Obama became president in 2009, partisanship in America exploded. Republican ideologues in Congress did everything possible to derail his agenda. Some of this was racism with refusal to accept leadership from an African-American and some was party based. Immigration reform was one subject that never got off the ground. The idea of deporting 11-12 million immigrants would have been costly and disastrous for the American economy, hurting agriculture, the hospitality and fast food industries. Hundreds of billions of dollars would be wasted if deportation was attempted. And analyses suggested Mexican immigration was already diminishing because of improvements in the Mexican economy and greater obstacles for undocumented immigrants to obtain jobs in the United States.[742] In fact, studies showed migration to the U.S. from Mexico had reversed, with more Mexicans heading for their homeland than coming to America.[743]

Besides immigration, issues generating the most partisan rancor during the Obama administration were passage of the Affordable Care Act and Iran Nuclear Accord. Partisan Republicans tried unsuccessfully numerous times to negate these actions, wasting time, effort, and funds. These measures were rallying cries for conservatives during the 2016 presidential campaign, instilling enthusiasm in GOP crowds. However, alternatives to provide health care for the uninsured were not suggested. Republicans also opposed the ACA as a job-killing program which turned out to be inaccurate, with 5.7 million private sector jobs added to the economy in the first two years after the start of ACA.[744]

In the early phases of the presidential campaign in the summer and fall of 2015, partisans in the GOP tribe soured on career politicians and their platitudes. However, some notions citizens held were divorced from reality, reinforced by their news sources and pundits followed on talk radio. A Public Policy Poll released in September showed 54 percent of Republicans still believed Obama was a Muslim.[745] And only 29 percent of Republicans thought Obama was born in America, just 12 percent of Trump supporters acknowledging Obama was Christian. Fox was the network of choice for Republicans, providing a conservative slant on the news. Interestingly GOP and Democratic tribes also watched different programs for entertainment according to a survey in the summer of 2019, perhaps a reflection of polarization or further enhancing it.[746] Looking at programs with similar audience numbers, liberals were enamored by Succession, a comedy-drama following a Murdoch like family controlling a media conglomerate. Conservatives and Trump supporters were glued to live wrestling on WWE Raw. Network programs had a similar split between liberals and conservatives.

Also in September, House Republicans voted to end funding for Planned Parenthood, knowing it would be filibustered in the Senate or vetoed by the president.[747] This was done to placate their base, infuriated by a video supposed to have shown personnel from Planned Parenthood selling body parts from aborted fetuses. (A Texas grand jury subsequently cleared Planned Parenthood of wrongdoing.[748]) The president's inability to obtain confirmation for a number of his ambassadorial nominees by the Senate was more evidence of partisanship.[749] As of December 2015, twelve of Obama's candidates had not been approved, including some to nations vital to American security. Polarization was interfering with U.S. foreign policy.

Further partisanship by Republicans in Congress was shown by a panel established to examine the 2012 attacks on American government posts in Benghazi, Libya.[750] Originally formed to analyze the causes of the assault and deaths of Ambassador Christopher Stevens and three other Americans, it evolved into a witch hunt tarring Hillary Clinton in her run for the presidency. In fact, one of the panel's investigators, a major in the Air Force Reserve, alleged in October 2015 he was fired by the committee because they opposed his desire to conduct a comprehensive study of the Benghazi attack.[751] They wanted to focus on the State Department and Hillary Clinton's role, hoping to demonstrate her failings as Secretary of State. That this was the committee's goal was reinforced by GOP House Majority Leader Kevin McCarthy who noted in a television interview that damaging Hillary Clinton's election prospects was a desirable byproduct of the investigation. The committee was also looking into Clinton's emails.

An overwhelming majority of Republicans believe balancing the federal budget is of utmost importance. However, GOP hypocrisy was shown with its plan in November 2015 to repeal spending cuts eliminating the crop insurance subsidy and saving $3 billion.[752] The Party's rural constituents had been angered by the cuts and plans to slash a total of $20 billion from farm programs. Large corporate farmers benefitted most from these programs which could truly be labeled 'corporate welfare.' However, though reducing government spending had been a constant mantra, the GOP was unwilling to upset their rural supporters by slicing their subsidies, as they wielded disproportionate political power because of gerrymandering.

The Senate's refusal to confirm Obama's candidate to replace Antonin Scalia on the Supreme Court with Merrick Garland, a centrist judge with impeccable credentials, was another example of GOP partisanship.[753] No other nominee for the Court had ever been rejected in a president's last year in office, but the Republican right-wing wanted to wait to choose a candidate after Obama was gone. GOP Senators were afraid Garland would tip the Court to the left. With the Court split between four conservatives and four liberals, four to four rulings were resulting in judicial paralysis.[754] Though a majority of Americans wanted the Senate to vote on Garland up or down for the Court, Republicans turned a deaf ear.

Republicans also obstructed federal court appointments recommended by Obama, causing difficulties in the courts' ability to function, with long delays handling cases.[755] As of February 2016, eleven federal district court nominees were awaiting votes by the full Senate and twenty-five judicial appointments had not yet passed the Judicial Committee.[756] Republicans also blocked Obama's attempts to fill vacancies on regional federal courts of appeal. Right-wing conservative groups pressured senators as well not to allow Obama to make any more appointments to the upper ranks of the judiciary, as these judges often are the final arbiters in cases the Supreme Court does not review. Additionally, there were 143 nominees for non-judicial federal jobs awaiting confirmation by the Senate, the GOP majority delaying installation of Obama's choices.[757]

The year 2015 saw the GOP with major infighting in the House between strongly right-wing conservative partisans and ordinary conservatives, the latter willing at times to compromise to allow government to operate. Extreme right-wingers forced out John Boehner as Speaker, a conservative they labeled as too moderate for his occasional willingness to deal with Democrats.[758] His apparent successor, Kevin McCarthy, was also considered too moderate by many extreme conservatives. Finally, they voted former vice-presidential candidate Paul Ryan to assume the mantle of Speaker. Two Republican groups in Congress that remained at odds were the Main Street Partnership, with over seventy members, who considered themselves moderate conservatives,[759] and the Freedom Caucus, uncompromising right-wingers, with about forty members.[760],[761]

Outside of Congress, Donald Trump and his populist, nativist base fomented another split within the GOP in 2016, with Trump's diatribes against Mexicans and Muslims that many citizens felt were un-American.[762] There were also questions about his conservative bona fides with his ideas of raising taxes on hedge fund managers and other wealthy people, and past comments on Planned Parenthood. However, he stepped back on higher taxes, with a pledge to try and lower them for every income group[763] and also flip-flopped on abortion.

A survey in early 2016 found a large portion of white, middle-class Americans were angry, sometimes almost rabidly so.[764] They believed they were living in a declining nation and life had not turned out as they had hoped. Hard work had not paid off, wage increases adjusted for inflation not keeping up with heightened GDP. Men felt they were working more for less reward. These beliefs were most pronounced in households with incomes of $50,000 to $75,000. Anger expressed at Trump rallies were about women and men of color elected to high offices as white men struggled to make a living.[765] At rallies, racial taunts, Nazi salutes, and threats to lynch blacks who opposed Trump were manifestations of feelings of rage and powerlessness.

(Interestingly, an increased death rate among middle-aged white men over a twenty-year period was noted by two economists in 2015.[766] The main causes were drugs, alcohol or suicides, and were most prevalent in men who had only graduated high school or had even less education.)

Washington had been ineffective in stimulating the economy and helping uneducated and unemployed white men under Obama because of unwillingness by GOP partisans in Congress to appropriate money.[767] With low interest rates and blue collar workers struggling, this would have been an ideal time to rehabilitate America's crumbling infrastructure. More programs to retrain the unemployed for the new jobs available would also have been beneficial for the nation.

The Occupy Wall Street 'people powered' movement formed as a left-wing answer to the Tea Party, starting with demonstrations in downtown New York in September 2011.[768] Members were protesting economic inequality and the 'corrosive power of major banks and multi-national corporations over the democratic process.' Though they garnered considerable publicity initially and sympathy in leftist political circles, the movement never really evolved.

With the Democratic Party split between centrists and progressives, the latter were more willing to compromise than their brethren in the GOP. The stalwarts of the left in the Senate included Elizabeth Warren of Massachusetts and Bernie Sanders of Vermont. In addition to dealing with inequality and regulation of big banks, a living minimum wage was important to them along with support for what remained of the union movement. Improving workman's compensation and protecting the safety net were other goals, along with keeping America out of another war in the Middle East.

In a discussion of partisanship in the United States, rulings of the federal judiciary and Supreme Court bear mentioning. While on some social issues like same-sex marriage and abortion rights the courts had leaned leftward, in cases with political consequences the courts were decidedly conservative, the one exemption being Justice Roberts affirmation of the Affordable Care Act.[769] However, Citizens United and the McCutcheon rulings were lauded by Republicans for virtually guaranteeing them unlimited funds for political campaigns. The Supreme Court also protected gun rights and aided corporations who faced suits from citizens requesting redress from duplicitous or egregious actions.

Judicial scholars believe the composition of the Roberts Court (prior to Scalia's death) was the most conservative court in the last seventy years.[770] Of forty-four justices who had sat on the Court since 1937, four of the six most conservative were presently serving, all Republican appointees. And though conservatives generally lament judicial activism and think Congress should write the laws rather than the justices, the Roberts Court has been overturning precedent and ruling laws unconstitutional. Both of these approaches are indicative of activism, which had taken a rightward turn. Nevertheless, some far right ideologues have been unhappy with Roberts, blasting him for not being conservative enough. His major failings of course, were not overturning the ACA and allowing gay marriage.

Partisanship in America is heightened by party primaries, where many of those who vote are ideologues holding extreme views. As a large portion of the GOP base are social conservatives, with evangelicals and other extremely religious individuals being active party members, they tend to choose candidates who take conforming positions. Gerrymandering has also given more power to rural conservatives. Similarly, many active Democrats are left-wing partisans. In campaigning for the primaries, candidates pander to their bases to show their partisan chops, with those at the far ends of the spectrum often winning primary contests. Right-wing talk show radio pundits are another driver of partisanship, with many listeners taking their discourses as gospel. Information from these shows is inevitably slanted in a partisan fashion and frequently far from the truth. Politically oriented cable TV shows are similarly partisan. But listeners to these programs may not be astute enough to discern what is opinion or propaganda and what is actually news. The hosts of these shows tend to be fanatical in their views of politicians they like or dislike, or positions of which they approve or disapprove.

Partisanship on both the left and right infecting a number of states has caused significant problems for citizens. While Republicans have pushed for smaller government, right-to-work laws, and lower taxes, Democrats have increased taxes, negotiated unaffordable pension benefits with public service unions, spent liberally and heightened deficits. States under GOP control have frequently followed the directives of ALEC, the American Legislative Exchange Council, which has extreme conservative views.[771] This has generally resulted in less money devoted to education, pre-school programs, and Medicaid. In addition, they have suggested curbing class action law suits and litigation, pushing pro-gun legislation, stringent voter IDs, and tax cuts.

In some states where Democrats are in the saddle, high taxes and unfunded obligations for state worker pensions make new businesses less likely to start and older businesses move away.[772] Affluent individuals have also migrated to lower-tax states to preserve assets for their families. An article in Forbes in August of 2013 asked how Connecticut had morphed into one of America's worst performing economies when it had had so many positive attributes. Connecticut ranked fiftieth in economic growth with government spending out of control, taxes upon taxes, and people and businesses leaving. The state had the fourth largest amount of debt per capita and the business climate was dreadful. Thus, partisans in control on either the left or right spelled trouble for the states involved.

Partisanship infecting America's political parties has made Washington the most dysfunctional of democratic capitals. Governing many states is only minimally easier. However, domination of the GOP by anti-government ideologues who will not compromise to allow the political system to work, and excessive spending by Democrats must be traced back to the voters. Too many citizens refuse to educate themselves about candidates and issues. A Pew Research Poll published in April 2016, found only 33 percent of Americans had a favorable impression of the Republican Party, 62 percent viewing it unfavorably. The Democratic Party was 45 percent favorable and 50 percent unfavorable. Neither party had much to brag about.

Notwithstanding GOP control of the majority of states, the future may look brighter for Democrats if they can pull the left and center together.[773] The percentage of minorities in the nation, (who tend to vote Democratic), is growing and millennials are more liberal on social issues and want greater government activism. One poll even showed them favoring socialism over capitalism, 49 to 46 percent. Republican millennials are also more liberal on social issues and feel that immigrants strengthen America, environmental laws are important, and corporate profits are too high. Millennials are "the most secular, most racially diverse and least nationalistic generation in American history."[774]

However, Republicans are doing everything possible at a state level to ensure they retain power even when defeated at the ballot box.[775] In

2016, Democrat Roy Cooper was elected governor of North Carolina. Prior to his inauguration, the Republican legislature and governor passed a series of laws taking various powers away from Cooper and handing them to the legislature, limiting what the Democrat could do. Some of these laws were overturned by the courts and in 2018 some were still being litigated. Seeing the GOP's success in North Carolina, Wisconsin and Michigan—where Democratic governors were elected in 2018--tried similar tactics to emasculate their newly elected governors.

Another indication that democracy is being suppressed by GOP actions is the fact that in Wisconsin, Republicans won 64 percent of State Assembly seats even though Democrats had beaten them in voting by a 54-46 percent margin. This was the result of markedly inequitable gerrymandering by Republicans when they controlled the legislature and governorship. While blatantly unfair, the question is whether this will be nullified by a conservative Supreme Court. In addition, the legislatures in a number of GOP controlled states have made it more difficult for minorities and students to vote by cutting down early voting and the hours and days when voting is possible. Voter ID laws are also being used to suppress minority voting. These actions are the result of unfettered partisanship, with no consideration given to how they damage democracy. Gerrymandering also diminished the number of Congressional seats the Democrats should have won in 2018. Despite the fact that they gained forty seats, on the basis of the percentage voting for Democrats nationwide, they should have taken even more.

Outside the political system, and generally disdainful of the workings of government and political parties, are extreme partisan organizations consisting of conspiracy theorists, militia members, neo-Nazis, white supremacists, secessionists, and similar groups, angry at the way America is evolving. Virtually all favor radical gun rights. Many trace their paternity to the anti-Communist John Birch Society founded in 1958, and to Senator Joseph McCarthy.[776],[777] The John Birchers who were beyond the political fringe, perceived liberals and even moderates as communists, suggesting President Eisenhower was an agent of an international communist conspiracy and demanding impeachment of Chief Justice Earl Warren.

Currently, anti-government activists and militias are trying to take over land in the West belonging to the federal government, whose ownership they do not recognize.[778] Some Congressional Republicans have considered setting up a land transfer fund to buy land from the federal government and sell it to the states, counties, or private buyers. Environmentalists are vehemently opposed to the sales as neither states nor counties have the funds to manage the land. In January 2016, Ammon Bundy, a rancher from Nevada, and a group of armed cohorts began occupying a wildlife refuge in Oregon to support a fellow rancher who had gone to prison for refusing to pay for grazing rights on public lands.[779],[780] Neighbors repeatedly asked the occupiers to leave, but they remained in place. Bundy preaches that the federal government is illegitimate and county governments are the highest power in the country.[781] The police did arrest some of the insurgents at a highway traffic stop at the end of January 2016 when they went off the refuge, killing one of the resisting members.[782] And other occupiers eventually left the wildlife sanctuary peacefully.

The number of armed anti-government militias ballooned after Obama was elected, with 276 groups noted in 2015 by a center that tracks extremists, the Southern Poverty Law Center (SPLC).[783] A former analyst with the Department of Homeland Security said that government is not doing enough to gather intelligence and combat potential danger from right-wing extremists. Domestic terrorism presents as much of a threat or more so than radical Islamic groups. Between 2002 and 2011, right-wing extremists were responsible for an average of 330 attacks a year, killing 250 people. Trump's election has encouraged alt-right and white supremacist groups.

European Democracies

As mentioned, the major fulcrum for partisanship has been the conflict between right and left on the role of government. However, there are other issues that produce partisan clashes. One of these has been the influx of migrants to Europe from the Middle East and Africa, many of whom are Muslim and some of whom are black. Immigration has been debated in Europe for decades (as in the U.S.), but a peak of urgency was reached in 2015 with people fleeing wars in Syria, Iraq, and Afghanistan, causing a humanitarian crisis. This wave of immigration opened a fissure between the wealthy nations of the north like Germany and the Scandinavian states willing to absorb migrants, and poorer countries of Eastern Europe that were resistant.

Unemployment has remained high in Southern and Eastern Europe and citizens did not want to have to compete for jobs with new arrivals. They also did not want to have to support the migrants. Thus, how to deal with immigration became a partisan problem for the E.U. as well as for individual countries. In addition to opposition on an economic basis, hostility was directed against the newcomers because of cultural differences, religion and race.

Political parties and groups opposed to Muslim immigration have existed in European nations for decades, exemplified by the National Front in France headed by Marine Le Pen.[784] (Some of these organizations were originally anti-Semitic.) The Freedom Group in the Netherlands, led by Gert Wilders, has gained adherents because of Dutch Islamists who joined ISIS and the assassination of film-maker Theo Van Gogh by a Muslim extremist. Anti-Islamist demonstrations have also taken place in Germany with thousands of participants under the banner of PEGIDA, a right-wing group claiming it is against extremism and for freedom for women.[785] Germany also has the AfD, a right-wing political party slowly gaining strength. Every European nation has political parties that take anti-immigration, anti-Muslim stances, their size and strength varying. With Europeans fearful of terrorism, the E.U.'s Open Borders policy has also become a contentious issue.

After terrorist attacks in Paris by Muslim adherents of ISIS that killed 130 people in November 2015, the right-wing National Front gained strength, leading the voting in regional elections taking place in December.[786] The Nice truck attack in July 2016 by a Tunisian further enhanced the French right, with unemployment running at over 10 percent and the economy still not fully recovered from the recession of 2007.

Strong right-wing governments have gained power in Poland and Hungary using immigration, economic growth, and unemployment as wedge issues. Autocratic actions by these governments have earned rebukes from the E. U. and revered political figures. Three ex-presidents of Poland, including Lech Walesa, issued warnings on the front page of the country's leading newspaper that government policies were a threat to democracy.[787] Hungary's president, Viktor Orban, and his Fidesz Party have also moved to consolidate their power, with Orban championing what he calls "illiberal democracy," the government becoming more intrusive in everyday life, and rewriting the history curriculum. Orban refuses to take non-Christian refugees as Hungary charts its own course independent of the E.U.

Language, culture, and historical grievances are also partisan issues in some nations, where integration and melding of different groups to forge national identities has been difficult. Belgium is divided between French-speaking Walloons and the Flemish who speak Dutch. This has caused conflict between the two groups and problems governing at times.[788] Similarly, Spain has had partisan problems with the Basque and Catalan regions.[789] Both areas would like to separate from Spain and Basque separatists mounted a violent campaign in the past in the name of freedom. As of 2019, the Catalan drive for independence was fully active and threatened to fragment the nation.[790]

Northern Ireland's partisan split is religious, with Catholics and Protestants fighting each other for a century. The Catholic Republicans want Northern Ireland to be part of the Irish nation, while Protestant Unionists want to remain in the United Kingdom.[791] Sectarian violence between Catholics and Protestants was constant during the time of The Troubles from 1968-1998. The Good Friday Agreement helped end the conflict with the two groups sharing power, but sporadic violence has continued.

European democracies have a parliamentary structure and in most countries a number of parties representing diverse views. Thus, partisan ideologues can create their own groups to have their voices heard. After elections, coalitions are formed to govern, involving parties with similar positions on important issues. Parties with strong ideological beliefs may or may not be included, depending on the needs of the coalition. But even outside of government, ideologues can continue working to increase party membership and attain greater representation in the future.

Africa

Where democracy exists in Africa, partisanship is usually defined by tribal allegiances. In Kenya, tribal violence is prevalent around the time of national elections, mainly between the Kikuyu and Kalenjins along with Luhya and Luo. This results in hundreds to thousands of deaths with each contest.[792] In South Africa, the African National Congress (ANC) has controlled the government for nearly a quarter of a century. Black advancement and the economy stand out as political issues with unemployment at 24 percent.[793] The main opposition party, the Democratic Alliance, which elected its first black leader, Mmusi Maimane, in May 2015, receives most of the white and mixed race votes.[794] However, it has been gaining support from blacks weary of ANC dominance with minimal economic improvement.[795]

In Nigeria, though there has been tribal fighting in the past between Igbos and Yorubas, much of the current conflict and partisanship is on a religious basis, between Christians and Muslims.[796] This is independent of the brutal insurgency in the Northeast by Boko Haram, the fundamentalist Islamic group. Thus far, the military has been unable to contain Boko Haram's insurrection. Given the level of corruption and the poor educational system, it has been nearly impossible to forge a Nigerian identity, which might make tribalism and religious differences less divisive.[797]

Tunisia is a nascent democracy in North Africa whose population is overwhelmingly Sunni. Partisan politics pits Islamists against moderate Muslims who would like a pluralistic democracy and a more secular state. However, extreme Islamists use assassination as a tool to eliminate secular politicians and journalists, hoping to turn Tunisia into a theocracy.[798]

The Middle East

The only Middle Eastern countries which are supposed democracies are Lebanon, Israel, and Iraq, the latter transformed from a dictatorship by American soldiers. Partisanship in Lebanon resides in religious differences among the Sunnis, Christians, and Druse, with the Shiites (Hezbollah) currently in control after a lengthy civil war. Rafik Harari, the Sunni Prime Minister, was assassinated by a huge car bomb in 2005, the perpetrators believed to have sourced from Hezbollah.[799] Intermittent bombings and shootings of opponents continue to occur. Syrian immigrants seeking safe haven poured into this small country since the start of the Syrian civil war.

In Iraq, partisan strife endures between the majority Shiites and Sunnis, with the Kurds another political force. In addition to religious and ethnic differences, tribalism contributes to partisanship. There is also a divide between moderate, secular Muslims and those favoring a theocratic state. Shootings and bombings by different religious groups are a part of daily life. A portion of the nation's territory and the city of Mosul ruled by ISIS was retaken by the Iraqi army and Shiite militias in 2017 with U.S. assistance. The inability of 'democratic' Iraqi politicians to forge an all-inclusive government with Shiites, Sunnis, and Kurds, allowed ISIS an opening. [800]

In addition to right-left, Israeli partisanship is between secular and religious citizens, the latter wanting their rabbis to control social institutions and the nation to adhere to Biblical law. Orthodox rabbis have been allowed by the government to define who are Jews and treatment of the Reform and Conservative denominations, whose rabbis are not recognized by the Orthodox. A long-standing split has also been present between Ashkenazi Jews who emigrated from Europe and Sephardic Jews from Middle Eastern countries. Divisions exist as well between nationalists who want to retain control of the West Bank and integrate it into Israel, and those who see the West Bank as a separate Palestinian mini-state. [801]

Turkey

Turkey is growing more autocratic daily under President Erdogan, an Islamist who has relegated secularists to the sidelines. Even insulting the president or criticizing officials is a crime which can result in a prison sentence.[802] The major split from a partisan standpoint is between secularists and Islamists, but also between those who favor giving Erdogan and his AKP Party more power and those who want to restrain him.[803] The split encompasses the rural population who tend to back Erdogan and urbanites who oppose him. Since a coup attempt in 2016, Erdogan has jailed many of his adversaries and Turkish intellectuals, firing teachers and holders of government jobs, and taking control of the media.

Asia

Pakistan

Pakistan's main partisan schism is between moderate Sunnis and extremists, the latter viewing Shiites, Sufi Muslims, and Christians as apostates who should be killed. Many members of these groups have been murdered by the Taliban and ISIS in car bombings, suicide attacks, and other acts of violence.[804] Politicians, journalists and those favoring a secular state have also been assassinated by Islamists who want Pakistan governed by Sharia. Sunni extremists use the country's blasphemy laws to terrorize members of other religions and secularists.[805]

India

This populous majority Hindu nation was founded as a secular state, with a large Muslim minority and other religious groups scattered throughout the country. There are two main partisan divides. One pits right-wing Hindus of the BJP Party against the Congress Party and secular groups who do not want religion to guide policy. For instance, the BJP in a number of Indian states protect cows from slaughter and prohibit the eating of beef.[806] This discriminates against Muslims and secular Indians for whom beef may be a staple. The second major partisan issue is related to caste, with special benefits (affirmative action?) provided to lower caste members in education, jobs, housing, and so forth.[807] This has led to protests by other castes who feel they have been denied equal access to higher education and employment.[808] President Modi and extremists in the BJP envision India as a right-wing Hindu state.

Japan

With the Liberal Democratic Party in control of government almost continuously since the end of American occupation, partisan divisions have been mainly intra-party. One major issue has revolved around nationalism and revelations about Japanese conduct during World War II. Though Prime Minister Murayama offered an official apology in 1995, as did Emperor Akihito, South Korea and China did not consider these adequate.[809] Japanese political figures continue to visit the Yasukuni Shrine where some war criminals are honored. And to placate Japanese nationalists, school textbooks whitewash the actions of the military during the war. Another partisan concern is whether to expand the Japanese Self-Defense Forces into a full-fledged military to neutralize Chinese dominance in the region and accept overseas missions.

Latin America

One of the significant partisan issues in a number of Latin American nations is the role the United States should be allowed to play. Because America supported a number of military coups in the past in opposition to leftist governments, the U.S. is not trusted to act in the best interests of Latin American states. This sentiment has blocked some joint commercial ventures, particularly in regard to oil and natural resources. Countries like Venezuela, Ecuador, Bolivia, and Nicaragua, blame the United States for their economic problems, used as an excuse for autocratic leaders of the left to grab more power. Widespread poverty and economic inequality are also partisan concerns, even in nations with left-wing governments. Recently, conservatives have gained power in voting in most major states. Any agenda to promote equality is difficult with deeply imbedded corruption in all nations.[810],[811],[812]

In many democracies, plutocracies develop, and the brightest and most educated, or those with hereditary wealth and connections rise to the top. This means that many citizens will be left behind, unable to successfully compete, inequality growing.[813] Eventually, they become resentful and envious of those who have 'made it.' The losers may turn to ethnic, blood and soil nationalism, to bolster feelings of belonging, rejecting accomplishment as a badge of excellence. Patriotism and ethnic partisanship are worshipped and substituted for competence--merit and talent no longer admired. Minorities are disparaged or worse, particularly if they have attained some degree of affluence or compete for employment. Nationalism and populism, as seen globally, become driving forces in the political system, at times leading to autocracy.

Partisan conduct by the political classes is a fact of life in most nations. However, when opponents refuse to compromise, government operations are impaired and economic growth stifled. Politicians cannot take unyielding positions on critical issues and must be open to negotiate with adversaries to find solutions in the interest of citizens.

Partisanship is another consequence of voters being uninformed, allowing them to be manipulated by politicians who insist their ideology is the only correct way for government to work. Voters must educate themselves about candidates and issues to reduce government dysfunction. Candidates are needed who will change the system to minimize corruption, inefficiency, and partisanship. It will entail changing the culture of government and the political processes.

9

Government Inefficiency

"Pride is thinking too highly of one's self from self-love."
Spinoza[814]

ACCORDING TO WEBSTER'S New Twentieth Century Dictionary, efficiency is the ability to produce the desired effect with a minimum of effort, expense, or waste.[815] This definition should hold whether applied to machines, individuals, businesses, or governments. However, when employed for government, efficiency should be considered as the ability to correctly perform designated functions in the shortest time frame, utilizing the fewest personnel possible, at the lowest cost conceivable. The way democracies are structured, with various checks and balances, and with voters as the ultimate arbiters of performance, can this form of government operate efficiently?

The major obstacles to efficiency are the remaining two thirds of the triad that shackles democracy: corruption and partisanship resulting from uninformed voters. In addition, the sheer number of government employees and apportioning of responsibilities among different divisions and layers cause problems. Further complicating matters, private contractors assume some roles government personnel would be expected to handle. Because of these factors, every democracy is inefficient to varying degrees. While one of the rationales for totalitarian regimes is their supposed efficiency, even there a wide variation exists, depending on the underlying culture of the nation's populace. (Fascism vs Communism: Hitler's Germany vs Stalin's Russia)

Some critics equate government size on a per capita basis with efficiency, believing larger ones cannot operate productively, their ranks bloated with unnecessary personnel. This has not been proven true. While it may seem counter-intuitive that a government employing a larger percentage of a nation's population can be as efficient, or more so, than one with fewer personnel per capita, it depends on the tasks government is expected to fulfill. A nation whose government has more obligations to its citizens than a neighboring state will require more staff to handle a greater workload.

However, there will always be citizens who do not want to pay higher taxes to support a bigger bureaucracy and want to minimize the role of government. They may believe the central government should handle defense, foreign relations, the currency, and perhaps trade with other nations, but should for the most part leave domestic affairs alone. The provinces or states can deal with infrastructure and local governments with education. In America, conservatives are adamant about downsizing the federal government, considering it too large, inefficient, and intrusive in citizens' lives. Conservatives also note voluminous waste in the operation of government and feel taxes could be put to better use in citizens' hands. In other democracies, where the culture and values are different, government efficiency is not as important as the maintenance of the safety net and protection for citizens. And some of these governments with more per capita employees function well.

There are economists, however, who believe government workers are invariably less productive than those in the private sector.[816] Unlike businesses, there are no incentives supplied by the profit motive. Secondly, government agencies are generally monopolies, so there are no competitive forces pressuring workers to perform better.

In addition, public employees are voters, so elected officials are often reluctant to render strict oversight. And governments may substitute non-monetary benefits for financial compensation, including liberal pensions and retirement awards, tenure, and job security. These benefits are given because voters react negatively to lofty salaries for government employees. This analysis would suggest the higher the percentage of government workers, the less efficient the economy would be, with a lower per capita GDP.

However, a brief review of data by Richard Posner in 2011 found no correlation between the fraction of a nation's population employed by government and its per capita GDP, examining twenty-seven nations.[817] Countries having the highest percentage of population employed by government were Sweden (33.87%), Denmark (32.3%), and Norway (29.25%). Japan, Singapore, and Taiwan had the fewest public sector workers, all below 10 percent. The United States (16.42%) was about the middle. Per capita income ranged from $17,537 in Poland to $53,478 in Norway. A regression analysis showed no relationship between the percentage of public sector employees and per capita GDP (treating Asian countries as a separate variable). Scandinavian nations, however, revealed a statistically positive relationship between the proportion of government workers and GDP, making it seem as if they might be more productive than their private counterparts.

Many democracies were not covered in Posner's study, but if his conclusions are correct, it appears that a nation can have a strong economy and prosperity with (or in spite of) a high percentage of public sector employees. The important variables not included in his evaluation were the types of jobs government workers performed in different countries and whether they contributed to productivity, or hindered growth. Workers may have included teachers, police officers, medical personnel, air traffic controllers, revenue agents, bank examiners, employees in government run companies, and so forth, (or licensing agents soliciting bribes, and politician's relatives benefitting from a spoils system of public employment). But why were Scandinavian nations with a high percentage of government workers and East Asian nations with a low percentage both so prosperous? Is there some inherent aspect of their cultures that determines productivity independent of ratios of public or private employment? What incentives drive public workers to perform their jobs well?

Other reports provide different statistics with wide variations regarding percentages of government employees, but may omit or include different groups as workers in the public sector. (For example, statistics may include only central governments, or add in provincial and municipal employees.) In 2012, a report by Business Insider showed that the percentage of the population employed by the U.S. government was unchanged since the 1970s. [818] (A Gallup Poll in 2010 had the number of U.S. public sector employees at 17 percent, with the Postal Service accounting for 23 percent of government jobs. [819])

The percentage of population working in the public sector in any democracy is actually immaterial. What really matters is whether employees perform their jobs well, maximize productivity, and little waste occurs. Citizens of every nation want to get the most bang for the bucks they provide government with their taxes: to know their money is not being squandered. Given the size and complexity of modern government, and with national, provincial, and local agencies having ample bureaucracies for various tasks, monitoring is necessary to know whether the vast government apparatus is efficient. But making it smaller does not mean it will be more productive. Governments must be able to meet the needs of citizens and bureaucrats must follow the mandates of elected officials in accomplishing assigned goals.

Democratic cultures in different nations raise different expectations regarding the role of government. American political culture focuses on individual self-sufficiency and smaller government--Europeans on larger governments to manage enhanced safety nets. But again, size is not the hallmark of efficiency. European democracies have chosen to pay higher taxes to enable governments to provide greater benefits, including social security, medical care, unemployment compensation, and so forth. Nations providing more benefits need more public sector workers to service the support system, and collect the taxes and fees necessary. Governments structured this way have done so with the desire and assent of their citizens.

The Greek government with patronage and excessive employment in the public sector has brought the country to the brink of bankruptcy because of inefficiency. In addition to employees occupying no-show jobs, the government subsidizes farmers who do not farm and provides benefits which if cut could save billions of euros.[820] Though 900,000 Greeks draw farming assistance, it is estimated only about 150,000 are eligible. But taking away privileges from citizens accustomed to them is difficult, despite the economic bailout Greeks have received.

Another illustration of government ineptitude is the pension crisis in Brazil.[821] Many public service workers retire in their forties and fifties with full benefits, some collecting multiple pensions, receiving over $100,000 annually. And after death, loopholes in the law may permit spouses or daughters to collect the pensions their entire lives. Young women may marry older men to receive their pension benefits after the men die. The situation is totally unsustainable economically, but politicians have not had the will to institute corrective measures.

With the profit motive gone and monopolies in services provided, how can public employees be induced to do their jobs well and maximize efficiency? Some people may be lazy and do not want to work hard or be pushed to increase output. They may perceive their positions as lifetime sinecures, merely waiting for retirement and expected pensions. And their jobs may be secure because of seniority, contracts, or union backing. However, the carrot as well as the stick may enhance workers' performances.

Executives and upper echelon personnel can establish competitions among employees to increase efficiency, rewarding them with days off or non-monetary bonuses. Productivity numbers, job performance, and customer satisfaction can be posted in public areas so everyone is aware who is doing a decent job and who is not. Then peer pressure may convince people to improve performance. Whatever stimulus executives utilize, we know public sector workers can be efficient, as shown by nations that have high GDPs with large proportions of their populations working for government. Proper leadership and supervision may be the key. Even in private industry, workers vary in productivity.

Those who complain that larger governments are less efficient and hurt entrepreneurship and growth in the private sector often point to more regulations 'big government' and excessive bureaucrats generate. A survey from the Philadelphia Federal Reserve in April 2016 revealed that companies in Mid-Atlantic states were spending more money complying with regulations than providing security for their data, networks, and physical plants.[822] However, America remains the global leader in entrepreneurship and private enterprise despite proliferation of rules and regulations. An entrepreneurial culture and the population's interest and support of innovation are more important than government size. It is true however that excessive rules and regulations can stifle private enterprise, as seen in the holding back of India's development.

In the United States, growth of licensing for various professions may also hinder the economy.[823] Almost 30 percent of America's work force currently needs licenses to work, while in 1970 it was 10 percent. Though it seems reasonable for professionals such as nurses, doctors, lawyers, pilots, contractors, architects, electricians, and so forth to be licensed, conservatives and liberals believe licensing has gotten out of hand. One of the reasons is that licensing provides income for states, counties, and cities. It also diminishes competition for those already covered and they lobby legislative and regulatory bodies to restrict licensing in their fields. Economists believe the profusion of licensing raises prices for consumers without upgrading services. However, licenses are rarely rescinded though areas covered may be bizarre, such as hair braiding, fruit packing, etc.

To demonstrate government inefficiency, various departments and sectors in the United States will be analyzed. In advanced nations, there are at least three separate levels of government: the central or federal government, states or provinces, and counties, cities, or municipalities. Their tasks include taxing and financing, building and maintaining infrastructure, preserving public order and security, monitoring safety of food, water, air and soil, supervision of financial institutions, licensing, maintaining educational standards, and so forth. In all democratic states, these obligations must be shared by the three layers of government, with funding also shared. Division of responsibility may lead to some overlap and duplication.

However, some functions are managed solely by one layer, such as defense and foreign affairs by the federal government, and sanitation by cities. There may also be elected members of school boards, water districts, and other public agencies with specific roles, that may have taxing powers. These organizations may work smoothly with other arms of government, but may clash at times if they believe their authority is being overlooked or bypassed. One can imagine the turf battles possible. Though analysis will focus on the United States, inefficiency is present in all democracies, indeed in every type of state, as with corruption and partisanship. And all nations have executive, legislative, and judicial branches supposedly designed to work in concert for the good of the people. They also have their bureaucracies, rules and regulations, required for any state to operate. Given these structures, some degree of inefficiency will invariably be present.

The European Union will be mentioned, however, as its Brussels bureaucracy and its plethora of rules and regulations, has raised inefficiency to new heights, causing hostility in many member states. Britain's vote to leave the E.U. can at least be partially blamed on its rejection of the need to conform to rules devised outside Britain that often seemed wasteful or silly. Because of the necessity to assuage sensibilities of all members of the E.U, decisions are sometimes made to hire extra employees to deal with problems that could be handled by far fewer.[824] This was seen when nine new judges were required to manage the backlog of cases in its highest appeals court. When agreement could not be reached on who the nine would be, twenty-eight justices were hired, one from each member nation, typical of how the E.U. works.

President Trump wants to make federal government smaller, cut employees and taxes, and reduce rules and regulations. This does not necessarily mean government will work better. Incentives must be built into government jobs to guarantee high levels of efficiency.

Federal Government

The checks and balances devised for the federal government by the Constitution almost guarantee inefficiency for legislation. In order for any bill to be established as the law of the land, all three divisions, the executive, legislative, and judicial branches play a role. Both chambers of the federal legislature, the Senate and House must pass the same versions of the bill. The president must then approve and sign it. The court system subsequently must hold the bill to be Constitutional if it is challenged by a person or group with standing. And the journey through the courts after a challenge may require years, until SCOTUS has the final say.

Executive Branch

The president and departments and agencies under his control are considered the executive branch and manage the government on the basis of laws enacted by Congress. While the president submits a budget to the legislative branch each year, the funds for departments to operate and purchase goods and services are authorized in appropriation bills by Congress. Agencies and departments may request additional sums if they are dissatisfied, but cannot raise or spend money on their own. Congress may purposely withhold funds from a department or agency if the Senate or House is controlled by a different political party than the president, or senators/representatives are unhappy with the agency's performance.

Emergency appropriations to supplement the budget may also be granted to departments if emergencies arise, such as earthquakes or hurricanes, terrorist incidents, military actions or wars. One can imagine the inefficiencies with revenue controlled by a different branch of the government than the operational unit. But it also provides safeguards to prevent overspending. Oversight of departments and agencies is an internal process with inspector generals and their staffs monitoring operations to be certain there are no illegal, unethical, or wasteful activities. Congress also has power of oversight. Congressional committees may use these powers to examine actions of personnel or operations in the executive branch, or to garner publicity for committee members.

Another aspect of the Constitution increasing government inefficiency is the mandate for the president's cabinet and other high officials to be confirmed by the Senate.[825] No doubt it would be easier for the chief executive to choose the individuals he will work with and who will run the various departments, unencumbered by political posturing and delays in confirmation. Indeed, it has become common for the Senate to stall approval of presidential appointments for political reasons, particularly if the opposing party is in control.[826] It may be done because of policy differences or hostility toward the nominee or the president but does not enhance smooth running of the government. The refusal to confirm Merrick Garland for the Supreme Court by a GOP controlled Senate in 2016 was purely political, but other officials in different agencies are not always approved. Obama tried to circumvent these actions through presidential appointments, but a federal appeals court ruled this unconstitutional.[827]

Change of administrations also lessens government efficiency. The new president has to fill about 4000 jobs, 1100 of which must be vetted by the Senate.[828] Civilian employment in the federal government alone in 2013 was 2,745,000 according to the census bureau.[829] (As noted, these numbers vary in different reports.) Defense and international relations encompassed 776,000 of that number, with several other departments having employees in the hundreds of thousands. Given the total quantity of workers, it is impossible for the president or secretaries of departments to be certain personnel are achieving their goals, being innovative when necessary, and generating customer satisfaction when there is interface with citizens. The president and department heads establish policy and objectives for each section, and senior executives in the departments have to be sure directives are followed.

Michele Flournoy, former Undersecretary of Defense for Policy under President Obama, critiqued the federal government after leaving.[830] She noted that while government workers are dedicated for the most part, and essential functions and services are provided for citizens, critical processes of many agencies were conceived fifty or sixty years ago. Flournoy believes most sectors of government lag behind private businesses in terms of efficiency and performance. While successful U.S. companies constantly transform strategies and the way they do business, many federal agencies are encumbered by out-of-date practices and outmoded infrastructure. Detractors of Flournoy say this is true of private companies as well.

The Heritage Foundation has defined six areas of unnecessary and wasteful spending by the federal government.[831] While they have a conservative view of government and would like to see it smaller, their suggestions have some validity.

Some programs can be transferred to state and local governments.
Some programs could be handled better by private industry.
Recipients not entitled to government benefits must be disqualified.
Outdated and unnecessary programs should be eliminated.
Duplicative programs should be sought out and eliminated.
Inefficiency, mismanagement, and fraud must be targeted.

Perhaps the biggest factor in government inefficiency is lack of the newest and best computer systems. There are thousands of different systems in agencies and departments that are obsolete and do not communicate with each other. Until Congress is willing to spend money to change this, inefficiency will be built in everywhere.

Department of Defense

The Defense Department (DOD) has the largest number of employees of any federal agency and a major part of the budget. The

Secretary of Defense and his deputies are in charge of America's military and help determine policy for the president in regard to security threats, maintenance and improvement of the armed forces, deployment of military personnel, procurement of weapons and equipment, and so forth. Having recently fought wars in Iraq and Afghanistan, American military advisors are still aiding these two nations, with American air power playing a significant role. Drones from the military and CIA, and Special Forces are active as well, battling terrorist forces in other nations in the Middle East and Africa.

Given its responsibility for national security, one would expect the DOD and military to perform efficiently. Unfortunately, this is not the case. The Pentagon is known for delays and cost overruns in development of armaments and exorbitant expenditures in purchases. And for decades, its computer management systems have been archaic and inefficient in gathering data. Whether the Secretary is a Democrat or Republican, the civilian bureaucracy and military personnel responsible for design and procurement remain the same. Waste involving mundane items like hundred dollar hammers and wrenches pale next to squandering hundreds of millions to billions of dollars on advanced weapons systems.

An article in 2012 detailed a number of absurdities in Pentagon expenditures.[832] In 2010, there were 963 active generals and admirals drawing salary and benefits, though analysts said only one third of these were needed. Many of them functioned as lobbyists, working Congress to try and obtain funds for various projects. The increase in rank meant higher pensions when the 'flag officers' retired, a long-term drain on taxpayers. And each of these officers had his or her entourage.[833] Benefits included private jets, their own chefs and valets, secretaries, security guards, and drivers. There were also palatial residences, police motorcades when traveling, musicians and special staff when entertaining. Cost of personnel for each general or admiral was over $1 million, excluding salary and housing. Some officers billed the government for vacations, along with the entourage accompanying them. There seemed to be a sense of entitlement disconnecting these military leaders from the real world.

The Pentagon also possessed an incredible 234 golf courses around the globe, the military function of which is unclear.[834] (Basic training or infiltration courses?) One can imagine the cost of maintenance for these facilities. ($400 toilet seats for one course.) Other resorts to entertain officers are rented or owned by DOD, with enhancements such as riding stables, hockey rinks, restaurants, and amphitheaters, aside from the usual Officer's Clubs. There is a ski lodge as well in the Bavarian Alps. While officers and enlisted men need rest and recreation, the Pentagon's real estate holdings, outside of bases and defense installations, seem quite excessive. A half billion dollars a year is also spent on marching bands, said to be for public relations.[835]

Adding to the cost of goods procured by DOD, retired generals are hired by defense corporations that sell products and service them for the military.[836] With these officers on board, businesses have access to top brass and civilian officials and are able to negotiate contracts favorable to the companies and expensive for government. One analyst noted that 70 percent of recently retired three and four star generals were quickly employed by major defense contractors. This also interferes with effective oversight of the companies. New laws are needed mandating a hiatus of three to five years before officers can work in the defense industry post-retirement.

Reports have also surfaced of serious errors by the armed services in inventory of weapons, ammunition, and equipment.[837] In order to coordinate what they were supposed to have with what they actually had on hand, data was often falsified. Monthly statements sent to the Defense Financing and Accounting Service, DOD's major accounting arm, were balanced with statements from the Treasury Department by inserting statistics with no basis in fact. False entries have been used for years because records of weapons and equipment were missing or inaccurate. There was also no way to tell how money was spent or from which Congressional appropriation items had been purchased.

Fudging accounts for the army, navy, air force and other defense agencies was and is standard procedure, with fabricated numbers used in place of missing information.[838] Oversight bodies reported to the Pentagon that its accounting practices were faulty, but these admonitions were disregarded. There was a backlog of over half a trillion dollars in unaudited contracts with private vendors in 2013, the department ignorant of whether goods and services had been provided. In 2012, DOD's budget was $566 billion, over half of all government spending. Billions of dollars of armaments and supplies were unaccounted for between 2003 and 2011.

The Pentagon is the sole government department unable to comply with a law mandating all agencies provide Congress with annual audits.[839] From 1996 to 2013, appropriations of $8.5 trillion for DOD were never reviewed for accuracy regarding purchases and services. Though Congress passed a law in 2009 demanding an accurate Pentagon audit by 2017, it is unlikely the objective was met. The Pentagon relies on thousands of outmoded and incompatible business-management systems in different administrative spheres, some being five decades old and using obsolete computer languages. The DOD is not even certain how many of these systems are employed and where and how they are being utilized.[840] Though billions have been spent to upgrade and centralize DOD computer systems to deliver correct data, much of the new technology has failed. And lack of knowledge about inventory has led to buying and storing equipment not needed, wasting millions to billions of dollars more. The problem had not been solved as of 2018, an internal audit showing the Defense Logistics Agency had lost track of more than $800 million in defense projects.[841] Strangely, America, the nation that masterminded the technology revolution, cannot seem to get its own house in order. Perhaps DOD should be taken over by Amazon which seems to have no problems with its accounting and inventory.

Another area of inefficiency is in procurement of equipment and weapons. Too often, goals are not met in terms of on-time availability and cost overruns. Part of the problem is cost-plus contracts with suppliers, who do not lose money if delivery is late or costs are higher. There are also failures by the Pentagon to anticipate needs of the troops.[842] During the Iraq War, thousands more armored Humvees were required to protect soldiers from improvised explosive devices. Many Americans died or were wounded because these were unavailable. At a meeting in Kuwait where a soldier raised this issue, Secretary of Defense Rumsfeld refused to recognize the danger troops faced, seeming to disregard the issue of fighters' safety.

Similarly, adequate body armor was lacking in the initial stages of the war and soldiers collected money to buy their own armor or asked families to send them the correct vests to diminish their vulnerability.[843] In fact, the DOD did have a supply of armored vests ready for use in 2003, but inserted ceramic plates for these vests did not cover enough area of the torso to maximize protection. A classified Pentagon report noted as many as 80 percent of Marines killed in Iraq by upper body wounds might have lived with proper body armor.

The way the Iraq War was run revealed disagreements between top military men and Rumsfeld and his civilian advisors. Rumsfeld constantly tried to pare down the number of troops requested, consistent with his theories of how a modern army should function.[844] He wanted light, mobile forces, able to strike quickly and surprise the enemy, winning the war with tactical advantages and overwhelming air power, insisting that 125,000, or even fewer troops, could do the job. Generals Shinseki and Zinni, and U.S. Central Command (CENTCOM) thought a force between 300,000 and 500,000 would be necessary to seal Iraq's borders and pacify the country after major battles were over.[845] The officers proved prescient. Of course, intelligence failures leading to the War were also signs of inefficiency.

Another example of DOD inefficiency involved the F-35 Joint Strike Fighter, which came in $163 billion over budget and seven years behind scheduled completion. [846] Military figures who oversaw the project are delighted with it despite cost and delays, saying it is far ahead of any other nation's aircraft. However, Frank Kendall, chief weapons purchaser for the Pentagon, described the price tag as "acquisition malpractice." Increased cost for each plane means fewer can be bought from the developer, Lockheed-Martin, and planes will be more difficult to sell to U.S. allies. Many minor mistakes, like tire problems and wingtip lights contributed to delays, as well as software glitches. Though a stealth craft, the F-35 has been noted to be heavy and sluggish.[847] The Pentagon anticipates buying nearly 2500 of these planes over the next twenty-two years for over a trillion dollars. [848]

The cost of the planes will make cuts in other military areas necessary. Critics have called the F-35 "overpriced and underperforming," and not needed to address our most urgent threats.[849] Costs have risen to $200 million for each plane. It is unclear whether Lockheed-Martin has been penalized in any way for the delays and cost overruns. Individuals in DOD responsible for new weapons systems seem to be enamored of the latest technology though they may not be required for the wars being fought. America can expect asymmetrical and guerilla warfare to be most challenging in the near future.

A troubling aspect of Pentagon procurement is that some defense contractors have few competitors and are considered essential for national security. This makes it difficult to impose major penalties on firms for fear it might put them out of business. Corporations that work for DOD also have stockholders to answer to, which means showing quarterly profits or suffering the consequences. During World War II, when America was in a life or death struggle, the military-industrial complex seemed to work better, competition greater with more firms to bid on projects. Currently, inefficiency in the Pentagon and by contractors seems to be widespread and accepted, no one cracking the whip to change the prevailing culture.

The Special IG for Afghanistan Reconstruction has found innumerable instances of fraud and misinformation in aid for Afghanistan, oversight by DOD and civilian agencies falling short.[850] Over $100 billion had already been spent by 2015. Aircraft had been purchased which the Afghanis were unable to fly, along with other instances of waste. Records had disappeared and metrics of progress in various areas were inaccurate. Part of the problem was reliance on local agencies and private contractors for data that they had reason to falsify.

In December 2016, an article by Craig Whitlock and Bob Woodward of the Washington Post revealed an internal Pentagon study finding $125 billion in administrative waste suppressed by senior defense officials.[851] The Defense Business Board, an advisory panel of corporate executives and consultants, generated the report after DOD had asked for help controlling their large bureaucracy. The study, completed in January 2015, showed nearly one quarter of the $580 billion budget went to overhead, business operations, human resources, property management, and logistics. There were 1,014,000 workers, including civilians, uniformed personnel, and contractors being used for back-office jobs, with 1.3 million troops on active duty, the lowest number since 1940. The study was kept under wraps because officials did not want Congress or the public to see the data.

In another instance of inefficiency, the United States has failed to keep pace with the global boom building icebreakers, with the Northwest Passage and Arctic increasingly accessible.[852] This area which may be available to drill for fossil fuels, shipping routes, leisure cruises, and fishing, has left the U.S. trying to catch up to Russia, China, and Chile in constructing icebreakers to guarantee passage in these semi-frozen waters. Outmoded icebreakers put America at a major disadvantage operating in the Arctic and Antarctic regions. The budget for the Coast Guard, which would be in charge of U.S. efforts, has been miniscule, with no planning by strategic thinkers about the necessity for ships and increased personnel.

Though the huge inefficiencies in DOD cannot be blamed on uninformed voters, they elect the officials who provide oversight and should be making certain that maximum efficiency is attained. Taxpayer money is used to sustain the inefficiencies noted.

State Department

The secretary of state determines foreign policy with the guidance and concurrence of the president. He or she also advises the president on appointment of ambassadors, ministers, consuls, and other diplomatic representatives.[853] State Department personnel in different countries promote American products, assist American businessmen and tourists, and try to increase trade with other nations. Diplomacy, the State Department's purview, is seen as a way to avoid conflict between the U.S. and nations with opposing concerns and values. In 2020, the Secretary of State was Mike Pompeo, a Trump appointee who followed Rex Tillerson when he was fired.

As of 2013, the State Department had 32,500 employees,[854] stationed domestically and in embassies and consulates in foreign nations. The embassies issue visas to citizens from other nations who want to vacation in the United States, study at American universities, or have job offers. A fixed number of citizens from each country may also receive documents allowing them to legally immigrate. In America, passports for travel may be issued to citizens. U.S. diplomats in other nations are tasked with protecting Americans, replacing lost or stolen passports and providing legal help to Americans accused of violating a country's laws. Department personnel negotiate treaties or agreements with other states at the behest of the president. Trump's initial budget drastically cut funding for the Department.

Inefficiency and waste would appear to be minimal at the State Department as its missions are well defined. However, in building new embassy compounds, excessive spending has been noted on construction and luxury items.[855] In some cases, funds to make compounds resistant to terrorist attacks have been used on esthetics that should have gone for security upgrades.[856] The Government Accountability Office in 2006 also described failure by the Department to change arms exports systems after 9/11 to prevent potential enemies from acquiring American weapons.[857] Problems included a lack of understanding regarding whether compliance with export rules and regulations were being followed. Limited resources and inadequate budgets were blamed for vulnerabilities, undermining guarantees that American interests were protected.

Since 2012, twenty critical audits and inspections had been conducted by the inspector general, in addition to identifying contracts worth about $6 billion where files were incomplete or could not be found. Grants were given by the Department to nearly 17,000 individuals and organizations in 2013, totaling $1.8 billion. State had only 570 grant overseers, 500 working abroad. Many of them were undertrained and overworked, or doing grant management part-time. Often, the awards could not be closed out because of missing documentation, suggesting possible fraud. In 2013, the IG reported the Department's office for cybersecurity was ineffective, with many Department systems vulnerable.[858] New policies and practices were suggested along with additional personnel.

As another example of government inefficiency, the State Department was tasked with fighting Internet censorship in 2010 and allocated $30 million.[859] Unfortunately, they did not have the technical personnel to do the job. However, another U.S. agency, the Broadcasting Board of Governors (that runs Voice of America and Radio Free Europe), had the technical expertise to provide unrestricted Internet access to populations lacking it, but did not have the funds. Therefore, nothing was done to further Internet freedom because the government was too dysfunctional to realize that two plus two equaled four.

On September 11, 2012, an attack on an American diplomatic compound in Benghazi, Libya, by Islamic militants killed four Americans, including Ambassador Christopher Stevens.[860] Afterwards, critics claimed State Department inefficiencies were responsible for the deaths because American forces were not sent to help. It was also suggested there had not been enough security at the compound and an American response team was not close enough to have made a difference in outcome. In June 2014, the leader of the attack, Ahmed Abu Khatallah, was captured in Libya and brought to the United States to stand trial.

There have also been questions about Hillary Clinton's tenure as secretary of state and her use of private emails.[861] Though she denied anything illegal was done, the Senate and House conducted investigations, the GOP hoping to embarrass Clinton during her bid for president. Since Trump's election, his policies and cuts in funding have resulted in senior personnel with knowledge of America's relationships with foreign nations resigning from the department. Trump appears not to care.

Department of Justice

The Department of Justice (DOJ) is responsible for prosecuting individuals thought to have committed federal crimes, including white collar offenses and terrorism, and gathering crime statistics. They also deal with civil rights and voting rights issues. The DOJ is headed by the attorney general with a deputy attorney general, an associate attorney general, and the solicitor general's office.[862] There are ninety-three federal prosecutors in judicial districts around the country, with numerous assistant United States attorneys and support personnel. In addition, there are 2300 prosecutor's offices managed by the states.[863] Also under DOJ's aegis are the Bureau of Alcohol, Tobacco, Firearms and Explosives (ATF) and FBI. William Barr is currently AG appointed by President Trump.

The New York federal prosecutor's office for the southern district, under Preet Bharara before his dismissal by Trump, handles most of the country's significant financial crimes, as its jurisdiction includes Wall Street, where major hedge funds, private equity funds, and big banks operate. Insider trading, manipulation of the markets, and manipulation of interest rates, are the type of crimes tried. Federal prosecutors also pursue corruption in local or state governments.[864]

A failure to prevent 9/11 has been ascribed to inefficiencies in the FBI and CIA, and their inability to communicate with each other.[865] U.S. intelligence and law enforcement agencies did not share information that might have provided advance warning.[866] And internally, the DOJ and FBI did not give priority to tips that might have aborted 9/11.[867] In August 2001, FBI agents in Minneapolis requested permission to search possessions of Zacarias Moussaoui, an Islamist attending flight school. Another FBI agent in New York asked for clearance to look for Khalid Almihdar, a known Al Qaeda operative at large in the U.S. Both requests were denied by bureaucrats. Almihdar was the pilot who flew American Airlines Flight 77 into the Pentagon.

Internal disputes in the FBI, CIA, and NSA also blocked a major intelligence coup.[868] The Taliban government in Afghanistan in 1998 and 1999 wanted to install a phone network using American equipment, awarding a joint venture to an Afghan-American entrepreneur and two British businessmen. Building extra circuits into the system, U.S. intelligence would have been able to eavesdrop on Afghan communications. But it was delayed for over a year because of infighting among the agencies over who was going to run the operation and never happened.

The degree of inefficiency, stupidity, and hubris by FBI and intelligence agencies in their failure to share information that would have prevented 9/11 was detailed by writer Lawrence Wright in 2006 who described their missteps as "dereliction of duty."[869] He ascribes the defective investigation of bombing of the USS Destroyer Cole in October 2000 as revelatory of flaws in the way American intelligence agencies operated. "Jealousy and turf wars"[870] prevented distribution of vital information. Wright strongly believes if U.S. intelligence agencies had been operating properly and working together, 9/11 would not have occurred. In June of 2005, the Justice Department's Inspector General released a report that the hijacking amounted to a "significant failure" by the FBI resulting from "widespread and longstanding deficiencies" in the way terrorism and intelligence cases were handled.[871]

The IG's report noted that before 9/11, the FBI had difficulty sharing information and did not give precedence to counterterrorism.[872] Problems with technology also plagued the FBI, making analysis and communication more difficult.[873] Inadequate IT prevented the Bureau from correlating data possessed by various sections. Personnel charged with modernizing IT were either not up to the job or did not remain long enough to get it done. In fact, in 2005, the Bureau had to scrap a $170 million software upgrade that did not perform well.[874] There was a continuing problem in recruiting qualified tech employees, analysts, and translators with knowledge of Arabic, Farsi, and Urdu.

In its report, the National Commission on Terrorist Attacks on the United States blamed a failure of imagination by the FBI and CIA for not preventing the 9/11 conspiracy, saying the gravity of the threat was not understood by the agencies.[875] Congress was criticized for a lack of oversight. The Commission suggested that a national counterterrorism center be established, with a director who would have power over all the nation's intelligence units. The Commission noted it had discovered no link between Al Qaeda and the Iraqi government, one of the reasons Bush used to initiate the war with Iraq and removal of Saddam Hussein.

Subsequent to 9/11, the situation did not rapidly improve, even with reorganization of the intelligence hierarchy.[876] Lines of responsibility remained muddied, bureaucratic cultures at each agency adhering to previous ideas that were flawed. As in the military, the prevailing attitude was CYA (cover your ass) so you are not blamed for any failures. On the other hand, smart, innovative, aggressive agents were usually not rewarded and often not allowed to put theories into action for fear of showing others up, or wasting funds and manpower.

A report by the FBI 9/11 Review Commission in 2015 described great progress made by the Bureau in counterintelligence efforts, but emphasized further improvement was needed.[877] It recommended hiring more linguists and cyber specialists and elevating the stature of the Bureau's analysts. This was required to meet increasingly complex national security threats by tech-savvy terrorists, computer hackers, and global cyber syndicates. The director of the FBI, James Comey, had put some of the suggestions into effect by the time the report was released.

The Bureau of Alcohol, Tobacco, Firearms and Explosives (ATF) revealed major inefficiencies when its Phoenix Field Division and other partners undertook Operation Fast and Furious to track illegal gun sales to Mexican cartels.[878] With this operation, an estimated 1400 weapons went missing in Mexico, two of which were found at the scene of the Arizona murder of Border Patrol agent, Brian Terry. Fast and Furious was part of an interagency program to monitor and fight

Mexican traffickers. Straw buyers would purchase firearms for others without required information on ATF forms. The Operation from 2009-2011 lasted about fifteen months, with thirty-four suspects indicted by a grand jury for drug and firearms trafficking. When Attorney General Holder appeared before the House Judiciary Committee in May of 2011, he said he had only learned of Fast and Furious a few weeks earlier.

An ATF agent testifying before the House Oversight Committee in June of 2011 declared the risk of having weapons possessed by violent criminals could not possibly "advance any legitimate law enforcement interest."[879] Four months later, investigators found memos showing Holder had been aware of Fast and Furious for nearly a year. The next month, five Mexican defendants were indicted by a grand jury for murder and conspiracy in the killing of Agent Terry. The following day, Holder described Fast and Furious to a Senate Committee as an operation flawed in concept as well as execution.[880] In February 2012 before a House committee, Holder denied a cover-up. However, the Oversight Committee in June 2012 recommended that Holder be held in contempt for withholding documents. The same day, Obama claimed executive privilege relating to records wanted by the House committee. This eliminated any possibility of Holder being prosecuted. Nevertheless, the House cited him for criminal contempt, the first instance an attorney general was held in contempt by Congress. In July, a joint staff Congressional report placed blame for the blunders of 'Fast and Furious' on acting ATF Director Kenneth Melson and Deputy Director William Hoover.

Probably one of the biggest failures of the DOJ has been its inability to indict and convict Wall Street traders, bankers, and executives whose corrupt acts, manipulation, and dishonesty were responsible for the financial crisis of 2008.[881] Inefficiency, laziness, and a fear of losing when prosecuting perpetrators were responsible for allowing these criminals to remain free, their reputations untarnished. Because of delays in investigations, statutes of limitation to bring charges ran out in many cases. [discussed under corruption] The DOJ seemed content it had collected nearly $190 billion in fines from forty-nine financial institutions since 2009.[882] This money was not obtained from perpetrators but from stockholders of the companies penalized.

Was the Justice Department so inefficient those guilty of crimes at banks, brokerage houses and rating agencies were let off the hook, instead settling for civil penalties?[883] Was this done to garner donations from Wall Street firms for political parties when attorney generals and prosecuting attorneys did not seek criminal indictments? During the eight years of the Obama administration, Democrats ran the DOJ, supposedly protectors of the little guy. But they were the ones unaggressive in pursuing the financial felons. (A prevalent theory is that perpetrators were not charged criminally because of fears it might endanger financial institutions deemed too big to fail.)

Veterans Administration

Inefficiencies and false record-keeping in the Veterans Administration (VA) were in the news for several years, with marked delays in veterans receiving care. The scandals caused the head of the Department, former General Eric Shinseki, to resign in May of 2014.[884] The VA official in charge of health affairs, Robert Petzel, had resigned earlier. Complaints about the delays in care initially came from the facility in Phoenix where the IG found false documents hiding the time veterans had to wait for appointments- 1700 veterans required an average of 115 days to see a physician. However, these problems were discovered to be systemic, with false records and unconscionable waits for appointments throughout the country.

With over 170 medical centers and 1063 outpatient sites providing care to 8.76 million veterans annually, the Veterans Health Administration is America's largest integrated health system.[885] Difficulties have been due to underfunding and lack of personnel. However, a year after the outcry regarding the VA's problems (June 2015), delays had grown worse.[886] There were 50 percent more veterans seeking care on wait lists greater than a month and a $3 billion shortfall in funds that needed to be explained. VAs managed 2.7 million more visits in 2015 than any previous year, while approving 900,000 visits to physicians outside the system. In total, 1100 new physicians, 2700 nurses, and 4700 other employees were hired by the VA during 2014-2015, and space devoted to clinical care was increased.[887] But this was still insufficient to handle the surge in outpatient visits. Congress needs to appropriate more funds for the VA, where veterans generally feel more comfortable and oversight of care is better. However, the Trump administration wants to place more medical care of veterans into private hands.

Department of Education

Trump's Secretary of Education is Betsy DeVos, a billionaire favoring charter schools and vouchers for private schools.[888] Education is the key to competing in today's world and standardized testing in K-12 to measure students' knowledge and progress is needed to shape effective educational programs. However, many parents and students are unhappy with standardized tests, believing teachers focus too much on preparing pupils for them. Parents also complain their children are not adept at tests, or they cause too much stress. Teachers claim it is not the way to evaluate their teaching ability and want other criteria employed.

In many states, large numbers of students are opting out of Common Core tests and politicians who once lauded these exams are now opponents.[889] Though some governors have eliminated Common Core tests and replaced them with state standards, the exams given are similar.[890] Federal funding requires some method of measuring student progress. The problem is the Department of Education has not done a good job selling the need for teaching specific materials along with uniform testing to parents, teachers, and politicians.[891] Students must have a certain body of information to function in the 21st century.

The Department of Education has failed as well to establish schools that will retain students and meet their educational needs. Not all students in high schools should be on a purely academic track

with college in mind. Some students are not interested in these prepa-
ratory subjects and some do not perform well in these subjects. About
one fifth of U.S. students do not graduate from high school in four
years, about one fifth have no further education, about one fifth do
not finish college, about one fifth are employed in a field unrelated to
the degree that have obtained, and about one fifth follow the career
path for which their education has prepared them.[892] Other options
should be offered to students in high schools as do other advanced
nations. For many students an apprenticeship track would be more
rewarding than an academic trajectory. More schools should focus on
vocational and technical training instead of academics, particularly in
fields that need workers. These courses would be more likely to keep
students in school and prepare them for the jobs available.

Many workers are now unemployed, with jobs going begging
because they do not have the necessary skills for these positions.
Rather than only spending more money on job retraining for laid off
unemployed workers, the Federal government should build and help
support technical and vocational schools for young students. These
could be utilized for job retraining of older workers as well. In addition,
companies could send their own workers to these schools to teach
toward their needs, or to learn new skills and techniques. This could
be supplemented with on the job training. Students and older workers
have to be taught the skills required for work in the 21st century, and
not all of it requires an academic degree.

Whether on an academic or vocational track, all students should
also be taught courses in civics and American history. They must learn
how the government is structured and how it works to prepare them
for their roles as citizens, so they will understand politics and the voting process. Perhaps this will kindle an interest in politics and they will
become more knowledgeable voters and participate in the political
process to help staunch democracy's decline.

The Department has also done poorly at overseeing college loans
and grants. Students may not be aware of loans available at low interest
rates and the best terms for repayment, usually provided by the federal

government or states.[893] Pell grants, grants for veterans, and other types of aid, along with scholarships from schools and other sources should be sought by students prior to taking out loans. Private universities and banks may advertise the availability of loans, but these are at higher interest rates, though they may be guaranteed by government. Seventy percent of students graduating from American universities have educational loan debt, an average of more than $28,000 in 2013,[894],[895] one in ten with more than $40,000 outstanding. In 2013, the Consumer Financial Protection Bureau declared student loan debt had cumulatively crossed $1.2 trillion, undoubtedly increasing since. That means student loans are the second highest type of consumer debt, lagging only mortgages. Besides being bad for individuals, it's bad for the economy, with less money to spend in other ways. Economic growth may slow under this burden, with fewer jobs created, higher interest rates, and capital more difficult to access. When people default, American taxpayers are hit.

For-profit schools and universities that graduate only a small percentage of students and do not get those the jobs promised, also have to be constrained. These schools have been protected by Republicans in Congress and by Trump, who see them as free-market entities. Unfortunately, young people who have done poorly in high school and cannot obtain admission to established universities view these for-profit schools as a way to get degrees and better jobs, not-withstanding the costs. They also provide more flexible schedules and on-line classes for working students or those with young children. As of 2013, 12 percent of post-secondary school students, 2.4 million, were enrolled in for-profit universities.[896]

The question of quality at these schools is constantly raised. Their primary goal is profit, education secondary. They are supported by $32 billion (2009-2010) in federal subsidies and Pell grants.[897] Advertising has increased the number of students in for-profit universities, while community and four year public colleges have been losing students.[898] A Senate investigation in 2012 found the profit margin at for-profits schools was 19.7 percent, 27 percent for the University of Phoenix which had 470,000 students enrolled in 2010.[899] Only 17.7 percent of income was spent on instruction, averaging $2050 per student compared to between $3344 and $11,128 at public schools. (The University of Phoenix spent only $892 per student.)

Approximately, 96 percent of students at for-profit colleges have to borrow money to attend compared to 13 percent at community colleges and 48 percent at four year public institutions. However, the most telling statistics are the drop-out rates of 54 percent, with 60 percent at the University of Phoenix. Nationwide, half of all default rates are from students from for-profit colleges, many of whom never attain degrees. Though the Education Department claims to have cracked down on predatory institutions, it continues to subsidize student 'education' at these schools.[900] "Hundreds of schools that have failed regulatory standards or been accused of violating legal statutes are still hauling in billions of dollars of government funds."[901]

As further evidence of inefficiency in handling student loans at for-profit institutions, whistle-blowers went to the government in 1999 claiming ITT Educational Services provided little education while increasing student debt through federal loans.[902] It took until 2016 for the Education Department to withdraw support for the company, forcing ITT into bankruptcy. In the meantime, the company had accumulated over $12 billion in revenue, 70 percent in government guaranteed loans. The top five executives of ITT made $117 million during this period. Trump University was another for-profit institution that ripped off students while providing little of educational value, costing Trump $25 million after the 2016 election to settle suits.[903]

Virtually all for-profit universities are scams perpetrated on America's youth. The Department of Education and Congress must change financial formulas that allow private schools to operate on the backs of young Americans grasping for higher education and better jobs, while putting taxpayers at risk. President Obama in 2014 put a plan into action by executive order called "Repaye" to help those with student loan debt.[904] Participants will have repayment capped at 10 percent of discretionary income and loan balances remaining will be forgiven after twenty years.

10

Additional Inefficiencies

"The state is an association intended to enable its members in their households and the kinships to live well; its purpose is a perfect and self-sufficient life." Aristotle[905]

INEFFICIENCIES IN THE structure of American democracy and a number of government departments have been described. Additional inefficiencies are portrayed below.

Security Agencies

Since 9/11, hundreds of billions of dollars have been spent by the Federal Government to try and make Americans safer and reduce terrorism.[906] This money has gone to the Department of Homeland Security, the FBI, CIA, NSA, the military, other government agencies, state and local police departments, and so forth. But are Americans safer? Though large-scale terrorist actions like 9/11 appear unlikely, lone wolf attacks are impossible to stop. And a number of security gaps present in 2001, remain.

With hordes of federal contractors competing for national security dollars and lobbyists coercing politicians on behalf of their clients, significant overlap and waste has occurred. Hundreds of millions of dollars to develop systems to contain bioterrorism were cancelled because they did not work. And political pressure diverted money from vulnerable places. Underpopulated states like Wyoming, with no large cities or terrorist targets, received federal dollars for protection instead of more funding for New York or Washington. Many small towns were given emergency vehicles and other equipment, though the likelihood of incidents was miniscule.

Though the TSA received over $2 billion to bolster security on checked bags, the new equipment was flawed. And a $5 billion program for border security awarded to Boeing, to replace a $2.5 billion system that failed to work, was itself faulty. Drive through radiation detectors at border crossings were also found to be defective after $230 million was spent. In general, money allocated to large cities did seem to make the cities safer. However, one estimate determined that between $100 billion to $150 billion was wasted on error-prone equipment or useless programs.[907]

The main area of vulnerability now is cybersecurity and government agencies that continue to be behind the curve. There is persistent hacking of data by individuals and groups, some of them foreign government actors from Russia, China and Iran.[908] Clinton's election campaign was disrupted by this hacking and the release of information from Wikileaks, Russia aiding Trump in the race for the presidency.[909] A critical vulnerability is the nation's infrastructure, 87 percent owned by private entities. This includes transmission lines, power plants, water companies, financial institutions, and so forth. Not only does government have to protect its own agencies and information, it has to pressure private corporations to spend money to make them safe. However, government efforts to guard its own digital infrastructure have so far failed. The Office of Personnel Management in 2014 and 2015 discovered 25 million records compromised. A $1 billion cybersecurity program designed by the DHS and labeled Einstein had been so ineffective it failed to pick up the hacking of OPM records.

Citizenship and Immigration Services is part of the DHS. Their inefficiency is breathtaking, with reports in 2016 that more than 200,000 approved Green Cards had not been sent to applicants awaiting them.[910] The agency also produced 19,000 cards over three years that were duplicates or contained misinformation. DHS's database had not been digitized or included nearly 150,000 older fingerprint records, and those involved in deportation proceedings were not sent to the FBI. Because of mishandling of fingerprint records, the DHS was unable to know if people were really who they said they were, allowing them to serve in the armed forces or police.

There has also been inadequate attention paid by the DHS and the FBI to domestic terrorism involving white supremacists. More deaths since 9/11 have been the result of domestic terrorism than caused by Islamic terrorists. However, President Trump and Congressional Republicans do not want to alienate white supremacists who support them at the ballot box.

Internal Revenue Service (IRS)

Brief mention should be made of inefficiencies of the IRS, brought on by Congressional Republicans who dislike and distrust the agency and have cut funding dramatically. The budget was lowered about 18 percent from 2010 to 2016 in spite of the fact the agency had new responsibilities due to enactment of the Affordable Care Act.[911] Because of cuts, the enforcement staff had been reduced 23 percent with audits dropping a similar amount. This resulted in more taxes being uncollected, an estimated $14 billion over two years. It also meant service was worse and taxpayers could not get answers to questions.

Budget cuts to the IRS passed by Republicans were in the service of their rich donors who are now less likely to be audited. ProPublica estimated that 18-20 percent of potential tax revenues annually are currently uncollected.[912] Tax loopholes are exploited and tax evasion by the richest Americans flourishes. Since more IRS tax collectors means more revenue for the Federal government, there was no reason for the GOP to cut the number of tax enforcers and auditors except to help the most affluent. And as the rich become richer, inequality grows. A study of IRS data has revealed that rich Americans are more likely to cheat with fewer audits occurring. And the IRS has about as many auditors as they had sixty years ago when America's population was half of what it is today. Just as recent Republican tax cuts have benefitted the wealthiest citizens and increased the nation's deficits and debt, cutting IRS personnel has done the same. As an example, IRS investigations in 2017 of people who did not file income taxes dropped to 362,000 from 2.4 million in 2011. $95 billion in uncollected funds has been left on the table since 2011.

Health and Human Services (HHS)

Only two aspects of HHS operations will be examined here- initiation of the Affordable Care Act and fraud in the Medicare and Medicaid programs.

To put it mildly, implementation of the Affordable Care Act (ACA, Obamacare) was a disaster, as HHS and the Obama administration bungled roll-out of the program.[913] This occurred even though more than three years elapsed between the bill's passage and its initiation. The website for millions of citizens to find available options then apply for and purchase insurance was an utter failure. In some cases, it did not work at all, in others it did not provide proper information, and for others it functioned at a glacial pace. Computer experts blamed the problems on numerous contractors employed to set up different aspects of the system and that some of the components were not compatible.

No matter what excuses were given, the ACA did not function as conceived. The website created to provide information to millions wanting health insurance did not do what had been expected.[914] Though the full force of the Obama team and HHS were thrown into repairing the HealthCare.gov site, the process required several months, by which time many potential clients were disgusted. Once the website was operational, the program ran into further difficulties when states controlled by Republicans refused to expand Medicaid or set up state insurance exchanges. The program had been tailored to be run jointly by the federal and state governments, but a number of states refused to play ball. As of the 2016 insurance year, some insurance companies had dropped out of the ACA, claiming to be losing money and the price of coverage had soared in some areas. The complexity of the ACA in an attempt to satisfy different constituencies made its operation a continuing nightmare. Trump and the GOP promised to repeal and replace the ACA, unsuccessfully as of 2019. At present in 2020, it appears to be running more efficiently.

Medicare and Medicaid are constantly burdened with fraudulent claims by health care providers attempting to obtain excessive reimbursement. Included are physicians, podiatrists, physical therapists, hospitals, nursing homes, rehabilitation centers, medical equipment companies, and pharmaceutical firms. Practitioners may upcode for services rendered to patients or procedures performed. Similarly, hospitals or other health care facilities may exaggerate services or the severity of patients' illnesses for which they are billing. This is a cat and mouse game played by providers with Medicare and Medicaid algorithms trying to pick out patterns of possible fraud. Whistleblowers also help HHS catch deceptive providers.

Estimates have states as well as the federal government losing billions of dollars each year through Medicaid fraud and abuse.[915] At times, insurance companies that reimburse Medicaid services can defraud government by overstating the cost of claims. Unnecessary duplicate services increase costs. Patients can cheat with providers by filing claims for services not rendered. Aside from upcoding and billing for unperformed services, doctors may falsify diagnoses, order excessive tests, and so forth. While patients are encouraged to report suspicious billing practices or expensive procedures they questioned, the states and federal government are using data mining to locate providers and billing that appear fraudulent.

The situation concerning Medicare fraud is worse than Medicaid, as more money is involved and the elderly may be easier to scam. Though the numbers are higher, the type of fraud and abuse are the same as with Medicaid. In 2014, estimates of improper payments for Medicare's fee-for-service sections (Parts A and B) came to $46 billion.[916] Part C (Medicare Advantage) and Part D (drug coverage) added another $15 billion. The numbers sound outrageous, but likely underestimate the losses to fraud, abuse and waste, along with bureaucratic incompetence. An analysis by Harvard's Malcolm Sparrow reports as much as 20 percent of all government spending on health care may be fraudulent, hundreds of billions of dollars annually.

Federal Election Commission

The Federal Election Commission (F.E.C.) was established by Congress in 1975 as an independent agency to enforce the Federal Election Campaign Act.[917] Members are appointed by the president and confirmed by the Senate. The F.E.C. is supposed to disclose campaign finance information in federal elections and enforce the limits and prohibitions on contributions, as well as manage public funding of presidential elections. However, the F.E.C. was structured as a six member body with three seats from each party, unable to take action unless four or more commissioners agreed (a bipartisan majority).[918] In this era of partisan politics, transgressions by candidates would have to be particularly egregious in order for members of his or her own party to sanction that person. More likely a deadlock would ensue or the action would not be voted on at all. The Commission was set up this way to be purposely inefficient and doomed to fail so politicians who broke the rules would not be penalized.

Securities and Exchange Commission (SEC)

The Securities and Exchange Commission is an independent agency. Its mission statement says its job is "to protect investors, maintain fair, orderly, and efficient markets, and facilitate capital formation."[919]

Though the SEC fined financial institutions that misled investors about CDOs and mortgage-backed securities that were a major cause of the 2008-2009 recession, they did nothing to prevent the crisis from occurring.[920] Sub-prime mortgages in bundled securities were a disaster waiting to happen, but the agency seemed content to watch rather than act to rein in these perilous investments. The SEC was totally ineffectual in monitoring the entities and did not warn investors of risks in purchasing these financial instruments.

After the damage had been done, the SEC levied relatively small fines on some of the companies that had engaged in deceptive practices.[921],[922] Standard and Poor's agreed to pay almost $80 million for fraudulent misconduct when rating CMBs- (commercial mortgage-backed securities).[923] Leading up to the last collapse on Wall Street, Citigroup devised a municipal bond strategy resulting in clients losing approximately $2 billion, though touted as a safe-money alternative.[924] The SEC fined Citigroup $180 million for deceiving clients, but did not reveal names of money managers who formulated the scheme and those who sold it to investors. Stockholders were left to foot the bill.

In April 2010, the SEC charged Goldman, Sachs and one of its vice presidents with defrauding investors,[925] the result of Goldman misstating and withholding information about a financial instrument tied to subprime mortgages. Goldman did not tell investors a major hedge fund, Paulson and Company, had paid Goldman to have a hand in choosing a CDO's securities and that the hedge fund had taken a short position against the CDO and sub-prime mortgage market. Goldman betrayed their clients and criminal charges should have been brought against their top executives. Though a fine was later imposed, none of their executives went to prison or were banned from the securities industry.

The SEC also missed landing a big fish when they ignored whistle-blowers about Bernie Madoff.[926] An attorney, Kathleen Furey, in the New York Regional Office, filed a complaint after the fact that she and twenty other lawyers who worked with her, were prohibited by their boss, Assistant Regional Director George Stepaniuk, from pursuing cases against investment managers like Madoff as a matter of policy. Two of the four main laws governing Wall Street gave the SEC jurisdiction over these cases. Problems within the SEC resulted not only from its failure regarding Madoff, but with other fraudulent investment managers as well, showing unusual ineptness.[927] As for Madoff, the SEC had received a detailed report on extensive fraud by Madoff from an investigator, Harry Markopolos, in 2000 and never followed through until the case exploded in December 2008.

Subsequent examination of Madoff's records showed he was not trading, but simply stealing money from investors in a straight Ponzi scheme.[928] If the SEC had investigated, they would have easily discovered how he had swindled his clients out of $60 billion. And instead of lauding Furey for her whistleblowing and alerting the SEC to its internal problems, she was demoted by her superiors even though outside auditors commended her work and ability. The same pattern of behavior led the SEC to disregard information from another whistleblower regarding the Alan Stanford Ponzi scheme in 2009.

The Legislative Branch- Congress

Given that recent sessions of Congress have been among the least productive in history, efficiency and Congress are two words that don't belong in the same sentence. The 112th Congress in 2011 and 2012 passed a total of 284 laws, the 113th Congress from 2013 and 2014 296 laws,[929] the 114th Congress 329 laws in 2015-2016.[930] This compares to 600-800 laws per session twenty to forty years earlier. The first year of Trump's White House sojourn, with the GOP controlling, Congress was even worse with only 123 laws enacted.[931]

All bills dealing with appropriations or revenue are supposed to originate in the House. Confirmations of cabinet members, judges, ambassadors, and treaties are within the province of the Senate through the Constitution's "advice and consent" provisions. The House is able to indict or impeach federal officials by a majority vote while the Senate has the power to try all impeachments and remove officeholders by a two thirds vote. The growth of Congressional inefficiency and Congress's inability to enact new laws is directly related to partisanship and the unwillingness of those with extreme ideologies to compromise.

Another critical factor undermining efficiency is the two year election cycle for the House. Every day Congress is in session, members of both parties use 'call time' to solicit funds from potential donors over the phone.[932] In addition, they attend fundraisers in the capital or in their districts. The quest for money never stops. An orientation session for freshman by the Democratic Congressional Campaign Committee anticipates a nine to ten hour working day for House members. Four hours are to be spent in 'call time' and an additional hour for 'strategic outreach' devoted to press contact and fundraisers. Another hour is set aside to 'recharge,' with three to four hours allotted for the real work of a lawmaker: hearings, discussions, votes on legislation and resolutions, and meetings with constituents. If the latter are potential donors, more time may be required to be spent with them.

Since the Senate has a six year election cycle, there is less pressure in terms of constant fundraising. Legislating, hearings, interacting with other senators, occasional trips back home to make appearances before constituents, and some fundraising are each part of a Senator's schedule. But as an election approaches, everything changes. According to former Democratic Majority Leader Tom Daschle, during the last two years of a senator's term, two thirds of every day is spent raising money.[933] Daschle noted Senators had to collect an average of $10,000 for every day of the six years they were in office to come up with the amount spent in most Senate contests. In both House and Senate, fundraising competes with the work of legislating, frustrating lawmakers who want to do a decent job.

The structure of Congress and practices with historical resonance also play a role in inefficiency. Bills may be introduced in either body of Congress and those ratified in the Senate or House proceed to the other branch. This usually results in some changes in wording or substance. Amendments not connected may also be attached to the original bill, members of Congress hoping to obtain quick passage of something unrelated. If there are great differences in Senate and House versions of the bill, it may go to a conference committee of the two branches to work out differences. Assuming the Speaker of the House and Senate Majority Leader believe the changes will result in passage, the bill then returns to each body of Congress for votes of approval.

Even if a bill has majority support in the House, if there is Republican control, a GOP Speaker may keep it from coming to the floor for a vote because of the 'Hastert Rule.' Formulated by Speaker Hastert in the mid-1990s, it requires a majority of the majority (the Republican caucus) to pass a bill before it is sent to the floor.[934] This means that even if Democrats and a minority of Republicans support a bill, it cannot be voted upon because consideration will not be allowed. The Speaker has significant power and may not permit bills to reach the floor if he or she opposes them. On the other hand, bills or resolutions may be rushed through the House if the Speaker favors them.

Usually, there is a lengthy process bills follow in the House before coming to the floor. A subcommittee of a standing committee with jurisdiction holds hearings, interviewing witnesses and possibly experts in the field. Sometimes jurisdiction over a measure is divided between two committees that may hold separate hearings. If the leader of the subcommittee and a majority of its members approve of a bill, it will be sent on to the full committee. Then further hearings may or may not take place before the full committee votes on the bill. Before or after a vote, the Chairman may keep the legislation bottled up in the committee if there are aspects he or she does not like. Special rules on legislation may be generated by the House Rules Committee, (controlled by the majority), when major bills are to be considered.[935]

The Rules Committee may also bring up bills for deliberation pending before Standing Committees, though this is rarely done.[936] Thirty days after a measure has been referred to a committee, a motion to discharge it and bring it to the House floor can occur with approval of 218 members. Filing a discharge petition, or threatening to do so, may hasten committee action on a bill, but it is unlikely to get to the floor over objection by the Committee Chairman. The Speaker of the House is also responsible for recognizing members, allowing them to speak, and ruling on points of order (which are rarely appealed). Because of the number of Representatives, time allocated to debate a measure is generally limited. Constitutionally, the Senate needs a majority of its hundred members to be in session. Because the Constitution mandated two senators from each state, senators from the twenty-six least populous states with 18 percent of the nation's citizens can decide legislation.[937] (Gerrymandering also allows House members representing a minority of citizens to control the legislative process.)

The Senate operates under different rules than the House.[938] The presiding officer is the vice president rather than the majority leader who refers legislation that has been introduced to the appropriate standing committee if it has not originated there. The chairman of the committee may direct the legislation to a subcommittee for hearings before it returns to the full committee. Once voted on by committee, the bill can be reported to the full Senate with approval of the majority and minority leaders. The majority leader picks the chairmen of the committees and appoints members from his party, the minority leader choosing committee appointees from his or her party. Senators with an interest in specific legislation are notified when a bill is in committee because measures are supposed to reach the floor by unanimous consent.

There are two unique powers Senators possess that no other legislative bodies have invested in their members.[939] These are the freedom of unlimited debate and the ability to offer unlimited amendments to legislation. If an individual speaks on the floor simply to delay passage of legislation it is called a filibuster and can be ended only by cloture which has to pass with a three fifths majority. Much of the Senate's business is conducted by unanimous consent to expedite action and limit debate, allowing a single member to delay enactment of a bill. Another prominent feature of the Senate is the practice of 'holds,' a request by a senator to his or her party leader to withhold floor consideration of legislation or nominations. The concept of 'holds' is not found in Senate rules or precedents, its origin uncertain.

The majority leader is responsible for scheduling Senate trans-actions.[940] This includes legislative business, which are bills and resolutions, and executive business, which are treaties and nomina-tions. Legislative or executive business when received from the House or the president usually is referred first to the standing committee with jurisdiction. Whenever possible, the majority leader tries to call up bills and resolutions by unanimous consent. If there are objections, it indicates senators oppose a measure and may filibuster or place a hold on it. Amendments to bills do not have to be "germane or rel-evant" according to Senate rules, except for appropriation bills and budget measures. If a committee does not report a measure out, any senator may submit its text as an amendment to any measure being considered.

Though it is obvious Congressional rules and precedents are quite complex and make legislating difficult, partisan conflicts cause most obstacles to passage of laws and confirmations. Whichever party is in control of Congress tries to assert its own agenda, while the party in the minority tries to block it. Compromise is not easy to achieve, as neither party wants the other to receive plaudits from the public over bills passed. When the two Houses are split between the parties, the legislative process is even more convoluted. Cooperation is necessary but may occur surreptitiously or not at all.

If the president hails from a different party than the one control-ling Congress, legislation may be vetoed if compromise is not reached beforehand. If there are enough votes in the Senate to sustain a veto, then there is no choice but compromise if critical legislation is to be enacted. However, there have been instances in recent years where extremists in the GOP shut down the government rather than agree-ing to compromise with Obama. Though Democrats had control of the Senate, in October 2013, government was shut down by GOP conservatives in the House who refused to pass a spending bill unless a measure to defund Obamacare (ACA) was included.[941] There were

800,000 government workers furloughed and the government flirted with default. The shutdown ended after sixteen days with a deal between the Senate majority and minority leaders, Harry Reid and Mitch McConnell.

As another example of Congressional inefficiency, House Republicans in the 113th Congress voted to repeal Obamacare fifty times by March of 2014.[942] These measures were debated and passed to assuage conservatives though it was certain the bills would not pass the Senate or be vetoed by Obama, a waste of time in each instance. The votes also cost taxpayers about $75 million. Mitch McConnell, the Senate minority leader when Obama was first elected in 2008 said his number one goal was to make sure Obama was a one-term president, more important than enacting any policies. This also made Congress less efficient. Though the Senate and House in the 114th Congress were both controlled by the GOP, they did not have enough votes to overcome presidential vetos. In December 2015, the Republican controlled Senate voted to end Obamacare, knowing Obama would veto the bill and there was not enough support to overturn it.[943] The bill was indeed vetoed in January of 2016, another useless bill highlighting the inefficiency and partisanship infecting Washington. [944]

Congressional inefficiency is also evident in the dearth of infrastructure repair and construction. Due to lack of funding, deaths have occurred because of bridge and highway hazards, railway accidents, and failure of dams and levees.[945] And infrastructure problems lead to a serious waste of time and money as citizens sit fuming in traffic or wait in overloaded airports. Yet Congress refuses to raise adequate sums to fix matters. The gasoline tax which supports the Highway Trust Fund has been stuck at eighteen cents since 1993. [946] The Department of Transportation declared that poor road conditions and design are involved in approximately 14,000 deaths annually. The medical cost of these accidents was $11.3 billion in 2013. An estimated $3.6 trillion was needed for a first class infrastructure by 2020 according to the Engineers' Society, including the high speed trains operating in Europe, China, and Japan. President Trump promised a trillion dollar boost for infrastructure, so far unfulfilled.

Congress neglects to adequately finance research and development as well. The private sector is less likely to spend money on basic research as returns may not materialize or may only be seen in the distant future. However, as the world becomes more dependent on technology and other nations are revving up spending on research, the GOP has been cutting appropriations for R and D across the board.[947] They do not view it as seed money that will bear fruit in the future. China is likely to control artificial intelligence because of lack of foresight by Congress.

The way a Senator's power contributes to inefficiency was seen in the obstruction of the Export- Import Bank (Ex-Im) by GOP Senator Richard Shelby of Alabama in 2016.[948] Shelby, Chairman of the Senate Banking Committee, claimed his mission was to cut "corporate welfare." But Shelby was hurting the U.S. economy by interfering with the functioning of Ex-Im, a government agency operating since the Depression. For a year, he blocked the Bank from helping to finance sales to foreign countries of products worth over $10 billion. These loans and insurance over the years have actually earned money for the bank and American taxpayers, and every other industrial country provides export loans to nations buying their products.

Because of Shelby's intransigence, GE moved thousands of jobs abroad to France, Czech Republic, Hungary, Britain, and China, whose governments were willing to provide the loans. Boeing lost contracts for satellites and planes to other bidders because the Ex-Im Bank could not render the necessary loans. The company subsequently negotiated with Britain to finance some of its planes using Rolls-Royce engines instead of American engines. Other companies needing the loans included Westinghouse, John Deere, and Caterpillar. Boeing has plants in Alabama which could shed jobs if Shelby continued his war on the bank. But Shelby would not budge, indifferent to his impact on the economy. John Engler, former GOP governor of Michigan and president of the Business Roundtable described opponents of the Ex-Im Bank as "economic illiterates."[949] How this was corporate welfare when the bank made money was not clear. On the other hand, conservatives in Congress were willing to provide major subsidies to large corporate farmers in states important to them politically. Jobs are being sent abroad and the economy bolstered in other nations due to one senator's obdurate stupidity.

States' ability to refuse to follow laws passed by Congress or executive orders and to sue to block these regulations is another problem increasing inefficiency. Even if the courts eventually side with the federal government, time and effort are wasted. States can also pass their own laws contrary to federal ones. This was seen in a number of states trying to halt implementation of the ACA.[950] States have also sued to block regulations ordered by the EPA.[951]

Judicial Branch

Federal courts handle cases questioning the constitutionality of laws, disputes between states or between states and the federal government, cases contesting laws and treaties of the nation, maritime laws, bankruptcy cases, and so forth.[952] The Supreme Court is the highest court and final arbiter of the constitutionality of a law. There are ninety-four district trial courts, and thirteen federal appeals courts below the Supreme Court. The ninety-four district courts are divided into twelve regional circuits, each with its own Court of Appeals with three sitting judges. There is also a Court of Appeals for the Federal Circuit which takes specialized cases, such as trade and patent laws. In addition, Bankruptcy Appellate Panels rule on cases heard by federal Bankruptcy Courts. (Both criminal and civil cases are handled by federal and state systems, but there may be specific courts to deal with particular problems such as bankruptcy, disability, domestic violence, mental health, drug use, traffic violations, etc.[953])

Inefficiency in federal and state judicial systems is manifest by delays in final adjudication of cases. Because cases may be settled before trial, judges may schedule multiple cases for the same time slots, assuming not all will go to trial. Then if more than one case needs to be tried, some have to be rescheduled. Time may also be needed for opposing attorneys to obtain information and depose witnesses. The interval between the start of a federal trial and the time an indictment was originally filed is often related to the intricacies and convolutions of a case. Another factor is choosing of a jury and how many potential jurors are disqualified by each side in the voir dire. (Failure of prosecutors to place African-Americans and Latinos on juries may be cause for an appeal.[954]) It is not unusual for start of a trial to take six months to a year.

Once a verdict is handed down by the jury, the losing or aggrieved party has thirty days to file an appeal.[955] For most cases, a federal appeal will require more than a year before final judgment. After the appeal is filed, a judge's clerk (an attorney or law student) will review it. While this is happening, the opposing party has thirty days to file a response. With the clerk's approval of the appeal, a hearing is scheduled, conducted by attorneys for the two sides. They present their arguments and then are questioned by the judges, who may decide to validate the original decision with damages to be paid or sentence confirmed. If the original verdict is overruled, a new judgment may be issued or a new trial ordered.

In special cases, further appeals by attorneys may take a case to the Supreme Court, if the Court is willing to accept it.[956]A petition for certiorari is filed with the Court, providing facts of the action, its history, and important legal issues. The opposing lawyer will likely enter a response. Parties with an interest may file a brief backing or opposing the petition. Supreme Court clerks will then review and summarize the data, recommending whether the action should be heard. The justices make the final decision. Only a small percentage of cases submitted are accepted, about eighty each year out of about ten thousand. The case must relate to an issue of federal law and be within the jurisdiction of the federal court system to be considered.

The legal process is particularly time-consuming and inefficient if a case goes to trial, made more so by a lack of judges on federal (and state) levels to handle cases in an expedited manner. The paucity of judges is because Congress and state legislatures do not wish to spend money on personnel to speed up the judicial process. In criminal cases, plea bargaining may take place, with prosecutors agreeing to charge the defendant with a less serious offense if he or she pleads guilty. This saves time and effort for the prosecutor and eliminates any possibility a jury might acquit the defendant. The defendant gains by pleading guilty because he or she stands to have a shorter prison sentence, fines, or other penalties if the crime is considered less serious.

If a plea bargain is not offered by the prosecutor or cannot be negotiated and a trial is necessary, the length of time required for any particular case is indeterminate. In addition to pre-trial depositions, there may be investigations needed and interviews of witnesses, so a while may elapse before a trial begins. Then its length depends on the case's complexity and number of witnesses. If a defendant is acquitted, the prosecution may find grounds for an appeal. If the defendant is found guilty, his or her lawyer may file an appeal. Acceptance of the appeal by the court adds further time for the case to be adjudicated.

To make the system more efficient, more judges are needed along with more prosecutors, more investigators, more Legal Aid Society attorneys, and an increase in fees paid to defense attorneys when defendants are destitute. Partisanship caused inordinate delays in confirmation of federal judges for open positions whose names were put forward by Obama.[957] As of November 2015, there were sixty-seven judicial vacancies in the federal courts, with nominees not acted upon by the GOP controlled Senate. There were not enough justices to begin with and the Senate's unwillingness to confirm judicial nominees because of partisan animus slowed the legal process even further. Trump's conservative nominees have been confirmed regularly by the Republican majority in the Senate, filling the open seats.

State court systems will not be discussed in depth. Needless to say, the states' legal system reflects its culture. For example, states may have restrictions on abortions and abortion clinics or not; speed limits on the roads vary; marijuana may be legal or allowed for medical reasons; guns may be carried in various places; stand your ground laws may be permissible, and so forth. There are also states like Delaware with a particularly business-friendly climate. However, whatever laws a state has enacted, they must be compatible with the Constitution.

An illustration of inefficiency of state court systems is the civil lawsuit brought by then New York Attorney General Eliot Spitzer in 2005 accusing Maurice Greenberg, former CEO of American International Group of accounting fraud.[958] As of August of 2015, the case was still not settled. (Andrew Cuomo and Eric Schneiderman followed Spitzer as New York attorney generals.) In 2014, the judge hearing the case, Charles Ramos, had frustratingly portrayed it as "a series of seemingly never-ending motions and appeals." Experts in litigation noted that the case was indicative of the way affluent defendants with top-notch lawyers can keep state attorneys at bay almost indefinitely, making a mockery of the legal system. David Boies, the head lawyer for the defense in this case, continuously found ways to delay trial and final decision, as Judge Ramos had ruled repeatedly against Greenberg. The S.E.C. had already fined Greenberg over the same issue and a class-action suit against him and another executive resulted in a $115 million settlement. The case was finally settled for $9.9 million after twelve years.

Boies was involved in a different case involving IBM that lasted even longer, and his wife participated in a price-fixing case that went on for fifteen years. The appeals process and the laws make inefficiency in the legal system almost inevitable, with defense lawyers paid more when cases last longer. A maxim ascribed to the British politician William Gladstone noted that "justice delayed is justice denied."[959] Though this is more evident for poor criminal suspects who cannot raise bail and who rot in jail, it is also true for civil plaintiffs in financial trouble needing restitution. Corporate lawyers may impede resolution of cases for years for various reasons.

In New York, the state has 175 days to bring felony suspects to trial.[960] Extensions can be granted to prosecutors for cause, extending the suspect's jail term for months to years. In a particularly egregious case, a juvenile named Kalief Browder spent three years in Riker's Correctional Institute on a felony robbery charge which he denied.[961] The prosecution delayed the trial numerous times, their one witness changing his story about the date of the robbery. Browder was markedly depressed, attempting suicide twice. Finally, 1,110 days after his arrest, on his 31st court date, the prosecution asked for a dismissal, knowing the burden of proof for conviction was lacking. The only witness could not be reached as he had returned to Mexico. Browder was released the next day, having served a three year sentence for no proven crime.

One must remember, as John Adams wrote in 1780, that America is supposed to have "a government of laws, not of men."[962] The fact the United States has been ruled by the same body of laws for over two hundred years, with some amendments whose passage has been arduous and infrequent, should be acclaimed, for it provides continuity of ideals and practices. Too frequent changes in the basic laws would be disorienting and confusing for the citizenry. As noted in The Federalist No. 62 written by Alexander Hamilton or James Madison- "It will be of little avail to the people, that the laws are made by men of their own choice, if the laws be so voluminous that they cannot be read, or so incoherent that they cannot be understood; if they be repealed or revised before they are promulgated, or undergo such incessant changes that no man, who knows what the law is today, can guess what it will be tomorrow."[963]

The inefficiencies of judicial systems in other democracies will be mentioned briefly. Those of Canada, Australia, and Western European nations are hobbled by similar problems as those in America. One advantage may be that most of these nations have the same code of laws throughout the country, instead of varied laws from province to province. Criminal cases may also come to trial more quickly in some of these countries, and rates of incarceration and length of sentences are less than the U.S. However, civil cases may also drag on through the court systems. In addition, there is the legal overlay of the European Union that must be considered in civil cases, as the losers may appeal to E.U. courts for relief. This may mean further delay, effort and funding to have these cases resolved.

The court systems of so-called democracies in the Middle East, Asia, and Africa besides being immensely inefficient are not equitable. Bribery, connections, religion, and tribal affiliations often determine how cases will be adjudicated. In a number of nations, judges pay to be appointed to the bench so they can collect bribes from defendants who come before them. In some districts of Muslim nations, Sharia law or tribal traditions may take precedence over the country's secular codes.[964] Women are not regarded as highly as men, and their testimony may not carry as much weight as men's. In Pakistan, Afghanistan, and other Muslim nations, vigilante justice often takes place on the streets when a person is accused of blasphemy, or desecration of the Koran.[965],[966] In India, extremist Hindus may lynch cow killers.

Japan, Taiwan, South Korea, and Singapore have modern legal systems with similar inefficiencies to those in the West. There are generally court hierarchies with supreme courts to finalize decisions.[967] South Korea, with a history of autocratic rulers and a relatively recent transition to democracy, has a court system still behind the curve in terms of protecting individual rights from government abuse and corporate interests.[968] Taiwan also was ruled by a single party with democracy taking hold about forty years ago. Because of this, there has been an overhang of autocratic conduct by judges and police brutality at times to extract confessions.[969]

In the executive, legislative, and judicial branches of all democratic nations, inefficiency is a major problem. Lack of knowledge by the electorate, who are uninformed about how their governments function and the positions of the officials they install in power, are responsible for much of the inefficiency that exists in all divisions of the government.

Inefficiencies in Government Financing

In America, financial boondoggles used by many states to kick the can down the road and dodge responsibility for debts is worthy of brief scrutiny. During 2009 and 2010, combined state sales, income, and corporate taxes dropped more than 10 percent.[970] In addition to diminished revenue due to the economic downturn, temporary gimmicks used to avoid tax increases or spending cuts, along with inadequate funding of public service employee pension plans, resulted in critical financial problems for a number of states. Many pension plans had shortfalls of tens of billions of dollars. Budgetary difficulties were not only on federal and state levels, but also involved dozens of municipal and county governments, highlighted by Detroit's bankruptcy.

The states' and municipalities' budget cuts and layoffs of public workers at that time heightened unemployment and prolonged the nation's economic pain. Educational systems were damaged by firing needed teachers, enlarging class sizes. While state and municipal officials could not have predicted the recession and drop in revenue, their reluctance to address past financial imbalances created many of the problems. Neither Republican nor Democratic leaders had been willing to make the hard choices necessary and talk to their constituents about requirements for higher taxes and reduced benefits to insure financial stability. This is further proof of inability of current political parties to govern responsibly. Decisions are made only in the face of emergencies, and even then ways are sought to delay the inevitable, solving immediate problems with trickery and artifice.

An outrageous incident related to financial difficulties occurred in Flint, Michigan, in state receivership from 2011 to 2015 and led by a state manager.[971],[972] To save money, the city was switched in April 2014 from its Detroit water supply to water from the Flint River. Within a short period, the poor, black residents began complaining that water had a funny taste. The state disregarded their concerns, even after testing raised questions about water quality. When bacteria were found in the water, chemical disinfectants were used that caused toxic contamination. Once that was resolved, residents still criticized the water. Eventually, pipes were discovered to have been corroded by the river water and increased levels of lead were in the water supply. Though the source was switched back to Detroit, Flint residents had dangerous amounts of lead in their bodies, which can cause brain and nerve damage, particularly in children.[973]

This event, endangering people's health and lives encompassed failure of government at all levels. That mainly minorities lived in Flint likely contributed to the inadequate response. Apparently, there were warnings to Republican Governor Rick Snyder of problems even before the water supply was switched, but those were ignored.[974] The state Department of Environmental Quality and federal Environmental Protection Agency also dropped the ball. Then, after the problems were identified, Republicans in Congress refused to appropriate adequate sums to mediate the trouble.[975] Subsequently, a number of other towns have found lead and other toxins in their water systems, as well as in paint in low-income housing.[976] In addition, at this time when drought is common, trillions of gallons of water are lost because of deterioration of reservoirs, pipes, and collecting systems for water.[977] And the longer repair is delayed, the more it will ultimately cost.

Nudges

The federal government under Obama worked with social and behavioral scientists to use small changes in interactions with citizens to try to make government more efficient.[978] These little 'nudges' are minor changes that get people to help themselves or the government. As an example, it was found Americans are more likely to enroll in 401(K) retirement plans when done automatically with opt out provisions, rather than having to opt in. This will make citizens more secure financially as they grow older. Some 'nudges' are opposed by one or the other political party depending what the objective is- for instance having people sign up for food stamps or enroll in Obamacare. The techniques, however, are employed by many corporate entities and should certainly be utilized if they can improve government efficiency and people's lives.[979]

Comparative Effectiveness

Members of legislative bodies and executives in democratic nations usually make decisions regarding policy and spending on ideological grounds or on the basis of how it will affect them politically. For the most part, solid data is not employed to determine efficacy of programs or how funds could maximize benefits of investments. If programs are effective and citizens feel they are getting their money's worth for the taxes they pay, less opposition can be expected to government spending. Of course, ideologues will continue to insist that many government activities can be handled better and less expensively by the private sector. However, as spending on medical care for older citizens through Medicare and Medicare Advantage have shown, this is not necessarily valid.[980] And employing private contractors to collect money from delinquent tax payers has been found to be more expensive and not as effective as utilizing I.R.S. personnel. Government programs and employees can be efficient and save money for taxpayers if programs are properly designed and responsibilities well defined. This is not always the case.

Moneyball For Government, a book published at the end of 2014 by a group of economists, politicians, and political scientists, puts forth prescriptions of how governments could use data to best spend funds and work more efficiently.[981] The model for this concept was the manner in which general manager Billy Beane of the Oakland Athletics baseball team produced a competitive crew year after year, able to win against organizations that generated more revenue and paid more for players. Employing data and statistics, Beane decided which ballplayers would help the Athletics at reasonable salaries, spending considerably less money than other teams and obtaining decent outcomes.[982] Why shouldn't governments be able to follow a similar strategy to cut costs and increase efficiency?

Peter Orszag (former director of the Congressional Budget Office) and John Bridgeland (former director, White House Domestic Policy Council, under George W. Bush), have calculated that "less than $1 out of every $100 of government spending is backed by even the most basic evidence that the money is being spent wisely."[983] Areas consuming the majority of government funds are health care, pensions, defense, welfare, and interest on the national debt.[984] Certainly, health care, defense, and welfare spending, and probably most expenditures (other than interest) can be regularly analyzed, employing specific metrics to determine where waste and inefficiencies exist, and then enact legislation to correct those problems.[985] However, though both parties claim they want government to be efficient and reduce waste, lawmakers are averse to legislate the small sums necessary to learn where money is well spent and where it is not.

Legislators are accustomed to renewing past programs almost automatically, employing intuition, partisan politics, personal rapport and friendships to decide on future programs and appropriations. They are afraid of diminished power if they depend on actual data to influence their choices, which may suggest eliminating programs or jobs they have supported. Prime examples of resistance to reliance on data were recommendations by the Defense Base Closure and Realignment Commission (BRAC) established by Congress. Five rounds of base closing ensued starting in 1988. BRAC concluded that various military installations were unnecessary and wasteful, but their proposals were ignored by Congress after several closings had occurred.[986] Over the years, members of Congress and Senators refused to follow BRAC's advice, as bases in their districts might be shut down and jobs lost.[987] In another illustration, money was cut from the Internal Revenue Service in 2014 and 2015, though data had shown that more funding for the IRS substantially increased government revenue.[988]

When dealing with social programs like welfare, social security, disability insurance, Workman's Compensation insurance, unemployment insurance, and so forth, it could be difficult to establish competing strategies to test efficacy. However, a minimum guaranteed income could replace many of the above programs, simplifying their administration and reducing the number of personnel necessary to run the programs. Government could be downsized if this worked. Running controlled studies on minimum guaranteed incomes versus some of these other arrangements over a period of several years could probably verify whether guaranteed incomes were efficacious and the way to go in the future. Both liberals and conservatives might be willing to support this controlled study for different reasons, with more efficient government resulting.

Comparative effectiveness studies focused on different aspects of government and programs in use or being considered are important to show taxpayers that government does care about cost and efficacy. The biggest hurdles for these studies are politicians concerned that jobs or money may be lost from their districts or states if programs are cut back or eliminated if shown to be inefficient or superfluous. However, politicians must decide whether they will keep mouthing platitudes about big government, excessive spending, and inefficiency, and do little or nothing about them, or whether they will take forceful action to see what policies work and are cost-effective. Informed voters would support these actions.

11

Whither Now

"In a democracy, enduring institutions depend upon the enduring support of ordinary citizens. And citizens are more likely to support those institutions they understand."
Justice Stephen Breyer[989]

AS SHOWN IN previous chapters, democracy is in trouble globally, its basic problem being uninformed or misinformed voters. This has led to the election of incompetent and venal officials, corruption, inefficiency, and partisanship, failing states and unhappy citizens. Automation and globalization have reduced jobs, with the working classes fearful of unemployment and feeling neglected by governments and the political establishment. Their anxiety has buoyed populism and nationalism in most democratic states with a number of autocrats gaining power. Citizens do not grasp the structure or function of their governments or the solutions offered by politicians. Of course, most politicians are infected with the virus of short-termism. They want to satisfy their constituents for the short term so they will be re-elected. Often, they are unwilling to spend money or increase taxes for projects that will not have an immediate impact but may generate future benefits for the nation and its citizens, when the politicians will no longer be running for office.

Promising pie in the sky, demagogues have taken advantage of voters' ignorance, citizens flocking to their banners, unaware they are being flimflammed. These demagogues ride the vehicles of nationalism and populism to ascend to power and possible autocratic rule. In fact, current developments cause countless people to wonder whether democracy is the proper political system for the twenty-first century or whether another form of government might be superior. Though enlightenment thinkers advocated freedom, tolerance, autonomy, and opportunity in democracies, and there was movement in that direction for a while, it seems as if reaction has now set in.

Fake news exacerbates unrest and disillusionment, some of it domestically produced and some originating from powers hostile to liberal democracy. In the Brazilian presidential election in 2018, right-wing ideologue Jair Bolsonaro was victorious, believed by some analysts to be due to fake information spread on social media, particularly WhatsApp owned by Facebook.[990] On a daily basis, Bolsonaro's adherents provided a flood of fake news and doctored photos that skewered the opposition and bolstered Bolsonaro on millions of cellphones. Of Brazil's 212 million citizens, 120 million use WhatsApp as an essential tool for communication. These text messages on WhatsApp were forwarded and re-forwarded millions of times, providing them with an increased aura of credibility.

Unfortunately, many politically uninformed citizens cannot distinguish between false and accurate information. Some turn only to sources that reinforce their biases and have been vetted by other members of their tribal cultures, the right and left unable to agree on the validity of facts. Even more politically sophisticated voters can be fooled by apparently factual data. To survive, democracy must be restructured to reduce the effects of political illiteracy and create more responsive and productive governments. And for democracy to work, the rule of law must be paramount, freedom of the press guaranteed along with freedom of speech. In addition, minority rights must be unquestionably protected.

As noted earlier, American democracy has some unique issues unrelated to uninformed voters that need to be addressed, with a system intentionally unfair to benefit particular political groups. Overwhelming partisanship in a number of states has caused gerrymandering of election districts or restricted the ability of some citizens to freely vote.[991] In addition, wealthy Americans spend unlimited funds to support candidates or parties espousing ideas congruent with their own. Lax laws and revolving doors allow former officials to become lobbyists, pushing bills and regulations that favor special interests. Right-wing propaganda has also made many Americans hostile to and afraid of government.

Though polls seem to show a preponderance of citizens backing progressive stances on many major issues (immigration, gun reform, health care, greater taxes on the wealthy, and so forth), the GOP controls the Senate and a majority of state governments and disregard citizens' wishes.[992] One reason is that fewer Americans who hold progressive positions vote. For instance, in the 2016 presidential election, millennials favored Clinton over Trump by a wide margin, but only 43 percent of them voted. Citizens over 65 backed Trump and 71 percent voted. Large numbers of ethnic citizens who supported Clinton also did not vote. Why progressives are less involved in the political process is unclear, but it may be partly because they believe their votes are insignificant given the avalanche of money that bolsters conservative candidates. There is also voter suppression and gerrymandering by Republican-controlled state governments that have disillusioned many progressives and have helped turn America from blue to red.[993]

The unusual aspects of the American political system that have made it unbalanced and unfair must be managed independently of initiatives to reduce the power of uninformed voters. Elections must be made impartial, discarding advantages for either party. If elections were truly equitable, many citizens wonder how Trump could have won the presidency with almost 3 million fewer votes than Hillary Clinton. A majority of Americans would like to see the popular vote determine the presidency and the Electoral College eliminated.[994]

No other democracy picks its leader in this blatantly unfair fashion[995] and it is the only office in the United States not chosen by popular vote.[996] In this system, small states have greater power than large states and the winner take all process makes voting unimportant in many states.[997] Currently, campaigning for president focuses on the swing states instead of the entire country which would change if the popular vote decided the victor. Many votes for president are devalued because of the Electoral College. There already is a movement attempting to negate the effect of the Electoral College called the National Popular Vote interstate compact.[998] States signing on have agreed to commit their electors to the winner of the overall popular vote when states with half of the nation's electoral votes are included. The movement is over 50 percent towards its objective but still needs additional states to agree. It is equitable and sensible, though many conservatives are opposed. Whether it will ever become a reality with the small rural states generally opposed is uncertain.

Gerrymandering must be eliminated as well and independent redistricting committees given power to redraw boundaries of congressional and legislative districts after each census. The issue is already before the Supreme Court and a group of Republicans as well as Democrats have filed briefs supporting the unconstitutionality of gerrymandering.[999] The Brennan Center for Justice estimates that Republicans currently hold 16-17 extra seats in the House because of gerrymandering.[1000] In addition to Congress, the GOP has taken over state legislatures by gerrymandering districts in their favor. If the Supreme Court does not abolish gerrymandering, a constitutional amendment will be necessary, which is unlikely. However, individual states could also eliminate gerrymandering through referenda.

Voter restrictions with ID laws that create hindrances for older people, minorities, and students must also be ended, making it easier to register and vote. States should have extended voting hours and more days to vote, mail-in ballots, and possibly Internet voting at home in the future using unique identifiers. States that suppress voters are restricting democracy for partisan reasons, all through legislatures controlled by Republicans. These laws are also being contested in the courts and a number of them have been overturned. Some analysts believe, however, that voter suppression is less of a problem than citizens who are able to vote not going to the polls.[1001] There were 231 million eligible voters in 2016 and 49.6 percent did not vote, many of them not even registered.

The length of campaigns for elected office should also be shortened and the power of money in politics curbed. Whether by legislation or constitutional amendment, Citizens United and the McCutcheon decisions must be overturned and restraints on spending reinstituted. According to a Pew Research Center poll in May 2018, 77 percent of Americans across party lines want limits on campaign spending.[1002] Almost three quarters of the citizenry do not want major donors to have increased political influence. Freedom of speech cannot be employed as a rationale to allow affluent citizens to control the elective process and have their ideas become the law of the land. American democracy is becoming a plutocracy and citizens must push back to make money less of a factor in elections.

The revolving door between elected officials, their staffers, and lobbying firms must be jammed as well, prohibiting these people from becoming lobbyists for a lengthy period, perhaps five years after leaving an office or staff positions. They should also be forbidden from joining corporations, industry groups or special interests if they sponsored or supported legislation benefitting the particular interest. These rules can be bypassed for non-profits.

Other changes are also needed in American democracy to improve its functioning and efficiency, but constitutional amendments would be required for these to become law. First of all, Supreme Court appointments (and other federal judgeships) should be limited to below twenty years, rather than a lifetime. Average life expectancy has more than doubled since the eighteenth century and tenure on the Court can last forty or more years, rather than the ten to twenty expected when the Constitution was written. Some analysts have suggested eighteen year terms for the nine justices, with appointments staggered to guarantee continuity. If a Justice's term is limited, the president and Senate can reappoint him or her when the term is over, but there should be some check on justices. Having a lengthy term should protect them from political pressure in their decisions, though their ideologies will still guide them.

Consideration should also be given to increasing the number of federal justices including those on the Supreme Court to handle more cases. While the population of the United States has exploded in the last century and a half, the number of Supreme Court Justices has remained at nine. The conservative majority on the Court at the end of 2019 included five justices who were appointed by presidents who gained office with a minority of the popular vote. And they were confirmed by Senate Republicans who represented a minority of the overall population.

There are some people and groups in the United States who would question the legitimacy of these appointments and the decisions they make. As an illustration of possible illegitimacy, after the Republican Senate refused to consider Obama candidate, Merrick Garland, for the Court, they confirmed Neil Gorsuch by a majority of Senators, 51 Republicans and 3 Democrats.[1003] However, the confirming Senators had only received 54 million votes when they were elected. The 45 Democrats who opposed Gorsuch received 73.4 million votes in their elections, an almost 20 million vote difference. And Trump, the president who nominated Gorsuch, lost the popular vote by almost 3 million. Was this process equitable?

Another suggestion for making the Court appointments more equitable would not require a constitutional amendment but the approval of Congress and the president. This would be to have every president nominate two candidates to the Court during each four year term.[1004] If the candidate was rejected by the Senate, the president would continue to put forth candidates until two were approved. With this method, the number of justices on the Court might fluctuate between seven and fourteen according to past data. But every president would have an equal opportunity to put his or her mark on the Court.

The number of justices previously has varied between five and ten and other smaller nations have more justices on their top courts than the U.S. does.

Another worthwhile change would be to increase the terms of members of Congress from two to three years. This would make fundraising less onerous and more time could be spent on legislating, committee work, and so forth. Whether to have term limits is an open question as it takes a while for new officials to learn the ins and outs of Washington. But five terms of three years for members of Congress seems reasonable along with three six-year terms for Senators. The number of members of Congress should also be expanded.[1005] The framers of the Constitution expected a Representative to have about 30,000 constituents. In 1911 the size of the House was established at 435, with one Representative having about 200,000 constituents. The number is now about 750,000 per member of Congress which makes it impossible for that person to stay on top of the needs of those in his or her district. Having one representative for every 30,000 citizens or even every 200,000 would make it far too unwieldy. However, many democracies have representative bodies that are approximately the cube root of the nation's population. That would add 158 members to Congress which would put the total at 593, which is quite reasonable.

Greater balance should also be considered to improve Senate representation. States that are more populous like California and Texas should have three or four Senators, instead of two. The difficulty with this concept is in devising a formula that would satisfy most states. But to have two Senators represent Wyoming with less than 600,000 residents and California with nearly forty million is not equitable. Obviously, the Senate is not the House, but some adjustments should be made to reduce the disproportionate power of less populous states and rural citizens. (Seventy percent of Americans live in metropolitan areas of 500,000 or more.[1006]) Though America is mainly an urban nation, in voting for Senators, one vote in Wyoming is worth more than sixty in California. It is unlikely the Founders or the creators of the XVII Amendment (direct election of senators) foresaw the degree of imbalance and unfairness that would evolve in Senatorial elections. Control of the Senate also has repercussions for confirmation of Supreme Court nominees, with the Court now majority conservative.

Taking the last three cycles of voting which elected all of the current Senators, the Democrats won 4.5 million votes more than their GOP counterparts.[1007] On average, each Democrat received about 30 percent more votes than their Republican colleagues. In the election of 2018, Democratic candidates received 45 million votes compared to 33 million for Republicans- 57 percent to 42 percent.[1008] Nevertheless, the GOP gained three seats. The Senate's party makeup in 2019 consists of 53 Republicans and 45 Democrats with two Independents who caucus with the Democrats. Political analysis reveals that GOP biases in both the Senate and the House elections are higher than at any previous time. White men, who constitute about a quarter of the population, overwhelmingly support Trump and Republicans. And their support elected Trump in 2016 and gave Republicans control of the Senate in 2018.

Barring an overwhelming blue wave election, it may be difficult for the Democrats to gain a majority in the Senate as the rural red states with mainly white populations will continue to back conservative GOP candidates for the Senate unless the format is changed.[1009] Though the population of the United States votes more Democratic than Republican, the Senate "is poised to serve as a reactionary rural veto on a center-left country, routinely thwarting efforts to address major issues such as immigration, climate change, the national debt, health care, international cooperation and wealth inequality."[1010] Filling judicial appointments and staff positions may also become increasingly difficult, as evidenced by the refusal of GOP Senators to vet Merrick Garland, an Obama nominee. The judiciary might turn even more politicized and conservative. For the United States to compete effectively in a complex world, government needs trained technocrats who make decisions on the basis of facts and Senators who will confirm them.

Future elections will heighten the anti-democratic tenor of the Senate as the distribution of the population changes.[1011] According to projections of the Weldon Cooper Center for Public Service of the University of Virginia, eight states will have almost half the population of the country by 2040. An additional fifth of the population will be in the next eight most populous states indicating nearly seventy percent of Americans will live in only sixteen states. Thus, 30 percent of Americans will control 68 percent of Senate seats. Given the concentration of the population in sixteen states, the remaining thirty-four states will be more rural, older and culturally different than their urban counterparts. Their Senators will be able to pass any laws and overcome any filibusters. The House will be much more representative of the population. To make government fairer, the composition of the Senate should be adjusted as previously mentioned. However, will the smaller rural states cede some of the power they have to make the political system more equitable?

A Pew poll in April of 2018 had 61 percent of respondents saying that "significant changes are needed in the fundamental design and structure of the American government to make it work better for current times."[1012] Though there is agreement that change is required, no proposals received bipartisan support. At present, a majority of citizens vetoed the idea of amending the Constitution to provide larger states with more Senate seats and there was little backing for enlarging the House of Representatives. Hopefully, that will change in the future as citizens recognize the inequity. There was support as before, however, (55 percent) for having the president elected by the majority of the population rather than through the Electoral College.

There are three other issues that merit study not involved with governmental processes or structure. One controversial proposal is having Universal National Service of a year or eighteen months for everyone between the ages of eighteen and thirty with reinstatement of the draft. This would provide citizens with greater understanding regarding America, would mix different classes and races, would have everyone give something back to the country, and would increase patriotism. National Service inductees could volunteer for the military, serve as auxiliary police, function as orderlies in hospitals, toil in the national parks, work for municipal or state governments, clean up the beaches, work as teacher's aides, and so forth. There is no reason for soldiers fighting the nation's wars to come overwhelmingly from impoverished backgrounds and National Service might provide a more diverse military by wealth and class and a shared obligation. If the draft had remained in place, the question arises whether we would have been fighting in Iraq and Afghanistan in such prolonged wars.[1013]

National Service could be deferred for students attending college or professional school and doctors, nurses, physician's aides, etc, could serve after their training. They could work in local health clinics or rural towns lacking medical personnel, or the armed forces. Lawyers could work for local governments or non-profits that help impoverished people. Teachers could teach in underperforming schools for a period. Americans are becoming too isolated in gated communities or particular neighborhoods and mixing young people and demanding service would be a valuable lesson for them and the nation. John Kennedy's inaugural words stand out- "Ask not what your country can do for you but what you can do for your country."

Another idea that will need to be considered in the near future is a universal guaranteed income. The world is reaching a point where work will soon be limited for many people because of automation and robots. Mass unemployment is just around the corner, suggested by Stephen Hawking, Bill Gates and Elon Musk.[1014] Evidence is already accumulating that robots are taking jobs and wages are falling because of them.[1015] However, people need an income to live in a modern society, whether they work full time, part time, or not at all. The consumer is also an important component of the capitalist system and needs to have money to spend. If the government provided everyone with a basic income, programs like unemployment insurance, Social Security, and so forth, could be cut, reducing the number of government employees and shrinking the size of government. This should be a program both the right and left could support, and indeed analysts from both sides of the aisle have been considering it.[1016] The question is where would the revenue come from? Bill Gates suggested taxing robotic workers and automated systems that perform the jobs humans once did.[1017] But in all likelihood, taxes on the rich would also have to be raised.

A futurist, Ray Kurzwell, who is chief engineer at Google has developed a thesis labeled The Law of Accelerating Returns.[1018] He believes that with computers and artificial intelligence, knowledge will expand exponentially rather than linearly as with human thinking. Moore's Law predicts that the number of transistors incorporated into computer chips will double every eighteen months. This is used as an example of accelerating returns. While this may be good for overall progress, it bodes ill for human employment, as computers and robots will be able to do more and more work that humans now do. Productivity will rise and hopefully this will be enough to support a basic universal income. But the growth in productivity should not just benefit the top 1 percent on the economic ladder, but should be distributed more equitably.

The third issue that needs to be addressed is the vast gulf of economic inequality between the top 0.01 percent and the bottom 99 percent. Dynastic wealth will lead to increasing oligarchy, with the mega-rich controlling society's political, social, and economic structures. The power of this group must somehow be curbed to allow advancement on the basis of merit rather than money. A democratic society should provide as much equality of opportunity as possible for its citizens. If economic inequality continues to grow, it will cause a social explosion at some point.

Ray Dalio, the CEO and Chief Investment Officer of Bridgewater Associates, one of the world's largest hedge funds, wrote an essay in April 2019 on reforming capitalism, concerned that the degree of inequality was going to destroy the system.[1019] Growing up in a middle class family in the United States, he became a billionaire but is unhappy with the way capitalism has evolved. Though he believes capitalism is an effective motivator for people and a good allocator of resources, it is not successful for the majority of Americans, with widening economic disparities between the haves and have-nots. There has not been significant growth in personal or family wealth since the 1970s for most of the population while it has skyrocketed for the top 1 percent. The bottom 60 percent can actually be considered poor. Economic mobility for the most part is a myth and many impoverished children are malnourished and poorly educated, their futures bleak. Family support for academic achievement is lacking.

To change the current situation, there must be more focus on educating those having difficulty with school, offering incentives and support to keep them from abandoning education.[1020] Much more money must be spent on teacher's salaries and on the worst performing school districts, making teaching a more attractive profession to improve its quality. Governments at all levels must also make certain that all children are receiving healthy, well-balanced diets, for one cannot learn and function well if one is malnourished. These changes, of course, will require higher taxes on the wealthiest citizens, needed to keep society vibrant and innovative, allowing those from the lower economic strata to reach their potential and benefit the nation. While affluent citizens may resist higher taxes, they are necessary for America to progress to a more equal, successful, and conflict free society. As Dalio says- "capitalists typically don't know how to divide the pie well and socialists typically don't know how to grow it well."

Because of the degree of inequality, populism is arising on the right and the left, and a future economic crisis could lead to a major confrontation. Working now to diminish inequality and increase optimism about the future by less affluent citizens could prevent open conflict. The pursuit of profit and efficiency by capitalists and capitalist companies must not cause further damage to those at the bottom rungs of the economic ladder. Otherwise, the ladder will be pulled out from under those entitled individuals on the higher rungs with the whole of society affected. The share of the economic pie that goes to the working and middle classes must be made more equitable.

Though President Trump denies the existence of global warming, it is still a reality and hopefully future American governments will aggressively work to lower carbon emissions and other greenhouse gases. This must be done if the world as we know it is to survive. And to keep the nation's economy strong, more federal funds must be devoted to research and development, and education from K-12 with a core curriculum and proficiency testing. If government efficiency, corruption and partisanship could be reduced by educating uninformed voters, more could be done to make citizens' lives happier and more fulfilling.

For the most part, uninformed citizens are not stupid. In general, ignorant or misinformed voters do not care about politics or believe the cost of obtaining political knowledge is greater than the potential benefits, and are not willing to spend the time or effort to learn about candidates and issues. The basic question in terms of the continuance and success of liberal democracy is how to entice voters to acquire the necessary information about candidates and issues before they cast their ballots in elections. How can this process be transformed in a way that makes citizens pursue political knowledge? It seems like an impossible task given that some individuals have not had the intellectual capacity, or the grit and fortitude to finish high school or seek further education, the key to earning power and lifestyle. In addition to diminished perseverance or cognitive ability, a certain percentage of the voting-age population is drug or alcohol dependent, mentally ill, with various learning disabilities, and other impairments. No matter what type of programs were initiated, these individuals would be unable to gain or retain the required information. Any mechanism used to modify democracy must take this into account.

However, democracy must evolve in an actively changing world, where the Internet, computers, and social media play a role in everyone's life. With news and information sites proliferating, cable news and television programs bloviating day and night, individuals must be able to differentiate between real and fake news, blocking out 'alternative facts.' A certain intellectual level will be required to be able to shed the cloak of political illiteracy: to know what is real and what is fantasy. The real world itself is increasingly convoluted, becoming more so every day, the flood of data overwhelming. Time to investigate and analyze news and information is needed, with many people already drowning in responsibilities and having little time to spare. And for others, entertainment of various sorts takes precedence. Still, if democracy is to survive and thrive, it is incumbent upon citizens to learn about the candidates and issues, including both sides of every question and the views of those whom they oppose.

In addition to populism and nationalism orienting democratic nations away from freedom of speech, a free press, freedom of assembly, and freedom of religion, demagogues attain power by scape-goating minorities and blaming the elites for existing problems. Those who are politically uninformed may accept the pledges of these demagogues of better lives for everyone, with more jobs, higher wages, lower taxes, and stronger safety nets. But it may not be clear how these goals will be accomplished and where the funding will be found. Knowledgeable voters ask these questions and expect answers before voting for these candidates, while the politically uninformed may take the statements at face value and become converts. In politics as in economics and life in general, if something seems too good to be true it usually is. But if people want to believe something, it may be hard to dissuade them. Emotions, particularly anger and rage, may be stronger drivers of support for candidates than reason and facts, especially if the latter are disputed.

Tony Blair has been quoted as saying- "The single hardest thing for a practicing politician to understand is that most people, most of the time, don't give politics a first thought all day long. Or if they do, it is with a sigh....before going back to worrying about the kids, the parents, the mortgage, the boss, their friends, their weight, their health, sex and rock 'n roll.... For most normal people, politics is a distant, occasionally irritating fog."[1021] However, some citizens in democracies now appear to be playing a greater role in politics, perhaps out of fear.

They are afraid of losing their jobs, unemployment compensation, health care, Social Security, and so forth, and are angry about the degree of inequality in society. Yet, despite activists pushing for change, the great mass of people seem indifferent to much of politics.

After the fall of the Soviet Union in 1989, it appeared that Western liberal democracy was going to be the way of the world.[1022]America was the hegemon that would guarantee the dominance of this system. However, populism, the growth of autocracies, and Trump's victory, have changed the world's calculus, threatening the disruption of alliances, reducing free trade, and disengaging the United States from the world to a large degree. And populism has not only engulfed Europe, but has crossed the Atlantic and swallowed America. The anger of the working class toward the affluent and the lack of shared prosperity propelled Trump and other populists forward, upsetting the ship of democracy. Workers' income has been curbed by less bargaining power, the result of crumbling unions, globalization and automation, making inequality more conspicuous. And the wealthy have been unwilling to part with any portion of their riches, even to promote social tranquility.

Workers see themselves as victims of an unfair economic system, blaming the political and financial elites for their circumstances, rather than castigating themselves for a paucity of education, or drug or alcohol dependence. Establishment institutions are all faulted for the lack of decent jobs and reasonable wages. According to the narrative of the populists, immigration and globalization have made the elites richer, while robbing many workers of employment. At the same time, the liberalization of abortion laws and same-sex marriage have ignored religious Americans and their views on what is proper. And white workers and rural Americans are concerned their guns will be taken if Democrats gain control of the government, convinced by the NRA, the gun lobby, and right-wing politicians. One can see the many reasons why discontent has flourished among uneducated workers. It is no wonder they supported a flawed candidate whose words resonated with them, who promised jobs as they dismissed his misogyny and sexual predation, his racism, narcissism and braggadocio, his hyperbole and frank lies. He gave vent to their anger unconstrained by political correctness. At least it was possible he would bring some change.

When democracies are analyzed, differences in perspectives and expectations regarding the role of government between Europeans and Americans become more evident. Undoubtedly, these contrasts reflect history: the way democracy was instituted in European states emerging from feudalism and monarchy or fascism, and was created in America by citizens who considered themselves free men. Protection of individual rights is more critical in America than European nations.[1023] Americans believe they control their own destinies and success is achieved by merit if people work hard. For Americans, individual liberty is vital, while Europeans require the state to guarantee that everyone has his or her basic needs met. The community is more crucial than the individual in European democracies. Offensive speech is tolerated to a greater degree in the U.S. than in Europe, and Europeans are more secular and less religious than Americans. These disparities have shaped European nations and America differently in terms of laws and norms. Still, freedom is freedom, a universal value that transcends time and place.

There are alternative forms of government now challenging Western enlightenment concepts of democracy that may appear more appealing to these who are downtrodden, naïve and unsophisticated politically. The totalitarian system of China has rapidly raised the standard of living in a third world country, utilizing a mix of centralized control of the economy with overt capitalism. However, every aspect of life in China is under the thumb of the Communist Party, with information and the Internet closed to free intercourse. Demonstrations protesting party policies are banned, private property may be appropriated by the state, and the rule of law is lacking. Courts decide cases on the basis of Communist directives rather than what is fair and just. And even discussions of democracy and freedom, or Western values and human rights, can lead to arrest. The Communist Party claims democracy inevitably causes chaos and conflicts and only an authoritarian system is capable of creating and maintaining peace and prosperity. But Xi and the ruling class is afraid to let the people choose how they want to be governed. And with Xi becoming China's president for life in February 2018 any hope for freedom was crushed.[1024]

The Russian model of autocracy arose from a transient democratic state, with the people placing a single strong man in charge to make all the important decisions for the country. Certain nations want and are accustomed to a strong leader and citizens may be willing to allow that person to dictate to them how their lives should be conducted. This may be associated with religious belief as in Iran, Turkey, and Saudi Arabia, or may be comfortable for the citizenry because of a nation's history, as in Russia and Belarus.

The year 2016 was not a good year for democracy, given Brexit and the election of Dutarte in the Philippines. However, the ascension of Trump to the U.S. presidency was the worst blow of all. Aside from these elections, the unspoken standards underpinning American democracy were further shattered in 2016 by the hammer of partisanship, the GOP placing power above allegiance to the nation and to democracy.[1025] Perhaps it started in the Senate where Republicans refused to consider or confirm Merrick Garland, a well-qualified candidate for the Supreme Court because he was suggested by Obama. Then there was Trump pledging to jail his opponent if he won and claiming he would not accept the outcome of the election if he lost because it was rigged. In addition, there was Russian interference in the democratic process, and Comey and the FBI playing a role in the election instead of trying to avoid affecting the results.

Obama may have violated democratic traditions with his executive orders on DACA, bank regulations, consumer protection, and immigration, but the GOP had previously threatened to shut down the government, threatened to default on the national debt, would not fill judicial and federal agency positions, and were responsible for nominating Trump in the first place. How could American voters have supported the Republican Party after all their actions infringing on the mechanisms of democracy? The only answer is that voters were politically uninformed.

Liberal Western democracy has been under severe pressure during recent decades, both from populism and nationalism within and imposed autocracies. Numerous states that were once democracies are now ruled by autocrats, chosen by supposedly free (but politically uninformed) electorates. It should be emphasized again that voters installed these autocrats in the seats of government in the first place and the officials then used their power to gain further control. However, restoration of freedom in these countries will not be an easy task, particularly since only a minority of the population seems concerned by what has happened. The only way to prevent a transition from democracy to autocracy is to have policies and candidates selected by voters who are politically knowledgeable when they cast their ballots.

Some social scientists believe that there are ingrained authoritarian voters who regularly support populist and nationalist candidates.[1026] These are citizens who want a strong man as leader who sets the rules for everyone. Law and order with a structured life is most important, and immigration to their countries is deplored. These citizens are determined to have a nation's population that is ethnically similar to them rather than to have diversity, with cultural, racial and religious differences that are unfamiliar and frightening. What percentage of the population fits the label of fixed authoritarian voter? And is it genetic in origin, learned behavior, or both?

Democracy is not performing as envisioned by the philosophers who believed universal suffrage would produce the optimum political system. What can be done to make it work better? How can the mass of voters be encouraged to become more astute, attentive, and caring about politics and government? Are small adjustments needed in the way government officials are chosen, or is a major overhaul of the process required? Various solutions will be discussed.

Education and the Politically Uninformed

Education is considered the answer to ignorance of any sort and political analysts saw education as necessary to provide people with information regarding the operation of their governments and to comprehend their responsibilities in a democratic state. John Stuart Mill noted in *Considerations on Representative Government-* "Universal teaching must precede universal enfranchisement," understanding that citizens must have a basic level of knowledge before being allowed to vote.[1027] And government aid for education through the years has been at least partially to develop a politically aware electorate. Civics was taught in the public schools to transmit information about how the political system worked to those who might soon be voting.

Unfortunately, heightened levels of education have not enhanced political insight.[1028] Though those who are highly educated appear to possess greater information about politics than the average citizen, additional years of education for the populace has not resulted in a burgeoning of political enlightenment, nor an apparent desire to learn more. Between 1972 and 1994, Americans over the age of thirty went from having an average of eleven years of education to thirteen, with measurements of political acumen basically unchanged.[1029] The reason for this failure is unclear. Perhaps citizens do not take advantage of opportunities to acquire political information because there is not enough personal benefit for them in doing so. Thus, the possibility that education alone will increase political acumen in the future is questionable.

However, schools have not been focusing enough on civics and history.[1030] Prior to the 1960s, students were generally required to take three courses in civics and government before leaving high school. Now, few states expect students to be knowledgeable in civics before graduating, though a report by the Educational Testing Service revealed that civics courses in the 8th and 12th grades were almost universal.[1031] But only around one fourth of students in the 4th, 8th, and 12th grades achieve test scores at or above proficiency in civics. This dearth of civic knowledge has repercussions for democracy. Less than half of citizens age 18-24 vote, while three quarters of those 55-74 cast ballots. And those who are less informed about civics are less likely to participate in community affairs and voting in the future.

Could the schools change their curriculum to provide greater instruction regarding politics and government so that students would become politically knowledgeable? Though civics, history, and government should be emphasized, politics is another story. It raises the question of indoctrination by teachers, as there would be subjectivity and possible bias in political discussions, conscious or not. It is also likely that information taught in high school would not be retained over a person's lifetime without episodic re-learning, which would necessitate self-education and the motivation to do so. Currently, most Americans do not know basic facts about the organization of their government and the nation's history.

Studies have found, however, that civic education if properly presented does influence the acquisition of political knowledge.[1032] Lectures and textbook utilization in civics can have a positive impact on learning information about political parties and processes. Discussing current events as well as classroom and community activities can be effective stimuli for students obtaining political insight. But the fact of the matter is that students now are not receiving adequate civics education, as the level of political illiteracy in the U.S. is astounding.

Current citizens given the tests required for new citizenship applicants did quite poorly compared to immigrants wanting to become citizens.[1033] Of one hundred possible questions, applicants had to answer six of ten questions correctly in order to pass–97.5 percent of immigrants were successful. On the other hand, one of three citizens failed, and if seven of ten correct answers had been required to pass, half of all citizens would fail. 85 percent did not know the meaning of 'the rule of law,' 82 percent could not name two rights in the Declaration of Independence, 75 percent did not know what the judiciary branch did, 68 percent did not know the number of justices on the Supreme Court, and 63 percent could not name one of their two U.S. senators.

If political information were taught in the schools, local, state, or the federal government may have set ideas about how this should be presented to students. This is already so in many states and localities where students are indoctrinated in certain concepts those in power favor. For example, the teaching of sexual, moral, and religious principles, patriotism and nationalism often reflect the state government's perspective in addition to the subjective leaning of teachers. Teaching of evolution and creationism, environmentalism and climate change, produces conflict in many school districts. Pressure groups outside of government may also influence school boards on local or state levels to have subjects taught with a particular emphasis. Even school textbooks on history are different in conservative and liberal states.

Voluntary adult education courses to refresh knowledge about government and its workings might be worthwhile for citizens wanting to recall information forgotten or never learned. Depending on demand, these courses could be scheduled regularly or just before elections. But civics and government should be taught first in K-12.

Interestingly, a group of Rhode Island high school students and parents are suing the state in federal court for a failure to teach students to prepare for citizenship, claiming that this deficiency violates their Constitutional rights.[1034] Social studies courses often focus on history, with little attention paid to civics, government or economics. The suit states that the Rhode Island school systems did not give all students the knowledge to function properly as citizens, being able to vote, serve on a jury, or understand the nation's political system. Nationally, both political parties are concerned about a lack of civic engagement and skills in young people, with low voter participation and an inability to discern false information on social media. Less than a quarter of eighth grade students throughout the country were proficient in civics on standard testing in 2014, reinforcing the fact that there will be problems later on.

Deliberation Day

Two political scientists, Bruce Ackerman and James Fishkin, have suggested that political knowledge could be increased by having a public holiday called Deliberation Day prior to presidential elections.[1035] On this holiday, Americans would gather in public spaces in large groups throughout the country to participate in structured debates about the positions of the candidates. Ackerman and Fishkin propose that each person who attended these meetings be given a stipend of $150 by the government. While this concept is certainly unusual, it would not work. You can lead a horse to water, etc, etc. And lawmakers would not be attracted to an idea that did not benefit them and would require considerable government spending. Deliberation Day does not seem to warrant further attention.

Restricting the Franchise

Another approach to the lack of political information would be to restrict the franchise, transferring power to citizens who are politically knowledgeable.[1036] The difficulty with this is determining who is informed and measuring it accurately. And is it fair? (This will be discussed in the section on Weighted Democracy.) The Founding Fathers limited the franchise to property holders or taxpayers in a republic rather than a democracy. But possessing property does not necessarily produce politically learned citizens or those who keep society's interests foremost. Restricting the franchise to college graduates or educated citizens might encompass a large segment of the population who were politically enlightened, but some in this group would not be, and some outside might be better informed regarding politics. Thus, using education as a marker of a citizen's political knowledge does not appear valid. Political theorists in the past, including John Stuart Mill, have suggested giving educated citizens more votes as a way of improving democracy. However, it is unlikely that citizens would be willing to surrender the franchise, or give those with more education more votes. And in America and other democracies, there is a bias against elites that would prevent restricting the franchise.

Transferring Power

Transferring power to unelected technocratic bodies of experts not controlled by politically deficient voters is another way that might improve government function. Agencies such as the Federal Reserve Board, the SEC, the EPA, the FDA, and some courts all play vital roles in making government operate efficiently. Experts in specific fields are responsible for formulating policies and acting upon them, rather than elected officials chosen by politically unenlightened voters. Elected officeholders may lack necessary knowledge, or may be totally incompetent aside from raising campaign funds and bonding with voters. Appointees to the courts, Federal Reserve and other agencies may have lengthy terms making them impervious to political pressure to a large degree, allowing them to do their jobs as they see fit.

However, members of the courts and government agencies may make mistakes in their policies and actions, no matter their level of experience and expertise. And there may be no oversight or accountability. These appointed experts have powers the public or their representatives are unable to contest or reverse. And judicial review of legislation may be influenced by a justice's political leanings, overturning or ratifying laws because of personal beliefs. The members of the boards of federal agencies may also make decisions reflecting partisan positions. After all, federal judges and high ranking officials of federal agencies were recommended by politicians prior to confirmation and are members of political parties. Also, deferring to experts to have a more efficient government and to have better decisions made, defeats the idea of democracy.

On the other hand, officials elected by politically uninformed voters may challenge the findings and solutions offered by experts in government agencies because the officeholders refuse to believe scientific data. This confrontation is being currently played out with members of Congress, Senators, and President Donald Trump who are denying the reality of global warming. Government agencies, including NASA, the Energy Department, NOAA, the EPA, the National Academy of Sciences, and multiple scientific bodies and government agencies have repeatedly demonstrated global warming as valid. The overwhelming consensus is that climate change is driven by human activity and presents a threat to the survival of mankind.[1037]

However, Trump still refuses to acknowledge global warming is real, ascribing it originally to a Chinese hoax to injure the American economy. And many other elected officials also reject climate change, related to religious beliefs or contributions from fossil fuel companies. So here we have experts saying vital scientific data is valid and officials elected by uninformed voters refusing to accept their findings. There are also some officeholders, including Trump, who reject scientific evidence that vaccinations do not cause autism or other disorders, and do not grasp why vaccinations should be mandatory to prevent communicable diseases. Fluoridation of the water supply to improve dental health was a matter of contention in the past that some citizens still cannot accept, thought by some right-wingers to be a Communist plot.

The Media and Improved Political Literacy

The media could be employed to increase citizens' political knowledge and interest in elections. Stations and networks could accept voluntary guidelines or legislation by Congress to change programming on radio and television for a few hours weekly to focus on politics and government operations. In addition, newspapers could provide necessary information. Though television and radio are corporate or private enterprises, they still operate on licensing from the government that allows them to use a portion of the radio frequency spectrum to broadcast. According to FCC rules, time must be regularly allotted for public service programming. Thus, the government could require television and radio broadcasters to devote a portion of air time to programs focusing on political information and civics for them to maintain their licenses. The time designated for political issues could be increased in the weeks or months preceding elections. However, that does not mean uninformed citizens would watch the programs earmarked for them if there were alternatives available in terms of entertainment, sports, movies and so forth. In addition, the Internet would be open to distract citizens.

And these programs on television or radio, or newspaper reports to help citizens learn about politics would have to be non-partisan, not skewing politics in a particular direction or promoting specific ideologies. One must remember that television and radio news and political discussions, including on cable outlets, have been around now for several decades, with some of the stations and networks covering politics 24/7. This has not improved political literacy, as these programs do not draw large segments of the population.

Networks and stations presenting politics in a partisan light also have greater appeal to the public than those that approach politics in an unbiased fashion. National Public Radio, public television programs and C-Span do not attract the numbers listening to Rush Limbaugh on radio, or watching the Fox Network or MSNBC on television. No authority can force citizens to tune to programs that would educate them about government and politics. Newspapers, television, and radio are all profit-making enterprises that have been losing eyeballs to the Internet in recent years, where many citizens now learn about politics. Much of the information is aggregated on social media, where fake news may be mixed in and the accuracy of information is variable. While hypothetically, the media could reduce political ignorance with interesting programming, in practice it would not work, as people freely choose what they want to listen to and watch. Motivation to learn about politics and government has to come from citizens, though government could provide incentives for citizens to learn.

Parliamentary versus Presidential System

Does it make a difference whether a democracy is structured as a parliamentary or presidential system in terms of political knowledge of the populace and the ease of transforming the state into an autocracy? From a practical standpoint, it does not seem to matter. Populism and nationalism can dominate politics in any nation, initiated by the grass roots or from the top down. A charismatic politician who trumpets populism and nationalism can easily develop a following if conditions are right. Given the ubiquity of the Internet and social media, his or her words can thrust this person into a position of leadership in a provincial or national government. That can be the first step on the road to autocracy.

Though it would seem that a presidential system of governance would be easier to change to autocratic rule, as a single figure already has a commanding status, this is not necessarily the case. Putin gained control of all the levers of power in Russia to make certain his party, United Russia, dominated the parliament (Duma) and backed all his actions.[1038] In reality, it is a puppet parliament where the members, ministers, and prime minister are all in thrall to Putin. Turkey was a parliamentary democracy when Erdogan decided he wanted more power through a strong presidency.[1039] He subsequently arranged to amend the Constitution which was approved by parliament and passed in a national referendum. This gave Erdogan complete control of Turkey, turning it into a dictatorship. The office of prime minister was abolished and the president allowed to appoint all the members of the cabinet, parliamentary oversight eliminated.

Politically uninformed voters played a large role in the loss of democracy in Russia and Turkey, but were not the only feature. Some politically sophisticated citizens also voted to remove democratic safeguards and checks on the power of the presidents because they wanted strong leaders who they believed would make their nations powerful and respected. However, once democratic safeguards are abandoned, they will not be easily reinstated if citizens are unhappy

with the direction of the country. With an autocratic leader controlling the media, the Internet, and all the elements of social intercourse,
the people will have difficulty taking back power once it has been
surrendered.

Compulsory Voting

To increase voter turnout with the hope that more citizens will educate themselves about the issues and candidates, some nations have
made voting compulsory. If citizens do not vote, they can be fined,
the effectiveness of this strategy perhaps depending on the amount
of the fine. In America, where voter turnout is poor, (around 60 percent in presidential years and 40 percent or less in off-years) there has
been little consideration given to compulsory voting.[1040] This is in spite
of the fact that the small percentage of voters in various elections,
particularly primaries, raise questions about the legitimacy of the outcomes, and it is likely the results of some elections would be different
if a higher percentage of the electorate voted.

However, some would view forcing citizens to vote as an infringe-
ment on liberty. In addition, Republicans in numerous states have
shaped laws to make voting more difficult, believing that minorities
most affected by restrictive laws tend to lean Democratic. If politicians
truly wanted more citizens to vote, they would make it easier for them
by extending voting hours, having more days available, more places
to vote, allowing absentee ballots, and more reasonable evidence of
identification. Also, having automatic voter registration would make
the process much simpler. Oregon did this through the DMV, with an
automatic vote by mail system, permitting people to opt out if they
so wished.[1041] However, some non-drivers and poor people may have
been missed even after follow-up.

Those recommending compulsory voting in the United States suggest it be started at a municipal level, then extended to states, and
finally to federal elections. Since cities contain more young people
and minority voters, it is likely Democratic registration would increase

initially. To balance this, Republican-leaning rural areas or entire states might adopt this system. However, this would be a drastic change in the way elections are conducted and it is unlikely this modification will occur since it would seem to be a violation of privacy and individual rights. In fact, state legislatures satisfied with the status quo could ban compulsory voting by municipalities and the ball would never get rolling. Conservative states are already taking pre-emptive measures against liberal cities to prevent various actions they oppose.[1042]

As of November 2016, twenty nations had some form of compulsory voting.[1043] But given secret balloting, it is really compulsory turnout that is being instituted as it cannot be known who voted and who did not. Still, one can assume the vast majority of citizens who showed up at the polling places actually did vote. Though a higher percentage of voters may participate in elections because of compulsory voting, this does not indicate they spent time studying the issues and candidates and were not politically uninformed when they stepped into the voting booth. This is certainly what has to be addressed even more than the level of voting itself.

Australia has one of the best-known mandatory voting systems with every citizen over age eighteen having to register to vote and appear at the polling place when there is an election, subject to being fined.[1044] The system has been in place since 1924. Prior to compulsory voting, the last voter turnout was 47 percent. Since then, it is generally in the range of 94-96 percent. Belgium and Brazil which also have compulsory voting have had turnouts at about 85 percent.[1045] However, not all Australians are in favor of compulsory voting, with the Australian Electoral Commission providing some of the arguments both pro and con as shown below.[1046]

Pro-

1) Voting is a civic duty comparable to other responsibilities like paying taxes, jury duty, and so forth.
2) Parliament reflects more accurately the will of the electorate.
3) Governments must consider the total electorate in formulating policy and management.

4) Candidates can concentrate their campaigning on the issues instead of encouraging their supporters to vote. (In the United States, significant energy and funds are spent by politicians on their 'ground games'- getting their base to cast their ballots.)

5) The voter isn't actually compelled to vote for anyone because the balloting is secret.

Con-

1) It is undemocratic, mandating that people vote and it infringes on their liberty.

2) The ignorant' and those with little interest in politics are being forced to vote.

3) It may increase the votes for a 'donkey'- a random candidate by people who feel they are being forced to vote.

4) It may increase the number of informal votes- ballot papers that are marked improperly by people who do not care.

5) It increases the number of safe, single-member electorates allowing political parties to concentrate on the more marginal electorates.

6) Resources must be allocated by the government to determine whether those who have failed to vote have done so for valid reasons.

The major reason why compulsory voting will not solve democracy's ills is the second one above- The 'ignorant' and those with little interest are being forced to vote. Since it has been shown that uninformed voters are the main flaw in the democratic process, it makes no sense to mandate voting by those who are uninterested or not attentive to the issues and candidates. In fact, it makes the situation worse, as many politically uninformed citizens normally do not vote and forcing them to do so increases their impact on the election. Democracy will not be aided if more politically oblivious citizens cast ballots. Compulsory voting is not the answer to the current failings of democracy.

12

Ideas Regarding Transformation

"Much here does seem to be arranged in such a way as to frighten people off, and when one is newly arrived here, the obstacles do appear to be completely insurmountable."
Franz Kafka, The Castle[1047]

WHILE EDUCATION IS important for citizens to learn about how their government functions, they must continue to gather information after leaving school. Being politically informed is a lifetime task and responsibility in a democracy. Mandatory voting is not an answer, as many citizens may be politically ignorant when they cast their ballots and may not support competent candidates.

This chapter will touch on other ideas for reforming democracy, some of which do not appear feasible or would not produce politically informed citizens. However, ranked choice voting and weighted democracy will also be discussed, which seem to offer positive change to recharge the current system.

Demeny Voting

Demeny voting, named after the demographer Paul Demeny, is a method of balancing increased voting power of elderly populations in Western democracies, whose proportion is growing because younger generations are having fewer children. In fact, in most democracies, there are not enough offspring being produced to replace the people who are dying.[1048] Older citizens vote in greater percentages than those younger, skewing spending to meet their needs rather than those of society as a whole. This means spending less on the requirements of children and the future of their nations, but more on the safety net for older citizens and lowering their tax burdens. With Demeny voting, custodial parents would receive extra votes related to the number of children they had, until the children themselves reached voting age. However, this system disregards the politically uninformed in its changes to the voting process and appears inadequate to eliminate the current failings of democracy.

Additional Political Parties

Another consideration for improving democracy is to increase the number of political parties, providing more choices for voters on critical issues. Currently, some people may not vote or participate in politics because they feel their views are absent from the political mix and their votes count for little. However, it is unlikely extra parties would decrease political ignorance and cause citizens to be more attentive to the issues and candidates. Extra parties may be an option where there are few currently, as in the United States with only two major political parties. In the U.S, though moderate and independent voters are a plurality, their views are not well represented. A Gallup poll in 2017 had 42 percent of respondents identifying as independents, the largest political group.[1049] Democrats were 29 percent and Republicans 27 percent.

In parliamentary democracies, the availability of multiple parties giving citizens more choices does not lead to more stable governments that function better. One only has to look to Greece, Italy and Spain as examples of nations where citizens have many parties from which to choose but lack durable governments. Multiple parties do not drive citizens to become more politically informed and select better candidates for office.

Ranked Choice Voting

Current elections in the United States are conducted with 'first past the post' voting. This means whoever gets the most votes wins, whether he or she has obtained a majority. Voting in this fashion supports the current two party system in the U.S., limiting the choices that voters have. Obviously, the full spectrum of views cannot be represented by just two candidates and fewer citizens may vote because of this arrangement. Ranked choice voting widens the array of candidates that voters may pick, helping independents or third or fourth parties vying for offices.[1050]

Ranked choice voting (RCV) is an electoral method currently being employed in some municipalities. In 2016, Maine became the first state to adopt RCV in election of its governor, members of Congress, and the state legislature.[1051] It had been used to select the mayor of Portland, Maine's largest city since 2011. Volunteers in Maine collected over 70,000 signatures to place RCV on the ballot and it was passed in a referendum by 52 percent of voters, the first use of RCV in statewide contests supposed to occur in 2018.[1052] However, state legislators voted in October 2017 to delay implementation of RCV until 2021 against the wishes of their constituents.[1053] They also vowed to repeal it if supporters were unable to have a constitutional amendment approved regarding this system. But another referendum in Maine reaffirmed RCV in 2018 and it was used statewide in elections that year.[1054] FairVote, the organization pushing ranked choice voting nationally, believes it is superior to the present mechanism and would like it to spread to other states and municipalities.

Proponents claim ranked choice increases fairness and improves government functioning.[1055] Howard Dean, the former governor of Vermont and a past Democratic candidate for president is a strong supporter of RCV.[1056] It does not favor a particular party, but can help third party or independent candidates gain more traction. The way RCV is structured, voters can rank as many candidates as they desire for a specific office on the ballot in the order of their preference. Candidates who tally a majority in the first round are obviously the winners. Those who have a large number of first choice supporters but not a majority may pick up additional backing as the second and third choices of voters that can propel them to a majority. The candidates with the lowest tallies are eliminated each round and their votes reapportioned.

In a Maine Congressional district in 2018, incumbent Republican Bruce Polquin won the first round of the November election but did not receive a majority.[1057] Subsequently, when two independent candidates were disqualified and their votes redistributed, the Democratic candidate, Jared Golden, was victorious by about 3500 votes out of over 200,000 cast. Polquin initially contested the result in court asking that only the first choice ballots be counted. When a federal judge rejected Polquins' demand, he dropped the case and conceded to Golden.

Ranked choice is particularly valuable when there are a large number of candidates for an office, which may be won by someone who only has a small plurality of the total vote. Instead, he or she has to be on a majority of the ballots to win if there is ranked voting. It can also be considered as an 'instant runoff' to elect officials rather than the necessity of a contest at a later date. Runoffs are wasteful, requiring greater effort and expenditures by candidates and government. When there is voting for multiple candidates, such as for city councils or state legislatures, RCV can represent the full spectrum of voting more equitably.

An area where RCV might be particularly useful is in party primaries, especially when many candidates are contesting an office. For instance, the Republican presidential primary in 2016 had seventeen candidates initially. A number of them dropped out early because they did not have the finances and believed their chances of attaining the nomination were minimal. If RCV had been utilized, more candidates might have remained in the race for longer periods, hoping they would receive second, third or fourth choices on enough ballots to win a few states and be in the running. Having RCV might have also scrambled the order in which the candidates finished, perhaps blocking Donald Trump from the nomination since he was not a choice of a majority of Republicans. The Democrats in the 2020 presidential race also had multiple candidates and RCV would have aided in the selection. Changing the format of the primaries, however, would be up to each party and the states.

Ranked choice voting would encourage more candidates to run for office at all levels as independents or nominees of newly formed and stronger third or fourth parties, challenging the dominance of Republicans and Democrats. A larger number of competent candidates might be willing to compete against incumbents if the process were fairer and with greater chances of success. At present, members in the tribal cultures of the GOP and Democrats are reluctant to vote for candidates of the other party. Without the overt hostility of a single opposing party, candidates of new parties might be named as choices lower down on the ballots and wind up being elected by garnering majorities with votes in the secondary rounds. It is likely there would be more comity in politics with RCV and possible that coalitions would have to be formed on a municipal, state, or federal level in order to pass legislation. Politicians would have to learn how to work together again.

Proponents of ranked choice voting believe it would also curb negative advertising and campaigning, as candidates would not want to risk the loss of critical second and third place votes by alienating supporters of other candidates. Elections would be more democratic as well with the winners having to be placed on a majority of ballots. Some backers of RCV think it would reduce legislative gridlock because candidates would try to appeal to a broader cross-section of the electorate, rather than small partisan groups. Thus, winners might be more moderate and open to compromise. Though RCV has been used in some municipal elections in the United States and parliamentary elections in Australia for a number of years, major benefits are uncertain to this point. Ireland also uses this system.

With an increased number of candidates to choose from with ranked choice voting, it is likely there would be fewer uninformed voters. Citizens would be better able to find candidates that truly represent them and more voters might be willing to spend time studying the candidates and issues. There is nothing in the Constitution that prohibits ranked choice voting and adopting this system nationwide could significantly improve the democratic process. Many incumbent officials might oppose RCV because it gives more power to the voting public by expanding the choices available to them at the ballot box.

Ranked Choice with Multi-Winner Districts

To further reduce partisanship and make citizens' votes more meaningful, a system of ranked-choice voting with multi-winner Congressional districts has been suggested.[1058] In fact, a bill called The Fair Representation Act was introduced in Congress by Democrat Don Beyer from Virginia that would switch to the above mechanism. Currently, the overwhelming majority of Americans live in landslide districts, where GOP or Democratic winners are victorious by overwhelming margins. In 2016, 98 percent of House incumbents were victorious with 402 of 435 districts won by more than 10 percent.

Replacing the present system with proportional representation in multi-winner districts would make every vote count in each election. This could be done by changing states like Connecticut with five Democratic members of Congress and Oklahoma with five Republicans members of Congress, all of whom won their districts by large margins. If districts were eliminated and all Representatives elected on a statewide basis with ranked choice voting, the Republicans in Connecticut and Democrats in Oklahoma, whose votes had been meaningless, would likely see their votes elect some members of Congress.

In small states with six or fewer members of Congress, the state could become a single district with multiple winners. In large states with more Congressional Representatives, the state would have to be divided into several districts, each with multiple winners, allowing minority parties to have some representation. With current winner-take all voting in single districts, up to 49.9 percent of the votes in Congressional elections may count for nothing. The same type of change could also be instituted for state legislative districts to make voters' ballots more significant. This process might get more citizens to vote, make them better informed about their choice of candidates, bring more comity into politics, and have more and better candidates running for office, either as independents or supported by third parties.

Open versus Closed Primaries

Changing the primary systems now in place might engender more interest in political campaigns and might induce more qualified individuals to try for office. But it would not reduce political ignorance and its effect on the outcome of general elections. Currently in the United States, there are open, closed, semi-closed, and other types of primaries in different states.[1059] The parties and states make the determinations about the type of primary employed, and it can be altered if there is dissatisfaction.

In open primaries, members of different parties or independents are eligible to vote in the contests of any party. When people register to vote, in many states they do not have to reveal party affiliations. Crossover voting is an area of contention in open primaries, where members of opposing parties may vote to try and influence who the nominee of their challenging party will be. As an example, Republicans in a Democratic district may vote for a more conservative nominee, while Democrats in a strongly GOP district may vote for a more moderate candidate. There is also 'party crashing' or sabotage where members of an opposing party vote for a weaker candidate to make it easier from a strategic standpoint for their party's nominee to win the general election.

In closed primaries, only registered members of that particular party are allowed to vote to choose candidates for the general election. Closed primaries ensure party members will be able to select the candidates. This format tends to produce more extreme candidates as only a small number of the most ardent members of the party's base tend to vote.

Unaffiliated voters in semi-closed primaries may select in which primary to vote on primary day, along with registered voters of that party. This is seen as a middle ground between open and closed primaries and does not lead to sabotaging of opposing parties.

Non-Partisan (jungle) Primaries

Non-partisan primaries are another way to conduct primaries with open voting. In this model, candidates of any political party or independents can run in the same primary for various government positions.[1060] If a candidate receives 50 percent or more of the vote, he or she would be declared the winner for that office. If no candidates attained 50 percent of the vote, the top two vote-getters would face each other in the general election, regardless of whether they had the same party affiliation or none at all. This mechanism might attract more voters to participate in primaries, which has woefully small numbers at present. Better candidates might also be willing to run in primaries structured in this fashion, where party labels might be less important. As of 2012, 80 percent of American cities had non-partisan elections to choose candidates for local office. Though this strategy has increased voter turnout where it is utilized, it does not increase voter knowledge.

One problem is that if too many candidates from one party run in a particular district, they may split the vote in smaller slices, allowing two candidates from the opposing party to be the finalists. In other words, in a strongly Republican district with many GOP candidates running, two Democrats may receive the highest vote counts and one of them will wind up representing a GOP district in Congress. (Four Republicans each: 16 percent of the vote. Two Democrats each: 18 percent of the votes.) The same situation could arise in a strongly Democratic district. Thus, it is not a fair way to manage elections.[1061]

Use of New Technology

The Founding Fathers of America were correct in their decision to form a Republic and prescient in seeing the problems that would arise in a democracy. Their concerns included capture of high offices by demagogues who promise the masses 'the moon' and are rewarded by politically uninformed voters unable to differentiate between valid pledges and unattainable assurances. Canny politicians, who read the mood of voters, may make promises to achieve national honor and greatness, heighten economic growth and bring back jobs, and emphasize racial or religious purity. Often, they use minorities or other nations as scapegoats for existing problems they guarantee to expunge. The wave of populism and nationalism now engulfing Europe and the United States as well as parts of Asia and Latin America has been harnessed by demagogues for their own ends. This is not to say that the mass of voters in these nations did not have compelling grudges against those wielding power. Inequality soared with automation, globalization, and multi-national corporations.

However, the men who created the American Constitution and the important documents of the new political system were mistaken in the solution they devised to evade the perils of democracy as they constructed their Republic. They selected wealth as the determinant of who should vote, giving the franchise to property-holders and taxpayers, believing they would make their choices in the interest of all citizens and the nation. In fact, the franchise was granted to men of their own class, disregarding the possibility they would vote in their own self-interest and not for the general welfare. Instead of using wealth or property to decide who should have the franchise, it would have been more reasonable to use political knowledge.

John Stuart Mill equated political knowledge with educational level, another false barometer of an individual's awareness regarding politics and government. Auto-didacts or non-college graduates with an interest in politics who are reasonably intelligent may have more political insight than some PhDs. In fact, college graduates may be deficient concerning politics or civic information, as a diploma alone is not a mark of political acumen. Though Mill believed in universal suffrage, he thought educated citizens should be allotted more votes than the general population, since he judged them more astute regarding politics. However, wealth, property, or education by themselves do not prove a person knowledgeable about politics or government. The mechanisms to rapidly assess a voter's grasp of civics and politics were not available when the United States was formed and the Constitution written. But that ability is available now. Thus, ways to restructure the voting process should be considered, so that political ignorance and political knowledge are not given equal weight in the voting booth. This is important to ensure that the process of democracy functions most effectively.

In a revamped system, no one need lose their vote, but additional votes could be allotted to individuals who were more informed about candidates and issues in each election. Knowledge could be judged by a short computerized test. Citizens would not have a fixed number of votes but would be tested on the issues and candidates in each election to decide how many votes they would be assigned before casting their ballots. This system can be labeled as 'weighted democracy' as voting power would be weighted in proportion to a person's political knowledge. It also could be called epistocracy, or governing by the knowledgeable.

All people are not equally intelligent or with similar interests. They are born into different environments and have different intellectual capacities. Democratic nations like to consider themselves meritocracies, where citizens can succeed on the basis of intelligence and effort. However, this is evidence of mass delusion. Other factors besides intelligence and hard work contribute to success in life, including parental guidance and help, connections, inherited wealth, education, luck (being in the right place at the right time), early childhood programs, health, and so forth. Society is unable to balance these complex factors to provide complete equity, but should provide equality of opportunity. No matter what government does, however, merit is not necessarily the defining element behind a person's station in life.

And political knowledge and interest are not necessarily attributes that remain static throughout an individual's years. Aging, injury, disease, or other factors may take a toll on a person's cognitive abilities or focus on politics. That is why, before voting in each election, citizens should be tested anew regarding their awareness of current politics and civics to decide how many votes they should be allocated. Different numbers of votes should also be granted for the election of different officials depending on the voter's knowledge about the specific nominees and their positions on the issues. Though this will be a major change in the democratic process, significant change is needed if democracy is to survive and flourish in some form.

New Visions for Democracy

The tools that can transform democracy and improve governing are in daily use worldwide- computers, the Internet, and social media. They have already changed the political landscape in terms of raising campaign funds, political advertising, gathering and disseminating political data, and recruiting and organizing volunteers. In all likelihood, they were responsible for electing Obama in 2008 and 2012, as well as candidates for other offices. The GOP employed the Internet and social media to help them gain control of Congress, multiple state legislatures and governorships, and to elect President Trump in 2016. (Hacking and use of social media by the Russians also influenced voters.) With computers and the Internet and building on the current civic framework, there are two general paths a new political order could follow in an attempt to revive democracy. But for either 'Direct' or Weighted' Democracies to be instituted, computers would have to be provided to citizens now lacking them, and people who were not adept with the technology would have to be trained in their use. Every citizen would also require a unique identifier when logging in to prevent voter fraud: fingerprints, iris scans, or facial recognition.

Direct Democracy

'Direct Democracy,' however equitable and impressive it sounds in theory, would be even less effective than the present system. In Direct Democracy, a nation's populace would cast votes in referenda on all issues of national importance, a permanent technocracy putting these decisions into effect. Some officials would also be elected to govern if decisions had to be made quickly between referenda. Direct Democracy could also be employed on a statewide, provincial, or municipal basis to decide local matters.

Though implementing Direct Democracy is certainly possible, it would not be an efficient way to govern and would not alleviate voters' lack of political information. In fact, if citizens with little political knowledge were voting on critical issues in various referenda, the outcomes could be worse than the current system. For some citizens, more frequent voting to determine policies might be considered an annoyance and they would not educate themselves about the issues and might not even vote.

Interestingly, after a number of state and municipal referenda in the last several years, elected officials have tried to reverse the results of the voting for various reasons, usually because it impacted them negatively in some way. Special interests also lobbied these officials in some instances to get them to change the new laws. For example, residents of Washington, D.C. passed a minimum wage law of $15 an hour (Initiative 77) in 2018 for restaurant workers and others, which was opposed by the food industry.[1062] Lobbyists convinced a majority of City Council members to reverse the measure. Over a two year period, legislators in different cities and states filled over 100 bills to reverse the outcomes of referenda, basically stealing power from the people. These were mostly progressive ideas, but regressive measures can also be passed by direct initiatives. The progressive ideas included expansion of Medicaid in Maine and a number of other states. Also passed by referendum were ethics reform, an independent ethics commission, limits on lobbying and campaign finance in South Dakota which was repealed by Republican legislators and a GOP governor who claimed that voters had been "hoodwinked by scam artists."[1063]

An article in Foreign Affairs by Yascha Mounk in 2014 noted- "Over the last two decades, populist movements in Europe and the United States have uprooted traditional party structures and forced ideas long regarded as extremist or unsavory onto the political agenda."[1064] As has been discussed, populists on both the left and the right have been raging against the establishment and control by the elites, evidenced by the election of Trump in the United States, Brexit in Great Britain, and a number of elections in continental Europe. The dangers of populism would be enhanced if direct democracy was employed by any nation to decide vital questions. Politically uninformed citizens could be convinced to vote one way or another by demagogic politicians and the media, as happened with Brexit.

In addition, people often tend to vote on the basis of their own interests rather than for society's long term needs. They may be unwilling to raise taxes or approve of actions that will cost money or inconvenience them (NIMBY). Thus, if revenue is required for education, infrastructure, or any functions of government, on a municipal, state, or federal level, it might not be authorized by citizens unaware of the need for funding or who do not care about how its lack will affect society. The impact of a particular law on the individual might be more important to that person than its societal benefits.

The prime example of this situation was Proposition 13 in California, an amendment to the state constitution enacted in 1978 by a direct vote of citizens in a statewide referendum.[1065] The initiative was passed by nearly two thirds of California voters, reducing property taxes by about 57 percent. It limited taxes on residential and commercial property to one percent of property value and restricted raises to the inflation rate or a maximum of 2 percent annually. And a two thirds majority of both Houses of the Legislature were necessary to elevate any tax rates. Local governments also had to have two thirds of voter approval for any taxes to be raised.[1066] Proposition 13 had a devastating effect on higher and K-12 education in California, as well as libraries, infrastructure, and other public services. Specific interest groups such as the older population (with Prop 13) who may be unconcerned about the school systems but worried about taxes, may be the deciding element in the outcome of a referendum to the detriment of society as a whole.

The Brexit referendum was another example of direct democracy, with uninformed voters in the driver's seat.[1067] In the referendum that took place in June 2016 on whether to leave or stay in the European Union, a majority of British citizens voted to leave, 52 to 48 percent. The tabloid newspapers in Britain pushed for separation, providing their readers with nationalist and populist rationales for doing so. The economic consequences were given short shrift by the media and political figures arguing for severance. The most important reasons given by the backers of detachment were to control immigration which had been open to E.U. citizens, to get out from under E.U. regulations, and to stop paying fees to the E.U. The biggest support for Brexit came from rural areas and white workers. However, E.U. immigrants had filled jobs British citizens did not want, or were incapable of doing, a number in high-tech fields vital to the British economy.

Shortly after Brexit passed, many who had voted to leave showed remorse, saying they had been unaware of the problems that could result, some asking for a second referendum. [1068] The ramifications of the split are still uncertain, but it will definitely affect banking, multinational corporations, manufacturing, and products that had open access to E.U. markets. It is also likely Scotland will separate from Great Britain at some point to remain in the E.U, and possible that Northern Ireland will unify with Ireland. And even Wales might split.

Great Britain will no longer be as 'great' because of Brexit. But politically uninformed citizens did not foresee the potential consequences of their votes.

To move toward a presidential dictatorship, the Turkish Parliament in January 2017 gave President Erdogan sweeping executive powers over the Turkish nation.[1069] This was ratified by a national referendum held in April. In a close vote questioned by the opposition, Turkish citizens who were politically uninformed voted to provide the Islamist Erdogan with all the power he desired, choosing to abandon the democratic system with its freedom and rule of law for a dictatorship.[1070] This is an example of a victory for uninformed voters when direct democracy is employed.

These illustrations show how direct democracy magnifies the basic flaw in the current system by giving politically uninformed voters more say in governing and more power. And if this system were employed, prior to every referendum advocates for and against each issue would need to advance their cases to citizens, on-line and by television, making this time-consuming. It is an inefficient way to run government and should not be considered as a solution for democracy's imperfections. On the other hand, having local referenda for local matters is certainly a reasonable exercise in direct democracy.

Weighted (Proportional) Democracy- Epistocracy

In his 2016 book, *Democracy and Political Ignorance*, Professor Ilya Somin noted that the long history of political ignorance and its apparent rational basis makes it a particularly difficult problem to attack.[1071] It is rational for many citizens because family, work or other concerns keep them from spending the necessary time learning about the candidates and issues. And it is rational for other citizens who recognize that 'big money' is a major factor determining most elections and their individual votes are unlikely to change the outcome of any contest (one vote among millions). Thus, whether they cast a ballot fortified by information does not matter. The Koch brothers stated in

June 2016 that their network planned to spend between $300 and $400 million to advance their policies and political ideas in the 2018 election cycle.[1072] Of course, this undermines the need for universal suffrage in democratic states and the responsibility of all citizens to vote regularly bolstered by the required knowledge.

An article in Foreign Policy in April 2018 by Dambisa Moyo argued that democracy did not deliver for the electorate because of endless elections, unqualified leaders, uninformed voters, and short-term thinking, all of which impacted economic growth.[1073] Among her suggestions to improve democracy were requiring voters to pass a civics test and then weighting the voting in favor of those who did well.[1074] This was criticized as being a system where those judged more qualified would have their votes count more than citizens shown to be less qualified. Regardless of the criticism, this appears to be a rational fix for democracy's major problem- uninformed voters, though her implementation of this process was unclear. Critics argue that weighting votes in favor of the elites might allow them to support their own short-term interests rather than the long-term needs of the nation. However, it makes sense to provide those with greater knowledge regarding government, the candidates and their positions more power in the voting process. And it does not have to be just the educated elites who gain more sway.

As noted, over the last half century, improvement in overall levels of education and the debut of new technology has not resulted in significant augmentation of political awareness by the general population. Though there are still some who believe political ignorance can be reduced and the range of political knowledge expanded among ordinary citizens, the fact that it has not yet happened makes it less likely. Theoretically, it could be done by providing the mass of voters with more valid incentives to help them focus and absorb political information prior to elections. But no obvious way of achieving this goal effectively, painlessly, and voluntarily has been suggested by political scientists who have studied this problem.

An alternative mechanism would be to aggregate political power mainly in the hands of citizens who are already well informed, since they would be more likely to vote for competent office-seekers and support issues that would further the interests of society. How this could be implemented with the agreement of a majority of voters in a democratic polity is unclear, though it is certainly feasible to measure an individual's political knowledge quickly and with reasonable accuracy. And there is little question that uninformed voters present a danger to democratic societies. However, people do not want to surrender power they have realized, even if it is not being utilized effectively.

The path to reducing or erasing uninformed voters might lie in education, providing knowledge about politics and government in a form that would capture people's attention and aid them in learning. It would probably be simplest to transmit data regarding politics and government through online programs, where an individual could view the information at his or her own convenience, at a pace that was comfortable, repeating it as often as necessary. Television programs might also be useful. But how could people be motivated to spend their time watching informational programs and trying to retain data, when much of the electorate believes their votes are meaningless. And there are many options for entertainment available that are more enjoyable.

For a number of citizens, knowing their votes were more valuable might induce them to learn about politics and government, candidates and issues. Weighted democracy, where votes would be apportioned according to voters' knowledge of the issues and candidates, could help correct the critical defect of uninformed voters in the present democratic system. People would be aware their votes were more significant than they had been because they had additional votes. Of course, for some citizens, it might not make any difference, while for others it would be worthwhile spending extra time to absorb the necessary information to maximize their voting power.

Why is political knowledge by the voters of such overriding importance in democracies that consideration should be given to transforming the mechanisms of politics and government now in place? We have shown that democracy is in trouble worldwide, having difficulty competing with alternative forms of governing, with populism and nationalism subverting its basic principles. In 2016, nearly one half of the world's nations could be considered as some sort of democracy, but only nineteen as full democracies according to The Economist.[1075] And the latter number has been decreasing. For voters to believe that a government "of the people, for the people, and by the people"[1076] is superior to other options, it must be changed to be made more effective and efficient in today's world, "so that it shall not perish from the earth."[1077]

Greater weight in voting must be given to those citizens who are politically informed, so officials will likely be chosen who are honest, forthright, and competent, and whose positions are most reasonable and favor advancement of society. As Professor Ilya Somin observed- "Accountability is difficult to achieve if voters do not know which officials are responsible for which issues."[1078] Political knowledge by voters is of critical importance for the survival of democracy. Thus, weighted democracy or epistocracy is suggested as a way to make political acuity more consequential in the voting process. Epistocracy, or government by the knowledgeable, is a system that provides extra voting power to those better informed about candidates, issues, and the way government functions. This makes more sense than the democratic methods now in place. Votes based on knowledge are more relevant than those cast randomly, or determined by factors unrelated to a candidate's presumed qualifications for office (looks, soundbites, race, religion, party, and so forth,) and the policies he or she supports.

David Estlund, who suggested 'epistocracy' as a term for governing by the knowledgeable, argued against putting it into practice, though philosophically he believed it to be more rational than democracy and would likely produce better outcomes for societies.[1079] Among his points in opposition, he said it could be "denied that truth was a suitable standard for measuring political judgement."[1080] He also rejected the notion that some citizens were more aware of what good government was than others and wondered whether greater political knowledge provided more political authority to that person than to another? In addition, he believed the process of screening voters for political acumen could be biased in ways not evident. He argued that democracy and universal suffrage were so engrained, that providing informed citizens with power over those who were politically oblivious would feel unjust. Despite these points, he thought a society granting greater influence to knowledgeable voters than those politically ignorant would operate more ably than today's democracies.

The political philosopher Jason Brennan avidly favored epistocracy over democracy, as did John Stuart Mill (though he did not know of the term). Brennan believed it was totally justifiable to restrict the authority that incompetent, inept, irrational, or ignorant voters had over those who were more informed and intelligent.[1081] Those who were uninterested or politically uninformed he labeled as hobbits, those with some political knowledge but highly biased in the way they interpreted this knowledge were labeled hooligans, and those with political acumen, open-mindedness and the ability to analyze as Vulcans.[1082]

Brennan felt epistocracy was more likely to improve the public welfare and contribute to the betterment of society than the current democratic system, which was more important than fairness or injured feelings. As support for limiting those who were politically uninformed from voting, Brennan used as an example the disqualification of cognitively impaired jurors or those with questionable morals. Arguments could be made on both sides of the ledger for epistocracy or garden variety democracy, but in today's world, the failings of democracy have become ever more evident. So why uphold a system that has not been working and may be less competitive with autocracies. Universal suffrage could be continued in an epistocracy as Mill envisioned, with a greater proportion of votes going to citizens who were politically informed (not merely educated) and relatively unbiased in their evaluation of political data.

In this format of weighted democracy, an independent body or committee, whose members were chosen by the candidates, would prepare a series of multiple choice questions regarding government, the candidates competing for each office and essential issues being decided. In the weeks prior to the election, voters would be able to take tests containing these questions at designated stations with banks of computers, signing in with their unique identifiers. (At some point, this could be done from home.) The number of ballots voters could cast in a particular contest would depend on how they performed on the test relating to that office. For example, if the test for a senate election contained ten questions and a voter answered eight of these correctly, he or she could be allotted eight votes to cast for that office. If there were twenty questions and a voter answered seventeen correctly, he or she could be given eight and a half votes.

The number of test questions would be decided by the independent body and could be adjusted in future elections if the design was felt to be too unwieldy or required too much time. The ratio of correct answers to votes allotted would also be determined by the committee, or perhaps by a national panel. The tests would be graded automatically and immediately by the computer so each individual would know how many votes he or she had acquired. All citizens, even if they did not answer any questions correctly, or chose not to take the test, would be able to cast one vote, guaranteeing that the universal franchise would not be withdrawn. No one would be compelled to take the tests if he or she were not so inclined. This concept is not being employed to prevent citizens from voting. Its main objective is to reduce uninformed voting to improve the way government functions, with democracy evolving into epistocracy. Though it entails an extra step for those casting ballots who wish to have more votes, it does not burden them excessively.

This system provides a major incentive for all citizens to become politically informed and actually vote. Weighed democracy would encourage voters to learn how government worked, and the histories of the candidates and their views, in order to have a greater impact on elections. This would be a partial solution to the problem of uninformed voters that is fair and reasonable. After all, should those who know little or nothing about the candidates and issues have the same voting power as those who are knowledgeable about the individuals running for offices and their positions? Necessary information on government, candidates and issues could be acquired through self-education or courses offered at local schools or community colleges. However, on-line courses would also be available for citizens to study at their own pace. Citizens with more than one vote would start to feel their votes were more important and that they had a greater say in determining the outcomes of elections.

Acquisition of the necessary knowledge would not be unduly onerous, and in any case, should be considered a citizen's duty in a democracy or epistocracy. It is important for voters to know about the operation of their government and how it is structured to help them understand the roles and responsibilities of elected officials. Multiple elections, i.e. president, senator, and member of Congress would necessitate more tests and learning more information, though candidates affiliated with the same parties usually have similar stances on issues. State and local officials would be part of the equation, though perhaps fewer questions could be employed for these contests, or their elections could be scheduled for off-years.

Because every person would have an equal chance to maximize his or her knowledge and maximize his or her voting power, testing to determine the number of votes allotted to each citizen would not be unfair. It is certainly more equitable and objective than basing this decision on arbitrary guidelines, such as wealth, taxes paid, or level of education. Individuals applying for American citizenship must first take an exam to show they are knowledgeable about the nation's system of government. Passing these tests allows immigrants to become citizens and vote in American elections. Voting is an important task for citizens and taking a short exam beforehand to ascertain a citizen's political knowledge is a reasonable idea. Why shouldn't a person's store of information about politics and government be the determining factor in the number of votes he or she is allocated? We want our physicians, attorneys, accountants, investment advisors, and so forth to pass tests affirming they are knowledgeable in their fields before they can practice their professions, and they need continuing education to keep up with new developments. The candidates Americans elect to government offices decide the nation's policies and how well the country will be managed, affecting all aspects of citizens' lives. Shouldn't informed individuals have more power to choose America's lawmakers than those who are politically inattentive?

In the first half of the 19th century, the franchise was extended in America to include working class white men, eliminating property requirements for voting and increasing the belief in equality expressed in the Declaration of Independence.[1083] Ninety percent of white men in America were allowed to vote by 1840, an unheard of expansion of the franchise in that era. Because of public schools and mandatory attendance which was put into effect in the latter half of the 19th century, American workers were more literate than working men in other nations.[1084]

Prior to elections in the 19th century, newspapers filled with stories about political figures and issues were read avidly by the voting public. Politics was like a form of entertainment when there was little else of interest or diversion occurring, especially in the small towns. When politicians came to visit and give speeches, the venues were always filled and there were a host of questions afterward that showed knowledge of the issues. And there were political discussions carried on in the local taverns. Of course, during this time there was no repetitious twenty-four hour news cycle to numb people's minds to politics and a functioning democracy was a new concept for the world that Americans wanted to succeed. Voters were also not as cynical and critical of government and politics as at present, seeing America as a land of boundless opportunity. Through most of the 19th century, eligible voter turnout was over 80 percent.[1085]

These men almost two centuries ago were not as educated as the population today, but were more politically aware. Men believed their votes important and they were proud to have the franchise. They paid attention to the candidates and issues to be sure their ballots were cast for what they believed. Now however, as previously shown, many citizens feel their votes are worthless and are not willing to take the time to educate themselves about office-seekers and critical matters before they vote, *if* they vote. There are also too many distractions that compete with politics for attention. But being politically knowledgeable and casting ballots are obligations that should be taken seriously by citizens in a democratic state. Unfortunately, this has not been the case, leading to the decline of democracy, with other forms of government favored in many nations.

Epistocracy, or weighted democracy, with more emphasis on voters being politically informed and rewarded for their knowledge with additional votes, would appear to be a sensible mechanism for revitalizing a failing system that is slowly losing influence and attraction for the world's population. As the English proverb has noted, nothing succeeds like success,[1086] and state capitalism under autocratic direction as practiced in China, seems to be riding a crest of worshipful admiration from developing societies.

Weighted democracy would rekindle citizens' interest in politics, the opportunity to have more voting power providing an impetus for voters to become more politically astute. The process of weighted democracy would only require minutes to complete the tests of political information prior to voting (if so desired), with testing stations open twenty-four hours a day. A knowledgeable electorate would be more attuned to corruption, partisanship, and inefficiency in government, and how to combat these defects. It is likely that individuals with higher levels of education and more interest in politics would be more willing to spend time acquiring information regarding the candidates, the issues, and government functions. But there is no reason why political knowledge would be limited to citizens with greater educational attainment, as the possibility to gain additional votes would be available for everyone. Only time and effort would be required.

Complaints would undoubtedly be raised that this system was too elitist and gave an advantage to those who were more educated or intelligent. However, the major factor in how many votes an individual could cast for a specific office would depend upon him or her learning about the candidates and their positions. Education outside of the usual political advertisements and sound bites would be necessary. A PhD who did not investigate the issues might wind up with a single vote for a particular office and a high school dropout who put in the time to acquire information might accrue the maximum number of votes. It might simply entail listening to different television stations, or perhaps taking courses or doing searches on the Internet. The objective of this system would be to ensure knowledgeable voters, so educational level, gender, race, wealth, or property would not matter regarding the number of votes an individual secured.

Because citizens would know their votes meant more and many would examine the records of candidates with greater skepticism than previously, political advertising and the money behind it would become less vital. Sound bites, statements from candidates, and orchestrated propaganda that sang a candidate's praises, would all slowly fade from their current roles prior to elections. As citizens became more educated politically, they would ignore political advertisements, realizing the announcements were dishonest or skewed the truth. Obtaining correct information would be critical for voters who wished to become knowledgeable and increase their voting power. And reducing politicians' debasing dependency on funding from lobbyists and special interests, and the time spent raising money, would in itself be a great step forward for democracy/epistocracy.

Because voter sophistication would increase, and a certain proportion of the population would have more votes and be more able to influence the outcome of elections, candidates might spend additional time trying to court this group. On-line approaches, targeted meetings, and other directed plans of action might be employed. But integrity and honest pronouncements by the candidates would be necessary, or these voters might be offended by those trying to obtain their votes. The whole tenor of the way elections were conducted would likely change for the better. Incumbency would also become less important, as voters would scrutinize the records of elected officials to see if they truly deserved to be supported instead of automatically returned to office. A more knowledgeable electorate would make decisions on the basis of views held by the candidates and what they had accomplished in office if they were incumbents. The political applecart would be turned upside down, with politicians having to defend their beliefs before a more discerning electorate.

Incumbent politicians and beneficiaries of the current process (lobbyists, special interests, affluent individuals, corporations) can be expected to oppose transformation to a system of weighted democracy. In addition, people satisfied with the status quo, or unwilling to spend time educating themselves before voting, might also be against this change. However, under this system, more qualified, competent individuals would run for office, no longer restrained by having to devote themselves to raising money and continuous campaigning. And citizens would realize that if they were willing to learn about the issues and candidates they could have a greater impact on elections. Officeholders would also know they would be rewarded by informed voters and re-elected if they performed well.

Some of the smaller nations that value education and might want a more effective political system, such as the Scandinavian countries, Singapore, South Korea, Taiwan, and so forth, might opt for a system of weighted democracy more easily than the United States, selling the idea to their citizens because it is fair and sensible. In fact, the infrastructure for epistocracy is already in place in Estonia, where every aspect of people's lives is digitized and can be conducted over the Internet, including voting and interactions with government.[1087] Licenses, insurance, banking, education, taxes, and so forth are all managed online. It would be simple enough to design a system to test citizens before they cast their ballots, allotting the number of votes on the basis of test results. And it is only a matter of time before all advanced nations adopt and build Estonia's digital infrastructure to make life easier and more efficient for citizens. These nations would also be set up for weighted democracy.

In the United States, if citizens of one county, municipality, or state were forward thinking and chose to experiment with epistocracy, it would provide the remainder of Americans with a prototype to decide if they favored this concept. Without question, there would be court challenges, and a constitutional amendment might be necessary to allow this change to the voting process. Realistically, if a system of weighted democracy is adopted by any nation, the United States is unlikely to be among the first. There are too many engrained interest groups devoted to the current system and knowledge is not held in high regard by much of the populace. Many citizens are hostile and afraid of experts and elites, as well as government.

Having knowledgeable voters making decisions about the candidates and issues should be the objective of any changes to the structure and practices of the world's democracies. Would such citizens have elected Erdogan as leader in Turkey, Dutarte in the Philippines and Trump as president of the United States? Would they tolerate the dysfunction and gridlock that binds Washington and prevents necessary legislation from being enacted? We will never know how informed voters would or would not act until the present democratic system is transformed, providing citizens who are politically aware with proportionately more voting power. Not only is it fair to do so, but it will improve governing. Astute voters are needed to transport democracy into the 21st century.

Combining epistocracy with ranked choice voting might be the optimal option, making the outcome of elections even fairer and quicker to determine winners. These systems could be employed in primary voting as well as for general elections. It is important, however, to ensure that hackers do not have opportunities to influence results. Maximum protection must be provided for computers involved in the voting process, and paper records should be kept. Barbara Simons, a prominent computer scientist, has studied electronic voting systems in the United States for years. She believes that the only safe voting technology at present is paper.[1088] External hackers from 'illiberal democracies' or autocracies like Russia want to poison the well of liberal democracies, as they are afraid that at some point their own people will demand the power to elect their leaders and control their own destinies.

Converting to a weighted system of voting does not impinge on American values of individualism, autonomy, and liberty. Citizens are not being forced to learn about candidates and issues if they are not so inclined, and will not be deprived of a vote if they do not educate themselves about politics. Attempts to increase the efficacy of the voting process to elect more competent officials should be lauded rather than fought. Though the mechanism is novel because of the availability of new technology, the idea of linking knowledge to political power has been considered by philosophers for centuries. Computerized testing now allows this to be accomplished. Party affiliation or structure will not be altered by this change and it does not interfere with progressive or libertarian views of the state. However, independent or third party candidates might be helped by this new process. Epistocracy should not be labeled elitist as maximum voting power can be attained by any citizen willing to learn about politics. But it is important that opportunities for citizens to educate themselves about politics and government be provided online and through courses at high schools and community colleges for those who feel they are politically uninformed.

Democracy is in distress worldwide, with corruption, inefficiency, and partisanship affecting democratic governments everywhere--the needs of the people going unmet. This has enhanced populism and nationalism as well as conversion to autocratic states. Being a citizen of a democratic state entails responsibility to be informed about the candidates and issues before voting, and this obligation is being ignored by many citizens. Epistocracy/weighted democracy reinforces and rewards citizen responsibility, giving those who are interested a louder voice in electing officials, enabling government to work more effectively. Transforming current systems of voting may seem utopian to most observers. However, weighted democracy is possible and makes sense as a way to improve governance. Democracy cannot continue its journey on the same road. The alternatives are autocratic states or plutocracies, where one man or wealthy individuals control the government. This has already happened in a number of nations, with voting cosmetic and meaningless. Change is necessary. More education about government and politics for children and adults, ranked choice voting, and weighted democracy all combined would provide a path to correct the current problems of democracy.

Democracy must evolve if it is to survive as a viable method of representative government, directing practices and protecting human rights. Politically informed citizens must have more influence to choose candidates and policies. It may not happen overnight, but we should start thinking in terms of modification and a better system. Perhaps another way will be advanced that is superior, but change is inevitable if democracy/epistocracy in some form is to overcome populism, nationalism and autocracy, returning power and equity to the people. The Corona virus pandemic presents great challenges to democracy as well. Hopefully, it will help in bringing about the necessary changes to revive and modernize democracy's current format.

References

1   Rousseau, Jean Jacques, The Social Contract and Discourses, Everyman's Library, E.P
    Duutton and Company, New York, 1950, Pg 66
2   Demokratia, Definitions, www.definitions.net/demokratia
3   Brennan, Jason, Against Democracy, Princeton University Press, 2016, Pg 8
4   Lichterman, Joseph, Nearly half of U.S. adults get news on Facebook,
    Pew says, NiemanLab, May 26, 2016, www.niemanlab.org/2016/05/
    pew-report-44%-of-u-s--adults-get-news-on-facebook/
5   Moyo, Dambisa, Why Democracy Doesn't Deliver, Foreign Policy, April 2018, https://
    foreignpolicy.com/2018/04/26/why-democracy-doesn't-deliver/
6   Fukuyama, Francis, The End of History, The National Interest, Summer 1989
7   Fukuyama, Francis, The End of History and the Last Man, Introduction, Penguin, 1992
8   Luhrman, Anna, and Wilson, Matthew, One third of the world's population lives in
    a declining democracy, Money Cage Analysis, Washington Post, July 4, 2018, www.
    washingtonpost.com/news/money-cage/wp/2018/07/03/ one-third-of-the-world's-
    population-lives-in-a-declining-democracy/?utm_term=.1.0a0053f3cb&wpirsc=nl_
    most&most&wpmm=1
9   Ibid
10 Hohmann, James, etal, The Daily 202: A poll commissioned by Bush and Biden
    shows Americans losing confidence in democracy, www.washingtonpost.com/news/
    powerpost/paloma/daily-202/2018/06/26/daily-202-a-poll-commissioned-by-bush-
    and-biden-shows-americans-lsing-confidence-in-democracy/
11 Mintz, Steven, Winning the Vote: A History of Voting Rights, History Now,
    downloaded May 24, 2017, www.gilderlehrman.org/history-by-era/
    government-and-civics/essays/winning-vote-history-voting-rights
12 Foner, Eric, and Garraty, John, The Reader's Companion to American History,
    Houghton, Mifflin Company, Boston, 1991, Pg 1043-1047
13 Madison, James, The Federalist, Number 10, The Modern Library, New York, 1937,
    Pg 56
14 Ibid

15   Brennan, Jason, Against Democracy, Princeton University Press, Princeton, NJ, 2016, Pg 8

16   Packer, George, The Populists, The New Yorker, September 7, 2015, Pg 23

17   Mahler, Jonathan, Trump's Message Resonates With White Supremacists, New York Times, March 1, 2016, Pg A15

18   Trotter, Gayle, Hillar Clinton's email, ethics eruptions and legal technicalities, The Hill, April 29, 2015, http://thehill.com/blogs/pundits-blog/presidential-campaign/240410-hillary-clintons-email-ethics-eruptions-and-legal

19   Steinmetz, Kathy, The 9%: Congress's Approval Rating Hits the Single Digits, Time, November 12, 2013, http://swampland.time.com/2013/11/12/the-9-congress-approval-rating-hits-the-single-digits/

20   Swanson, Emily, Major survey finds record low confidence in government, AP, March 12, 2015, http://news.yahoo.com/major-survey-finds-record-low-confidence-government-194703854

21   Rehm, Todd, Rasmussen: low approval ratings, for Congress, Senate, gapundit.com/2013/03/11/Rasmussen-low-approval-ratings-for-congress-senate/

22   Public Trust in Government: 1958-2017, Pew Research Center, May 4, 2017, www.people-press.org/2017/05/03/public-trust-in-government-1958-2017/?utm_source=Pew+Research+Center&utm_campaign=be5de05165-EMAIL_CAMPAIGN_2017_05_04&utm_medium=email&utm_term=)_3e95369b70-be5de05165-400219269

23   www.polifact.com/truth-o-meter/statements/2014/nov/11/facebook-posts/congress-has-11-approval-ratings-96-incumbets-re-e/

24   Salam, Reihan, and Richie, Rob, How to Make Congress Bipartisan, OpEd, New York Times, July 8, 2017, Pg A19

25   Ibid

26   Appelbaum, Yoni, Is the American Idea Over, The Atlantic, November 2017, Pg 17

27   Longo, Nicholas, and Meyer, Ross, College Students and Politics: A Literature Review, Circle Working Paper 46, May 2006, www.civicyouth.org/popups/workingpapers/wp46longomeyer.pdf

28   Appelbaum

29   Brennan, Against Democracy, Pg 200-201

30   Flam, Faye, Trump's 'Dangerous Disability'? It's the Dunning-Kruger Effect, Bloomberg News, May 12, 2017, www.bloomberg.com/view/articlesd/2017-05-12/trumps-dangerous-disability-it-s-the-dunning-kruger-effect

31   Porter, Eduardo, The Government Check Disconnect, New York Times Business, December 22, 2018, Pg B1

32   Short, John Rennie, Why There's A Globalization Backlash, US News, November 29, 2016, www.usnews.com/news/national-news/articles/2016-11-29/why-theres-a-globalization-backlash/

33   Starr, Kelsey Jo, Tepid support for democracy among both young and old in Central and Eastern Europe, Pew Research Center, June 8, 2017, www.pewresearch.org/fact-tank/2017/06/08/tepid-support-for-democracy-among-both-young-and-old-in-central-and-eastern-europe/?utm_source=Pew+Research+Center&utm_campaign=490a9a6cc9

34   Leahy, Joe, and Schipani, Andres, Culture of corruption engulfs Brazilian elite, Financial Times, May 25, 2017, www.ft.com/content/3490dbb8-4050-11e7-9d56-25f963e998b2

35   Piketty, Thomas, Capital in the Twenty-First Century, Belknap Press, Cambridge, Massachusetts, 2014, Pg 248, Table 7.2

36   Somin, Ilya, When Ignorance Isn't Bliss- How Political Ignorance Threatens Democracy, Policy Analysis #525, September 22, 2004, Cato Institute

37   Owen, Diana, et al, Civic Education and Knowledge of Government and Politics, paper prepared for Annual Meeting of the American Political Science Association, Seattle, Washington, September 1-4, 2011

38   Krugman, Paul, Knowledge Isn't Power, New York Times, July 31, 2014, OpEd

39   Johnson, Fawn, Obama: Infrastructure a Top Priority, National Journal, October 25, 2010, http://transportation.nationaljournal.com/2010/10/obama-infrastructure-a-to-pri.php

40   Spiegel, Peter, Berlin attacks EU's easing of austerity demands, Financial Times, February 28, 2014, www.ft.com/intl/cms/s/0/d7b79578-a000-11e3-9c65-00144fe-ab7de.html#axzz3L3kliOMZ

41   Werleman, C.J, Americans Are Dangerously Politically Ignorant- The Numbers Are Shocking, Alternet, September 4, 2014, www.alternet.org/print/news-amp-politics/americans-are-dangerously-politically-ignorant-the-numbers-are-shocking/

42   Ewing, Tom, Dismal Civics Knowledge Linked to Decline in Voting, Volunteering Among Young, ETS News May 23, 2012, http://news.ets.org/news/dismal-civics-knowledge-linked-to-decline-in-voting-volunteering-among-young

43   Network To Up Its Spending, Politico, January 29, 2017

44   Stohr, Greg, Bloomberg Poll: Americans want Supreme Court to Turn Off Political Spending Spigot, September 8, 2015, www.bloomberg.com/politics/article/2015-09-28/bloomberg-poll-americans-want-supreme-court-to-turn-off-political-spending-spigot

45   Brennan, Jason, Against Democracy, Princeton University Press, 2016, Pg 110

46   Blumenthal, Mark, What Americans Know: Pew Research Finds Most Can Identify Where Parties Stand, Huffington Post Pollster, www.huffington-post.com/2012/4/11/what-americans-know-pew-research-party-positions-leaders_n_1418489.html

47   Romano, Andrew, How Ignorant Are Americans, Newsweek, March 22, 2011, www.newsweek.com/how-ignorant-are-americans-665053?om_nd=CTiCsY&om_mid=BNhmKiB8ZvuD37#

48   Werleman, C.J., Alternet, Americans Are Dangerously Politically Ignorant, June 17, 2014, www.alternet.org

49   Ibid

50   Current Knowledge of Current Affairs Little Changed by News and Information Revolutions, Pew Research, Center for the People and the Press, April 2007, www.people-press.org/2007/04/15/public-knowledge-of-current-affairs-little-changed-by-news-and-information-revolutions/

51   Will, George, Political Ignorance Is Alive and Well, January 2, 2014, www.newsmax.com/GeorgeWill/Political-Ignorance-Democracy-Somin/2014/01/02

52   CNN Poll: Americans flunk budget IQ test, April 2, 2011, www.cnn.com/2011/POLITICS/04/01/americans.flunk.budget.iq/index.html

53   Egan, Timothy, Why Do We Re-elect Them?, OpEd, New York Times, October 8, 2104

54   Just 63% Know Which Parties Control House and Senate, Rasmussen Reports, September 11, 2014, www.rasmussenreports.com/public_content/politics/general_politics/september_2014/just_63_know_which_parties_control_house_and_senate

55   Dorning, Mike and Woellert, Lorraine, Weak Wages Stir Voter Ire at Obama Amid Gridlock, Bloomberg, October 31, 2014, www.bloomberg.com/news/print/2014-10-31/weak-wages-stir-voter-ire-at-obama-amid-gridlock.html

56   Edelman, Adam, Many Louisiana Republicans blame President Obama for Hurricane Katrina response, New York Daily News, August 21, 2013, www.nydailynews.com/news/poliotics/louisiana-republicans-blame-president-obama-hurricane-katrina-response

57   Ross, Janell, How come 53 percent of Republicans think the unemployment rate has risen under Obama, The Fix, The Washington Post, November 20, 2015, www.washingtonpost.com/news/thefix/wp/2015/11/20/the-amount-of-misinformation-about-our-economy-is-amazing/?utm_term=.2fdf65a40d4f

58   Bryan, Bob, The Verdict, A comprehensive look back at Obama's job record, Business Insider, January 6, 2017, www.businessinsider.com/obama-jobs-report-labor-market-participation-rate-2017-1/#since-obama-took-offfice-in-january-2009-the-us-economy-has-added-11250000-people-to-total-nonfarm-payrolls-1

59   Big Gaps Found in College Students' Grasp of Current Affairs, New York times, April 18, 1993, www.nytimes.com/1993/04/18/us/big-gaps-found-in-college-students-grasp-of-current-affairs.html

60   Dye, Thomas, What Florida University Graduates Don't Know About History and Government, James Madison Institute, March 1996, Madison OpEd Series

61   Surowiecki, James, Trump's Budget Bluff, The New Yorker, February 13 & 20th, 2017, Pg 34

62   Stephens, Bret, Climate of Complete Certainty, OpEd, New York Times, April 29, 2017, Pg A23

63   Newport, Frank, In U.S., 42% Believe Creationist View of Human Origins, June 2, 2014, http://news.gallup.com/poll/170822/believe-creationist-view-human-origins.aspx

64   Anderson, Kurt, How America Lost Its Mind, The Atlantic, September 2017, Pg 76

65   Lockie, Alex, Poll: A majority of Republicans think Trump won the popular vote, Business Insider, December 18, 2016, www.businessinsider.com/poll-trump-popular-vote-republicans-hillary-clinton-2016-12

66   Horsey, David, Americans who voted against Trump are feeling unprecedented dread and despair, Los Angeles Times, December 21, 2016, www.latimes.com/opinion/topoftheticket/la-na-tt-american-dread-20161220-story.html

67   Anderson

68   Jensen, Tom, Trump Remains Unpopular; Voters Prefer Obama on Scotus Pick, Public Policy Polling, December 9, 2016, www.publicpolicypolling.com

69   Price, Greg, The Deep State Controls Government Policy in US, Most Americans Believe In New Poll, Newsweek, March 19, 2018, www.newsweek.com/deep-state-us-real-control-851006

70   Fitz, Nicholas, The American people are clueless: Why income inequality is so much worse than we realize, Scientific American, Salon, April 1, 2015, www.salon.com/2015/04/01/the_american_people_are_clueless_why_income_inequality_is_so_much_worse_than_we_realize_partner?

71   Pew Research Center, From Brexit to Zika: What Do Americans Know, July 25, 2017, www.people-press.org/2017/07/25/from-brexit-to-zike-what-do-americans-know/

72   Tappin, Ben, et al, Your Opinion Is Set In Stone, New York Times Sunday Review, May 28, 2017, Pg 8

73   Mitchell, Amy, et al, Distinguishing Between Factual and Opinion Statements in the News, Pew Research Center, June 18, 2018, www.journalism.org/2018/06/18/distinguishing-between-factual-and-opinion-statements-in-the-news/

74   Levinthal, Dave- Center for Public Integrity, Nasty Attacks Dominate Airwaves In Senate Battleground States, Huffington Post, October 16, 2104, www.huffington-post.com/2014/10/16/2014-elections_n_5995810.html

75   Tarlo, Shira, Democrats demand recount after indicted GOP congressman wins re-election, Salon, November 7, 2018, www.salon.com/2018/11/07/democrat-demands-recount-after-indicted-gop-congressman-wins-re-election/

76   Sherman, Amy, Rick Scott 'oversaw the largest Medicare fraud in the nation's history,' Florida Democratic Party says, Tampa Bay Times/ Miami Herald, March 3, 2014 PoliFact Florida, www.polifact.com/flordia/statement/2014/mar/03/florida-democratic-party/rick-scott-rick-scott-oversaw-largest-medicare-fra/

77   Caputo, Marc and Smith, Adam, How Rick Scott won reelection as Florida governor, Miami Herald, November 5, 2014, www.miamiherald.com/news/politics-government/article3589527.html

78   Sack, Kevin, and Mazzei, Patricia, Ultrawealthy Candidate Set Up A Blind Trust That Wasn't Blind, New York Times, October 18, 2018, Pg A1

79   Mazzei, Patricia, et al, Scott Unseats Senate Democrat After a Manual Recount in Florida, New York Times, November 19, 2018, Pg A11

80   Lubin, Gus, The 14 Most Corrupt Members of Congress Who Aren't Charlie Rangel, Business Insider, July 26, 2010, www.businessinsider.com/the-14-most-corrupt-members-of-congress-who-arent-charlie-rangel-2010-7?op=1

81   Kane, Paul, Rep. Charlie Rangel found guilty of 11 ethics violations, Washington Post, November 16, 2010, www.washingtonpost.com/wp-dyn/content/article/2010/11/16/AR2010111604000.html

82   Durden, Tyler, Presenting 2011's Top 10 Most Corrupt American Politicians, Zero Hedge, January 2, 2012, www.zerohedge.com/news/presenting-2011s-top-10-most-corrupt-american-politicians

83   Surowiecki, James, The Corruption Conundrum, The New Yorker, February 6, 2017, Pg 19

84   Hussey, Kristin, Joseph Ganim, Disgraced Ex-Mayor of Bridgeport, Conn., Wins Back Job, New York Times, November 4, 2015

85   Bornemeier, James, New Details Released in House Check Scandal, Los Angeles Times, April 2, 1992, http://articles/latimes.com/1992-04-02/local/me-258_1_overdrafts

86   Standard Eurobarometer 79, Spring 2013, http://ec.europa.eu/public_opinion/archives/eb/eb79_first_en.pdf

87   Does Political Knowledge Increase Support for Europe?, CES info Working Papers, http://papers.sssm.com/sol3/papers.cfm?abstract_id=1785254

88   McVeigh, Karen, and Fishwick, Carmen, Kelvin MacKenzie is far from the only one with Brexit buyer's remorse, The Guardian, June 27, 2016, www.theguardian.com/politics/jun27/eu-referendum--kelvin-mackenzie-brexit-buyers-remorse

89   Friedman, Thomas, The U.K. Has Gone Mad, New York Times, OpEd, April 3, 2019, Pg A23

90   Stephens, Bret, An Antidote to Idiocy in a New Book About Churchill, OpEd, New York Times, December 15, 2018, Pg A26

91   Cigainero, Jake, Who Are France's Yellow Vest Protesters, And What Do They Want, NPR, December 3, 2018, www.npr.org/2018/12/03/67286235/who-are-frances-yellow-vest-protesters-and-what-do-they-want

92   Associated Press, Brazil: Former President Lula da Silva Convicted of Corruption, NBC News, July 12, 2017, www.nbcnews.com/news/latino/brazil-former-president-lula-da-silva-convicted-corruption-n782291

93   Fisher, Max, and Taub, Amanda, Why Uprooting Corruption Has Thrown Brazil's Political System Into Upheaval, New York Times, July 15, 2017, Pg A6

94   Vaishnev, Milan, When Crime Pays: Money and Muscle in Indian Politics, Quoted in The Atlantic, June 2017, Pg 17

95   Pew Poll, April 15, 2007, www.people-press.org/2007/04/15/public-knowledge-of-current-affairs-little-changed-by-news-and-information-revolutions/

96   Owen, Diana, et al

97   Carter, Bill, and Steel, Emily, It's Muted, But Buzz for Fall TV Returns, New York Times, B1, September 22, 2014

98   Hsu, Tiffany, Big Spenders on Small Screens Worry as Digital Backlash Grows, New York Times, January 6, 2020, Pg B2

99   National Voter Turnout in Federal Elections: 1960-2012, Infoplease, www.infoplease.com/pa/A0781453.html

100 Domonoske, Camila, A Boatload of Ballots: Midterm Voter Turnout Hits 50-Year High, NPR, November 8, 2018, www.npr.org/2018/11/08/665197690/a-boatload-of-ballots-midterm-voter-turnout-hit-50-year-high

101 Friedman, Howard Steven, American Voter Turnout Lower Than Other Wealthy Countries, Huff Post Politics, 9/09/12, www.huffingtonpost.com/howard-steven-friedman/voter-turnout-europe-america_b_1660271.html

102 Wallace, Gregory, Voter turnout at 20-year low in 2016, CNN Politics, November 30, 2016, www.cnn.com/2016/11/11/politics/popular-vote-turnout-2016/

103 Voter Identification Requirements, NCSL, National Conference of State Legislators, June 25, 2014, www.ncsl.org/research/elections-and-campaigns/voter-id.aspx

104 Krugman, Paul, The G.O.P. Goes Full Authoritarian, OpEd, New York Times, December 11, 2018, Pg A26

105 Fausset, Richard, Court Says District Map Can Stand For Midterms, New York Times, September 8, 2018, Pg A15

106 Jacobs, Tom, The Policy Consequences of Partisan Gerrymandering, Pacific Standard, October 4, 2017, https://psmag.com/news/the-policy-consequences-of-partisan-gerrymandering

107 Gallup Polls, American Dissatisfaction, New York Times, Match 17, 2016, Pg A21

108 Study: US is an oligarchy, not a democracy, Echo Chambers, BBC, April 17, 2016, WWW.bbc/news/blogs-echochambers-27074746

109 The mid-terms produce a divided government for a divided country, The Economist, November 8, 2018, www.economist.com/2018/11/08/the-mid-terms-produce-a-divided-government-for-a-divided-country

110 Hamilton, Alexander, The Federalist Papers, Number 1, New American Library, New York, 1961, Pg 35

111 Plato, Republic, VIII, Vintage Books, New York, Pg 321.

112 Aristotle, The Politics, Penguin Books, London, 1988, Definitions of Democracy and Oligarchy, Pg 245

113 Ibid 251
114 Ibid, Principles and Practices of Democracy, Pg 362
115 Machiavelli, Niccolo, The Prince, Bantam Classics, New York, 2003, Pg 106
116 Hobbes, Thomas, Leviathan, Penguin Classics, New York, 1986, Pg 185
117 Spinoza's Political Philosophy, Stanford Encyclopedia of Philosophy, October 7, 2013, 4.3.3, https://plato.stamford.edu/entries/spinoza-political/#Dem
118 Kirsch, Adam, What Makes You So Sure? The New Yorker, September 5, 2016, Pg 71, Quote Spinoza- Theological-Political Treatise
119 Locke, John, Two Treatises of Government, Orion Publishing Group, London, 1993, Pg 164 (paragraph 97)
120 Ibid, Pg 211 (Paragraph 192)
121 Adams, John, 1814 letter, Ketchum, Dan, Why Did John Adams Say That Democracy Never Lasts Long, http://classroom.synonym.com/did-john-adams-say-democracy-never-lasts-long-7843.html
122 John Stuart Mill, Stanford Encyclopedia of Philosophy, downloaded May 30, 2017, http://plato.stanford.edu/entries/mill/
123 Ibid, Pg 18 (Utilitarianism, X:237)
124 Ibid, Pg 29, (Liberty XVIII:269)
125 Ibid, Pg 29 (Considerations, XIX:473)
126 Ibid, Pg 30 (Considerations XIX: 478)
127 Estlund, David, Why Not Epistocracy/, Desire, Identity and Existence, Essays in honor of T.M. Penner, Academic Printing and Publishing, 2003, Pg 53-69
128 Brennan, Jason, Against Democracy, Princeton University Press, 2016
129 Caplan, Bryan, The Myth of the Rational Voter, Princeton University Press, 2007
130 Ibid, Pg 112-113
131 Lewis, Michael, The Undoing Project, WW Norton & Company, New York, 2017
132 Kahneman, Daniel, Thinking Fast and Slow, Farrar, Strauss and Giroux, New York, 2011
133 Irrational decisions driven by emotions, University College London, August 3, 2006, www.ucl.ac.uk/media/library/decisionbrain
134 Fernbach, Philip, and Sloman, Steven, The Knowledge Illusion, Riverhead Books, New York, 2017
135 Taub, Amanda, Partisanship as a Tribal Identity, New York Times, April 13, 2017, Pg A10
136 Jacobs, Tom, Racism, Xenophobia, and Trump's Win, Pacific Standard Magazine, November 10, 2016, https://psmag.com/racism-xenophobia-and-trumps-win-cbe07344e75c#.15ekqjv5a
137 Beck, Julie, Understanding America's Moral Divides, The Atlantic, December 14, 2016, www.theatlantic.com/science/archive/2016/12/the-psychology-of-moral-divides/510569/?utm_source=nl-atlantic-daily-121416
138 Sullivan, Andrew, Democracies end when they are too democratic, New York Magazine, May 2, 2016, Pg 31
139 Brands, Hal, and Edel, Charles, The End of History Is the Birth of Tragedy, Foreign Policy, May 29, 2017, http://foreignpolicy.com/2017/05/29/the-end-of-history-is-the-birth-of-tragedy/?utm_source=Sailthru&utm_medium=email&utm_campaign=New%20Campaign&utm_term=Flashpoints
140 Kottasova, Ivana, Trump criticized NATO spending. Here's what's really going on, CNN Money, May 25, 2017, http://money.cnn.com/2017/05/25/news/nato-trump-defense-spending/index.html

141 Editorial, Donald Trump's Insult to History, New York Times, May 31, 2017, Pg A 20

142 Hacker, Jacob, and Pierson, Paul, American Amnesia, Simon and Schuster, New York, 2016

143 Smith, Adam, The Wealth of Nations, Bantam Dell, New York, 2003, (originally published 1776), Pg 195

144 Ibid, Pg 1042-43

145 Hayek, F.A., The Road to Serfdom, University of Chicago Press, 1944, Pg 148

146 Ibid

147 Somin, Ilya, Democracy and Political Ignorance, Stanford Law Books, 2016, Pg 2

148 Ibid, Pg 229

149 Ibid, Pg 232

150 Gearin, Mary, Vladimir Putin accused of using Soviet-style propaganda strategy to control Russian media, ABC News, September 16, 2014, www.abc.net.au/news/2014-09-16/putin-accused-of-manipulating-media-by-critics/5748440

151 Gedmin, Jeffrey, It's Not Just Ukraine, Politico Magazine, November 30, 2014, www.politico.com/magazine/story/2014/11/its-not-just-ukraine-113164_full.html#.VlHHnxNOzq5

152 Aratunyan, Anna, Putin's move on Crimea bolsters popularity back home, USA Today, March 19, 2014, www.usatoday.com/story/news/world/2014/03/18/crimea-ukraine-putin-russia/6564263/

153 Kotkin, Stephen, Russia's Perpetual Geopolitics, Foreign Affairs, May/June 2016, Pg 2

154 Hille, Kathrin, FT Big Read. Russia, Putin's Balance Sheet, Financial Times, March 8, 2016, Pg 7

155 Ibid

156 Birnbaum, Michael, How to understand Putin's jaw-droppingly high approval ratings, Washington Post, March 6, 2016, www.washingtonpost.com/world/europe/how-to-understand-putins-jaw-droppingly-high-approval-ratings/2016/03/0517f5d8f2-d5ba-11e5-a65b-587e721fb231_story.html

157 Gvosdev, Nikolas K, The Bear Awakens: Russia's Military Is Back, The National Interest, November 12, 2014, http://nationalinterest.org/commentary/russias-military-back-9181

158 Luhn, Alec, Stalin, Russia's New Hero, New York Times Sunday Review, March 13, 2016, Pg 7

159 Giraldi, Philip, Turkey in Conflict, Assyrian International News Agency, January 20, 2014, www.aina.org/news/20140120143013.htm

160 Steinvorth, Daniel, Erdogan and the Traitors: Scandals and Protests Threaten Turkey's AKP, Spiegel Online International, March 19, 2014, www.spiegel.de/interntaional/europe/turkish-prime-minister-facing-corruption-scandal-protests-a-959453.html

161 Turkey's War of Distraction, Editorial, New York Times, August 31, 2015, Pg A14

162 Cook, Steven, What Turkey's election surprise says about the troubled country, Fortune Insider, November 2, 2015, http://fortune.com/2015/11/02/turkey-election-akp/

163 Yeginsu, Ceylan, A Comment in Turkey About Hitler Stirs Alarm, New York Times, January 2, 2016, Pg A4

164 Arrango, Tim, and Yeginsu, Ceylan, Parliamentary Election Victory Bolsters Turkish President's Bid to Add Power, New York Times, November 3, 2015, Pg A9

165 Akarcesme, Sevgi, Despotic Zeal in Turkey, New York Times OpEd, March 9, 2016, Pg A21

166 Editorial, Democracy's Disintegration in Turkey, New York Times, March 8, 2016, Pg A 26

167 Arrango, Tim, and Yeginsu, Ceylan, Needing Help, Europe Ignores Turkish Abuses, New York Times, March 9, 2016, Pg A1

168 Cockburn, Patrick, President Erdogan could be using the coup against him to turn Turkey towards full-scale Islamisation, Independent, July 18, 2016, www.independent.co.uk/news/world/europe/turkey-cou-president-erdogan-islam-akp-government-a7142836.html

169 Tharoor, Ishaan, What Erdogan's narrow referendum victory means for Turkey, The Washington Post, April 17, 2017, www.washingtonpost.com/news/world-views/wp/2017/04/17/what-erdogans-narrow-referendum-victory-means-for-turkey/?utm_term=18ea81572c42

170 Berendt, Joanna, Polish Government Undermines Democracy, E.U. Says, New York Times, April 14, 2016, Pg A8

171 Polish President Vetoes Bill to Purge Supreme Court Judges, YouTube, July 25, 2017, www.youtube.com/watch?v=Yiol3Cz_y

172 Markovic, Frank, Hungary's Democratic Standards: a Slippery Slope to Autocracy, European Public Affairs, March 26, 2014, www.europeanpublicaffirs.eu/hungarys-democratic-stands-a-slippery-slope-to-autocracy/

173 Viktor Orban wins four more years, Euronews, June 4, 2014, www.euronews.com/2014/04/06/hungarian-elections-2014-live-coverage/

174 Rodriguez, Andrea, and Sanchez, Fabiola, Venezuelan President Moves Swiftly Against The Opposition, Huffington Post Latino Voices, March 21, 2014, www.huffingtonpost.com/2014/03/21/venezuelan-president-opposition_n_5007473.html

175 Romero, Simon, A Polarizing Figure Who Led a Movement, New York Times, March 5, 2013, www.nytimes.com/2013/03/06/world/americas/hugo-chavez-venezuelas-polarizing-leader-dies-at-58.html?_r=0

176 Wilson, Peter and Gupta, Girish, Venezuela's Maduro narrowly wins presidency, USA Today, April 15, 2013, www.usatoday.com/story/news/world/2013/04/15/maduro-wins-venezuela-presidency/2083457/

177 Neuman, William, 9 Opposition Candidates Barred From Venezuela's December Ballot, New York Times, August 24, 2015, Pg A4

178 Kryl, Jeremy, Has Venezuelan President Maduro Gone Insane, The Daily Beast, September 27, 2105, www.thedailybeast.com/articles/2015/09/27/has-venezuelan-president-maduro-gone-insane/

179 Azocar, Geraldine, and Atencio, Mariana, 'Mother of All Marches' Turns Violent in Venezuela, NBC News, April 19, 2017, www.nbcnews.com/storyline/venezuela-crisis/mother-of-all-marches-turns-violent-venezuela-n748396

180 Dwyer, Colin, Photos: As Anti-Maduro Protests Swell in Venezuela, Death Toll Mounts, npr, April 14, 2017, www.npr.org/sections/thetwo-way/2017.04/14/523922534/phtos-as-anti-maduro-protests-swell-in-venezuela-death-toll-mounts.

181 Sanchez, Ray, Venezuela: How Paradise Got Lost, CNN, July 27, 2017, www.cnn.com/2017/04/21/americas/venezuela-crisis-explained/

182 Morales, Neil, Philippines' election victor Dutarte plans government overhaul, Reuters World News, May 11, 2016, www.reuters.com/articles/us-philippines-election-idUSKCN0XZ02N

183 Curato, Nicole, All Dutarte's People, OpEd, New York Times, June 1, 2017, Pg A23

184 Shirer, William L, The Rise and Fall of the Third Reich, Chapters 7 and 8, Pg 263-381, Ballantine Books, New York,, 1960

185 Benito Mussolini, History, BBC, www.bbc.co.uk/historic_figures/mussolini_benito.shtml

186 Thorne, John, Political assassination unsettles fragile Tunisian democracy, Christian Science Monitor, July 26, 2013, www.csmonitor.com/World/Middle-East/2013/0726/Political-assassination-unsettles-fragile-Tunisian-democracy

187 Thomason, Andy, Islamic-Studies Professor, Accused of Blasphemy, Is Assassinated in Pakistan, The Chronicle of Higher Education, September 18, 2104, http://chronicle.com/blogs/ticker/jp/Islamic-studies-professor-accused-of-blasphemy-is-assassinated-in-pakistan

188 India's middle class population to touch 267 million in 5 yrs, The Economic Times, February 6, 2011, http://articles.economictimes.indiatimes.com/2011-02-06/news/28424975-1-middle-class-population-to-touch-267-million-in-5-years/

189 BBC News Business, India's economic growth disappoints, May 30, 2104, www.bbc.com/news/business-27638906

190 Harris, Gardiner, 'Superbugs' Kill India's Babies and Pose an Overseas Threat, New York Times, December 4, 2014, Pg A1

191 Chotiner, Isaac, India's Election: The Next Prime Minister Is a Dangerous man, New Republic, May 16, 2104www.newrepublic.com/article/117783/narendra-modis-election-and-future-india

192 Najar, Nida, Rumors of Cow Killings in India Deepen Rift Between Hindus and Muslims, New York Times, October 14, 2015, www.nytimes.com/2014/10/15/world/rumors-of-cow-killings-in-india-deepen-rift-between-hindus-and-muslims.html

193 Outspoken Indian scholar killed by gunmen, Al Jazeera, August 30, 2015, www.aljazeera.com/news/2015/08/outspoken-indian-scholar-rationalist-killed-150830093019963.html

194 Barstow, David, and Raj, Suhasini, Indian Writers Spurn Awards as Violence Flares, New York Times, October 18, 2105, Pg A1

195 Pandit, Eesha, The modern horrors of India's ancient injustice: How a government has abandoned millions- and they are fighting back, Salon, October 22, 2015, www.slaon.com/2015/10/22/the_modern_horrors_of_india's_ancient_injustice_how_a_government_has_abandoned_millions_and_they_are_fighting_back

196 Fackler, Martin, Japan's Election Returns Power to Old Guard, New York Times, December 16, 2012, www.nytimes.com/2012/12/17/world/asia/conservative-liberal-democratic-party-nearing-a-return-to-power-in-japan.html?pagewanted=all

197 Fackler, Martin, With Bad Economic News for Japan, Abe's Magic Seems to Evaporate, New York Times, November 20, 2014, Pg A13

198 Fixes for Japan's Economy, Editorial, New York Times, September 10, 2014

199 Harding, Robin, and Jones, Claire, Soaring yen defies Tokyo's effort to spur growth and head off deflation, Financial Times, April 8, 2016, Pg 1

200 Saito, Mary, and Slodkowski, Antoni, Japan says Fukushima leak worse than thought, government joins clean-up, Reuters, August 7, 2013, www.reuters.com/article/2013/08/07/us-japan-fukushima-pm-idUSBRE97601K20130807

201 Fackler, Martin, Rewriting War, Japanese Right Goes on Attack, New York Times, December 3, 2014, Pg A1

202 Cochrane, Joe, Singapore: Victory for Governing Party, New York Times, September 12, 2015, Pg A7

203 Cochrane, Joe, Suspense in Singapore Vote Is the Strength of a Long-Governing Party's Grip, New York Times, September 10, 2015, Pg A10

204 Democracy in Crisis: Freedom House Releases Freedom in the World 2018, http://freedomhouse.org/article/democracy-crisis-freedom-house-releases-freedom-world-2018

205 Kreig, Gregory, President Trump has a long history of praise for autocrats, dictators and strongmen, CNN Politics, April 18, 2017, www.cnn.com/2016/07/06/politics/donald-trump-favorite-dictators-and-strongmen/

206 Thompson, Mark, and Ghosh, Bobby, Did Waterboarding Prevent Terrorism Attacks? Time Magazine, April 21, 2009, http://content.time.com/nation/article/0,8599,1892947,00.html

207 Goldsmith, Jack, The Terror Presidency, WW Norton and Company, New York, 2007

208 Hersh, Joshua, Extraordinary Rendition Report Finds More Than 50 Nations Involved In Global Torture Scheme, Huffington Post, TheWorldPost, February 4, 2013, www.huffingtonpost.com/2013/02/04/extraordinary-rendition-torture-report_n_2617809.html

209 Goldman, Adam, Six Guantanamo detainees transferred to Uruguay as Obama works to close prison, Washington Post, December 7, 2014, www.washingtonpost.com/world/national-security/sxi-guantanamo-detainees-transferred-to-uruguay-as-obama-works-to-close-prison/2014/12/07/18f8ca3c-7c03-11e4-9a27-6fdbc612bff8_story.html

210 Ricks, Thomas, Fiasco- The American Military Adventure in Iraq, Penguin Press, New York, 2006

211 Mehsud, Saud, U.S. drone strikes in Pakistan kill at least eight suspected militants, Reuters, October 7, 2014, www.reuters.com/article/2014/10/07/us-pakistan-drones-idUSKCN0HW0NZ20141007

212 Walt, Vivienne, European Officials Infuriated by Alleged NSA Spying on Friendly Diplomats, Time, June30, 2013, http://world.time.com/2013/06//30/european-officials-infuriated-by-alleged-nsa-spying-on-friendly-diplomats/

213 Bartolomeo, Liz, The Political Spending of 501(c)(4) Nonprofits in the 2012 Election, Sunlight Foundation, May 21,2013, http://sunlightfoundation.com/blog/2013/05/21/the-political-spending-of-501c4-nonprofits-in-the-2012-election/

214 Sorkin, Andrew Ross, and Thee-Brenan, Megan, Many Feel American Dream Is Out of Reach, Poll Shows, New York Times, December 11, 2014, Pg B1

215 Lauter, David, and Ulloa, Jazmine, Family separations at the border: How did we get here? Los Angeles Times, June 19, 2018, www.latimes.com/politics/la-na-pol-family-separation-q-a-20180618-story.html

216 Goodman, David, China's middle class may be rising, but not in revolt, South China Morning Post, October 28, 2013, www.scmp.com/comment/insight-opinion/article/1339795/chinas-middle-class-may-be-rising-not-revolt

217 Walker, Peter, and Taylor, Matthew, Far right on rise in Europe says report, , The Guardian, November 6, 2011, www.theguardian.com/world/2011/nov/06/far-right-rise-europe-report

218 Turning Right, The Economist, January 4, 2014, www.economist.com.news/briefing//21592666-parties-nationalist-right-are-changing-terms-european-political-debate-does

219 Kern, Soeren, European Concerns Over Muslim Immigration Go Mainstream, Gatestone Institute, August 15, 2011, www.gatestoneinstitute.org/2349/european-concerns-muslim-immigration

220 Lyman, Rick, and Smale, Alison, Defying Soviets, Then Pulling Hungary to Putin, New York Times, November 7, 2014, www.nytimes.com/2014/11/08/world/europe/viktor-orban-steers-hungary-towards-russia-25-years-after-fall-of-the-berlin-wall.html

221 AP, Bolivia: President's Supporters Aim To Alert Constitution to Allow 4th Term, New York Times, September 10, 2015, Pg A8

222 Mussolini, Benito, Interview by Edwin James of the New York Times, 1928, http://thinkexist.com/quotes/benito_mussolini

223 Wallace, Gregory, Voter turnout at 20-year low in 2016, CNN Politics, November 30, 2016, www.cnn.com/2016/11/11/politics/popular-vote-turnout-2016/

224 Kuhn, David Paul, Bigotry Didn't Elect Trump, New York Times, OpEd, December 27, 2016, Pg A19

225 Grynbaum, Michael, Trump Calls Media the 'Enemy of the American People,' New York Times, February 18, 2017, Pg A15

226 Clinton, Trump voters sharply diverged on seriousness of an array of problems, Pew Research Center, November 10, 2016, www.people-press.org/2016/11/10/a-divided-and-pessimistic-electorate/1-11/

227 Vitali, Ali, Trump Says He Could Shoot Somebody and Still Maintain Support, NBC News, January 23, 2016, www.nbcnews.com/politics/2016-election//trump-syas-he-could-shoot-somebody-and-still-maintain-support-n502911

228 2016 Iowa Caucus, February 2, 2016, http://2016iowacaucus.com/cruz-defeats-trump/

229 New Hampshire Primary Results, NBC News, February 9, 2016, www.nbcnews.com/politics/2016-election/primaries/NH

230 Ibid

231 Bump, Phillip, Hillary Clinton just clinched the Democratic nomination. Here's the math behind it, Washington Post, June 6, 2016, www.washingtonpost.com/news/the-fix/wp/2016/06/06/make-no-mistake-hillary-will-clinch-the-democratic-nomi-nation-on-tuesday/?utm_term=.40eb74d5b4d0

232 Ibid

233 TPP: What is it and why does it matter?, BBC News, November 22, 2016, www.bbc.com/news/business-32498715

234 Hofstadter, Richard, The Paranoid Style in American Politics, Harper's Magazine, November 1964, https://harpers.org/archive/1964/11/the-paranoid-style-in-american-politics/

235 Thrall, Trevor, and Goepner, Erik, Trump terrorism fear-mongering versus the facts, New York Daily News, February 22, 2017, www.nydailynews.com/opinion/trump-terrorism-fearmongering-facts-article-1.2979567

236 Gonzalez-Barrera, Ana, More Mexicans Leaving Than Coming to the U.S, Pew Research Center, November 9, 2015, www.pewhispanic.org/2015/11/19/more-mexicans-leaving-than-coming-to-the-u-s/

237 Crime Trends, http://victimsofcrime.org/docs/default-sourcencvrw/2015/2015ncvrw_stats_crimetrends.pdf?sfvrsn=2

238 Patterson, Thomas, Pre-Primary News Coverage of the 2016 Presidential Race: Trump's Rise, Sander's Emergence, Clinton's Struggle, Shorenstein Center on Media, Politics, and Public Policy, June 13, 2016, https://shorensteincenter.org/pre-primary-news-coverage-trump-clinton-sanders/

239 Ibid

240 Ibid

241 Ibid

242 ibid

243 Peters, Jeremy W, Primary Process Has Many Voters Feeling Sidelined, New York Times, April 10, 2016, Pg 1

244 2016 Election Timeline, AOL, www.aol.com/2016-election-timeline/

245 Catanese, David, DNC Chair Debbie Wasserman Schultz resigns as tensions threaten to roil convention, AOL News, July 24, 2016, www.aol.com/article/2016/07/24/dnc-chair-debbie-wasserman-schultz-resigns-as-tensions-threaten/21438130/

246 Steakin, William, Newly released emails show State Department ties with Clinton Foundation, Aol News, August 10, 2016, www.aol.com/articles/2016/08/10/newly-released-emails-show-state-department-ties-with-clinton-fo/21449011/

247 Vogel, Kenneth, Clinton Foundation in campaign tailspin, Politico, April 30, 2015, www.politico.com/story/2015/04/clinton-foundation-bill-hillary-chhelsea-117505

248 Rushton, Christine, Campaign 2016 updates: Hillary Clinton: Donald Trump isn't going to change, Los Angeles Times, August 17, 2016, www.latimes.com/nation/politics/trailguide/la-na-trailguide-updayes-lewandowski-new-trum-advisors-will-1471438244-htmlstory.html

249 Logan, Bryan, Hillary Clinton pegs half of Donald Trump's supporters as a 'basket of deplorables', September 10, 2016, www.businessinsider.com/hillary-clinton-basket-of-deplorables-donald-trump-2016-9?utm_source=referral&utm_medium=aol

250 CNN, Who won the presidential debate?, CNN News, September 27, 2016, www.cnn.com/2016/09/27/opinions/hillary-clinton-donald-trump-debate-opinion-roundup/index.html

251 Darcy, Oliver, Focus Groups: Hillary Clinton was the clear winner of the first presidential debate, Business Insider, September 26, 2016, www.businessinsider.com/focus-groups-who-won-clinton-trump-debate-polls-2016-9

252 New York Times: Trump's 1995 tax records suggest no federal taxes for years, Aol News, October 2, 2016, www.aol.com/article/2016/10/02/new-yok-times-trumps-1995-tax-records-suggest-no-feral-taxes/21484678/

253 Salinger, Tobias, Wikileaks releases emails with excerpts from Hillary Clinton's Wall Street speeches, Daily News, October 7, 2016, www.nydailnews.com/news/politics/wikileaks-releases-excerpts-clinton-wall-street-speeches-article-1-2822032

254 Cox, Jeff, Clinton speech to Deutche Bank worried her staff: Wikileaks, CNBC, October 17, 2016, www.cnbc.com/2016/10/17/clinton-speech-to-deutsche-bank-worried-her-staff-wikileaks.html

255 Dorell, Oren, Russia engineered election hacks and meddling in Europe, USA Today, January 9, 2017, www.usatoday.com/story/news/world/2017/01/09/russia-engineered-election-hacks-europe/96216556/

256 Timm, Jane, Trump on a hot mic: "When you're a star. you can do anything to women," NBC News, October 7, 2016, www.aol.com/article/2016/10/07/trump-on-hot-mic-whenyoure-a-star-you-can-do-anything-t21576949/

257 Caldwell, Leigh Ann, Six takeaways from the second presidential debate, NBC News, October 10, 2016, www.aol.com/article/news/2016/10/10six-takeaways-from-the-second-presidential-debate/21578039/

258 Palmer, Anna, and Sherman, Jake, Poll: Hillary Clinton won the second debate, Politico, October 11, 2016, www.politico.com/story/2016/10/clinton-trump-debate-poll-229581

259 Johnson, Alex, Reports: Four women accuse Trump of inappropriate touching them years apart, NBC News, October 12, 2016, www.aol.com/article/news/2016/10/12/four-women-accuse-trump-of-inappropriately-touching-them-years-a/21581448/

260 Agiesta, Jennifer, Hillary Clinton wins third presidential debate, according to CNN/ORC poll, CNN Politics, October 20, 2016, www.cnn.com/2016/10/19/politics/hillary-clinton-wins-third-presidential-debate-according-to-cnn-orc-poll/index.html

261 CNN Wire, Take the poll: Who won the third debate?, Fox 61, October 19, 2016, http://fox61.com/2016/10/19/who-won-the-third-presidential-debate/

262 Fact checks of the Third Presidential Debate, New York Times, October 19, 2016, www.nytimes.com/interactive/2016/10/19/us-elections/fact-check-debate.html?_r=0

263 Krugman, Paul, How to Rig An Election, New York Times, OpEd. November 7, 2016, Pg A23

264 Hamid, Shadi, The End of the End of History, Foreign Policy, November 15, 2016, http://foreignpolicy.com/2016/11/15/the-end-of-the-end-of-history/?utm_source=Sailthru&utm_medium=email&utm_campaign=New%20Campaign&utm_term=%2AEditors%20Picks

265 MacGillis, Alec, The Revenge of the Forgotten Class, Pacific Standard Magazine, November 17, 2016, https://psmag.com/the-revenge-of-the-forgotten-class-ee14a3a56bfa?source=rss-2cf906365a55-4

266 Carnes, Nicholas, and Lupu, Noam, It's time to bust the myth: Most Trump voters were not working class, Washington Post, Monkey Cage, June 5, 2017, www.washingtonpost.com/news/monkeycage/wp/2017/06/05/its-time-to-bust-the-myth-most-trump-voters-were-not-working-class/?utm_term=60228a112678

267 Beinart, Peter, Fear of a Female President, The Atlantic, October 2016, Pg 15

268 Hunt, Kasie, The FBI will re-open the investigation into Hillary Clinton's email server, NBC News, October 28, 2016, www.aol.com/article/2016/10/28/the-fbi-will-re-open-the-investigation-intio-hillary-clintons-em/215942213/

269 Westcott, Lucy, 2016 Presidential Polls For October 28, 2016, Newsweek, October 28, 2016, www.newsweek.com/2016-election-polls-october-28-trump-clinton-514519

270 Steakin, William, Trump climbs back into contention as Clinton email investigation looms, AOL News, October 31, 2016, www.aol.com/article/news/2016/10/31/trump-climbs-in-polls-against-clinton-in-final-days/21595019/

271 Stephenson, Lauren, Fox News Anchor apologizes for misleading indictment statement, AOL News, November 4, 2016, www.aol.com/article/news/2016/11/04/fox-news-anchor-apologizes-for-misleading-indictment-statement/21599160/

272 Loffredo, Nicholas, Presidential Election Polls For November 5, 2016, Newsweek, November 5, 2016, www.newsweek.com/presidential-election-polls-november-5-2016-517411

273 Darcy, Oliver, FBI Director James Comey: Review of new Clinton emails has not changed our original conclusion against charges, Business Insider, November 6, 2016, www.aol.com/article/news/2016/11/06/fbi-director-james-comey-review-of-new-clinton-emails-has-not-c/21599833/

274 Steakin, William, Donald Trump projected to be the next president of the United States, AOL News, November 9, 2016, www.aol.com/article/news/2016/11/09/donald-trump-projected-to-be-the-next-president-of-the-united-st/21601910/

275 Wines, Michael, 5 Numbers That Give Clearer View Of Election, New York Times, March 18, 2017, Pg A9

276 Mayer, Jane, Trump's Money Man, The New Yorker, March 27, 2017, Pg 34

277 Wines, Michael

278 Voting Turnout Statistics, Statistic Brain, November 22, 2016, www.statisticbrain. com/voting-statistics/

279 Wright, David, Poll: Trump, Clinton score historic unfavorable ratings, CNN Politics, March 22, 2016, www.cnn.com/2016/03/22/politics/2016-election-poll-donald-trump-hillary-clinton/index.html/

280 Remnick, David, Comment- One Hundred Days, The New Yorker, May 1, 2017, Pg 17

281 Surowiecki, James, Trump's Budget Bluff, The New Yorker, February 13, 2017, Pg34

282 Rattner, Steven, Voodoo Economics, Then and Now, New York Times OpEd, May 2, 2017, Pg A27

283 Le Miere, Jason, Popular Vote Recap: Donald Trump Set For Inauguration Despite Losing to Hillary Clinton By Huge Margin In Election 2016, International Business Times, January 20, 2017, www.ibtimes.com/

284 Seipel, Arlene, Fact Check: Trump Falsely Claims A Massive Landslide Victory, NPR, December 11, 2016, www.npr.org/2016/12/11/505182622/fact-check-trum-claims-a-massive-landslide-victory-but-history-differs

285 Greenhouse, Steven, What the Unions Got Wrong, New York Times, November 27, 2016, Sunday Review Pg 2

286 McWilliams, James, The Miracle of Trump: Why Did Evangelicals Deliver the Votes for a Sinner, Pacific Standard Magazine, February 13, 2017, https://psmag.com/the-miracle-of-trump-why-did-evangelicals-deliver-votes-for-a-sinner-f0769bce9684#.(mn7k50t)

287 Frydenborg, Brian, A Brief History of the First Russo-American Cyberwar, War Is Boring, December 16, 2016, https://warisboring.com/a-brife-history-of-the-firstrusso-american-cyberwar-75077194988b#.eqk52meg3

288 Entous, Adam, and Nakashima, Ellen, FBI in agreement with CIA that Russia aimed to help Trump win White House, Washington Post politics, December 16, 2016, www.washingtonpost.com/politics/clinton-blames-putins-personal-grudge-against-her-for-election-interference/2016/12/16/12f36250-c3be-11e6-8422-eac61c0ef74d_story.html?utm_term=.e638c660293e

289 Mr. Obama Punishes Russia, At Last, Editorial, New York Times, December 30, 2017, Pg A22

290 Flegenheimer, Matt, Despite Democrats Demands, a Broad Investigation Into Russian Ties Isn't Assured, New York Times, February 16, 2017, Pg A16

291 Yglesias, Matthew, Donald Trump ditched free market ideology for nationalism- and its working, Vox, March 1, 2016, www.vox.com/2016/3/1/11135756/donald-trump-nationalism

292 Trump's Triumph, The Economist, May 7, 2016, www.economist.com/node/21698251/print

293 Daily Presidential Tracking Poll, Rasmussen Reports, January 16, 2017, www.rasmussenreports.com/public_content/obama_administration/prez_track_jan16

294 Agiesta, Jennifer, CNN/ORC Poll: Confidence drops in Trump Transition, CNN Politics, January 17, 2017, www.cnn.com/2017/01/17/politics/trump-administration-approval-ratings-inauguration/index.html?adkey=bn&via=newsletter&source=CSAMedition

295 Jackson, David, Trump: Approval rating polls are rigged, too, USA Today, January 17, 2017, www.usatoday.com/story/news/onpolitics/2017/01/17/donald-trump-polls-rigged-approval/96660980/

296 NBC/WSJ Poll: Trump Approval Rating at 44%, January 18, 2017, www.msnbc.com/mtp-daily/watch/nbc-wsj-poll-trump-transition-approval-rating-at-44-856694339548

297 Jackson

298 Agiesta

299 Greenwood, Max, NBC/WSJ poll: Seven in ten Americans don't approve of Trump's Twitter use, The Hill, January 18, 2017, www.thehill.com/blogs.blog-briefing-room/news/314762/nbc-wsj-poll-seven-in-ten-americans-dont-approve-of-trumps

300 Harwood, John, 52% of Americans disapprove of Trump's preparations for the Oval office, says NBC-WSJ poll, CNBC Politics, January 18, 2017, www.cnbc.com/2017/01/17/52-of-americans-disapprove-of-trumps-preparations-for-the-oval-office-says-nbc-wsj-poll.html

301 Low Marks for Major Players in 2016 Election- Including the Winner, Pew Research Center, November 21, 2016, www.people-press-org/2016/11/21/low-marks-for-major-players-in-2106-election-including-the-winner/?utm_source=Pew+Research+Center&_utm_campaign=9e40b867cf-weekly_Nov_23_201611_22_2016&utm_medium=email&utm_term=)_3e953b9670-9e40b867cf-400219269

302 Traub, James, Donald Trump: Making the World Safe for Dictators, Foreign Policy, January3, 2017, http:forignpolicy.com/2017/01/03/Donald-trump-is-making-the-world-safe-for-dictators/?utm_source=Sailthru&utm_medium=email&utm_campaign=FP%20Jan%204&utm_term=Flashpoints

303 Trump: Flag-Burners Should Be Jailed, The Daily Beast, November 29, 2016, www.thedailybeast.com/cheats/2016/11/29/trump-flag-bruners-should-be-jailed.html?via=desktop&source=copyurl

304 Hobbes, Thomas, Leviathan, Penguin Classics, New York, 1981, (originally published 1651), Pgs 336-338

305 Cohen, Patricia, Need to Hide Some Income? Forget About Panama, Try Delaware, New York Times, April 8, 2016, Pg A1

306 Watkins, Thayer, Political Bosses And Machines in the U.S, downloaded April 27, 2105, www.sjsu.edu/faculty/watkins/bosses.htm

307 Karabell, Zachary, Chester Alan Arthur, Times Books, 2004, from daily@delancy-place.com

308 Holan, Angie Drobnic, All Politicians Lie. Some Lie More Than Others, New York Times Sunday Review, December 13, 2015, Pg 4

309 Konnikova, Maria, Trump's Lies vs. Your Brain, Politico Magazine, January/February 2017, www.politico.com/magazine/2017/01/trumps-lies-liar-affect-brain214658

310 Morris, Roy, Fraud of the Century, Simon and Schuster, New York 2004

311 Wormser, Richard, Hayes-Tilden Election 1876, The Rise and Fall of Jim Crow, downloaded April 28, 2015, www.pbs.org/wnet/jimcrow/stories_events_election.html

312 Greenberg, David, Was Nixon Robbed? Slate, October 16, 2000, www.slate.com/articles/news_and_politics/history/lesson/2000/10/was_nixon_robbed.single.html

313 Fenton, Ben, Why A Beaten Richard Nixon Accepted Losing Fixed Election in 1960, Rense.com, 11-10-00, http://rense.com/general5/fixed.htm

314 Summary of the 2000 Presidential Election, Presidential Election, Washington Post, October 17, 2012, www.2000presidentialelection.com?

315 en.wikipedia.org/wiki/U.S._presidential_election_2000

316 Bush v Gore, Legal Information Institute, downloaded April 30, 2015, www.law.
     cornell.edu/supct/html/00-949.ZPC.htm;
317 McBride, Alex, Bush v. Gore, Landmark Cases, Supreme Court, downloaded, April
     30, 2015, www.pbs.org,wnet/supremecourt/future/landmark_bush.html
318 Mcbride
319 Hicken, Jackie, 2000: George W. Bush vs. Al Gore, Deseret News, November 5,
     2012, www.deseretnews.com/1093/9/2000-George-W-Bush-vs-Al-Gore-10-of-the-
     closest=presidential-elections-in-United-States-history.html
320 Ibid
321 Bibby, John, and Maisal, Sandy, Two Parties or More, Westview Press, Boulder, CO,
     2ⁿᵈ edition, 2003, Pg 42
322 2000 General Election Results- Florida, downloaded May 6, 2015, http://uselection-
     atlas.org/RESULTS/state.php?f=0&fips=12&year=2000
323 Basinger, Scott, and Rottinghaus, Brandon, Skeletons in White House Closets: A Dis-
     cussion of Modern Presidential Scandals, Political Science Quarterly, Volume 127,
     Number 2, 2012, Pg 213-239
324 Watergate Scandal, History, downloaded May 3, 2015, www.history.com/topics/
     watergate
325 Sabato, Larry, and Simpson, Glenn, Dirty Little Secrets, The Persistence of Corrup-
     tion in American Politics, Times Books, New York, 1996, Pg 14
326 Sabato, Larry, and Ernst, Howard, Encyclopedia of American Political Parties and
     Elections, Facts on File, 2006, Pgs 111-12
327 Watergate Scandal, History
328 Ibid
329 Ibid
330 Ibid
331 Hudson, William, American Democracy in Peril, Chatham House Publishers, New
     York, 2001, Pg 54
332 Richard M..Nixon- The resignation of vice president agnew, Profiles of U.S. Presi-
     dents, downloaded May 4, 2015, www.presidentialprofiles.com/Kennedy-Bush/
     Richard-M-Nixon-The-resignation-of-vice-president-agnew.html
333 Sabato, Larry, and Ernst, Howard, Encyclopedia of American Political Parties and
     Elections, Pg 425
334 Reagan, The Iran-Contra Affair, PBS, downloaded May 5, 2015, www.pbs.org/wgbh/
     americanexperience/features/general-article/reagan-iran/
335 Iran Hostage Crisis, World History Project, downloaded May 5, 2015, http://world-
     historyproject.org/topics/iran-hostage-crisis
336 PBS
337 Encyclopedia of American Political Parties and Elections, Pg 426
338 Maraniss, David, and Schmidt, Susan, Hillary Clinton and the Whitewater Controver-
     sy: A Close-Up, Washington Post, June 2, 1996, www.washingtonpost.com/wp-srv/
     politics/special/whitewater/stories/wwtr960602.htm
339 Ibid
340 Roberts, Joel, Clintons Cleared on Whitewater, CBS, March 20, 2002, www.cbsnews.
     com/news/clintons-cleared-on-whitewater/
341 Gennifer flowers, 'mistress' of Bill Clinton, says they ended 12-year affair be-
     cause of Chelsea and that Hillary is bisexual, news.com.au, September 19,

2013, www.news.com.au/world/gennifer-flowers-mistress-of-bill-clinton-says-they-ended-12-year-affair-because-of-chelsea-and-that-hillary-is-bisexual/story-fndir2ev-1226723165907

342 Time Staff, Where Are They Now: The Clinton Impeachment, Time, January 9, 2009, http://content.time.com/time/specials/packages/article/0,1870544_1870543_1870458,00.html

343 A Chronology: Key Moments in the Clinton-Lewinsky Saga, All Politics CNN, downloaded May 6, 2015, www.cnn.com/ALLPOLITICS/1998/resources/lewinsky/timeline/

344 Lewinsky scandal, infoplease, downloaded May 6, 2015, www.infoplease.com/encyclopedia/history/lewinsky-scandal.html

345 Pooley, Eric, The Lewinsky Scandal Is Not Comparable to Watergate, Political Scandals Opposing Viewpoints, Greenhaven Press, San Diego, California, 2001, Pgs 89-98

346 infoplease

347 John Edwards life and political career, Washington Post, downloaded May 7, 2015, www.washingtonpost.com/politics/the-political-career-of-john-edwards/2007/03/09/AGIRtGBH_gallery.html

348 Larson, Leslie, John Edwards talks return to law after scandal-plagued political career, New York Daily News, July 24, 2014, www.nydailynews.com/news/politics/john-edwards-talks-returning-law-article-1.1878459

349 Stuart Taylor, Jr, "The Man Who Would Be King," The Atlantic Monthly, April 2006, Pg 25

350 Scott Shane, Behind Power, One Principle as Bush Pushes Prerogatives," New York Time, December 17, 2005, Pg A1

351 Scott Shane, "Behind Power, One Principle as Bush Pushes Prerogatives," New York Times, December 17, 2005, Pg A1

352 Scott Shane, December 17, 2005

353 Adam Liptak, "The Court Enters the War, Loudly," New York Times, July 2, 2006," Week in Review, Pg 1

354 David E. Sanger," Congress and Courts Try to Restore Balance," New York Times, July 14, 2006, Pg A15

355 Editorial, New York Times, September 15, 2006, Pg A24

356 Kate Zernike, "Lawyers and G.O.P. Chiefs Resist Tribunal Plan," New York Times, September 8, 2006, Pg A1

357 Im Ruttenberg and Sheryl Gay Stolberg, "Bush Says G.O.P. Rebels Are Putting Nation At Risk," New York Times, September 16, 2006, Pg A12

358 Jack Goldsmith, "The Terror Presidency," W.W. Norton and Company, New York, 2007

359 Robert Pear, "Legal Group Faults Bush for Ignoring Parts of Bills," New York Times, July 24, 2006, Pg A12

360 Gary R. Hess, "Presidents and the Congressional War Resolutions of 1991 and 2002," Political Science Quarterly, Volume 121, Number 1, 2006, Pg 93-118

361 Ibid, Pg 111

362 Rob Warmowski, "President Obama's Clear Abuse Of Power Cited By...President Obama," The Huffington Post, June 27, 2009, www.huffingtonpost.com/rob-warmowski/president-obamas-clear-ab_b_221836.html

363 The Pendleton Civil Service Reform Act (1883), downloaded May 10, 2015, www.authentichistory.com/1865-1897/3-gilded/3-arthur/1883_Pendleton_Act.html

364 Teapot Dome Scandal, United States History, downloaded May 10, 2105, www.u-s-history.com/pages/h1377.html

365 Justice Blinked for Michael Deaver, New York Times Opinion, September 28, 1988, www.nytimes.com/1988/09/28/opinion/justice-blinked-for-michael-deaver.html

366 Dehaven, Ted, HUD Scandals, Downsizing the Federal Government, The CATO Institute, June, 2009, www.downsizinggovernment.org/hud/scandals

367 Ibid

368 Ibid

369 I. Lewis Scooter Libby, downloaded May 12, 2015, Sourcewatch, The Center for Media and Democracy, www.sourcewatch.org/index.php/_Lewis_Scooter_Libby

370 Let Inspectors General Do Their Jobs, Editorial, New York Times, March 9, 2016, Pg A20

371 "Statement of the OCE Regarding Evidence Collected in OCE's PMA Investigation," May 27, 2010, http://oce.house.gov/

372 Michael Mcauliff, "Scandal-plagued Rep. Charles Rangel struggles in latest fundraising period," NYDailyNews.com, April 15, 2010, www.nydailynews.com/news/politics/2010/04/16/2010-4-16_cash_woes_for_Rangel.html.

373 Ethics committee won't review allegations against Rep. McMorris Rodgers, The Spokesman-Review, March 25, 2014, www.spokesman.com/stories/2014/mar/25/ethics-committee-wont-review-allegations-against/

374 Lichtblau, Eric, Paralyzed F.E.C. Can't Do Its Job, Chairwoman Says, New York Times, May 3, 2015, Pg A1

375 Ravel, Ann, How Not to Enforce Campaign Laws, OpEd, New York Times, April 3, 2014, A27

376 Associated Press, "Ex-Congressmen gets 13 years in freezer cash case," USAToday.com, November 13, 2009, USAToday.com/news/nation/2009-11-13-jefferson-bribe-sentence_n.htm.

377 Eric Lipton, "20 in Black Caucus Ask For Curbs on Ethics Office," New York Times, June 2, 2010, A17.

378 Batley, Melanie, Harry Reid Wants to Bring Back Pork-Barreling, Newsmax, June 26, 2014, www.newsmax.com/Newsfront/Reid-earmarks-GOP-Democrats/2014/06/26/id/579427/

379 "Prospects for Ethics Reform in the 110th Congress," Source Watch, July 12, 2007, www.sourcewatch.org/index.php?title=Prospects_for_Ethics_Reform_in_the_110th_Congress.

380 Parti, Tarini, $7 billion spent on 2012 campaign, FEC says, Politico, January 31, 2013, www.politico.com/story/2013/01/7-billion-spent-on-2012-campaign-fec-says-87051.html

381 Thomas B. Edsall, Sara Cohen, and James V. Grimaldi, "Pioneers Fill War Chest, Then Capitalize," Washington Post, May 16, 2004, A01.

382 Eduardo Porter, "The Cost of a Vote Goes Up," New York Times, Week in Review, November 7, 2010, 7.

383 Cillizza, Chris, The 2014 election cost $3.7 billion. We spend twice that much on Halloween, Washington Post, November 6, 2014, www.washingtonpost.com/blogs/the-fix/wp/2014/11/06/the-2014-election-cost-3.7-billion-we-spend-twice-that-much-on-halloween/

384 Dunbar, John, The 'Citizens United' decision and why it matters, The Center for Public Integrity, October 18, 2012, www.publicintegrity.org/2012/10/18/11527/citizens-united-decision-and-why-it-matters

385 AP, McCutcheon v. FEC: Supreme Court Strikes Down Overall Limits On Campaign Contributions, Huffington Post, April 2, 2014, www.huffingtonpost.com/2014/04/02mccutcheon-v-fec_n_5076518.html

386 Paul Krugman, "The K Street Prescription," *New York Times*, OpEd, January 20, 2006, A17.

387 "John Ashcroft," http://en.wikipedia.org/wiki/John_Ashcroft, downloaded May 20, 2010.

388 Elizabeth Brown, "Lobbying FAQ: What is Permissible? Out of Bounds? Punishable?" The Center for Public Integrity, January 18, 2006, http://publicintegrity.org/lobby/report.aspx?aid=775.

389 Aron Pilhofer, "Revolving Doors Spin Open Once Again," *New York Times*, November 12, 2006.

390 Hubert B. Herring, "Lobbying Scandals? They Can't Slow This Juggernaut," *New York Times*, August 6, 2006, Business, 2.

391 "Campaign contributions of selected industries," OpenSecrets.org, Center for Responsive Politics, www.opensecrets.org/pres08/select.asp?Ind=B12, downloaded June 3, 2010.

392 "Lobbying Spending Database," OpenSecrets.org, Center for Responsive Politics, April 25, 2010, www.opensecrets.org/lobby/top.php?showYear=2009&indexType=i.

393 Lobbying Database, OpenSecrets.org, www.opensecrets.org, lobby/

394 Larry J. Sabato and Bruce Larson, *The Party's Just Begun*, Longman Press, New York, NY, 2002, 85.

395 Vandewalker, Ian, Outside Spending and Dark Money in Toss-Up Senate Races: Post-election Update, Brennan Center For Justice, November 10, 2014, www.brennancenter.org/print/12870

396 Michael Luo and Stephanie Strom, "Donor Names Remain Secret as Rules Shift," *New York Times*, September 20, 2010, A1.

397 Gaines, Jim, A constitutional amendment to take Big Money out of politics dies quickly, Reuters, September 12, 2014, http://blogs.reuters.com/james-gaines/2014/09/12/nearly-80-percent-of-americans-want-it-but-their-chances-of-getting-it-just-took-another-hit/

398 George Childs Kohn, "House Overdraft Scandal," *The New Encyclopedia of American Scandal, Facts on File*, New York, 2001, 189.

399 Ibid., "Charles Keating," 217.

400 Leiby, Richard, To the players in Abscam, the real-life 'American Hustle,' the bribes now seem quaint, Washington Post, December 26, 2013, www.washingtonpost.com/lifestyle/style

401 Hamilton, Alexander, Federalist Papers, Number 15, New American Library, New York, 1961, Pg 110

402 Calabrese, Erin, and Greene, Leonard, Grimm easily wins re-election as trial looms, New York Post, November 5, 2104, http://nypost.com/2014/11/05/grimm-easily-wins-re-election-despite-looming-trial/

403 Bash, Dana, and Jaffe, Alexandra, Michael Grimm announces resignation, CNN, December 30, 2014, www.cnn.com/2014/12/29/politics/michael-grimm-to-resign-soon/imdex.html

404 Delaney, Arthur, Trey Radel, Busted On Cocaine Charge, Voted For Drug Testing Food Stamp Recipients, Huffington Post, November 19, 2013, www.huffingtonpost.com/2013/11/19/trey-radel-drug-testing_n_4305348.html

405 Yglesias, Matthew, Everything you need to know about Senator Robert Menendez corruption scandal, Vox, April 2, 2015, www.vox.com/2015/4/2/8336147/robert-menendez-scandal

406 Confessore, Nicholas, and Apuzzo, Matt, Menendez Case Focuses On Role of Super PACs, New York Times, April 3, 2015, Pg A15

407 Wagner, Dennis, Arizona's ex-Rep. Rick Renzi gets 3-year prison term, USA Today, October 28, 2013, www.usatoday.com/story/news/politics/2013/10/28/rick-renzi-arizona-prison-sentence/3288937/

408 Crabtree, David, One on One With Frank, Balance, WRAL.com, January 14, 2008, www.wral.com/news/loca/blogpost/2300620/

409 Merica, Dan, Lazo, Larry, and Bentz, Leslie, Jesse Jackson Jr. going to prison says he 'manned up', CNN, Augist 14, 2013, www.cnn.com/2013/08/14/justice/jesse-jackson-jr-sentencing/index.html

410 Pennsylvania Democrat Chaka Fattah Found Guilty, The Atlantic, June 21, 2016, www.theatlantic.com/politics/archive/2016/06/chaka-fattah-guilty-house/488087/?utm_source=nl-atlantic-daily-062116

411 Bidgood, Jess, and Seelye, Katherine, Top Republicans Call On Congressman to Serve His Party by Resigning, New York Times, May 20, 2015, Pg A17

412 Breshnahan, John, et al, Bill Shuster admits 'private and personal relationship' with airline lobbyist, Politico, April 16, 2015, www.politico.com/story/2015/04/bill-shuster-admits-personal-relationship-with-lobbyist-117054

413 AP, Aaron Schock Indicted on 24 Counts, The Daily Beast, November 10, 2016, www.thedailybeast.com/cheats/2016/11/10/attprneys-aaron-schock-to-be-indicted.html.via=desktop&source=copyurl

414 Haag, Matthew, Ex-Congresswoman Who Ran Fraudulent Charity is Sentenced to 5 years in Prison, New York Times, December 5, 2017, Pg A18

415 Knickerbocker, Brad, Dennis Hastert sex scandal widens with allegations from a second accuser, Christian Science Monitor, June 6, 2015, www.csmonitor.com/usa/Politics/2015/0606/Dennis-Hastert-sex-scandal-widens-with-allegations-from-a-second-accuser-video

416 Ornstein, Norm, This Isn't Dennis Hastert's First Scandal, The Atlantic, June 3, 2015, www.theatlantic.com/politics/archive/2015/06/dennis-hastert-scandal/394754/

417 Hulse, Carl, Now, Hastert Seems an Architect of Congressional Dysfunction, New York Times, May 3, 2016, Pg A14

418 Berman, Russell, The Atlantic, October 15, 2015, www.theatlantic.com/politics/archive/2015/10/a-guilty-plea-for-speaker-hastert/410749/

419 Levy, Gabrielle, Dennis Hastert Sentenced to 15 Months in Prison, US News and World Report, April 27, 2016, www.usnews.com/news/articles/2016-04-27/dennis-hastert-sentenced-to-15-months-in-prison

420 Bruni, Frank, The Many Faces of Dennis Hastert, New York Times Sunday Review, May 1, 2016, Pg 3

421 Silva, Christina, Nevada Sen. John Ensign announces resignation, Yahoo News, April 21, 2011,http://news.yahoo.com/Nevada-senator-jogn-ensign-announces-resignation-225711708.html

422 Terbush, Jon, How David Vitter got on top of his sex scandal, The Week, January 22, 2014, http://theweek.com/articles/452538/how-david-vitter-got-sex-scandal

423 Senator, Arrested at Airport, Pleads Guilty, New York Times, August 28, 2007, www.nytimes.com/2007/08/28/washington/28craig.html?_r=0

424 Hess, Hannah, Judge Rules Larry Craig Must Repay Campaign Funds Used in Bathroom Scandal, Roll Call, Hill Blotter, September 30, 2014, http://blogs.rollcall.com/hill-blotter/judge-rules-larry-craig-must-repay-campaign-funds-used-in-bathroom-scandal/

425 Skoloff, Brian, Former Congressman Mark Foley Breaks Silence On Sex Scandal, Huffington Post, December 13, 2008, www.huffingtonpost.com/2008/22/12/former-congressman-mark-f_n_143196.html

426 Editorial, After Conventions, a Debt to Donors, New York Times, May 11, 2016, Pg A22

427 David Johnston, "FBI's Focus on Public Corruption Includes 2000 Investigations," New York Times, May 11, 2006, A32.

428 Wilson, Reid, The most corrupt state(s) in America, The Washington Post, January 22, 2014, www.washingtonpost.com/blogs/govbeat/wp/2104/01/22//the-most-corrupt-states-in-america

429 Ibid

430 AP, Illinois Governors In Prison, 4 of State's Last 7 Governors Were Convicted, Imprisoned, Huffington Post, January 30, 2013, www.huffingtonpost.com/2013/01/30/illinois-governors-in-pr_n_2581182.html

431 Ochsner, Nick, Ex-Va gov sentenced to 2 years in prison for corruption, USA Today, January 6, 2015, www.usatoday.com/story/news/politics/2015/01/06/bob-mcdonnell-sentencing/21321365/

432 Teachout, Zephyr, There's No Such Thing as a Free Rolex, New York Times OpEd, April 29, 2016, Pg A21

433 Ibid

434 Gerstein, Josh, Supreme Court overturns Bob McDonnell's corruption convictions, Politico, June 27, 2106, www.politico.com/story/2016/06/supreme-court-overturns-bob-mcdonnells-corruption-convictions-224833

435 Hulse, Carl, Is the Supreme Court Naïve About Corruption? Ask Jack Abramoff, New York Times, July 6, 2016, Pg A15

436 Camia, Catalina, McDonnell to join infamous club of governors who have gone to prison, Onpolitics, USA Today, January 6, 2015, http://onpolitics.usatoday.com/2015/01/06/governors-prison-bob-mcdonnell/

437 Perez-Pena, Richard, Corruption Guilty Plea Reached in Rhode Island, New York Times, March 4, 2014, Pg A19

438 Camia

439 Ibid

440 Hussey, Kristin, and Santora, Marc, Judge Sends Ex-Connecticut Governor Back to Prison for 30 Months, New York Times, March 19, 2015, Pg A19

441 Fernandez, Manny, Securities Fraud Charges Bring Texas Attorney General to County Jail, New York Times, August 4, 2015, Pg A14

442 Texas AG Charged With Federal Securities Fraud, The Daily Beast, April 11, 2016, www.thedailybeast.com/cheats/2016/04/11/texas-ag-charged-with-federal-securities-fraud.html

443 AP, Pennsylvania Attorney General Faces Arraignment, New York Times, August 9, 2015, Pg 14

444 Perez-Pena, Richard, Pennsylvania Takes Steps To Remove Top Lawyer, New York Times, November 26, 2015, Pg A24

445 Wines, Michael, and Bidgood, Jess, Attorney General's Conviction Unlikely to End Scandal in Pennsylvania, New York Times, August 17, 2016

446 AP, A Top New Mexico Official Is Charged With Financial Misdeeds, New York Times, August 29, 2015, Pg A11

447 Santos, Fernanda, Scandals Multiple in New Mexico, New York Times, September 9, 2015, Pg A24

448 Eliot Spitzer Biography, bio, downloaded June 16, 2015, www.biography.com/people/eliot-spitzer-279076

449 Fenton, Reuven, Ex-NY Comptroller Alan Hevasi out of prison after serving 20 months in pension scandal, New York Post, December 13, 2012, http://nypost.com/2012/12/13/ex-ny-comptroller-alan-hevasi-out-of-prison-after-serving-20-months-in-pension-scandal/

450 Rashbaum, William, Ex-Speaker of Assembly Is Indicted, New York Times, February 20, 2015, Pg A20

451 Orden, Erica, Former N.Y. Assembly Speaker Sheldon Silver Found Guilty in Corruption Trial, Wall Street Journal, November 30, 2015, www.wsj.com/article/n-y-assemblyman-sheldon-silver-found-guilty-in-corruption-trial-1448917663

452 Siegel, Fred, Sheldon Silver Gets 12 Years in Prison, The Daily Beast, May 3, 2016, www.thedailybeast.com/cheats/2016/05/03/

453 Kaplan, Thomas, and Craig, Susan, Charges of Corruption Topple Another of Albany's Leaders, New York Times, May 12, 2015, Pg A1

454 McDemid, Brendan, Ex-NY Senate Leader Guilty of Corruption, Reuters, December 11, 2015, www.thedailybeast.com/cheats/2015/12/11/ex-ny-senate-leader-guilty-of-corruption.html?via=newsletter&source=CSPMedition

455 Profiting From His Mother's Crime, Editorial, New York Times, April 22, 2105, Pg A22

456 Buettner, Russ, Speaker's Tab Includes, Cars, Clubs, and 'Other', New York Times, June 9, 2015, Pg A1

457 Weiser, Benjamin, et al, U.S. Attorney Says Trails Offer Solutions to a Corrupt Albany, New York Times, December 14, 2015, PgA1

458 New York Governor Cuomo's office intervened in corruption probe: New York Times, Reuters, July 23, 2014, www.reuters.com/article/2014/07/23/us-usa-new-york-cuomo-idUSKBN0FS1J920140723

459 Rashbaum, William, and Craig, Susanne, U.S. Attorney Criticizes Cuomo's Closing of Panel, New York Times, April 9, 2104, Pg A1

460 Kaplan, Thomas, and McKinley, Jesse, Corruption Panel's Report Offers Look at the Payback Culture in Albany, New York Times, December 4, 2013, PgA25

461 Kelly, Brian, and Leathersich, Joe, Upstate developers, Cuomo aide, indicted for bribery, fraud, The Daily News, September 23, 2016, www.thedailynewsonline.com/bdn01/upstate-developers-cuomo-aide-indicted-for-bribery-fraud-20160923

462 Yee, Vivian, Who's Taking On Ethics in Albany? Not the Ethics Panels, New York Times, January 20, 2016, Pg A19

463 Kaplan, Thomas, Effort to Cut Off Pensions For Corrupt Officials Stalls, New York Times, May 4, 2015, Pg A16

464 Editorial, The Revenge of Scott Walker, New York Times, October 27, 2015, Pg A26

465 Britt, Bill, Will 2016 be a turning point, Alabama Political Reporter, May 30, 2016, www.alreporter.com/will2016-be-a-turning-point/

466 Robertson, Campbell, Inquiries Ensnare Leaders of 3 Alabama Government Branches, New York Times, May 17, 2016, Pg A9

467 Steere, Tom, Alabama Gov. Robert Bentley Resigns, April 10, 2017, Industry News, www.bizjournals.com/birminghamnews/2017/04/10/alabam-gov-robert-bentley-to-resign-.html

468 Robertson, Campbell, Alabama Lawmaker Sentenced to Prison, New York Times, July 9, 2016, Pg A9

469 CBS News, 60 Minutes, Did Ex-Alabama Governor Get A Raw Deal, February 21, 2008, www.cbsnews.com/news/did-ex-alabama-governor-get-a-raw-deal/

470 Racioppi, Dustin, Bridgegate trial: Christie taking heat from defense, prosecution, USA Today, September 25, 2016, www.usatoday.com/story/news/nation-now/2016/09/25/bridgegate-trial-christie-taking-heat-defense-prosecution/91096566/

471 Katersky, Aaron, et al, 2 Former Aides to Chris Christie Found Guilty in Bridgegate Trial, ABC News, November 4, 2016, http://abcnews.go.com/us/jury-reaches-verdict-bridgegate-trial/story?id=43303262

472 Palast, Greg, Commentary: Here's how Brian Kemp is stealing the Georgia election, Salon, November 9, 2018, www.salon.com/2018/11/09/commentary-heres-how-brian-kemp-is-stealing-georgias-election/

473 Berman, Ari, Blocking the Ballot Box, Opinion, New York Times Sunday Review, October 28, 2018, Pg 1

474 Rozsa, Matthew, Missouri's GOP governor is trying to block voter-approved limits on lobbyists, gerrymandering, Salon, December 27, 2018, www.salon.com/2018/12/27/missouris-gop-governor-is-trying-to-block-voter-approved-limits-on-lobbying-gerrymandering/

475 Millhiser, Ian, Supreme Court's Judge-For-Sale Case Is Just The Tip Of A Larger Iceberg, Huff Post Politics, May 25, 2011, www.Huffingtonpost.com/ian-millhiser/supreme-courts-judeg-for_b_171498.html

476 Jenkins, Jeff, Federal prosecutors turn attention to shareholders statement in Blankenship trial, Metro News, November 8, 2015, http://wvmetronews.com/2015/11/08/federal-prosecutors-turn-attention-to-shareholders-statement-in-blankenship-trial/

477 Smith, Mitch, Partisanship a Worry in Wisconsin Supreme Court Election, New York Times, April 6, 2015, Pg A3

478 Millheiser

479 Secrecy in Panama and Beyond, Editorial, New York Times, April 8, 2016, Pg A24

480 Warren, Senator Elizabeth, One Way to Rebuild Our Institutions, OpEd, New York Times, January 29, 2016, Pg A29

481 Keefe, Patrick Radden, Limited Liability, The New Yorker, July 31, 2017, Pg 28

482 Tillman, Robert, and Pontell, Henry, Corporate Fraud, Criminal Time, OpEd, New York Times, June 29, 2016, Pg A25

483 Pettinger, Tejvan, The great recession 2008-2013, Economics help, May 16, 2013, www.economicshelp.org/blog/7501/economics/the-great-recession/

484 Young, Angeko, Cheney's Halliburton Made $39.5 billion on Iraq War, International Business Times, March 20, 2013, http://readersupportednews.org/news-section2/308-12/16561-focus-cheneys-halliburton-made-395-billion-on-iraq-war

485 Cheney/Halliburton Chronology, Citizens Works.org, downloaded April 11, 2016, www.halliburtonwatch.org/about_hal/chronology.html

486 Welch, William, Tauzin switches sides from drug industry overseer to lobbyist, USA Today, December 15, 2004, http://usatoday30.usatoday.com/money/industries/drugs/2004-12-15-drugs-usat_x.htm

487 Stiglitz, 6 ways to radically reform our corrupt financial system, Salon, March 29, 2016, www.salon.com/2016/03/39/6_ways_to_reform_our_corrupt_financial_system_partner/

488 Gordon, Rebecca, We're living in a kleptocracy: America robs from its poor- while its infrastructure crumbles, Salon, November 29, 2015, www.salon.com/2015/11/29/were_living_in_a_kleptocracy-america_robs-from_its_poor_while_its_infrastructure_crumbles?source=newsletter

489 Machiavelli, Niccolo, The Prince, Bantam Classics, New York, 2003, Pg 90

490 Silverstein, Ken, Mossack Fonseca's Willful Ignorance, Foreign Policy, April 6, 2016, http://foreignpolicy.com/2016/04/06/mossack-fonsecas-willful-ignorance/?utm_source=Sailthru&utm_campaign=New%20Campaign&utm_term=Flashpoints

491 Gramer, Robbie, Bribery Is on the Rise Worldwide, and It Costs A Lot More Than Just Money, Foreign Policy, December 1, 2016, http://foreignpolicy.com/2016/12/01/global-bribery-corruption-scandal-worldwide-index-infographic/?utm_source=Sailthru&utm_medium=email&utm_campaign&utm_term=%2AEditors%20Picks

492 Widening Cracks, The Economist, May 25, 2013, www.economist.com/news/americas/21578444-bizarre-drug-scandal-distracts-voters-prime-ministers-problems-widening-cracks

493 Austen, Ian, Canadian Senators Face Wide Corruption Inquiry, New York Times, June 10, 2015, Pg A8

494 Ibid

495 Osborne, Louise, Europe widespread corruption 'breathtaking', USA Today, February 4, 2014, www.usatoday.com/story/news/world/2014/02/04/europe-corruption/5206501/

496 Hjelmgaard, Kim, France's ex-president Sarkozy held in corruption probe, USA Today, July 1, 2014, www.usatoday.com/story/news/world/2014/07/01/former-president-sarkozy-held/11862633/

497 Sayare, Scott, Out of Office, Sarkozy Is Still Front and Center, New York Times, March 16, 2014, PgA4

498 Murray, Don, Nicholas Sarkozy corruption probe a European trend, CBC News World, July 7, 2014, www.cbc.ca/news/world/nicholas-sarkozy-probe-a-european-trend-1.2696859

499 Ibid

500 Murray

501 Dowell, William, Le Monde raises government hackles with diamond scandal questions, Christian Science Monitor, November 18, 1980, www.csmonitor.com/1980/1118/111831.html

502 Nossiter, Adam, French Nepotism Scandal Incriminates Political Elite, New York Times, February 4, 2017, Pg A6

503 Murray

504 Schwarz, Peter, Financial scandal envelops former German Chancellor Helmut Kohl, wsws, December 4, 1999, www.wsws.org/en/articles/1999/12/ger-d04.html

505 Murray

506 Osborne

507 Ibid

508 Abdelal, Rawi, etal, Corruption in Germany, Harvard Business Review, July 30, 2008, http://hbr.org/product/corruption-in-germany/an/709006-PDF-ENG

509 Humborg, Christian, In The Fight Against Corruption, Germany Falls Behind, Transparency International, May 16, 2011, http://blog.transparency.org/2011/05/16/in-the-fight-against-corruption-germany-falls-behind/

510 Paterson, Tony, Gerhard Schroeder's birthday party with Vladimir Putin angers Germany, The Telegraph, April 29, 2014, www.telegraph.co.uk/news/worldnews/europe/ukraine/10795042/Gerhard-Schroeders-birthday-party-with-Vladimir-Putin.html

511 Smale, Alison, German Politician's Rush to Lobbying Brings Scorn, New York Times, January 4, 2014, PgA6

512 Smale, Alison, Critics Link German Scandal to Government's Close Ties With Industry, New York Times, October 2, 2015, Pg A14

513 Higgins, Andrew, In Europe, Fighting Rules at Every Turn, New York Times, September 29, 2015, Pg B1

514 UK Corruption, Transparency International, UK, downloaded May 16, 2016, www.transparency.org.uk/our-work/uk-corruption

515 Smith, Andrew, Corruption in high places: Britain's involvement in the arms trade, New Internationalist blog, July 7, 2014, http://newint.org/blo/2014/07/14/britain-arms-trade-corruption/

516 Evans, Becky, UK corruption getting worse poll finds, Daily Mail, July 9, 2013, www.dailymail.co.uk/news/article-2358665/UK-corruption-getting-worse-poll-finds-20-britons-admit-bribing-public-service-officials.html.

517 Corruption in the UK government, downloaded May 17, 2015, http://blogs.hindustantimes.com/terminal-3/2012/03/26/corruption-in-the-uk-government

518 Loughran, Gerry, Cash for access sting traps two ex-ministers, Daily Nation, March 7, 2015, www.nation.co.ke/oped/Opinion/Corruption-Scandal-Malcolm-Rifkind-Jack-Straw/-/440808/2645718/-/2kgj9mz/-/index.html

519 Martin, Iain, MPs' expenses: A scandal that will not die, The Telegraph, April 13, 2014, www.telegraph.co.uk/news/newstopics/mps-expenses/10761548/mps-expenses-A-scandal-that-will-not-die.html

520 Hooper, John, Berlusconi's scandals- timeline, The Guardian, October 14, 2011, www.theguardian.com/2011/oct/14/berlusconi-scandals-timeline

521 Silvio Berlusconi Biography, Bio, downloaded May 17, 2015, www.biography.com/people/silvio-berlusconi-9209602

522 Murray

523 Pullella, Philip, Italy's Andreotti, leading postwar politician, dead at 94, The Guardian, May 6, 2013, www.theguardian.com/article/2013/05/06/us-italy-andreotti-death-idUSBRE9450BC20130506

524 Ibid

525 Willan, Philip, Bettino Craxi, The Guardian, January 19, 2000, www.theguardian.com/news/2000/jan/20/guardianobituaries.philipwillan

526 Italy-Clean Hands, Global Security.org, downloaded November 22, 2015, www.globalsecurity.org/military/world/europe/it-clean-hands.htm

527 Robinson, Andy, Political Corruption and Media Retribution in Spain and Greece, The Nation, February 21, 2013, www.thenation.com/article/173044/political-corruption-and-media-retribution-spain-and-greece

528 Ibid

529 Duffy, Sean, Corruption in Spain: Something rotten in the state of democracy, the corner, downloaded June 20, 2015, www.thecorner.eu/news-europe/corruption-spain-something-rotten-state-democracy/41548/

530 Robinson, Andy

531 Kitsantonis, Niki, Greek Prosecutors Focus on Corruption at the Top, New York Times, January 18, 2014, www.nytimes.com/2014/01/19/world/europe/greek-prosecutors-focus-on-corruption-at-the-top.html?_r=0

532 Wakefield, Adam, South Africa: Government in Denial About Corruption- Alliance, news24wire, June 16, 2015, http://allafrica.com/stories/201506161547.html

533 Time for South Africa's President to Step Down, Editorial, New York Times, April 2, 2016, Pg A16

534 Gegout, Catherine, Buhari wins-but new president of Nigeria faces enormous challenge, Open Security, March 31, 2015, www.opendemocracy.net/opensecurity/catherine-gregout/buhrai-wins%E2%80%94but-new-president-of-nigeria-faces-enormous-challenge

535 Business Corruption in Nigeria, Norad Business Anti-Corruption Portal, May 2014, www.business-anti-corruption.com/country-profiles/sub-saharan-africa/nigeria/business-corruption-in-nigeria.aspx

536 Kenya, TI, Corruption Rising, Kenyans Reluctant To Report Bribery Incidents, Transparency International- Kenya, April 14, 2015, http://tikenya.org/index.php/press-releases/351

537 The Facts About Corruption In Kenya, Kenya-Advisor.com, 2007-2014, www.kenya-advisor.com/corruption-in-kenya.html

538 Ibid

539 Perry, Alex, Kenya's Election: What Uhuru Kenyatta's Victory Means for Africa, Time, March 9, 2013, www.time.com/2013/03/09/kenyas-election-what-kenyattas-victory-means-for-africa/

540 Gettleman, Jeffrey, An Anticorruption Plea in Kenya: Please, Just Steal a Little, New York Times, November 5, 2015, Pg A4

541 Gettleman, Jeffrey, Evidence of Graft Paints Congo's Leader Into a Corner as His Term Ends, New York Times, December 18, 2016, Pg 6

542 Cook, Stephen, and Koplow, Michael, How Democratic Is Turkey? Foreign Policy, June 3, 2013, http://foreignpolicy.com/2013/06/03/how-democratic-is-turkey/

543 Aranogo, Tim, Turkish Leader Disowns a Part of His Legacy, New York Times, February 27, 2014 Pg A1

544 Steinworth, Daniel, Erdogan and the Traitors: Scandal and Protests Threaten Turkey's AKP, Spiegel Online International, March 19, 2014, www.spiegel.de/international/europe/turkish-prime-minister-erdogan-facing-corruption-scandal-protests-a-959453.html

545 Arango, Tim, and Yeginsu, Ceylan, As Turks Prepare to Vote, Polls Point to Inconclusive Results and More Instability, New York Times, October 31, 2015, Pg A4

546 Akarcesme, Sevgi, Despotic Zeal in Turkey, New York Times OpEd, March 9, 2016, Pg A23

547 Hume, Tim, and Tuysuz, Gul, Turkish Prime Minister Ahmet Davutoglu to step down this month, CNN, May 5, 2016, www.cnn.com/201605/05/europe/turkey-prime-minister-to-resign/index.html

548 Peker, Emre, Turkish Parliament Votes to Strip Lawmakers' Immunity, Wall Street Journal, May 20, 2016, www.wsj.com/articles/trukish-parliament-votes-on-bill-that-would-strip-lawmakers-immunity-1463735376

549 Dolan, David, and Solaker, Gulsen, Turkey rounds up plot suspects after thwarting coup against Erdogan, Reuters, July 16, 2017, www.reuters.com/article/us-turkey-security-primeminister-idUSKCN0ZV2HK

550 Bruno, Greg, et al, Iran's Revolutionary Guards, Council on Foreign Relations, June 14, 2013, www.cfr.org/irans-revolutionary-guards/p14324

551 Karami, Arash, Iranian economist: I can't recollect such 'corruption and plunder', Iran Pulse, February 7, 2104, http://iranpulser.al-monitor.com/index.php/2014/02/3852/iranian-economist-i-cant-recollect-such-corruption-and-plunder/

552 Israel among most corrupt of OECD countries, Jerusalem Post, December 26, 2015, www.jpost.com/National-News/Israel-among-most-corrupt-of-OECD-countries-319315

553 AP, Israeli Minister Will Resign Amid Misconduct Inquiry, New York Times, December 21, 2015, Pg A6

554 Kershner, Isabel, Israeli Court Cuts Sentence of Ex-Premier, New York Times, December 30, 2015, Pg A10

555 Patience, Martin, Israel faces corruption 'epidemic', BBC News, September 24, 2007, http://news.bbc.co.uk/2/hi/middle_east6276071.stm

556 Controversy deepens over French tycoon's payments to Netanyahu, Expatica, June 7, 2016, www.expatica.com/news/Controversy-deepens-over-French-tycoons-payments-to-Netanyahu_697677.html

557 Avishai, Bernard, Benjamin Netanyahu's Art Of Avoidance, The New Yorker, February 16, 2017, www.newyorker.com/news/news-desk/benjamin-netanyahus-art-of-avoidance

558 Heller, Aron, Israeli government falls, early elections called for April, AP, December 24, 2018, https://apnews.com/6db1e4d5ecc04c78ac5dca34a2407ed9

559 Editorial, Pakistan's corruption problem, The Express Tribune, December 17, 2102, http://tribune.com.pk/story/480473/pakistans-corruption-problem/

560 AP, Pakistan among 'most corrupt' countries, Dawn, May 21, 2014, www.dawn.com/news/1107732

561 Overview of corruption in Pakistan, U4 Anti-Corruption Resource Center, downloaded May 19, 2015, www.u4.no/publications/overview-of-corruption-in-pakistan/

562 Walsh, Declan, Pakistan's Chief Justice Leaves a Legacy of Independence and Failings, New York Times, December 14, 2013, Pg A4

563 Reflections on the Electoral History of Pakistan (1970- 2008), Pakistan Institute of Legislative Development and Transparency, PILDAT, January 2008, www.pildat.org?Publications/Publication/elections/HowElectionsStolen.pdf

564 Masood, Salman, Pakistani Leader Leaves Country Amid Questions Over Family's Wealth, New York Times, April 15, 2016, Pg A10

565 Masood, Salman, Graft Case Forces Out Pakistani Premier, Roiling Fragile System, New York Times, July 29, 2017, Pg A1

566 Corruption in India, Causes of Instability & Inequalities, Poverties org, April, 2012, www.poverties.org/corruption-in-India.html

567 Xu, Beina, Governance in India: Corruption, Council on Foreign Relations Backgrounders, September 4, 2014, www.cfr.org/corruption-and-bribery/governence-india-corruption/p31823

568 Sharma, Ashok, India's Anti-Corruption Party Deals Huge Blow To Modi's Government, The World Post, February 10, 2105, www.huffingtonpost.com/2015/02/10/india-anti-corruption_n_6651966.html

569 Barstow, David, Longtime Critic of Modi Is Now a Target, New York Times, August 19, 2015, www.nytimes.com/2015/08/20/world/asia/teesta-setalvad-modi-india.html?ref=world&_r=0

570 Xu

571 Business Corruption in South Korea, Business Anti-Corruption Portal, Jan 2014, www.business-anti-corruption.com/country-profiles/east-asia-the-pacific/republic-of-korea/snapshot.aspx

572 Business Anti-Corruption Portal, general information

573 Sang-Hun, Choe, South Korea: Ex-Premier Indicted, New York Times, July 3, 2015, Pg A10

574 Choe, Sang-Hun, South Koreans 'Ashamed' Over Secret Advisor, New York Times, November 6, 2016, Pg 4

575 Park-Geun-hye: South Korea lawmakers vote to impeach leader, BBC News, December 9, 2016, www.bbc.com/news/world-asia-38259984

576 Choe, Sang-Hun, South Korean Leader Digs In Against Rising Calls for Impeachment, New York Times, November 28, 2016, Pg A1

577 Sang-Hun, Choe, Ex-President Jailed in South Korea, but It's Business as Usual, New York Times, April 8, 2018, Pg 10

578 Mulgan, Aurelia George, How significant was the LDP's victory in Japan's recent general election, East Asia Forum, December 31, 2012, www.eastasiaforum.org/2012/12/31/how-significant-was-the-ldps-victory-in-japans-recent-general-election/

579 Corruption and Government Scandals in Japan, Facts and Details, downloaded May 20, 2015, http://factsanddetails.com/japan/cat22/sub146/item799.html

580 Ibid

581 Ibid

582 Ibid

583 Ibid

584 Inoue, Makiko, and Ueno, Hisako, Japan's Minister for Economic Growth Resigns Amid Scandal, New York Times, January 29, 2016, Pg A4

585 Corruption in Indonesia, Indonesia Investments, downloaded June 24, 2015, www.indonesia-investments.com//business/risks/corruption/item235

586 Editorial, Countering Corruption in Indonesia, July 3, 2014, www.nytimes.com/2014/07/04/opinion/countering-corruption-in-indonesia.html

587 Philippines- Corruption, Global Security, downloaded June 25, 2015, www.globalsecurity.org/military/world/philippines/corruption.htm

588 Ibid

589 Ibid

590 Business Corruption in the Philippines, Norad Business Anti-Corruption Profile, downloaded June 25, 2015, www.business-anti-corruption.com/country-profiles/east-asia-thepacific/philippines/snapshot.aspx

591 Whaley, Floyd, Central Figure in Philippine Graft Case Surrenders, New York Times, August 20, 2013, Pg A10

592 Maresca, Thomas, Rodrigo Duterte inaugurated as Philippines president, USA Today, June 30, 2016, www.usatoday.com/story/news/world/2016/06/30/ rodrigo-duterte-philippines/86544354/

593 AI slams Duterte over claims on killing criminals, Inquirer, December 14, 2016, http:// newsinfo.inquirer.net/853730/ai-slams-dutarte-overclaims-on-killing-criminals

594 Mohamad Mahathir, bio, downloaded November 11, 2015, www.biography.com/ people/mahathir-mohamad-9395417

595 Story, Louise, U.S. Investigating Malaysian Leader Over Property Deals, New York Times, Septmber 22, 2015, Pg A4

596 Fuller, Thomas, 'Road Show' Seeks Inquiry of Malaysian Leader, New York Times, September 13, 2015, Pg 4

597 Vasagar, Jeevan, and Kerr, Simeon, Mayasia's IMDB board offers to resign, Financial Times, April 8, 2016, Pg 2

598 Paddock, Richard, Malaysian State Bars Opposition Candidate From Campaigning, New York Times, May 4, 2016, Pg A7

599 Associated Press, The Latest: Suu Kyi Ally Says Election Results Looking Good, ABC News, November 8, 2015, http://abcnews.go.com/International/wireStory/ latest-suu-kyi-ally-election-results-good-35047618

600 Rohingya crisis: Humanitarian situation catastrophic, UN says, BBC News, September 14, 2017, www.bbc.com/news/world-asia-41260767

601 Artunes, Anderson, The Cost Of Corruption In Brazil Could Be Up To $53 Billion Just This Year Alone, Forbes, November 28, 2013, www.forbes.com/site.andersonartunes/2013/11/28/ the-cost-of-corruption-in-brazil-could-be-up-to-53-billion-just-this-year-alone/

602 Ibid

603 AP, Brazil's top court Oks investigation into dozens of top politicians in Petrobras graft scandal, Fox News, March 6, 2015, www.foxnews.com/world/2015/03/06/ brazil-top-court-oks-investigation-into-dozens-top-politicians-in-petrobras/

604 Romero, Simon, Brazil Bribery Inquiry Targets Top Politicians, New York Times, March 7, 2015, Pg A10

605 AP, Politicians face investigation in Brazil's biggest ever corruption scandal, The Guardian, March 6, 2015, www.theguardian.com/world/2015/mar/07/ brazilian-court-approves-investigation-into-politicians-inpetrobras-scandal/

606 Romero, March 7, 2105

607 Romero, Simon, Expanding Web of Scandal in Brazil Threatens Further Upheaval, New York Times, August 22, 2015, Pg A6

608 Romero, A Swift Fall From Grace for Brazil's President, New York Times, March 21, 2015, Pg A4

609 Chandler, Adam, Brazil's Corruption Scandal Has It All, The Atlantic, March 17, 2016, www.theatlantic.com/international/archive/2016/03/ brazil-corruption-lula-rouseff/474258/

610 Romero, Simon, Faced With Many Crises, Brazil Focuses on Corruption, New York Times, December 4, 2015, Pg A8

611 Romero, Simon, and Sreeharsha, Vinod, Trying to Oust Brazil's Leader, Yet Facing Trial, New York Times, April 15, 2016, Pg A1

612 Romero, Simon, Lawmaker Trying to Oust Brazil's Leader Is Told to Step Down, New York Rimes, May 6, 2016, Pg A4

613 Fisher, Max, Taub, Amanda, Why Uprooting Corruption Has Thrown Brazil's Political System in Upheaval, New York Times, July 15, 2017, Pg A6

614 Osborn, Catherine, Are These Lawmakers Ready to Replace Rousseff, Foreign Policy, April 21, 2016, http://foreignpolicy.com/2016/04/21/brazil-dilma-rousseff-cunha-temer-pmdb/

615 Romero, Simon, Recording Spurs Brazil's Anticorruption Minister to Resign, New York Times, May 31, 2016, Pg A6

616 Romero, Simon, As Brazilians Mourn, Legislators Gut Graft Bill, New York Times, December 1, 2016, Pg A10

617 Londono, Ernesto, Brazilian Lawmakers Reject Bribery Prosecution of President, New York Times, August 3, 2017, Pg A7

618 Fisher, and Taub

619 Londono, Ernesto, and Darlington, Shasta, Leftist Lion and Far-Right Hawk Vie for Brazil Presidency, New York times, January 21, 2018, Pg 1o

620 Romero, Simon, Brazil's Power Dynamics Shifting Amid Scandals, New York Times, April 27, 2015, Pg A4

621 Romero, April 15, 2016

622 Romero, April 27, 2016

623 Romero, Simon, Murder of Brazilian Journalist Furthers Alarming Trend, New York Times, August 8, 2015, Pg A7

624 Ferreira do Vale, Helder, Bolsonaro wins Brazil election, promising to purge leftists from the country, The Conversation, October 28, 2018, http://theconversation.com/bolsonaro-wins-brazil-election-promises-to-pureg-leftists-from-country-105481

625 Editors' Picks, Our coverage of the Brazilian election, Foreign Policy, October 27, 2018

626 Hootsen, Jan-Albert, Searching for Mexico's Disappeared, Newsweek, April 7, 2015, www.newsweek.com/2015/04/17/searching-mexicos-disappeared-320026.html

627 Glenny, Misha, Supplying the High, New York Times Book Review, March 13, 2016, Pg 12

628 Fugitive Mayor, Wife Nabbed After 43 Students Disappear in Mexico, NBC News, November 4, 2014, www.nbcnews.com/news/world/fugitive-mayor-wife-nabbed-after-43-students-disappear-mexico-n240686

629 Villegas, Paulina, Experts Reject Official Account of How 43 Mexican Students Were Killed, New York Times, September 7, 2015, Pg A4

630 Rama, Anahi, and Diaz, Lizbeth, Mexico hampered probe into apparent student massacre, panel says, Reuters, April 25, 2016, www.reuters.com/article/us-mexico-violence-idUSKCN0XL0VX

631 How bad is Mexican political corruption, Yo Expert, downloaded M1y 22, 2015, http://worldnews.yoexpert.com/latin-american/how-bad-is-mexican-politica-corruption-15303.html

632 Archibold, Randal, A Quandary for Mexico as Vigilantes Rise, New York Times, January 16, 2104

633 Azam, Ahmed, and Schmitt, Eric, The stunningly efficient killers unleashed in Mexico's drug war: Marines kill 30 for every one they injure, National Post, May 27, 2016, www.nationalpost.com/m/wp/news/blog.html?b=news.news.nationalpost.com/news/world/the-stunningly-efficient-killers-unleashed-in-mexicos-drug-war-marines-kill-30-for-everyone-they-injure&pubdate=2016-05-28

634 Ahmed, Azam, Mexico Spends Big on Ads to Tame the News Media, New York Times, December 25, 2017, Pg A1

635 Malkin, Elizabeth, Journalistic Freedom Scrutinized in Mexico After Reporter's Firing, New York Times, March 29, 2015

636 Malkin, Elisabeth, Mexican Official Quits Over Helicopter Ride, New York Times, April 10, 2015, Pg A8

637 Malkin, Elisabeth, and Minder, Raphael, A Former Mexican Governor Is Arrested, but Not by His Own Country, New York Times, January 22, 2016, Pg A4

638 Malkin, Elizabeth, and Villegas, Paulina, Warrant for Vanished Ex-Official Is Seen as a Step in Mexico's Graft Fight, New York Times, October 21, 2016, Pg A11

639 Feuer, Alan, Al Chapo Trial Reveals An Abyss of Corruption, New York Times, December 29, 2018, Pg A22

640 Barnes, Luke, The agenda for Mexico's new leftist president is ambitious. But is it doable/ Think Progress, December 1, 2018, https://thinkprogress.org/the-agenda-for-mexicos-new-leftist-president-is-ambitious-but-is-it-doable-672ae7296c3a/

641 Kurtz, Michael, Corruption in Argentina, Politics & Policy, March 6, 2012, http://politicsandpolicy.org/article/corruption-argentina

642 Gilbert, Jonathan, Argentina's Vice President Charged in Corruption Case, June 28, 2014, www.nytimes.com/2014/06/29/world/americas/argentine-official-charged-with-bribery.html?_r=0

643 Associated Press in Buenos Aires, South China Morning Post, World, December 18, 2013, www.scmp.com/news/world/articles/1384971/corruption-scandal-swirls-around-argentine-leader

644 Gilbert, Jonathan, Prosecutor May Add Ex-President to Inquiry, New York Times, April 10, 2016, Pg 11

645 Gilbert, Jonathan, Ex-Leader of Argentina Is Indicted on Financial Charge, New York Times, May 14, 2016, Pg A3

646 Associated Press, Cristina Fernandez de Kirchner indicted in Argentina corruption case. The Guardian, December 27, 2016, www.theguardian.com/world/2016/dec/27/cristin-fernandez-de-kirchner-indicted-corruption-argentina

647 Martin, Abby, Scioli Sets New Promises Ahead of Argentina Presidential Runoff, Telesur, November 11, 2015, www.telesurtv.net/english/news/Scioli-Sets-New-Promises-Ahead-Of-Argintina-Presidential-Runoff-20151111-0017.html

648 Silverstein, Ken, Foreign Policy, April 6, 2016

649 Lopez, Virginia, and Watts, Jonathan, Nicholas Maduro declared Venezuela election winner by thin margin, The Guardian, April15, 2013, www.theguardian.com//world/apr/15/nicholas-maduro-wins-venezuela-election

650 Gallagher, J.J., Victory behind bars, How imprisoning politicians in Venezuela could backfire, Christian Science Monitor, www.csmonitor.com/World/Americas/2015/05/20/Victory-behind-bars-How-imprisoning-politicians-in-Venezuela-could-backfire

651 Sanchez, Maria Isabel, Venezuela opposition files 2 mn signatures for recall vote, Yahoo News, May 2, 2016, www.yahoo.com/news/venezuelas-maduro-calls-rebellion-opposition-recall-succeeds-091526014.html

652 Torres, Patricia, and Malkin, Elizabeth, Electoral Panel Halts Effort to Recall Venezuelan Leader, New York Times, October 22, 2016, Pg A6

653 Romero, Simon, Chile Joins Latin American Countries Shaken by Scandal, New York Times, April 10, 2015, Pg A8

654 Bonnefoy, Pascale, Daughter-in-Law of Chile's Leader Faces Corruption Charge, New York Times, January 30, 2016, Pg A6

655 Romero, April 10, 2015

656 Bonnefoy, Pascale, Chilean Journalists Face Restraints at a Busy Time, New York Times, April 8, 2016, Pg 3

657 Zarate, Andrea, and Casey, Nicholas, Ex-President of Peru Is Dead After Shooting Himself During Arrest, New York Times, April 19, 2019, Pg A11

658 Churchill, Winston, www.goodreads.com/quotes/5980-the-best-argument-against-democracy-is-a-five-minute-conversation-with-the-avergae-voter

659 Diggles, Michelle, and Hatalsky, Lanae, The State of the Center, May 15, 2104, www.thirdway.org/report/the-state-of-the-center

660 A Deep Dive Into Party Affiliation, Pew Research Center, April 7, 2015, www.people-press.org/2015/04/06/a-deep-dive-into-party-affiliation/

661 Doherty, Carroll, and Kiley, Jocelyn, Kew facts about partisanship and political animosity in America, Pew Research Center, June 22, 2016, www.pewresearch.org/fact-tank/2016/06/22/key-facts-partisanship/?utm_source=Pew+Research+Center&utm_campaign=7732039071_Weekly_June_23_20166_23_2016&utm_medium=email&utm_term=o_3e953b9b70-7732039071-400219269

662 Wagner, John, and Clement, Scott, It's just messed up: Most think political divisions as bad as Vietnam era, new poll shows, The Washington Post, National, Analysis, October 28, 2017, www.washingontpost.com/graphics/2017/national/democracy-poll

663 Anderson, Meg, Report: Partisan Bad Blood Highest In Decades, NPR, June 22, 2016, www.npr.org/2016/06/22/482970864/report-partisan-bad-blood-highest-in-decades?utm_source=Pew+Research+Center&utm_campaign=7732039071_Weekly_June_23_20166_23_2016&utm_medium=email&utm_term=o_3e953b9b70-7732039071-400219269

664 Lukianoff, Greg, and Haidt, Jonathan, The Coddling of the American Mind, The Atlantic, September 2015, Pg 42-52

665 French, David, Mueller Won't Shake Trump's Base, New York Times OpEd, October 31, 2017, Pg A23

666 Austin, E,G, Taking it to the people, The Economist, September 20, 2011, www.economist.com/blogs/democracyinamerica/2011/09/art-compromise

667 Rosenfeld, Steven, 8 ways the super rich make life miserable for the rest of us, Alternet/Salon, December 3, 2015, www.salon.com/2015/12/03/8_ways_the_super_rich_make_life_miserable_for_the_rest_of_us_partner/?source=newsletter

668 Brooks, Arthur C, Bipartisanship Isn't for Wimps, After All, New York Times Sunday Review, April 10, 2016, Pg 7

669 Rosenberg, Tina, Debates Do Matter, New York Times Sunday Review, November 15, 2015, Pg 3

670 Choi, Charles, Politics on the Brain: Scans Show Whether You Lean Left or Right, Live Science, April 7, 2011, www.livescience.com/13608-brain-political-ideology-liberal-conservative.html

671 Levitz, Eric, America Is Not Center-Right, OpEd, New York Times, November 2, 2017, Pg A27

672 Webster's New Twentieth Century Dictionary, Second Edition, William Collins Publishers, Inc, 1979, Pg 1307

673 Goldwater, Barry- 1964 Acceptance Speech, Republican Presidential Nomination, www.nationalcenter.org/Goldwater.html/

674 Alexander, Michelle, The New Jim Crow, Chapter 3, The Color of Justice, The New Press, New York, 2012 Pg 97-109

675 Ciaramella, C.J, Criminal Justice Reform Brings Together Liberals, Conservatives, The Washington Free Beacon, November 20, 2014, http://freebeacon.com/issues/criminal-justice-reform-brings-together-liberals-conservatives/

676 Federal Government Shutdown: Biggest News Stories of 2013, US News, December 20, 2013, www.usnews.com/news/special-reports/articles/2013/12/20/federal-government-shutdown-best-of-2013

677 Jacobs, Tom, The Policy Consequences of Partisan Gerrymandering, Pacific Standard, October 4, 2017, https://psmag.com/news/the-policy-consequences-of-partisan-gerrymandering

678 Brunius, Harry, Percentage of Republicans who believe in evolution is shrinking, The Christian Science Monitor, December 31, 2015, www.csmonitor.com/USA/Society/2013/1231/Percentage-of-Republicans-who-believe-in-evolution-is-shrinking

679 Jones, Robert, Southern Evangelicals: Dwindling- and Taking the GOP Edge With Them, The Atlantic, October 17, 2014, www.theatlantic.com/politics/archives/2014/10/the-shrinking-evangelical-voter-pool/381560/

680 Brunius

681 Pew Poll, April 7, 2015

682 Abramowitz, Alan, How race and religion have polarized American voters, The Washington Post, January 20, 2104, www.washingtonpost.com/blogs/monkey-cage/wp/2014/01/20/how-race-and-religion-have-polarized-American-voters/

683 Smith, Gregory, and Martinez, Jessica, How the faithful voted: A preliminary 2016 analysis, Pew Research Center, November 9, 2016, www.pewresearch.org/fact-tank/2016/11/how-the-faithful-voted-a-preliminary-2016-analysis/

684 Hamburger, Tom, Christian conservative group announces support for Trump as evangelical leaders remain divided over candidacy, The Washington Post, May 10, 2016, www.washingtonpost.com/news/post-politics/wp/2016/05/10/christian-conservative-group-announces-support-for-trump-as-evangelical-leaders-remain-divided-over-candidacy/

685 Editorial Board, The Truth of 'Black Lives Matter', New York Times, September 3, 2015, www.nytimes.com/2015/09/04/opinion/the-truth-of-black-lives-matter.html

686 Alexander, Michelle, The New Jim Crow, New Press, New York, 2012, Chapter 3, Pg 97-139

687 Abramowitz, Alan

688 Fiorina, Morris, and Abrams, Samuel, Americans aren't polarized, just better sorted, The Washington Post, January 21, 2015, www.washingtonpost.com/blogs/monkey-cage/wp/2014/01/21/americans-arent-polarized-just-better-sorted/

689 Aldrich, John H, Why Parties, University of Chicago Press, Chicago, 1995, Pg 10

690 Politics stops at the water's edge, April 15, 2009, www.barrypopik.com/index.ohp/new_york_city/entry/politics_stops_at_the_waters_edge/

691 Miller, Jake, Boehner invites Benjamin Netanyahu to address Congress, CBS News, January 21, 2015, www.cbsnews.com/news/john-boehner-invites-israeli-prime-minister-benjamin-netanyahu-to-address-congress/

692 Robinson, Eugene, Boehner's invitation to Netanyahu backfires on them both, Opinion, Washington Post, January 29, 2105, www.washingtonpost.com/opinions/

eugene-robinson-pboehners-invitation-to-netanyahu-backfires-on-them-both/2015/01/29/4636fbf0-a7f4-11e4-a06b-9df2002b86a0_story.html

693 Barrett, Ted, etal, Senate Democrats protect Obama on Iran vote, CNN Politics, September 10, 2015, www.cnn.com/2015/09/10/politics/iran-nuclear-deal-congress/index.html

694 Andelman, David, Iran should call Trump's bluff on nuclear deal, CNN, October 13, 2017

695 Annas, George J, Culture of Life Politics at the Bedside- The Terry Schiavo Case, New England Journal of Medicine, 2005, 352;16:1710

696 Bendery, Jennifer, Ted Cruz Is Vowing To Block A Bunch Of Obama's Nominees… Again, Huffington Post Politics, July 17, 2015, www.huffingtonpost.com/entry/ted-cruz-obama-nominees_55a936a0e4b04740a3dfd82a

697 Kapur, Sahil, Ted Cruz to Star in Government Shutdown, the Sequel, Bloomberg Politics, September 8, 2015, www.bloomberg.com/politics/articles/2015-09-08/ted-cruz-to-star-in-government-shutdown-the-sequel

698 Lieberman, Jethro K, The Evolving Constitution, Random House, New York, 1992, Pg 385

699 Hicks, John D, cited by Lisa Jane Disch in The Tyranny of the Two Party System, Columbia University Press, New York, 2002, Pg 4-5

700 Hudson, William, American Democracy in Peril, Third Edition, Chatham House Publishers, New York, 2001, P2 29

701 Excerpts from George Washington's Farewell Address, September 19, 1796, thirty-thousand.org, www.thirty-thousand.org/pages/Baneful_Parties.htm

702 Elections, 1792, The Readers Companion to American History, Foner, Eric, and Garraty, John, Houghton Mifflin Company, Boston, 1991, Pg 331

703 Kerwin C. Swint, "Mudslingers- The Top 25 Negative Political Campaigns of All Time," Praeger Press, Westport, Connecticut, 2006, Pg 183-191

704 John H. Aldrich, Pg 77

705 Eric Foner and John Garraty, "The Reader's Companion to American History," Houghton Mifflin Company, Boston, 1991, "Andrew Jackson," Pg 579

706 Robert North Roberts, "Ethics in U.S. Government, "Greenwood Press, Westport, Connecticut, 2001, Introduction, Pg VII

707 Ibid

708 Ibid, Pg 25

709 Aldrich, Pg 101

710 Ibid, "Republican Party," Pg 932

711 Roberts, "Buchanan Administration Corruption Scandals," Pg 33-34

712 Bibby and Maisel, Pg 28

713 Foner and Garraty, "Republican Party," Pg 932

714 Ibid, Pg 33

715 Foner and Garraty, "Dixiecrat, Party," Pg 290

716 Aldrich, Pg 163

717 Foner and Garraty, "Lyndon B. Johnson," Pg 600

718 Bibby and Maisel, Pg 38

719 Foner and Garraty, "George C. Wallace," Pg 1127

720 Bibby and Maisel, Pg 38

721 Foner and Garraty, "Richard M. Nixon," Pg 794

722 Aldrich, Pg 254, 255

723 Frankl, Viktor, Man's Search for Meaning, Simon and Schuster-Touchstone, 1984, Pg 133

724 Foner and Garraty, The Reader's Companion to American History, Houghton Mifflin, 1991, "Ronald Reagan, Pg 915

725 John F. Bibby and L. Sandy Maisel, *Two Parties or More?* Westview Press, Boulder, CO, 2nd ed., 2003, 41.

726 Hershey, 303.

727 1995-96 Government Shutdown, Slaying the Dragon of Debt, downloaded September 15, 2015, http://bancroft.berekley.edu/ROHO/projects/debt/governmentshutdown.html

728 What Bush did to McCain in the 2000 S.C. primary, downloaded September 15, 2015, www.bartcopnation.com/dc/dcboard.php?forum=8&topic_id=522&az=show_topic

729 Breaux, John, and Frist, Bill, Medicare Part D: A health care success, Politico, November 16, 2009, www.politico.com/story/2009/11/medicare-part-d-a-health-care-success-029545

730 Ibid.

731 Adam Nagourney, "Theme of Campaign Ads: Don't Be Nice," *New York Times*, September 27, 2006, A1.

732 John Broder, "As Election Nears, Groups Plan Negative Ads," *New York Times*, October 11, 2006, A27.

733 Sky, Emma, Iraq After the Surge, Foreign Affairs Video, June 5, 2015, www.foreignaffairs.com/videos/2015-06-05/emma-sky-iraq-after-surge

734 Federal Election Commission, Campaign Finance Reports and Data, Summary Reports Search Results 2007–2008 Cycle, http://query.nictusa.com/cgi-bin/cancomsrs/?_08+00+PR.

735 Bob Willis and Danielle Ivory, "Republicans Aren't Seeking Shutdown, Budget Chairman Ryan Says," Bloomberg, February 21, 2011, http://www.bloomberg.com/news/2011-02-21/republican-lawmakers-say-house-majority-isn-t-seeking-government-shutdown.html.

736 Steven Greenhouse, "Strained States Turning to Laws to Curb Labor Unions," *New York Times*, January 3, 2011, A1.

737 Nicholas Riccardi and Abigail Sewell, "Controversial collective-bargaining measure clears Wisconsin Assembly," *Los Angeles Times*, February 25, 2011, http://articles.latimes.com/2011/feb/25/nation/la-na-midwest-union-20110225.

738 MSNBC.com staff and AP, "Wis. governor refuses to budge on budget bill," msnbc.com, 2/22/2011, www.msnbc.msn.com/cleanprint/CleanPrintProxy.aspx?1298836740301.

739 Barro, Josh, Yes, if You Cut Taxes, You Get Less Tax Revenue, New York Times, June 27, 2014, www.nytimes.com/2014/06/27/upshot/kansas-tax-cut-leaves-brownback-with-less-money.html?_r=0

740 Hiltzik, Michael, How Tea Party tax cuts are turning Kansas into a smoking ruin, Los Angeles Times, June 10, 2014, www.latimes.com/business/hltzik/la-fi-mh-kansas-smoking-ruin-20140709-column.html

741 Shorman, Jonathan, How you could be affected by Kansas' new tax increases, Witchita Eagle, June 6, 2017

742 Meacham, Carl and Graybeall, Michael, Diminishing Mexican Immigration to the United States, Center for Strategic and International Studies, July 2013, http://csis.org/files/publication/130711_Meacham_DiminishingMexImm_WEB.pdf

743 Return Migration, Pew Study, April 23, 2012, www.pewresearch.org/subjects/ return-migration/

744 Krugman, Paul, The Time-Loop Party, OpEd, New York Times, February 8, 2016, Pg A25

745 Trump Supporters Think Obama is A Muslim Born in Another Country, Public Policy Polling, September 1, 2015, www.publicpolicypolling.com/main/2015/08/trump-supporters-think-obama-is-a-muslim-born-in-another-country.html#more

746 Savitsky, Shane, 1big thing: Two Americas, tuning each other out, Axios AM email, August 31, 2019

747 Herszenhorn, David, House Republicans Vote to Stop Funding Planned Parenthood, New York Times, September 19, 2015, Pg A13

748 Carter, Virginia, Planned Parenthood plot twist: 10 things to know about who was indicted, Gosport Times, January 28, 2016, http://gosporttimes.com/2016/01/28/ planned-parenthood-plot-twist-10-things-to-know-about-who/

749 Mondale, Walter, America's Empty Embassies, OpEd, New York Times, December 29, 2015, Pg A19

750 Lipton, Eric, et al, Benghazi Panel's Mission Evolved in Its 17 Months, New York Times, October 12, 2015, Pg A1

751 Scheiber, Noam, et al, Former Benghazi Investigator Claims House Committee Fired Him Illegally, New York Times, October 11, 2015, Pg 23

752 Calmes, Jackie, Crop Insurance Subsidy Reflects a Budget Reality, New York Times, November 27, 2015, Pg A24

753 Craig, Gregory, Playing Politics With the Court, New York Times OpEd, March 18, 2106, Pg A27

754 Editorial, A Partisan Prescription for Paralysis, New York Times, March 22, 2016, Pg A24

755 Everett, Burgess, GOP senators aim to confirm judges-just not for SCO-TUS, Politico, February 28, 2016, www.politico.com/story/2016/02/ courts-gop-senate-confirmation-nominees-219850

756 Savage, Charlie, Battle Over Bench Started Well Before Scalia's Death, New York Times, February 16, 2016, Pg A1

757 Editorial, A Partisan Prescription for Paralysis

758 Hulse, Carl, and Herszenhorn, David, After Boehner, House Hard-Liners Aim to Weaken Speakership Itself, New York Times, October 11, 2015, Pg 25

759 Kabaservice, Geoffrey, Anarchy in the House, New York Times OpEd, September 29, 2015, Pg A27

760 Gehrke, Joel, Meet the Freedom Caucus, National Review, January 26, 2015, www. nationalreview.com/article/397170/meet-freedom-caucus-joel-gehrke

761 Chait, Jonathan, The House's Right Flank Finally Got Boehner's Scalp, New York Magazine, Intelligencer, October 5, 2015, Pg 13-14

762 Ball, Molly, I'm Against the Muslims, Trump's Supporters and the Republican Divide, The Atlantic, December, 2015, www.theatlantic.com/politics/archive/2015/12/ the-split-within-conservatism/419400/

763 Lawder, David, and Dunsmuir, Lindsay, Trump changes tune on tax hikes for wealthy Americans, Reuters, May 9, 2016, www.reuters.com/articles/ us-usa-election-trump-idUSKCN0XZ013

764 Editorial, Angling for the Hopping Mad, New York Times, January 5, 2015, Pg A22

765 Traister, Rebecca, The Dying of the White Male Light, New York Magazine, December 28, 2015-January 10, 2016, Pg 9

766 Starr, Paul, A Shocking Rise in White Death Rates in Midlife- and what It Says About American Society, The American Prospect, November 2, 2015, http://prospect.org/articles/shocking-rise-white-death-rates-midlife-and-what-it-syas-about-american-society

767 Rattner, Steven, Who's Killing Global Growth, OpEd, New York Times, March 10, 2016, Pg A23

768 Occupy Wall Street Home Page, downloaded September 24, 2011, http://occupywallstree.org/about/

769 Parton, Heather Digby, John Roberts' right-wing crucifixion: How conservatives turned their back on Ronald Reagan's truest heir, Salon, October 1, 2015, www.salon.com/2015/10/01/john_roberts_right_wing_crucifixion_how_conservatives_turned_their_back_on_ronald_reagans_truest_heir/?source=newsletter

770 Ibid

771 ALEC, Model Policies, downloaded May 13, 2016, www.alec.org/model-policy/

772 Powell, Jim, How Did Rich Connecticut Morph Into One Of America's Worst Performing Economies, Forbes, August 1, 2013, www.forbes.com/sites/jimpowell/2013/08/01/how-did-rich-connecticut-morph-intoone-of-americas-worst-performing-economies/#21d91b2b270e

773 Beinart, Peter, Why America Is Moving Left, The Atlantic, January/February 2016, Pg 61-69

774 Ibid

775 Chait, Jonathan, The Bad News Since the Blue Wave, The National Interest, New York Magazine, December 10-23, 2018, Pg 23

776 Mallon, Thomas, A View From the Fringe, The New Yorker, January 11, 2016, Pg 63

777 Joseph McCarthy biography, bio, downloaded January 26, 2016, www.biography.com/people/joseph-mccarht-9390801

778 Healy, Jack, and Johnson, Kirk, A Quieter Push to Get Control of U.S. Lands, New York Times, January 11, 2016, Pg A1

779 Turkewitz, Julie, Fervor at an Oregon Wildlife Refuge, Concern Just Outside it, New York Times, January 13, 2016, Pg A10

780 Surowiecki, James, Bundynomics, The New Yorker, January 25, 2016, Pg 23

781 Tirado, Linda, Behind the Scenes in Oregon, Bundy Preaches Revolution, The Daily Beast, January 10, 2016, www.thedailybeast.com/articles/2016/01/10/behind-the-scenes-in-oregon-ammon-bundy-preaches-revolution.html

782 Bundys Nabbed, I Dead- But Militia Still Occupies, The Daily Beast, January 27, 2016, www.thedailybeast.com/cheats/2016/01/26/ammon-bundy-arrested.html?via=newsletter&source=CSAMedition

783 Nixon, Ron, Homeland Security Should Be Doing More To Fight Militias, a Former Analyst Says, New York Times, January 9, 2016, Pg A11

784 Clavel, Geoffroy, Marine Le Pen Decides 99 Percent of Incoming Refugees Are Men, Opposes Giving Them Political Refugee Status, WorldPost, September 9, 2015, www.huffingtonpost.com/2015/09/09/marine-le-pen-refugees_n_8110376.html

785 Germany Pegida protests: Rallies over 'Islamisation,' BBC News, January 6, 2015, www.bbcnews.com/news/world-europe-30685842

786 Rubin, Alissa, France's Far-Right Front Gains in Regional Elections, New York Times, December 6, 2015, www.newyorktimes.com/2015/12/07/world/europe/fraces-far-right-national-front-gains-in-regional-elections-.html?_r=0

787 Bramson, Dara, Ex-Presidents Of Poland Issue Rebuke To Government, New York Times, April 26, 2016, Pg A4

788 Belgian, Countries and their Cultures, downloaded September 18, 2015, www. everyculture.com/A-Bo/Belgium.html

789 Barnes, Ryan, Basque and Catalan Nationalism: An Evolution, Fair Observer, January 10, 2013, www.fairobserver.com/region/europe/basque-and-catalan-nationalism-evolution/

790 Minder, Raphael, Catalan Independence Drive Looms Over Spain's Coalition Talks, New York Times, January 12, 2016, Pg A6

791 The Economist Explains, Why is Northern Ireland part of the United Kingdom? The Economist, November 7, 2013, www.economist.com/blogs/economist-explains/2013/11/economist-explains-4

792 Rosell, Tarris, and Buttry, Dan, A Peacemaker in Kenya, Interfaith Peacemakers, downloaded September 21, 2015, www.readthespirit.com/interfaith-peacemakers/wilson-thiongo-gathungu/

793 Rogo, Paula, Anti-immigrant violence spreads to South Africa's largest city, Christian Science Monitor, April 17, 2015, www.csmonitor.com/World/Africa/2015/0417/Anti-immigrant-violence-spreads-to-South-Africa-largest-city-video

794 Onishi, Norimitsu, First Black Leader of South Africa's Opposition Seeks to Unseat the A.N.C, July 24, 2015, www.nytimes.com/2015/07/25/world/africa/mmusi-maimane-south-africa-democratic-alliance-anc-html?_r=0

795 Associated Press, South African Opposition Party Elects First Black Leader, New York Times, May 10, 2105, www.nytimes.com/world/africa/ap-af-south-african-opposition-leader.html?_r=0

796 Roots of Igbo-Yoruba conflict in Nigerian politics, Vanguard, May 2, 2014,www.vanguardngr.com/2014/05/roots-igbo-yoruba-conflict-nigerian-politics/

797 Ogundamisi, Kayode, What does it mean to be Nigerian? Al Jazeera, August 24, 2015, www.aljazeera.com/indepth/opinion/2015/08/nigerian-150824071305081.html

798 Gall, Carlotta, Second Opposition Leader Assassinated in Tunisia, New York Times, July 25, 2013, www.nytimes.com/2013/07/26/world/middleeast/second-opposition-leader-killed-in-tunisia.html

799 AP, Trial starts of suspects in Harari assassination, USA Today, January 16, 2014, www.usatoday.com/story/news/world/2014/01/16/harari-assassination/4548915/

800 Iraqi forces take control of Mosul Airport, Al Jazeera, February 23, 2017, www.aljazeera.com/news/2017/02/iraqi-forces-control-mosul-airport-170223085238235.html

801 Hadid, Diaa, Video Indicates Jewish Extremists Celebrated Palestinian Boy's Death, New York Times, December 25, 2015, Pg A6

802 Rogers, Katie, Is Gollum Good, or Evil? Turkish Doctor's Fate Rests on Answer, New York Times, December 6, 2015, Pg 6

803 Pamuk, Humeyra, Turkey's main opposition accuses Erdogan of blocking coalition efforts, Reuters, August 3, 2015, www.reuters.com/article/2015/08/03/us-turkey-politics-idUSKCN0Q80TJ20150803

804 Banerji, Rana, Deepening Sectarian Schisms In Pakistan, Mumbai Mirror, September 14, 2105, www.mumbaimirror.com/columns/comment/Deepening-sectarian-schisms-in-Pakistan/articleshow/48951704.cms

805 Taseer, Aatish, My Father's Killer's Funeral, New York Times Sunday Review, March 13, 2016, Pg 10

806 Mustafa, Faisan, The holy cow and the judiciary, The Tribune, September 14, 2015, www.tribuneindia.com/news/comment/the-holy-cow-and-the-judiciary/132655.html

807 Rout, Bharat Chandra, Patel quota row: The political economy of India's reservation policy, dna India, September 21, 2015, www.dnaindia.com/analysis/standpoint-patel-quota-row-thepolitical-economy-of-india-s-reservation-policy-2127039

808 Barstow, David, and Raj, Suhasini, Indian Writers Spurn Awards as Violence Flares, New York Times, October 18, 2015, Pg 1

809 Japan and the Power of an Apology, The Journal of Diplomacy and International Relations, September 15, 2015, http://blogs.shu.edu/diplomacy/2015/09/japan-and-the-power-of-an-apology/

810 Brazil impeachment: Rousseff attacks cabinet for being all male and all white, BBC News, May 14, 2016, www.bbc.com/news/world-latin-america-36292137

811 Casey, Nicholas, Venezuelan Courts Chip Away at Opposition's Power, New York Times, April 13, 2016, Pg A4

812 Maduro's Constituent Assembly seizes power from Venezuelan legislature, France 24, August 18, 2017, www.france24.com/2017/08-18-venezuela-maduro-new-constituent-assemply-seizes-power-opposition-legislature

813 Brooks, David, The Rise of the Resentniks, OpEd, New York Times, November 16, 2018, Pg A25

814 Spinoza, Baruch, The Ethics of Spinoza, The Citadel Press, Secaucus, New Jersey, 1976, Pg 68

815 Webster's New Twentieth Century Dictionary, Unabridged, Second Edition, William Collins, Publishers, Inc, New York, Pg 578

816 Too Many Government Workers?-Posner, The Becker-Posner Blog, September 26, 2011, www.becker-posner-blog.com/2011/09/too-many-government-workersposner.html

817 Ibid

818 Blodget, Henry, Guess What Percentage Of Americans Work For The Government Now Versus The Late 1970s, Business Insider, July 24, 2014, www.businessinsider.com/percentage-of-americans-work-for-the-government-2012-7

819 Morales, Lymari, Gov't Employment Ranges From 38% in D.C. to 12% in Ohio, Gallup, August 6, 2010, www.gallup.com/poll/141785/Gov-Employment-Ranges-Ohio.aspx

820 Daley, Suzanne, and Bounias, Dimitris, Rooting Out the Greeks Who Farm Mainly On Paper, New York Times, October24, 2015, Pg A5

821 Romero, Simon, An Exploding Pension Crisis Feeds Brazil's Political Turmoil, New York Times, October 21, 2015, Pg A4

822 Reuters, U.S. manufacturers spend more on regulations than security- Philly Fed, Yahoo Finance, April 21, 2016, http://finance.yahoo.com/news/u-manufacturers-spend-more-regulations-144215623.html

823 Cohen, Patricia, Horse Rub? Where's Your License? New York Times Business, June 18, 2016, Pg B1

824 Kanter, James, E.U.'s Ballooning Bills Are Stirring Fury, New York Times Business, June 18, 2016, Pg B1

825 Applebaum, Yoni, Our Fragile Constitution, The Atlantic, October 2015, Pg 20-23

826 Min Kim, Seung, and Everett, Burgess, Angry GOP freezes out Obama nominees, Politico, October 14, 2015, www.politico.com/story/2015/10/gop-senate-barack-obama-cotton-214700

827 Pear, Robert, President Protests Limits On His Power to Fill Posts, New York Times, February 29, 2016, Pg A10

828 An Administration of Empty Desks, Editorial, New York Times, January 23, 2017, Pg A22

829 American Fact Finder, United States Census Bureau, March 2013, http://factfinder. census.gov/faces/tableservices/jsf/pages/productview.xhtml?src=bkmk

830 Joyner, James, Is Government Inefficient, Outside the Beltway? August 23, 2012, www.outsidethbeltway.com/is-government-inefficient/

831 Riedl, Brian, 50 Examples of Government Waste, The Heritage Foundation, October 6, 2009, www.heritage.org/research/reports/2009/10/50-examples-of-government-waste#_edn4

832 Gottesdiener, Laura, Alternet, 7 absurd ways the military wastes taxpayer dollars, Salon, December 12, 2012, www.salon.com/2012/12/12/7_absurd_ways_the_military_wastes_taxpayer_dollars/

833 Ibid

834 Ibid

835 Ibid

836 Ibid

837 Paltrow, Scott, Special Report: The Pentagon's doctored ledgers conceal epic waste, Reuters, November 18, 2103, www.reuters.com/article/2013/11/18/us-usa-pentagon-waste-specialreport-idUSBRE9AH0LQ20131118

838 Ibid

839 Ibid

840 Ibid

841 Bender, Bryan, Exclusive: Massive Pentagon agency lost track of hundreds of millions of dollars, Politico, February 5, 2018, www.politico.com/story/2018/02/05/pentagon-logistics-agency-review-funds-322860

842 Thompson, Mark, et al, How Safe Are Our Troops? Why the Pentagon ended up with a shortage of armored vehicles for U.S. soldiers in Iraq, Time Magazine, December 20, 2004, reprinted GlobalSecurity.org, www.globalsecurity.org/news/2004/041220-armored-vehicles.htm

843 Moss, Michael, Pentagon Study Links Fatalities to Body Armor, New York Times, January 7, 2006, www.nytimes.com/2006/01/07/politics/07armor.html?pagewanted=all&_r=0

844 Ricks, Thomas, Fiasco: The American Military Adventure in Iraq, Penguin Press, New York, 2006, Pg 42-43 and other sites.

845 Gordon, Michael, and Trainor, General Bernard E, Cobra II, Pantheon Press, New York, 2006, 26, 101-103

846 Drusch, Andrea, F-35 fight plane cost overruns detailed, Politico, February 16, 2014, www.politico.com/story/2014/02/f35-fighter-plane-costs-103579.html

847 F-35 Brief, Defense Issues, March 16, 2013, http://defenseissues.wordpress.com/tag/lockheed-martin/

848 Lott, Maxim, F-35 fighters plagued with delays, cost overruns, federal report says, Fox News April 3, 2014, www.foxnews.com/tech/2014/04/03/f35-fighters-plagued-with-delays-cost-overruns-federal-report-says/

849 McGarry, Brendon, Report: Pentagon to Buy Fewer F-35s in 2015, DODBuzz, February 18, 2014, www.dodbuzz.com/2014/02/18/report-pentagon-to-buy-ferwer-f-35s-in-2015/

850 Nixon, Ron, Inspector Keeps a Watchful Eye on U.S. Spending in Afghanistan, to Dramatic Effect, New York Times, August 25, 2015, Pg A6

851 Whitlock, Craig, and Woodward, Bob, Pentagon buries evidence of $125 billion bureaucratic waste, The Washington Post, December 6, 2016, Pg 1

852 Johnson, Keith, and DeLuce, Dan, U.S. Falls Behind in Arctic Great Game, Foreign Policy, May 24, 2016, http://foreignpolicy.com/2016/05/24/u-s-falls-behind-in-arctic-great-game/

853 Duties of the Secretary of State, January 20, 2009, www.state.gov/secretary/115194.htm

854 Chapter 11, Table 11-2, Federal Civilian Employees in the Executive Branch, Budget of the United States FY 2013, Analytical Perspectives, www.whitehouse.gov/sites/default/files/omb/performan e/chapter11-2013.pdf

855 Flint, Laura, CBS Covers Inefficiencies In State Department, mrc TV, June 4, 2014, www.mrc.org/videos/cbs-covers-inefficiencies-in-state-department

856 Flint, Laura, CBS: Obama State Department Wasting Millions on Embassy Aesthetics at Cost of Security Upgrades, mrc newsbusters, June 4, 2014, http://newsbusters.org/blogs/laura-flint/2014/06/04/cbs-covers-inefficiencies-state-department

857 Defense Trade: Arms Export Control Vulnerabilities and Inefficiencies in the Post 9/11 Environment, GAO, April 7, 2006, fas.org/asmp/resources/govern/109th/GAO05468R.pdf

858 Schneier, Cogan, State's cybersecurity office 'ineffective,' inefficient, Federal News Radio, July 25, 2013, http://federalnewsradio.com/technology/2013/07/states-cybersecuity-office-ineffective-inefficient/

859 Inefficiencies In The American Political System: A Threat To Freedom?, New Threats to Freedom, downloaded August 7, 2015, http://newthreatstofreedom.com/news/inefficiencies-in-the-american-political-system-a-threat-to-freedom/

860 Bacon, John, Five things to know about the Benghazi attack, USA Today, June 17, 2014, www.usatodat.com/story/news/world/2014/06/17/benghazi-attack-five-things/10676869/

861 Nicholas, Peter, Sen. Grassley Vows to Hold Up State Dept. Nominations Over Clinton Inquiry, Wall Street Journal, August 7, 2015, http://blogs.wsj.com/washwire/2015/08/07/sen-grassley-vows-to-hold-up-state-dept-nominations-pending-clinton-records/

862 Office of the United States Attorneys, United States Department of Justice, downloaded August 8, 2015, www.justice.gov/usam/usam-1-2000-organization-and-functions

863 Prosecutors Offices, Bureau of Justice Statistics, Downloaded August 8, 2015, www.bjs.gov/index.cfm?ty=tp&tid=27

864 O'Brien, Rebecca Davis, and Orden, Erica, Federal Prosecutors Launch Assault on Public Corruption in New York State, Wall Street Journal, March 6, 2015, www.wsj.com/articles/federal-prosecutors-launch-assault-on-public-corruption-in-new-york-state-1423534577

865 FBI and CIA were too busy fighting each other to avert 9/11, RT.com, March 28, 2012, www.rt.com//usa/fbi-fighting-911-agency-675/

866 Sharing Law Enforcement and Intelligence Information, CRS Report for Congress, February 13, 2007, http://fas.org/sgp/crs/intel/RL33873.pdf

867 MacDonald, Heather, Why the FBI Didn't Stop 9/11, City Journal, Autumn 2002, www.city-journal.org/html/12_4_why_the_fbi.html

868 Cobain, Ian, US acted to conceal evidence of intelligence failure before 9/11, The Guardian, March 27, 2012, www.theguardian.com/world/2012/mar/27/us-intelligence-failure-911-fbi-cia

869 O'Connor, Rory, How 9/11 Could Have Been Prevented, Alternet, August 7, 2006, www.alternet.org/story/40005/how_911_could_have_been_prevented

870 Ibid

871 Eggen, Dan, Pre-9/11 Missteps By FBI Detailed, Washington Post, June 30, 2005, www.washingtonpost.com/wp-dyn/conetnt/article/2005/06/09/AR2005060902000.html

872 Ibid

873 Cumming Alfred, and Masse, Todd, FBI Intelligence Reform Since September 11, 2001: Issues and Options for Congress, April 6, 2004, http://fas.org/irp/crs/RL32336.html#_1_27

874 Eggen

875 Tully, Andrew, U.S. Panel Cites Lack Of Imagination In Failure to Prevent 9/11 Attacks, Radio Free Europe, July 22, 2004, www.rferl.org/content/article/1053897.html

876 O'Connor

877 Schmidt, Michael, Report Credits F.B.I. With Progress Since 9/11, but Says More Is Needed, New York Times, March 25, 2015, www.nytimes.com/2015/03/25/us/fbi-911-review-commission-releases-report.html?_r=0

878 Operation Fast and Furious Fast Facts, CNN Library, Updated April 21, 2015, www.cnn.com/2013/08/27/world/americas/operation-fast-and-furious-fast-facts/index.html

879 Ibid

880 Ibid

881 Cohan, William D, How The Bankers Stayed Out Of Jail, The Atlantic, September 2015

882 Ibid

883 Cohan

884 Zezima, Katie, Everything you need to know about the VA- and the scandals engulfing it, Washington Post, May 30, 2014, www.washingtonpost.com/news/the-fix/2014/05/21/a-guide-to-the-va-and-the-scandals-engulfing-it/

885 Veterans Health Administration, downloaded August 13, 2005, www.va.gov/health/

886 Oppel Jr, Richard A, Wait Lists Grown as Many More Veterans Seek Care and Funding Falls Far Short, New York Times, June 21, 2015, Pg 12

887 Editorial, Ever-Growing Wait for Veterans' Care, New York Times, July 8, 2015, Pg A20

888 Flores, Reema, Donald Trump taps Betsy DeVos for education secretary, CBS News, November 23, 2016, www.cbsnews.com/news/donald-trump-taps-betsy-devos-for-education-secretary/

889 Harris, Elizabeth, 20% of New York State Students Opted Out of Standardized Tests This Year, New York Times, August 12, 2105, www.nytimes.com/2015/08/12/nyregion.new-yorl-state-students-tests.html

890 Ellenberg, Jordon, Meet the New Common Core, New York Times, June 16, 2105, OpEd, Pg A27

891 Editorial, New York Times, August 15, 2015, Pg A22

892 Brooks, David, What the Working Class Is Trying to Say, OpEd, New York Times, November 9, 2018, Pg A31

893 Federal Student Aid, An office of the U.S. Department of Education, downloaded August 13, 2015, http://studentaid.ed.gov/sa/types

894 Carrns, Ann, A Revised Program For Student Loan Debt, New York Times, August 15, 2015, Pg B5

895 Denhart, Chris, How The $1.2 Trillion College Debt Crisis Is Crippling Students, Parents And The Economy, Forbes, August 7, 2013, www.forbes.com/sites/specialfea-

tyres/2013/08/07/how-the-college-debt-is-crippling-students-parents-and-the-economy/

896 For-Profit Colleges and Universities, National Conference of State Legislatures, July 3, 2013, www.ncsl.org/research/education/for-profit-colleges-and-universities.aspx

897 Ibid

898 The Hechinger Report, Students Are Returning to For-Profit Colleges, US News and World Report, February 24, 2015, www.usnews.com/news/articles/2015/02/24/students-are-returning-to-for-profit-colleges

899 Hanford, Emily, The Case Against For-Profit Colleges and Universities, American Radioworks, downloaded August 14, 2015, http://americanradioworks.publicradio.org/features/tomorrows-college/phooenix/case-against-for-profit-schools.html

900 Cohen, Patricia, For-Profit Colleges Fail Standards, but Get Billions, New York Times, October 13, 2015, Pg A1

901 Ibid

902 Morgenson, Gretchen, Whistle-Blowers Spoke Up; 17 Years Later, ITT Collapsed, New York Times, Business, October 23, 2016, Pg 1

903 Isikoff, Michael, Trump University lawsuits for $25 million, Yahoo News, November 18, 2016, www.yahoonews/com/news/trump-settles-trump-university-lawsuits-for-25-million-215707514.html

904 Carrns, Ann, A Revised Program For Student Loan Relief

905 Aristotle, The Just Distribution of political Power, The Politics, Penguin Classics, 1988, Pg 198

906 Brill, Steven, Are We Any Safer, The Atlantic, September 2016, Pg 61

907 Ibid

908 Ibid

909 Fox News, Wikileaks, Clinton campaign in Twitter war over latest leaks, Fox News, October 11, 2016, www.foxnews.com/politics/2016/10/11/wikileaks-clinton-campaign-in-twitter-war-over-latest-leaks.html

910 Nixon, Ron, Immigration Agency's Green Card Errors Said to Be Worse Than First Thought, New York Times, November 22, 2016, Pg A16

911 Rattner, Steven, Airport Lines and Budget Lies, OpEd New York Times, July 9, 2016, Pg A21

912 Editorial, A Gutted I.R.S. Makes the Rich Richer, New York Times, December 26, 2018, Pg A18

913 Cohen, Tom, CNN Politics, October 23, 2013, www.cnn.com/2013/10/22/politics/obamacare-website-four-reasons/index.html

914 Young, Jeffrey, Obamacare Website Failure Threatens Health Coverage For Millions of Americans, Huff Post Business, October18, 2013, www.huffingtonpost.com/2013/10/18/obamacare-train-wreck_n_4118041.html

915 Medicaid Fraud and Abuse, National Conference of State Legislators, downloaded December 1, 2015, www.ncsl.org/research/health/medicaid-fraud-and-abuse.aspx

916 De Rugy, Veronique, Medicare Waste, Fraud, and Abuse Means the System Needs Reform, Reason, November 26, 2015, http://reason.com/archives/2015/11/26/medicare-waste-fraud-and-abuse-means-the

917 About the FEC, Federal Election Commission, downloaded January 22, 2016, www.fec.gov/about.shtml

918 Goodman, Lee, The FEC's Problems Aren't with the GOP, Politico Magazine, May 10, 2015, www.politico.com/magazine/story/2015/05/thefecs-problems-arent-with-the-gop-117798

919 Introduction, U.S. Securities and Exchange Commission, downloaded August 26, 2015, www.sec.gov'about'whatwedo.shtml

920 SEC Enforcement Actions- Addressing Misconduct that Led To or Arose From the Financial Crisis, statistics through May 26, 2015, www.sec.gov/spotlight/enf-actions-fc-shtml

921 Hedge Fund Advisory Firm to Pay the SEC $5 million to Settle Fund Valuation Scam Allegations, Institutional Investor Securities Blog, July 1, 2015, www.institutionalinvestorsecuritiesblog.com/mortgagebacked_securities/

922 SEC Settles With Ex-Freddie Mac Executives Over Allegations They Mislead Investors Over Mortgage Risks, April 15, 2015, Institutional Investor Securities Blog, www.institutionalinvestorsecuritiesblog.com/mortgagebacked_securities/

923 Standard and Poor's to Pay Almost $80 million to Resolve SEC Charges Over Ratings Fraud Involving CMBs, January 21, 2015, www.institutionalinvestorsecuritiesblog.com/mortgagebacked_securities

924 Morgenson, Gretchen, Neglecting To Name The Names, New York Times, August 30, 2015, Business 1

925 SEC Charges Goldman Sachs With Fraud in Structuring and Marketing of CDO Tied to Subprime Mortgages, April 16, 2010, www.sec.gov/news/pres//2010/2010-59.htm

926 Taibbi, Matt, Why Didn't the SEC Catch Madoff? It Might Have Been Policy Not To, Rolling Stone, May 31, 2013, www.rollingstone.com/politics/news/why-didnt-the-sec-catch-madoff-it-might-have-neen-policy-not-to-20130531

927 Ibid

928 Ibid

929 Bills by Final Status, Statistics and Historical Comparisons, govtrack.us, downloaded August 14, 2015, www.govtrack.us/congress/bills/statistics

930 Congress Bills, Statistics and Historical Comparisons, downloaded February 26, 2017, gov track/ www.govtrack.us/congress/bills/statistics

931 Statistics and Historical Comparison, Congress, govtrack, downloaded 2/ 8/18, www.govtrack.us/congress/bills/statistics

932 Grim, Ryan, and Siddiqui, Sabrina, Call Time For Congress Shows How Fundraising Dominates Bleak Life, Huffington Post, January 8, 2013, www.huffingtonpost.com/2013/01/08/call-time-congressional-fundraising_n_2427291.html

933 Goldmacher, Shane, Former Senate Leader Says Senators Spent Two Thirds of Time Asking for Money, National Journal, January 16, 2015, www.nationaljournal.com/congress/former-senate-leader-says-senators-spent-two-thirds-of-time-asking-for-money-20140116

934 Political Dictionary, Taegan Goddard, downloaded August 14, 2015, http://political-dictionary.com/words/hastert-rule/

935 Schneider, Judy, House and Senate Rules of Procedure: A Comparison, Congressional Research Service, Update April 16, 2008, www.senate.gov/reference/resources/pdf/RL30945.pdf

936 Ibid

937 Senate Legislative Process, United States Senate, downloaded August 17, 2015, www.ussenate.gov/legislative/common/briefing/Senate_legislative_process.htm

938 Schneider

939 Senate Legislative Process

940 Ibid

941 Yan, Holly, Government shutdown: Get up to speed in 20 questions, CNN Politics, www.cnn.com/2013/09/30/government-shutdown-up-tp-speed/index.html

942 McCarter, Joan, House Republicans reach pathetic milestone: 50th Obamacare repeal vote, Daily Kos, March 5, 2014, www.dailykos.com/story/2014/03/05/1282420/House-Republicans-reach-pathetic-milestone-50th-Obamacare-repeal-nbsp-vote#

943 Herszenhorn, David, Not Even Catharsis Is Seen in Senate Vote to Repeal Health Law, New York Times, December 5, 2015, Pg A12.

944 Harris, Gardiner, As Expected, Obama Vetoes Repeal of Health Law, New York Times, January 9, 2016, Pg A14

945 Nixon, Ron, Human Cost Rises as Infrastructure Withers, New York Times, November 6, 2015, Pg A12

946 Mooney, Chris, The gas tax has been fixed at 18 cents for two decades. Now would be a great time to raise it, Washington Post, December 3, 2014, www.washingtonpost.com/news/wonk/wp/2014/12/03/why-now-would-be-a-very-good-time-to-raise-the-gas-tax/

947 Southall, Ashley, Spending Cuts Threaten to Delay Research, Obama Tells Scientists, New York Times, April 29, 2013, http://thecaucusblogs.nytimes.com/2013/04/29/spending-cuts-threaten-to-delay-research-obama-tells-scientists/?_r=0

948 Calmes, Jackie, Inflexibility of Senator Stymies Ex-Im Bank, New York Times Business, June 28, 2016, Pg B1

949 Calmes, Jackie, New York Times, September 16, 2015

950 Fox, Maggie, State Efforts to Block Obamacare Are Working, Study Finds, NBC News, January 14, 2014, www.nbcnews.com/health/health-care/state-efforts-block-obamacare-are-working-study-finds-n9596

951 Davenport, Coral, Numerous States Will Sue To Stop New Climate Rules, New York Times, October 23, 2015, Pg A22

952 Court Role and Structure, About Federal Courts, United States Courts, downloaded August 18, 2018, www.uscourts.gov/about-federal-courts/court-role-and-structure

953 Specialized Courts, National Institute of Justice, downloaded August 20, 2015, www.nij.gov/topics/courts/pages/specialized-courts.aspx

954 Liptak, Adan, New Questions On Racial Gap In Filling Juries, New York Times, August 17, 2105, Pg A1

955 FreeAdvice Staff, How long does a federal appeal take, FreeAdvice, downloaded August 19, 2015, http://freeadvice.com/litigation/appeals/federal_appeal.htm

956 How Does the U.S. Supreme Court Decide Whether to Hear a Case, FindLaw, downloaded August 19, 2015, http://litigationfindlaw.com/lega-system/how-does-the-u-s-supreme-court-decide-whether-to-hear-a-case.html

957 Editorial, New York Times, Confirm President Obama's Judges, New York Times, November 13, 2015, Pg A34

958 Smith, Randall, Case Limps On For a Decade, By Legal Design, New York Times, August 7, 2015, Pg B1

959 Justice Delayed Is Justice Denied, Project Censored, January 17, 2015, www.project-censored.org/justice-delayed-is-justice-denied/

960 Criminal Justice System: How It Works, The New York County District Attorney's Office, downloaded August 22, 2015, http://manhattanda.org/criminal-justice-system-how-it-works?s=38

961 Ibid

962 Tapscott, Mark, Whatever happened to a 'government of laws, not of men, The Washington Examiner, November 1, 2012, www.washingtonexaminer.com/whatever-happened-to-agovernment-of-laws-not-of-men/article/2512346

963 Hamilton, Alexander, or Madison, James, The Federalist No. 62, 1787-1788, The Modern Library of New York, Random House, Pg 406

964 McCoy, Terrence, In Pakistan, 1000 women die in 'honor killings' annually. Why is this happening, Washington Post, May 28, 2014, www.washingtonpost.com/news/morning-mix/wp/2014/05/28/in-pakistan-honor-killings-claim-1000-womens-lives-annually-why-is-this-still-happening/

965 Haq, Riaz, Can Secular Laws Promote Tolerance in Pakistan? Haq's Musings, June 3, 2010, www.riazhaq.com/2010/06/can-secular-laws-promote-tolerance-in.html

966 Agencies, Mob beats woman to death for burning the Koran in Afghanistan, The Telegraph, March 18, 2015, www.telegraph.co.uk/news/worldnews/asia//afghanistan/11484431/Mob-beats-woman-to-death-for-burning-the-Koran-in-Afghanistan.html

967 The Secretariat of the Justice System Reform Council, The Japanese Justice System, July 1999, http://japan.kantei.go.jp/policy/sihou/singikai/990620_e.html

968 Brown, Ben, Korean justice system, The Korea Times, August 5, 2010, www.korea-times.co.kr/www/news/opinon/2010/08/137_70900.html

969 Keating, Jerome, Taiwan's Court Reform A Matter For Everyone, The Wild East Magazin, January 11, 2015, www.thewildeast.net/tag/justice-system-in-taiwan/

970 Editorial, "The Looming Crisis in the States," New York Times, December 25, 2010, Week in Review, 13.

971 Bosman, Julie, et al, Crises in Two Cities Test Michigan's Governor, New York Times, January 21, 2016, Pg A1

972 Bellinger, David, Lead Contamination in Flint- An Abject Failure to Protect Public Health, New England Journal of Medicine, March 24, 2016

973 Editorial, How Michigan Failed the City of Flint, New York Times, January 15, 2016, Pg A30

974 Oosting, Jonathan, et al, 'Disaster' warning preceded Flint water switch, Detroit News, March 11, 2016, www.detroitnews.com/story/news/politics/2016/03/10/disaster-warning-preceded-flint-water-switch/

975 Editorial, The Republican Refusal to Aid Flint, New York Times, February 6, 2016, Pg A22

976 Lartey, Jamiles, US government investigating blood lead levels in New York's public housing, The Guardian, March 17, 2016, www.theguardian.com/us-news/blood-lead-levels-new-york-city-public-housing-investiagtion

977 Schaper, David, As Infrastructure Crumbles, Trillions Of Gallons of Water Are Lost, NPR, April 29, 2014, www.npr.org/ 2014/10/29/as-infrastructure-crumbles-trillions-of-gallons-of-water-lost

978 Fox, Craig, and Tannenbaum, David, The Curious Politics of the 'Nudge', New York Times Sunday Review, September 27, 2015, Pg 9

979 Wolfers, Justin, Making Government Work More Like Google, New York Times Sunday Review, September 27, Pg 6

980 Levine, Robert A, Shock Therapy for the American Health Care System, Praeger Press/ABC-CLIO, Santa Barbara, California, 2009, Chap 2, Pg 32-33

981 Nussle, Jim, and Orzag, Peter, Editors, Moneyball For Government, Disruption Books, 2014

982 Lewis, Michael, Moneyball- The Art of Winning an Unfair Game, W.W. Norton and Company, New York, 2004

983 Bridgeland, John, and Orszag, Peter, Can Government Play Moneyball, The Atlantic, July 2013, www.theatlantic.com/magazine/archive,2013/07/can-government-play-moneyball/309389/

984 Estimated vs. Actual Federal Spending for Fiscal Year 2014, USgov spending, www.usgovernmentspending.com/federal_budget_estimate_vs_actual

985 Bridgeland, John, and Orszag Peter, A moneyball approach to government, Politico, October 18, 2013, www.politico.com/story/2013/10/opinion-john-bridgeland-peter-orszag-moneyball-approach-to-government-98498.html

986 Defense Base Closure and Realignment Commission, downloaded 2-16-15, www.brac.gov/

987 Carney, Jordain, Pentagon Asks Congress for Permission to Close Military Bases, National Journal, February 25, 2014, www.nationaljournal.com/defense/pentagon-asks-congress-for-permission-to-close-military-bases-20140225

988 IRS BUDGET: The IRS Desperately Needs More Funding to Serve Taxpayers and Increase Voluntary compliance, www.taxpayeradvocate.irs.gov/userfiles/file/2013Fullreport/IRS-BUDGET-The-IRS-Desperately-Needs-More-Funding-to-Serve-Taxpayers-and-Increase-Voluntary-Compliance.pdf

989 Breyer, Stephen, Making Our Democracy Work, Alfred A. Knopf, New York, 2010, Pg 161

990 Belli, Luca, WhatsApp skewed Brazilian election, proving social media's danger to democracy, The Conversation, December 5, 2018, http://theconversation.com/whatsapp-skewed-brazilian-election-proving-social-medias-danger-to-democracy-106476

991 Waxman, Simon, Ranked-Choice Voting Is Not the Solution, Democracy, November 3, 2016, http://democracyjournal.org/arguments/ranked-choice-voting-is-not-the-solution/

992 Leonhardt, David, If Liberals Voted..., OpEd, New York Times, June 20, 2017, Pg A27

993 Kolbert, Elizabeth, Drawing The Line, The New Yorker, June 27, 2016, Pg 68

994 Swift, Art, Americans' Support for Electoral College Rises Sharply, Gallup Politics, December 2, 2016, www.gallup.com/poll/198197/americas-support-electoral-college-rises-sharply.aspx

995 Desilver, Drew, Among democracies, U.S. stands out in how it chooses its head of state, Pew Research Center, November 22, 2016, www.pewresearch.org/fact-tank/2016/11/22/among-democracies-u-s-stands-out-in-how-it-chooses-its-head-of-state/#

996 Alberta, Tim, Is the Electoral College Doomed? Politico Magazine, 9/8/17, www.politico.com/magazine/story/2017/09/05/electoral-college-national-popular-vote-compact-215541

997 Finkelman, Paul, The Proslavery Origins of the Electoral College, June 9, 2002, http://people.uncw.edu/lowery/pls/01/wilson_chapter_outlines/The%20Proslavery%20Origins%20of%20the%20Electoral%20College.pdf

998 Wagstaff, Keith, We're halfway to eliminating the Electoral College, The Week, August 2, 2013, http://theweek.com/articles/461444/halfway-eliminating-electoral-college

999 Levine, Sam, McCian, Whitehouse, Make Bipartisan Appeal to SCOTUS Against Wisconsin Gerrymandering, HuffPost, September 5, 2017, www.huffingtonpost.com/entry/mccain-whitehouse-wisconsin-gerrymander_us_59af13c3e4b03570184e440d

1000 Editorial, When Politicians Pick Their Voters, New York Times, May 30, 2017, Pg A20

1001 Keller, Jared, How Voter Suppression Really Works, Pacific Standard, November 11, 2016, https://psmag.com/how-voter-suppression-really-works-3f094c84151f#.bfrou3250

1002 Jones, Bradley, Most Americans want to limit campaign spending, say big donors have greater political influence, Pew Research Center May 8, 2018, www.pewresearch.org/fact-tank/2018/05/08/most-americans-want-to-limit-campaign-spending-say-big-donors-have-greater-political-influence/

1003 McMahon, Kevin, Is the Supreme Court's legitimacy undermined in a polarized age? The Conversation, July 7, 2018, https://theconversation.com/is-the-supreme-courts-legitimacy-undermined-in-a-polarized-age-99473

1004 Elliot, E. Donald, Fixing a broken process for nominating US Supreme Court justices, The Conversation, October 15, 2018, https://theconversation.com/fixing-a-broken-process-for-nominating-us-supreme-court-justices-104629

1005 America Needs a Bigger House, Editorial, New York Times Sunday Review, November 11, 2018, Pg 8

1006 Krugman, Paul, Real America Versus Senate America, New York Times OpEd, November 9, 2018, Pg A31

1007 Markovits, Daniel, and Ayres, Ian, The U.S. is in a state of perpetual minority rule, Opinion, Washington Post, November 8, 2018, www.washingtonpost.com/opinions/the-us-is-in-a-perpetual-state-of-minority-rule/2018/11/08/9fqf38a0

1008 Tomasky, Michael, Democrats Need a Rural Strategy, OpEd, New York Times, November 8, 2018, Pg A23

1009 Stromberg, Stephen, Millennials political nightmare is coming, Opinion, Washington Post, November 7, 2018, www.washingtonpost.com/opinions/millennials-political-nightmare-is-coming/2018/11/07

1010 Ibid

1011 Bump, Philip, In about 20 years, half the population will live in eight states, Washington Post, July 12, 2018, www.washingtonpost.com/news/politics/wp/2018/07/12/in-about-20-years--half-the-population-will-live-in-eight-states/

1012 The Public, the Political System and American Democracy, Pew Research Center, April 26, 2018, www-people-press.org/2018/04/26/the-public-the-political-system-and-american-democracy

1013 Schmemann, Serge, A Public Service Message From the Class of '67, OpEd, New York Times Sunday Review, June 11, 2017, Pg 8

1014 Larson, Quincy, A warning from Bill Gates, Elon Musk, and Stephen Hawking, Medium, February 18, 2017, https://medium.freecodecamp.com/bill-gates-and-elon-musk-just-warned-us-about-the-one-thing-politicians-are-too-scared-to-talk-8db98i5fd398#.t620f3nd8

1015 Acemoglu, Daron, Restrepo, Pascusal, Robots and jobs: Evidence from the US, Vox, April 10, 2017, http://voxeu.org/article/robots-and-jobs-evidence-us

1016 Universal basic incomes, The Economist, June 6, 2016, www.economist.com/economist-explains/2016/06/economist-explains-4

1017 Larson

1018 Baer, Drake, Google's genius futurist has one theory that he says will rule the future- and it's a little terrifying, Business Insider, May 27, 2015, www.businessinsider.com/ray-kurzwell-law-of-accelerating-returns-2015-5

1019 Dalio, Ray, Why and How Capitalism Needs to Be Reformed, Linkedin, April 5, 2019, www.linkedin.com/pulse/why-how-capitalism-needs-reform-parts-1-2-ray-dalio/?ulm_source=newsletter&utm_medium=email&utm_campaign=newsletter_axiousam&stream=top

1020 Ibid

1021 Blair, Tony, A Journey- My Political Life, quoted in, Somin, Ilya, Democracy and Political Ignorance, Stanford University Press, Stanford, CA, 2016, Pg 74

1022 The Trump Era, The Economist, November 12, 2016

1023 Wike, Richard, 5 ways Americans and Europeans are different, Pew Research Center, April 19, 2016, www.pewresearchcenter.org/fact-tank/2016/04/19/5-ways-americans-and-europeans-are-different

1024 Xi Jinping, President for Life, Editorial Board, Wall Street Journal, February 25, 2018, www.wsj.com/articles/xi-jinping-president-for-life-1519598379

1025 Masket, Seth, The Toughest Death of 2016: the Democratic Norms that (Used to) Guide Our Political System, Pacific Standard, December 27, 2016, http://psmag.com/the-toughest-death-of-2016-the-democratic-norms-that-used-to-guide-our-political-system-cc7f6b4361fa#.jnmopeqi3

1026 Worthen, Molly, Is There Such a Thing as an Authoritarian Voter, New York Times Sunday Review, December 16, 2018, Pg1

1027 Mill, John Stuart, Considerations on Representative Government, Chapter 8, Of the Extension of the Suffrage, The Project Gutenberg, www.gutenberg.org/cache/epub/5669/pg5669.txt

1028 Somin, Ilya, Political Ignorance and Democracy, Stanford Law Book, Stanford, California, 2016, Pg 198

1029 Ibid

1030 Egan, Timothy, Look in the Mirror: We're With Stupid, OpEd, New York Times, November 18, 2017, Pg A18

1031 Fault Lines in Our Democracy, ETS, downloaded March 6, 2018, www.ets.org/s/research/19386/rsc/pdf/18719_fault_lines_report.pdf

1032 Owen, Diana, et al, Civic Education and Knowledge of Government and Politics, Paper presented at the Annual Meeting of the American Political Science Association, September 1-4, 2011, www.civiced,org/pdfs/Civics%20Education%20and%20Knowledge%20of%20Government%20and%20Politics.pdf

1033 Americans failing citizenship test again, AEI Citizenship, April 30, 2012, www.citizenship-aei.org/2012/04/americans-failing-citizenship-test-again/#.WahylYfD-hc

1034 Goldstein, Dana, Lawsuit Says Rhode Island Failed to Teach Students to be Good Citizens, New York Times, November 29, 2018, Pg A12

1035 Ackerman, Bruce, and Fishkin, James, Deliberation Day, Yale University Press, 2005,www.goodreads.com/book/show/208252.Deliberation_Day

1036 Ibid

1037 Scientific consensus: Earth's climate is warming, Global Climate Change, downloaded February 1, 2017, http://climate.nasa.gov/scientific-consensus/

1038 Gregory, Paul Roderick, Opinion- Putin Changes September Election Rules, Forbes, March 14, 2016, www.forbes.com/sites/paulroderickgregory/2016/03/14/putin-changes-september-election-rules-to-prop-up-his-united-russia-party/#7b10c0d58a2e

1039 Feldman, Noah, Turkey's New Constitution Would End Its Democracy, Bloomberg, January 17, 2017, www.bloomberg.com/news/articles/2017/01/22/turkey-s-new-constitution-would-end-it-sdemocracy

1040 Stephanopoulos, Nicholas, A Feasible Roadmap to Compulsory Voting, The Atlantic, November 2, 2015, www.theatlantic.com/politics/archives/2015/11/a-feasible-roadmap-to-compulsory-voting/413422/

1041 Berman, Russell, Should Voter Registration Be Automatic?, The Atlantic, March 2015, www.theatlantic.com, politics/archive/2015/03/should-voter-registration-be-automatic/388258

1042 Quinton, Sophie, Expect More Conflict Between Cities and States, Stateline, January 25, 2017, www.pewtrusts.org/en/research-and-analysis/blogs/stateline/2017/01/25/expect-more-conflict-between-cities-and-states

1043 Rosenberg, Matt Compulsory Voting, About Education, November 30, 2016, http://geography.about.com/od/politicalgeography/a/compulsoryvote.htm

1044 Ibid

1045 Stephanopoulos

1046 Rosenberg

1047 Kafka, Franz, The Castle, Vintage Books, Alfred A. Knopf, New York, 1974, Pg 333

1048 Douthat, Ross, Power to the Parents, OpEd, New York Times Sunday Review, March 4, 2018, Pg 9

1049 Jones, Jeffrey, Americans Identification as Independents Back Up in 2017, Gallup, January 8, 2018, https://news.gallup.com/poll/225056/americans-identification-independents-back-2017.aspx

1050 De Loera-Brust, Andres, The Independent's Case for Ranked Choice Voting, Unite America, May 13, 2018, www.unitedamerica.org/the-independents-choice-for-ranked-choice-voting

1051 Ibid

1052 Seelye, Katherine, Maine Adopts New Way of Counting Ballots, New York Times, December 4, 2016, Pg 27

1053 Hawk, Thomas, Voters Betrayed: Maine Politicians Set Ranked Choice Voting Up For Repeal, Electoral Reform, October 23, 2017, http://ivn.us/2017/10/23/voters-betrayed-maine-lawmakers-set-ranked-choice-voting-repeal/

1054 Taylor, Kate, Maine Republican Concedes, Ending Voting Law Dispute, New York Times, December 25, 2018, Pg A16

1055 Ranked Choice Voting/ Instant Runoff, Fair Vote, downloaded January 17, 2017, www.fairvote.org/rcv/#rcvbenefits

1056 Dean, Howard, How to Get Beyond Two Parties, OpEd, New York Times, October 8, 2016, Pg A21

1057 Taylor

1058 Salam, Reihan, and Richie, Rob, How to Make Congress Bipartisan, OpEd, New York Times, July 8, 2017, Pg A19

1059 Primaries, FairVote, downloaded January 28, 2016, www.fairvote.org/primaries#open_and_closed_primaries

1060 Mastro, Randy, Make Elections Nonpartisan, OpEd, New York Times, June 26, 2012, www.ntyimes.com/roomfordebate/2012/06/26/waht-can-get-more-new-yorkers-to-vote/make-elections-nonpartisan

1061 Kousser, Thad, California's jungle primary sets up polarized governor's race for November, The Conversation, June 6, 2018, https://theconversation.com/california-jungle-primary-ste-up-polarized-governors-race-for-november

1062 Greve, Joan, The Daily 202: By overturning ballot initiatives, more lawmakers are rejecting the will of their voters, Washington Post, August 14, 2018, www.washingtonpost.com/news/powerpost/paloma/daily-202/2018/08/14/daily-202-will-of-the-voters/

1063 Ibid

1064 Mounk, Yascha, Pitchfork Politics, Foreign Affairs, September/October 2014, Pg 27

1065 Proposition 13, Howard Jarvis Taxpayers Association, downloaded January 28, 2017, www.hja.org/propositions/proposition 13/

1066 Glyn, Noah, and Drenkard, Scott, Prop 13 in California, 35 Years Later, June 6, 2013, https://taxfoundation.org/prop-13-california-35-years-later

1067 Robins-Early, Nick, Brexit Wins As The UK Votes To Leave EU In Historic Referendum, The Huffington Post, June 23, 2016, www.huffingtonpost.com/entry/brexit-results-referendum_us_576c37d5e4b0f1683238e3d9

1068 Sparrow, Andrew, 26 % of voters want second referendum on final Brexit deal, poll suggests- as it happened, The Guardian, January 23, 2017, www.theguardian.com/politics

1069 Hacaoglu, Selcan, and Kozok, Firat, Turkey Parliament Triggers Referendum on Presidential System, Bloomberg, January 20, 2017, www.blommber.com/news/article/2017-01-21/turkey-parliament-triggers-presidential-system-iy6kd8n6

1070 Fox, Kara, ey al, Turkey referendum: Erdogan declares victory, CNN, April 17, 2017, www.cnn.com/2017/04/16/europe/turkey-referendum-results-erdogan/

1071 Somin, Ilya, Democracy and Political Ignorance, Stanford Law Books, Stanford, California, 2016, Pg 197

1072 Robillard, Kevin, Koch network ramps up political spending while trying to push Trump, tea,. Politico, June 24, 2017, www.politico.com/story/2017/06/24/koch-brothers-spending-pence-trump-239928

1073 Moyo, Dambisa, Why Democracy Doesn't Deliver, Foreign Policy, April 2018, https://foreignpolicy.com/2018/04/26/why-democracy-doesnt-deliver/

1074 Crabtree, James, Should Democracy Favour the Elite, The Financial Times, May 3, 2018, www.ft.com/content/48cee200-46df-11e8-8c77-ff51caedcde6

1075 Democracy Index 2016, The Economist Intelligence Unit, downloaded March 3, 2018, www.eiu.com/public/topical-_report.aspx?campaignid=DemocracyIndex2016

1076 Lincoln's Gettysburg Address, November 19, 1863, www.abrahamlincolnonline.org/lincoln/speeches/gettysburg.htm

1077 Ibid

1078 Somin, Ilya, Pg 2

1079 Estlund, David, Why Not Epistocracy?, Desire, Identity and Existence, Essays in honor of T.M. Penner, Academic Printing and Publishing, 2003

1080 Crain, Caleb, None of The Above -The Case Against Democracy, The New Yorker, November 7, 2016, Pg 67

1081 Brennan,, Jason, Against Democracy, Princeton University Press, Princeton, NJ, 2016

1082 Somin, Ilya, Democracy vs. Epistocracy, Washington Post, September 3, 2016, www.washingtonpost.com/news/vo/oth-conspiracy/wp/2016/09/03/democracy-vs-epistocracy/

1083 The Expansion of the Vote: A White Man's Democracy, Politics and the New Nation, downloaded January 30, 2017, www.ushistory.org/us/23b.asp

1084 Compulsory Education Laws, FindLaw, downloaded February 3, 2017, http://education.findlaw.com/education-options/compulsory-education-laws-background.html

1085 Schulman, Marc, Voter Turnout In The United States, History Central, downloaded March 3, 2018, www.historycentral.com/elections/Voterturnout.html

1086 The Phrase Finder- English Proverbs, downloaded July 4, 2017, www.phrases.org.uk/meanings/261100.html

1087 Heller, Nathan, The Digital Republic, The New Yorker, December 18, 2017, Pg 84

1088 Simons, Barbara, Guardian of the Vote, The Atlantic, December 2017, Pg 16

Index

CPSIA information can be obtained
at www.ICGtesting.com
Printed in the USA
LVHW111006130520
655512LV00001B/52

9 781977 224460